EXPLORING
NEW YORK CITY

FODOR'S TRAVEL PUBLICATIONS, INC.

NEW YORK • TORONTO • LONDON • SYDNEY • AUCKLAND

HTTP://WWW.FODORS.COM/

Copyright © The Automobile Association 1998
Maps copyright © The Automobile Association 1998

All rights reserved under International and Pan-American Copyright conventions. Distributed by Random House, Inc., New York. No maps, illustrations, or other portions of this book may be reproduced in any form without written permission from the publishers.

Published in the United States by Fodor's Travel Publications, Inc.
Published in the United Kingdom by A.A. Publishing.

Fodor's and Fodor's Exploring Guides are registered trademarks of Fodor's Travel Publications, Inc.

ISBN 0-679-03559-1
Third Edition

Fodor's Exploring New York

Author: **Mick Sinclair with additional 'Hotels and Restaurants' material by Mitchell Davis**
Series Adviser: **Ingrid Morgan**
Joint Series Editor: **Susi Bailey**
Revisions Editor: **Sean Connolly**
Cartography: **The Automobile Association**
Cover Design: **Louise Fili, Fabrizio La Rocca**
Front Cover Silhouette: **Robert Kristofik/Image Bank**

Special Sales
Fodor's Travel Publications are available at special discounts for bulk purchases for sales promotions or premiums. Special editions, including personalized covers, excerpts of existing guides, and corporate imprints, can be created in large quantities for special needs, For more information, contact your local bookseller or write to Special Markets, Fodor's Travel Publications, 201 East 50th Street, New York, NY 10022.

Printed and bound in Italy by Printer Trento srl.
10 9 8 7 6 5 4 3 2

How to use this book

This book is divided into five main sections:

❏ Section 1: *New York Is*
discusses aspects of life and living today, from streetlife to art.

❏ Section 2: *New York Was*
places the city in its historical context and explores those past events whose influences are felt to this day.

❏ Section 3: *A to Z Section*
covers places to visit, including walks and excursions, and lists itineraries, tips for those on a tight budget and sightseeing ideas for children. Within this section fall the Focus-on articles, which consider a variety of subjects in greater detail.

❏ Section 4: *Travel Facts*
contains the strictly practical information vital for a successful trip.

❏ Section 5:
Hotels and Restaurants
lists recommended establishments throughout New York, giving a brief summary of their attractions.

How to use the star rating
Most of the places described in this book have been given a separate rating:

▶▶▶ **Do not miss**

▶▶ **Highly recommended**

▶ **Worth seeing**

Not essential to see

Map references
To make the location of a particular place easier to find, every main entry in this book has a map reference to the right of its name. This comprises a number, followed by a letter, followed by another number, such as 176B3. The first number (176) refers to the page on which the map can be found; the letter (B) and the second number (3) pinpoint the square in which the main entry is located. The map on the inside front cover and inside back cover is referred to as IFC and IBC respectively.

Contents

Sign-cleaning on the corner of Seventh Avenue and Broadway

Quick reference

This quick-reference guide gives the features of the book you will use most: the maps; the introductory features; the Focus on articles; the walks and the excursions.

Statue of Liberty

7

New York fire engine

My New York by Mick Sinclair

Mick Sinclair has made a career out of examining the inner workings of some of America's major cities from the traveler's point of view. Chicago, Miami, and San Francisco have featured in other guidebooks he has authored. He has also written at length about California, Florida, Denmark, Finland, and Iceland, and his magazine and newspaper reviews and features on travel, culture, and the arts have appeared all over the world.

Whether they love it or loathe it, few can deny that New York is the most stimulating city in the world, and the only one where so much is so familiar even at first sight. The Statue of Liberty, the Empire State Building, and Central Park are just three New York landmarks well known to visitors before they set eyes on them. Equally familiar are the New York sights—such as bagels with cream cheese, and yellow cabs—that could exist anywhere but which the media has made iconographic images of the city.

It could be said that there is nothing new for an author to say about the city, but writing about New York provides the challenge to make the familiar suddenly seem less familiar. It means pounding the streets and combing the archives to dig up the inside stories that swiftly make visitors realize that, for all their preconceptions, they never really knew New York at all.

A closer look at New York opens up a great metropolis built on madness and mayhem fortuitously coupled to sufficient money to buy it the kind of things rival cities can only dream about. New York museums are vast, and reflect the achievements of every culture. New York buildings might be places in which to live and work, but are frequently also groundbreaking architecture. New York's stores hold everything anyone could ever want to buy, while New York's rich seem wealthy beyond the limits of earthbound accountancy.

Everyone recognizes the Statue of Liberty, but how many know it was originally intended for the Suez Canal? Who can name the hard-headed 19th-century financier who consulted an astrologist for assistance with decision-making? And how many visitors can explain how profits from the notorious slum tenements of the Lower East Side were instrumental in giving New York one of the world's greatest reference libraries?

In finding the answers, I was able to steadily peel back the layers of superficiality to reach the city beneath. New York stripped naked is not always a pretty sight, but it is one that is ultimately much more believable than the city of myth. If only to encourage others to find something new in this seemingly familiar, but also strange and mysterious, place, the undertaking was a worthwhile one.

NEW YORK IS

■ **Great museums, fantastic architecture, luxurious hotels, and every imaginable kind of restaurant—New York has them all. But only by stepping out among the sights, smells, and sounds that fill its streets will you begin to feel the true pulse of the mighty city.** ■

Nonstop streets A New York street can be a lonely place but seldom—morning, noon, or night—is it an empty one. Around 5 AM, the first batches of briefcase-carrying commuters emerge from the city's subway stations, just in time to see the nightclubbers heading for home.

A few hours later, young people make their way to school; soon after, the first lunch-seeking office workers begin filing onto the sidewalks. By early afternoon, the early-rising commuters are already making for the stations and by dusk Midtown Manhattan is buzzing with pretheater diners. In Greenwich Village, meanwhile, the bars and clubs prepare for another long, busy night.

New York without traffic jams is unthinkable

❏ The 12,000 yellow taxis that cruise New York's streets are much more than merely a quick (traffic permitting) way of traveling from A to B. Enshrined in city mythology, taxis have inspired a T.V. series (*Taxi*, which made a star of Danny DeVito), been represented as small yellow rectangles in a major painting—Mondrian's *Broadway Boogie-Woogie* (displayed at New York's Museum of Modern Art)—and, like taxis the world over, are infamously hard to find when it rains.

But why are they yellow? Because John Hertz, who founded the Yellow Cab Company in 1907, read a survey carried out by the University of Chicago that found that yellow was the color most people found easiest to spot. ❏

Off the street One contributory factor to the round-the-clock hubbub on New York's streets is the size and price of the apartments that rise above them. Most Manhattan apartments are small and, except for a few rent-controlled properties, extremely expensive. Rather than stay indoors cooking in a tiny kitchen, New Yorkers will welcome any opportunity to eat, drink, and socialize outside their apartments.

Street deals Free enterprise rules the New York streets. An abundance of foodstands can be found all around the city, and appetites can be satisfied—often surprisingly well—without ever venturing inside a restaurant. Bookworms can shop at makeshift outdoor tables, which offer for sale all kinds of reading material ranging from brand-new discounted hardbacks to used paperbacks. Many New York apartments have been furnished by various purchases from street markets, where the merchandise ranges from eccentric lumps of junk to pieces of matching furniture.

Even if it rains, there is no need to duck inside for shelter. As the first drops start to fall, street-corner traders appear, seemingly from nowhere, bearing armfuls of inexpensive umbrellas.

Tompkins Square Park. Street culture comes in many guises

Street traffic Listen to bike riders and truck drivers locked in verbal combat at traffic lights, after jostling for prime position the length of the last block. Careful eavesdropping may even provide you with useful ammunition if you ever find it necessary to exchange insults with a New Yorker.

Watch out for rollerbladers who tempt death by weaving through Fifth Avenue's frantic rush-hour traffic—sometimes they will even grab hold of passing vehicles for a free tug.

Dirty streets With federal funding cut by 20 percent in the years since 1980, the U.S.'s most glamorous city is, sometimes literally, falling to pieces. Many city bridges are in urgent need of maintenance; emergency repairs to these vital traffic points complicates rush-hour traffic. Potholes are common on many streets—some neighborhoods are littered with them.

In a bizarre twist to the city's garbage-disposal problems, the New York Sanitation Department loses two or three of its 18-ton refuse trucks to thieves every year. Each vehicle is worth $110,000.

❏ Everyone knows New York is nicknamed the Big Apple but nobody is sure of the origins of the term. Musicians, gangsters, and horse-racing devotees have all been cited as its source, but the phrase's recent popularity stems from a tourism campaign launched in 1971. ❏

Mean streets Through the 1990s, levels of crime in New York fell dramatically. Between 1993 and 1995 there was a 27.4 percent drop in reported crime while, below ground, subway offences declined by 64.3 percent in five years. Nonetheless, visitors should heed the Survival Guide on pages 54–55. As in most of the world's big cities, it is wise to be cautious, but New York is not particularly unsafe.

11

■ **For anyone, anywhere, with aspirations and dreams, New York is the place to be. Whether you want to sing and dance your way to fame, make a mint on Wall Street, or start a new life in a new land, New York is—as it has always been—the beacon of opportunity.** ■

High finance For those who can stand the stresses and strains, the heady world of New York high finance offers rewards unimagined and a level of power few outside the realms of international politics ever experience.

Take one look at the glass-and-steel high-rise towers of the Manhattan skyline, and it should be no surprise that New York provides 3.5 million people with jobs and holds more than 200,000 businesses, among them some 700 insurance companies, 5,000 law firms, and around 400 foreign banks.

Cab driving: a steady living

Industrial giants such as international oil companies may have blue-collar work forces around the globe but their companies are driven by decisions made in the penthouse boardrooms of their Manhattan headquarters. These decisions not only directly affect the livelihoods of millions but indirectly influence the well-being of the country's—and the world's—economy.

❏ During the 1980s, a surging New York Stock Exchange helped create the yuppie and the junk-bond millionaire. Following the stock-market crashes of 1987 and 1989—when a few of the more unscrupulous went to jail—overnight fortunes have been harder to find. Nonetheless, the New York Stock Exchange continued to be globally preeminent, and was at the heart of the "bull market" of the mid-1990s, when stock prices soared. Wall Street made a record $12.5 billion profit in 1996 and its rewarding of workers with performance bonuses—estimated to average $54,000 per person—created a chain reaction across the city as the money was lavished on goods and services. ❏

Taxi drivers It may not be the most glamorous occupation, but shortly after the internal combustion engine replaced the horse on the New York streets, driving a taxi became the staple first job of arriving immigrants.

Currently, less than 11 percent of applications for cab-driving jobs are from native-born New Yorkers. More immediately noticeable in some instances is a cab driver's less than fluent command of English.

Many of these newly arrived taxi-drivers may have a university degree or years of experience in accounting, medicine, or some other profession in their native land. Being a cabbie in New York, however, means steady wages and a chance to provide their children with a standard of education not available back home.

Unconventional lifestyles Many come to New York simply for the opportunity to live as they want to Multicolored hair and bizarre attire seldom raise eyebrows on Manhattan's seen-it-all-before streets. Avid nightclubbers can enjoy themselves every night, sleep all day and never feel that New York life is passing them by.

New York also promises a support-

New Yorkers have learned to take the eccentric in stride

ive infrastructure for gays and lesbians, many of whom come to escape discrimination in jobs and housing elsewhere.

Publishing The New York-based *Wall Street Journal* and *The New York Times* lead the country for quality reporting and carry journalism's most prestigious jobs—coveted by ambitious news-gatherers across the

❏ An estimated 770,000 college graduates move to New York annually. ❏

country. Some New York-based magazines enjoy worldwide esteem. In recent years, the *New Yorker*, *Vanity Fair* and *Vogue* have had little trouble in luring overseas talent and have raised some eyebrows by appointing British editors, such as Tina Brown, Liz Tilberis and Anna Wintour, to their most coveted jobs.

Most of the country's major publishers are based in New York, which attracts writers —both American and émigré to the city and gives editors the chance to work with some of the world's most celebrated literary names.

The stage Those intent upon a career in the performing arts ignore New York at their peril. A major early boost is being one of the thousand accepted every year into the city's highly rated Juilliard School of Music and Performing Arts.

For thespians, there is no disputing New York's place at the heart of U.S. theater, whether it is Broadway blockbusters or the dozens of Off-Off-Broadway productions. New York offers acting opportunities away from live audiences, too: the majority of T.V. soap operas and commercials are cast in Manhattan, even though most T.V. and film work is centered in Los Angeles.

New York's ballet, orchestras, and opera companies, meanwhile, are among the world's most highly rated.

13

■ **Everybody knows, or thinks they know, New York long before they actually arrive there, having seen the city depicted—be it lovingly or with loathing—in innumerable movies. Here is a highly selective list of the most revealing, famous, or simply the most enjoyable, films set in New York. (Woody Allen's New York films are detailed on page 188.) ■**

Breakfast at Tiffany's (1961). On screen New York has never appeared more romantic than in this adaptation of the Truman Capote novella; Audrey Hepburn stars as the free-spirited Holly Golightly who—dressed in a chic black evening gown—drinks coffee shortly after dawn as she admires the jewels in the shop window of Fifth Avenue's Tiffany and Company.

Crossing Delancey (1988). Woody Allen gets a sideways acknowledgment in this tale of an unlikely Manhattan romance between an Upper West Side literary type and a Lower East Side pickle seller, engineered by the former's Jewish grandmother.

The Crowd (1928). Two years after Fritz Lang's futuristic *Metropolis*, inspired by the Manhattan skyline, came King Vidor's expressionistic study of the ordinary man's struggle in the seething city: memorable New York scenes abound.

King Kong (1933). The conflict between man and nature reaches its climax as the giant ape of the title

❏ Thomas Edison may have electrified the city but a combination of factors—royalties due on Edison-patented cinematic equipment, the demands of actors' unions, and inclement weather—encouraged fledgling filmmakers to leave New York (where movies were a natural offshoot of Broadway theaters) in the early 1900s for the sunshine of southern California. ❏

swats planes while flirting with Fay Wray beside the then infant Empire State Building.

The Lost Weekend (1945). The bar in which Billy Wilder's alcoholic weekend began still exists—P. J. Clarke's, Third Avenue at 55th Street.

Mean Streets (1973). Martin Scorsese had a bigger hit in 1976 with *Taxi Driver*, but this contrasts the New York of hippies and flower-power with the macho traditions of young Italian-Americans on the make.

Metropolitan (1990). This witty drawing-room comedy focuses on the alternately comic and poignant adventures of a West Side intellectual who befriends a group of rich Upper East Side young people in the midst of attending Manhattan debutante balls at Christmas time.

On the Town (1949). One of the first MGM musicals shot on location, this fast-paced film follows three sailors (Gene Kelly, Frank Sinatra, and Jules Munshin) on a 24-hour pass as they dash around the city, stopping at Rockefeller Center, the Statue of Liberty, the Bronx Zoo, the Brooklyn Bridge, and other key sights.

Portrait of Jennie (1948). A lovely and appropriately haunting film in which a troubled artist is enchanted by a young girl in Central Park and later discovers that she is a ghost.

Q—The Winged Serpent (1982). Witty, low-budget piece in which a giant bird flies out of Aztec mythology to terrorize sunbathing New Yorkers.

The city's best-known screen moment: King Kong and Fay Wray in 1933

It lays an egg inside the tower of the Chrysler Building, only to be discovered by a hoodlum who tries to cash in on his amazing find.

Saturday Night Fever (1977). A product of 1970s disco mania that gives a taste of the culture of young Italian-Americans in Brooklyn's Bensonhurst neighborhood.

Serpico (1973). In real life, Frank Serpico was an honest cop whose efforts to stamp out corruption in the New York police force met with intimidation and violence. Serpico's stand eventually led to a massive clean-up campaign—and to Al Pacino playing him in this highly charged thriller, which has great location shots.

Seven Year Itch (1955). Probably Marilyn Monroe's finest screen moment, this film is known for one of her most enduring images: her skirt is lifted by air rising from the subway grate at the junction of 52nd Street and Lexington Avenue.

Sweet Smell of Success (1957). A brilliant Tony Curtis stars as the sleazy press agent currying favor with a powerful and sinister Broadway gossip columnist, played by Burt Lancaster.

When Harry Met Sally (1989). Katz's Deli on the Lower East Side was a New York legend even before this film's fake orgasm scene was shot there; an enjoyable but lightweight comedy romance in which the Metropolitan Museum of Art's Temple of Dendur steals a scene.

> ❑ An unknown 18-year-old actress called Lauren Bacall was crowned Miss Greenwich Village in 1942. ❑

Saturday Night Fever *in Brooklyn*

■ Beneath its veneer of glamour and afflu-ence, New York is a city wrenched asunder by social problems—chiefly stemming from racial intolerance, homelessness, and drug use. Despite constant media attention and the seemingly endless rhetoric of politicians, New York's troubles seem unlikely to go away. ■

Racial tensions New York's 7 million inhabitants span a multitude of nationalities, colors and religions, but while it may appear to be the world's greatest melting pot, racial tensions frequently surface here and often escalate into violence.

In 1986, 23-year-old black Michael Griffiths was killed after being chased by a white mob wielding baseball bats. The car Griffiths had been traveling in had broken down in a white area—Howards Beach, Queens—and he had left the vehicle to find a public telephone to call a mechanic.

Three years later, a black youth, Yusuf Hawkins, was shot dead by young Italian-Americans in white, middle-class Bensonhurst in Brooklyn. Along with three friends, Hawkins was in the area to look over a bike that he had seen advertised.

The Bensonhurst incident contributed to the election of New York's first black

mayor, David Dinkins, in the hope that he could quell the city's racial strife.

Dinkins' first test came a few months later, when years of feuding between the predominantly black residents of the depressed Crown Heights district of Brooklyn and the neighborhood's ultra-strict, politically active Lubavitcher Jews exploded after a black child was killed by a car driven by a member of the sect. Soon after, black protesters killed a rabbinical student and four days and nights of violence ensued.

Mayor Dinkins' hesitance at order-ing police to quell the disturbance brought the charge that he was showing favor to blacks, outraging both the city's Jewish com-munity and his political oppo-nents.

Harlem riots in 1964 and (below) opti-mism from Mayor Dinkins

Police tactics have often inflamed racial tensions

In 1992, the police shooting of a suspected drug dealer in the Hispanic neighborhood of Washington Heights incited more street violence, and allegations of racism led to the city's police force coming under scrutiny.

Homelessness Numbering approximately 100,000, New York's homeless population was swelled by the razing of single-room occupancy hotels—generally occupied by poor people on a long-term basis—and the mass discharge of mental hospital patients in the 1960s.

In 1992, a survey revealed some 6,000 homeless people were living beneath the city in branches of the subway system. Among the homeless are victims of A.I.D.S., for whom the city—despite a $14 million initiative in the early 1990s—provides little care.

Drugs Mind-altering drugs and narcotics are great social levelers. On the one hand, drugs have long provided recreation for New York's hip rich. But on the other hand, drugs also provide a means of escape from the drudgery of life in the city's slums—either by consuming them or by dealing in them.

In 1985, the city's drug problems worsened with the arrival of crack cocaine. Easier and cheaper to make and supply than heroin, crack brought immense profits to dealers, some of whom started as schoolchildren carrying bags of the drug to users.

An estimated 70 percent of the city's 5,000 prostitutes are thought to be crack addicts. They are also the fastest-growing group found to be H.I.V.-positive.

Zero tolerance Taking office in 1994, Mayor Giuliani launched a policy of "zero tolerance" intended to tackle New York's crime problems. Based on the idea that stopping small crimes prevents bigger ones, police cracked down on "quality of life" offences such as graffiti and unlicensed street vending. Increased random street searches of individuals yielded unexpected quantities of drugs and weapons (prompting protests from civil liberties groups), while many people arrested on minor offenses were subsequently found to be wanted for major ones. The mayor was quick to cite zero tolerance as underpinning the city's greatly reduced crime figures of the mid-1990s, though an enlarged police force and a new system of police accountability for local crime were also regarded as contributory factors, as were the demographic factors which saw crime levels fall in most major American cities.

❏ To prove how easy it was to buy crack on New York's streets, Senator Alfonse D'Amato went undercover in 1986 and, watched by a T.V. crew, bought a $20 bag of the drug in Washington Heights. ❏

■ **Few areas of New York stay the same for long. Not only do entire districts undergo staggering transformations— socially, architecturally, and commercially—within a few years, but sometimes a whole new neighborhood can suddenly rise up where previously there was nothing but a hole in the ground.** ■

Times Square and 42nd Street The 1970s saw Times Square and the adjacent stretch of 42nd Street—on the borders of Broadway—being taken over by porno theaters, massage parlors and adult bookstores. Drug dealers and prostitutes plied their trade; homeless people were a common sight, and the pedestrian congestion was ideal for pickpockets.

A major program of regeneration and development got underway in the mid-1980s, under the banner of the Times Square Business Improvement District. The now considerably transformed area—patrolled by its own security force and kept clean with frequent garbage collection—succeeds in its intention of being safe and welcoming to shoppers, tourists, and legitimate businesses. New construction work has seen high-rise hotels, shopping complexes, and office buildings appear but the new-look square has drawn a mixed response from New Yorkers. While most are happy to see crime levels reduced and relish a much-improved subway station, many fear Times Square's "Disneyfication," its character buried beneath theme restaurants and major retail franchises. Many New Yorkers are skeptical about the scheme's chances of success, happy to lose the sleaze but fearful at the same time of trading Times Square's legendary vitality for a sterile landscape of modern towers.

Battery Park City The sleekest testament to New York's powers of metamorphosis is Battery Park City, a $4-billion project combining commercial, residential and recreational areas on a 92-acre landfill site on the western edge of the Financial District.

Conceived in the 1970s, Battery Park City gave a new lease of life to an abandoned stretch of Hudson River waterfront, while finding a use for the thousands of tons of earth and rock excavated during the building of the World Trade Center.

Like Rockefeller Center (to which it is frequently compared), Battery Park

Will Times Square lose its grit?

City is evolving through the labors of several architects working within a single master plan, which is intended to re-create the atmosphere of an elegant, traditional Manhattan neighborhood.

Of the commercial architecture, Cesar Pelli's World Financial Center, completed in 1986, was well received for its palm-decorated Winter Garden atrium, but encountered a mixed response overall.

❏ "A sobering effect"—the architects' intended impact of Times Square Center on seething Times Square. ❏

More popular is the mile-long Esplanade, restoring public access to this section of the Hudson River for the first time in decades. Victorian-style lampposts and benches heighten the leisurely ambience. The residential buildings are luxury apartments.

Chelsea Approximately bordered by 14th and 29th streets, and Sixth Avenue and the Hudson River, Chelsea began collecting the residential overspill from the increasingly upscale Greenwich Village through the 1980s. By the early 1990s, the neighborhood—a prominent shopping area during the 1890s and now mixture of townhouses and apartment buildings,

The Esplanade along the Hudson

industry and commerce—was an increasingly important nightlife and restaurant area, with a strong gay contingent among its residents and business owners. Many early landmarks remain, not least the Chelsea Hotel (page 85) and those of the Chelsea Historical District (page 153).

East Village As Greenwich Village moved out of the price range of all but the most established writers and artists, the city's creative spirits crossed Broadway into the less costly East Village. Unlike former commercial areas such as SoHo and TriBeCa, however, the East Village already had its own population with deep roots, among them a sizable Ukrainian community. This prevented the area moving headlong into gentrification.

❏ The continuing eastward migration of New York's unknown and lesser-known artists from Greenwich Village, through SoHo and the East Village, now finds them across the East River, creating loft studios in the former factories of Brooklyn's Williamsburg. Here they form a striking contrast to the area's concentration of orthodox Jews. ❏

■ **Thanks to a unique combination of wealthy collectors and a wartime influx of modern European artists, New York has not only amassed some of the world's finest pieces of art—displaying them in several world-class museums—but has also evolved into a renowned showcase for new artistic ideas and directions.** ■

First collections Founded in 1804, the **New-York Historical Society** became the city's first repository for art, acquiring a singular collection of Early American works, including many originally commissioned by Robert Lehman, a New Yorker who opened part of his town house as a gallery and brought American artists such as Thomas Cole to public attention.

The paintings collection of New York's **Metropolitan Museum of Art** (pages 142–148) began with a modest purchase of 174 Dutch and Flemish canvases in 1870 and grew—aided by bequests and donations—into a world-class stock, including many major pieces by Van Gogh, Turner, El Greco, and Vermeer.

Businessmen become collectors Having amassed wealth through their control of the industralization of the United States, and with newly built Fifth Avenue mansions

in need of decoration, New York's 19th-century millionaires began raiding the art collections of Europe. One such was Henry Clay Frick, who acquired the phenomenal hoard now known as the **Frick Collection** (see page 110).

Patrons Many affluent New Yorkers indulged themselves by commissioning artists to paint their portraits, but one who did a great deal more to encourage the creativity of American artists was Gertrude Vanderbilt Whitney. Displaying and promoting emergent artists such as Edward Hopper and John Sloan, Whitney also established an influential Parisian-style salon during the early 1900s. Her legacy, the **Whitney Museum of American Art** (page 191), continues to champion the country's unknown artists regardless of prevailing fashions, and has many of the finest

The Metropolitan Museum of Art

Art for Sale—a private SoHo gallery

❏ New York is said to be home to 90,000 artists and to hold 500 art galleries. A new and controversial form of New York art emerged in the 1970s when complex and colorful graffiti began appearing in public places, such as subway trains, created with paint sprayed from cans and signed by its makers only with a distinctive symbol or "tag." ❏

American artists of the 20th century represented among its permanent stock.

As Gertrude Whitney was furthering appreciation of American art, wealthy industrialist Solomon R. Guggenheim was discovering the art and artists of modern Europe. Guggenheim's purchases of early Cubist and abstract canvases were displayed on the walls of his suite at the Plaza Hotel, and later became the basis of the **Guggenheim Museum** (pages 122–124). Frank Lloyd Wright designed the building, which is as remarkable as the innovative works of art it holds.

An international art center As war loomed in Europe, New York found itself acquiring not only European art but European artists as well. By the 1940s, many of modern art's major names resided in the city. They were to have a colossal impact on the New York art scene.

New York surpassed Paris (then under Nazi occupation) as the center for international art dealing and the city's preeminence was confirmed by the emergence of abstract expressionism (see pages 128–129). Meanwhile, the **Museum of Modern Art** (see pages 158–160), founded in 1929, was evolving into the world's most prestigious modern art museum.

New York now New York spawned pop art, op art and minimalist art during the 1960s, and by the late 1970s the shabby warehouses of SoHo (see page 175) had been transformed into pristine galleries showcasing new trends and new talents.

In the economically buoyant 1980s, New York art became big business. The artists in vogue then—Julian Schnabel, David Salle and Eric Fischl—could expect poverty to be a thing of the past.

Today, many artist-run galleries can be found in the East Village, Chelsea, and on the Lower East Side. While still energetically showcasing emerging New York artists, the larger galleries are reflecting growing interest in the art of South and Central America.

❏ Among the most remarkable of New York's many plaza sculptures is Jean Dubuffet's *Group of Four Trees*, in the Chase Manhattan Bank in the Financial District. ❏

■ **Not only is New York the center of U.S. publishing, it has also provided more material for 20th-century writers than perhaps any other city. Literary landmarks are liberally strewn about, and several New York neighborhoods have carved out special places for themselves in the annals of literary achievement.** ■

A publishing capital Geography made New York the publishing capital of the U.S. in the 1850s. Before the U.S. recognized international copyright laws in 1891, any book could be copied, printed, and sold, earning its publisher fat profits as no royalties were due.

To maximize earnings, publishers vied with one another to be first with the latest foreign manuscripts. As New York became the nation's major seaport, the city's publishers could get their hands on new books and pirate them faster than rivals elsewhere.

The city observed New York has long provided rich pickings for observant writers. From a barstool vantage point in the early 1900s, O. Henry (the pen name of William Sydney Porter) produced short stories drawing on the seamy side of city life. In a similar vein a few decades later,

Damon Runyon

Damon Runyon described the characters on the fringes of Broadway theaterland. The dark side of the jazz age was illustrated by F. Scott Fitzgerald's *The Great Gatsby*, while Truman Capote's *Breakfast at Tiffany's* was fine-tuned to 1950s New York high life.

The stresses of 1980s New York underpinned Tom Wolfe's comic novel, *Bonfire of the Vanities*, and the same decade saw the emergence of writers such as Tama Janowitz and Jay McInerney, whose ambivalent prose dwelt on the selfishness and conceits of contemporary New York. Their cocaine-fueled tales were followed in the 1990s by more introspective, if similarly drug-centred work, such as Elizabeth Wurtzel's *Prozac Nation* and Linda Jablonky's *The Story of Junk*.

❏ Born in Manhattan in 1783, Washington Irving might well be considered New York's first home-grown writer. His satirical *A History of New York* was written under the memorable pseudonym of Diedrich Knickerbocker. ❏

Literary neighborhoods In the mid-1880s, New York literary life revolved around the fashionable drawing-rooms of Greenwich Village town houses, where heavyweights like James Fenimore Cooper rubbed shoulders with the publishers of literary journals. Such times were described in Edith Wharton's *The Age of Innocence* and by Henry James in *Washington Square*.

Washington Square and (below right) Henry James

As Greenwich Village rents fell, the area drew a host of talented but impoverished writers—as diverse as Willa Cather, John Reed, Theodore Drieser, John Dos Passos, Robert Frost, Eugene O'Neill, and Thomas Wolfe—who between them left Greenwich Village filled with literary landmarks (see pages 112–118).

The East Village and the Lower East Side began attracting impecunious scribes in the 1950s, when Beat writers like William Burroughs and Allen Ginsberg moved in alongside émigrés such as W. H. Auden. Another arrival was Norman Mailer, who formerly lived in Brooklyn Heights (and lives there now). Mass African-American migration into Harlem helped stimulate the Harlem Renaissance of the 1920s, bringing black writers such as Langston Hughes and Zora Neale Hurston to public notice. In the 1950s, Harlem-born James Baldwin created a stir with *Go Tell It on the Mountain*, though not before leaving Harlem for Europe. More recently, Chester Himes used Harlem as the setting for a series of thrillers.

The history of New York's Jewish population can be traced through such works as *World of Our Fathers*, by Irving Howe; *Call It Sleep*, by Henry Roth; *The Promise*, by Chaim Potok; *The Assistant*, by Bernard Malamud; and *Enemies, a Love Story*, by Isaac Bashevis Singer.

❑ Rejected writers in New York have included some notable names. Born in Lower Manhattan in 1819, Herman Melville was a customs officer on the East River after his *Moby Dick* received scathing reviews. Only after his death was it acclaimed as a masterpiece. Edgar Allan Poe's poems and short stories were admired in Europe, but in New York he scraped a living from journalism before dying in a state presumed to be drunkenness. Walt Whitman penned eulogies to Manhattan and the Brooklyn Bridge in the 1840s, but every publisher in the city turned down *Leaves of Grass*, eventually acknowledged as one of the great works of American poetry. ❑

For architecture enthusiasts, the Manhattan skyline is the stuff of dreams. The city's colonial structures may have almost vanished, but New York's existing buildings are a thrilling mixture, encompassing styles from the country's formative years to the contemporary adventures in postmodernism. ■

The Federal style From 1760 to 1830, the Federal style became the first genuine American building style, though it drew heavily on British Georgian and treated public buildings to columns and domes reminiscent of ancient Rome: **City Hall** (see page 89) is a prime example.

Federal-style residential architecture was distinguished by semi-detached houses of brick and wood, with fanlights above the entrances and dormer windows. **Gracie Mansion** (see page 111) is one example. A grander specimen is the former James Watson residence, now the **Shrine of Elizabeth Ann Seton** (see page 66).

❏ The zoning law of 1916, which outlawed new buildings rising sheer from their plot to rob neighboring buildings and streets of light, shaped the look of the Manhattan skyscraper. The law lead to the widespread use of cutbacks (also called step-backs), a tapering effect interpreted by architects in various ways and perhaps most memorably demonstrated by the profile of the Empire State Building. ❏

Revivals As New York enjoyed an economic surge during the 19th century, the Greek revival style—bringing porticos and floral-patterned ironwork to the façades of the new rows of town houses, such as those facing **Washington Square Park**—was the first of a spate of revivals, which included Italianate, Renaissance, and Gothic. Examples of all these are widely found.

Brownstones A cheap form of sandstone quarried in New Jersey, brownstone was used to build swiftly and at low cost in the mid-1800s, and brownstone town houses became the main residences of the middle classes. Held in little affection at the time, brownstones enjoyed a surge of popularity from the 1950s and the many that remain—especially in Midtown—are highly prized, both as residences and offices.

Luxury apartment houses By the turn of the century, property prices in Midtown Manhattan had risen beyond the pockets of the middle classes, who began colonizing the new luxury apartments on the Upper West Side. Sumptuously appointed and with anything up to 10 rooms, the apartments also boasted futuristic extras such as built-in refrigerators and pneumatic mail-delivery systems. The still-standing **Dakota** (see page 96) was the first such building; several others remain near by.

Early skyscrapers The 1902 **Flatiron Building** (see page 106) was the city's first "world's-tallest" structure and was also the first to be supported by a steel frame—a technique that showed the way for creating even taller buildings. A 1920s building

boom gave Manhattan the **Chrysler** and **Empire State buildings**, both of which not only reached record heights but bore the hallmarks of art deco (see pages 162–163)

The International style The towers of steel and glass that rise above Manhattan resulted from the arrival in New York of Europe's most creative architects, who fled Nazism and brought with them the antitraditional ideas of the International style.

The **Museum of Modern Art** (see pages 158–160), its original façade designed by Goodwin and Stone in 1939, gave New York a taste of the International style. Among the many examples that followed was Mies van der Rohe's 1958 **Seagram Building** (Park Avenue between 52nd and 53rd streets), which gave New York its first plaza—an open space where the public could stroll, sunbathe, and eat a snack. By the late 1970s, plazas were incorporated into every high-rise plan, some being enclosed to form atriums.

❏ The beaux-arts style arrived in New York in 1890 and is exemplified by Carrère and Hastings' **New York Public Library** (see page 168), Cass Gilbert's **U.S. Custom House** (see page 190), and works by the firm of McKim, Mead, & White, such as Washington Memorial Arch (see page 116). ❏

25

The 1980s boom With the 1980s construction boom, Manhattan gained its first modern buildings not bearing the international-style stamp. Philip Johnson's **A.T. & T. Building** (on Madison Avenue between 55th and 56th streets) became known as the Chippendale skyscraper; **Trump Tower** (see page 183) rose as a shrine to vulgar consumerism, and the **World Financial Center** filled its atrium with palm trees.

The Chrysler Building and its futuristic neighbors

■ Rare is the visitor who manages to be in New York when there is not some kind of festival taking place, whether a traffic-stopping parade along Fifth Avenue or a low-key neighborhood get-together. These are just a few highlights from an exceptionally busy festivals and events calendar. For precise dates and details, check the local newspapers or contact the New York Convention and Visitors' Bureau (festivals hotline tel: 397–8200). ■

January
Chinese New Year (The date depends on the lunar cycle; sometimes this takes place in early February.) Celebrated by giant dragon and lion dances in the streets of Chinatown. Festive banquets are offered by the neighborhood's restaurants.

Chinese New Year celebrations: the Lion Dance

❑ With a 150-year history, the St. Patrick's Day Parade (along Fifth Avenue between 44th and 86th streets) is by far the biggest of New York's parades.

Green proliferates in many of the city's bars, which often mark the day with special events, as do other institutions through the city.

Tens of thousands take part in the parade itself, and many more join in other St. Patrick's Day-related activities. ❑

Winter Antiques Fair At Seventh Regiment Armory, Park Avenue at East 66th Street. Upscale antiques and their dealers; browsers are also welcome (see also page 226).

February
Black History Month Lectures and exhibitions on African-American themes held throughout the city.
Empire State Building Run-Up Indoor joggers dash from the landmark building's lobby to its 86th floor by way of 1,575 stairs; the winner usually completes the course in 12 minutes.

March
Greek Independence Day Parade On Fifth Avenue between 59th and 79th streets. Honors the regaining of Greek independence in 1821: a sea of blue and white as school bands

and Greek-Americans in national costume march jovially along the route.

Parade of Circus Animals
Creatures from the Ringling Bros. and Barnum & Bailey Circus trek from a railroad siding at Twelfth Avenue and 34th Street to Madison Square Garden.

St. Patrick's Day Parade (see previous page).

The St. Patrick's Day Parade is New York's largest street parade

❏ The Puerto Rican Day Parade, along Fifth Avenue between 44th and 86th streets on the first Sunday in June, brings New York's huge Puerto Rican population onto the streets to celebrate their nation's Independence Day. Red, white, and blue Puerto Rican flags are everywhere, traditional foods are sold from stalls, and live bands playing on floats provide a nonstop soundtrack of salsa music to wildly appreciative audiences. ❏

April
Easter Day Parade Participants stroll on Fifth Avenue near St. Patrick's Cathedral wearing extravagant Easter bonnets. On the Saturday before Easter a children's egg-rolling contest takes place on Central Park's Great Lawn. Check out Macy's ground floor the week before the holiday—it's wall-to-wall flowers.
Japanese Cherry Blossom Festival Highlights bloomtime in Central Park's Conservatory Garden and at the Brooklyn Botanic Garden.

May
Martin Luther King Memorial Day Parade Along Fifth Avenue from 44th to 86th streets. Marchers celebrate the life and achievements of the civil rights leader and highlight other African-American issues.
Ninth Avenue International Food Festival A two-day feast of the city's ethnic cuisines, on Ninth Avenue between 37th and 57th streets.
Ukrainian Festival In the East Village along 7th Street on the weekend closest to May 17: traditional foods, crafts and folk dancing.
Washington Square Outdoor Arts Show A gathering of local artists showing and selling their wares over three successive weekends.

June
American Crafts Festival Lincoln Center. Over two successive weekends, exhibitors from all over the country show their skills.
Welcome to Brooklyn Festival Stalls and events along Eastern Parkway provide a focal-point while happenings throughout the borough mark local history and culture.
Feast of St. Anthony of Padua Little Italy. More restrained than the neighborhood's Feast of St. Gennaro (see September), with food stalls along Sullivan Street, the feast culminates with an image of the saint carried through the streets after dark.
Puerto Rican Day Parade See box.
Lesbian and Gay Pride Day Parade Along Fifth Avenue to Washington Square Park and around Greenwich Village. New York's gay and lesbian community stands together for this assertion of strength through unity.

27

Museum Mile Celebration The museums of Fifth Avenue's Museum Mile hold special events and stay open later than usual.

The Metropolitan Opera Free performances in city parks, including Central Park; continues all summer.

Shakespeare in the Park Works by the bard staged for free at Central Park's Delacorte Theater, continues all summer.

July

Feast of O-Bon Japanese music and dance in the Upper West Side's Riverside Park, marking the full moon.

Independence Day celebrations Including Macy's firework display, the site of which varies.

Mostly Mozart Festival At Lincoln Center's Avery Fisher Hall (see page 235); continues into August.

28

The horrors of Halloween

August

Harlem Week A two-week celebration of Harlem's history and culture.

New York Philharmonic Open-air concerts in city parks.

September

Labor Day Parade Along Fifth Avenue. Ostensibly to celebrate the American worker, really just an excuse to mark the end of summer with a parade.

New York Is Book Country Fifth Avenue between 48th and 59th streets. All the major—and many minor—publishers are represented at stalls; many well-known authors give readings and signings.

New York Film Festival At Lincoln Center (see page 234).

Feast of St. Gennaro Lasts ten days along Little Italy's Mulberry Street. Makeshift kitchens serve sausages and hunks of pizza; final night sees a shrine to the saint carried through the streets and showered with dollar bills. (See also page 135.)

Washington Square Outdoor Art Show Stands with locals' artworks and ethnic food sold from stalls.

October

Columbus Day Parade Fifth Avenue between 44th and 72nd streets. As awareness of indigenous American cultures grows throughout the U.S., this parade to commemorate Christopher Columbus' "discovery" of the New World has become increasingly controversial. Many Native American and Hispanic groups—and others—oppose the event.

Halloween Parade Outrageous drag queens and others in freakish costumes parade through Greenwich Village to Washington Square Park Memorial Arch.

New York Marathon Run from Verrazano-Narrows Bridge to Central Park's Tavern on the Green (occasionally early November).

November

Macy's Thanksgiving Day Parade Along Central Park West and Broadway starring the famous helium-filled balloons—more spectacular than you can imagine. Their inflation draws mobs to the area around the American Museum of Natural History.

December

Rockefeller Center The lighting of the Rockefeller Center Christmas Tree in early December kicks off NYC's Christmas season, when many stores mount magical window displays.

❑ Thousands of New Yorkers gather in Times Square to see in the New Year. As midnight approaches, an illuminated ball (disguised as a big apple) slides down Times Tower. ❑

■ During the 16th century, the eastern seaboard of North America was steadily explored by European seafarers, not with the expectation of locating the site of the future world's greatest metropolis but in the hope of finding the North West Passage—a shortcut to the spice islands of the Pacific. Many years were to elapse between the European discovery of the land that now holds New York and its eventual settlement. ■

Early explorers The first European sighting of what became New York was made in 1524 by Giovanni da Verrazano, a Florentine merchant employed by the French. Verrazano described the land he found as having "commodiousness and beauty" and its native inhabitants uttering "loud cries of wonderment" as they spotted the vessels of the Europeans.

It was not until 1609 that a more thorough navigation of the area was made, this time by Henry Hudson, an Englishman working for the Dutch East India Company. Hudson's voyage was made along the river that now bears his name as far north as present-day Albany.

Nieuw Amsterdam (New York), 1673

❑ Before European settlement, the New York area was inhabited by several Native American groups, most being of the Algonquin tribe. The Native Americans, who lived by farming, hunting, and fishing, did not share the European concept of land ownership—the root of many future disputes—but they did share the European enthusiasm for trading, which helped keep early relations fairly cordial.

A sustained series of Dutch-led attacks eventually forced the natives away from the settled areas. European diseases, to which Native Americans lacked immunity, also took their toll. ❑

Like Verrazano, Hudson failed to find the fabled North West Passage, but he did note that the Native Americans were rich in beaver, mink, and otter pelts and were also eager to trade them.

The first New Yorkers Attracted by the prospect of commerce with the Native Americans, the Dutch West India Company was founded in Amsterdam and launched several North American settlements. In 1625, one such settlement—named

The arrival of Henry Hudson in 1609 at the mouth of what is now the Hudson River

New Amsterdam—was founded in what is now Lower Manhattan. It was made up of Dutch and French-speaking Walloon families and their African slaves. In 1626, the leader of the Dutch colony, Peter Minuit, bought Manhattan (a native term possibly meaning "Island of Hills") from a local tribe for a box of tools and trinkets worth the equivalent of $24.

Nieuw Amsterdam onlangs Nieuw Jorck genant : ende hernomen bij de Nederlanders op den 24 Aug: 1673 : eindelijk aan de Engelse weder afgestaan

■ **Though established as a colonial trading base, Dutch New Amsterdam—soon to become British New York—quickly acquired a character of its own, partly through the ethnic and religious diversity of its inhabitants and partly through the fact that many of them came to share a desire to rid themselves of their Old World links for good.** ■

New Amsterdam—success and failure Much to the delight of the Dutch West India Company, New Amsterdam soon began to flourish as a trading center. New settlers arrived, taking advantage of the company's generous land grants. Some came here to escape religious persecution in their homeland, seeking the freedom of worship that the company had promised.

New Amsterdam was far from being the tranquil replica of a Dutch town that the company might have hoped for, however. Violence and lawlessness were rife, unmarried couples cohabited, pigs ran wild in the streets, and—with a tavern for every 12 adults—many of the population spent their spare time drinking to excess.

A new governor In 1647, the corrupt governor was dismissed and the job of bringing order to bear on the wayward colony was given to Peter Stuyvesant, a noted disciplinarian. Under his iron rule, and with a new city charter providing for elected officials, New Amsterdam doubled in population and in size, gaining its first hospital, prison, school, and post office, and its first real commercial institutions.

The colony also gained a protective wall to its north, which would later prove ineffectual at halting British advances but did give rise to the thoroughfare named Wall Street.

Peter Stuyvesant

The British arrive Stuyvesant's unpopularity, coupled with excessive tax demands by the Dutch West India Company, caused the population of New Amsterdam to offer no resistance when four British warships blockaded the harbor in 1664. Under British rule, the colony was renamed New York, after James, Duke of York, brother of King Charles II.

Set between the major British bases to the south and north, and at the mouth of the strategically important Hudson River, it is not surprising that New York became a prominent seaport. Nonetheless, the British proved no more able to stamp their authority on the everyday life of the colony than had the Dutch, and New York remained as socially robust as ever.

By 1700 New York had acquired a population numbering 20,000, composed of a mix of nationalities and religions.

The American Revolution After the 1763 Treaty of Paris confirmed their dominance over the 13 American colonies, the British imposed a series of punitive taxes on the settlements. Previous anticolonial uprisings had been violently quashed by the British, but with the world entering a postcolonial age and the theories of republicanism being universally discussed, the idea of independence became increasingly

Declaration of Independence

> ❏ When the Declaration of Independence was publicly read at New York's Bowling Green in July 1776, the excited crowd overturned the green's equestrian statue of King George III. Legend has it that the lead statue was melted down and turned into bullets, subsequently used against the British. ❏

attractive to the 13 by now economically thriving colonies.

Following the Declaration of Independence in 1776, General George Washington led the war against the British. Many British troops were billeted in New York, where they commandeered food supplies, terrorized locals, and imprisoned captured rebel prisoners on board ships in which hunger and disease were rife.

New York was to remain the last toehold of British rule in the New World. Although the 1783 Treaty of Paris formally ended the War of Independence, not until Washington's march from Harlem into the Bowery in November of that year were the remaining British troops finally withdrawn. Their last act of defiance was to grease the flagpole to hinder the raising of the Stars and Stripes.

■ **As the country's major seaport, New York was the gateway to the New World. Through the 19th century it was on the receiving end of the largest migration in human history; a mass movement of people which not only transformed the city but shaped the future of the entire nation.** ■

New York's population had been markedly cosmopolitan from the earliest days of settlement, and a steady influx of immigrants continued after the Revolution.

Some new arrivals were attracted by the prospect of shaping the first democratic mixed-nationality society, others were radical intellectual rebels driven into exile by governments who feared them, and a few were simply adventurers or fortune-seekers.

In the mid-19th century, however, came the great waves of mass immigration that were to change the city completely.

Mass migrations There were three major factors which contributed to the mass waves of European migration into New York during the first half of the 19th century: the social upheaval which had been caused by the Napoleonic wars, the potato famines in Ireland and Germany, and the industrial revolution, which spread across Europe and robbed many skilled craftsmen and smallholding farmers of their livelihoods.

Arriving in the New World: an engraving of 1892

Immigration into 19th-century New York:
1820s 150,000
1840s 1.7 million
1850s 2.5 million

On the receiving end of a mass movement of people on a scale never before known, New York's overstretched Castle Garden (now called Castle Clinton) immigrant processing center was replaced in 1890 by the federally funded Ellis Island complex. The new receiving center, which was a pristine, state-of-the-art affair, was a far cry from the slums that awaited most new arrivals once they set foot in New York as U.S. citizens.

While not all of the new arrivals stayed in New York, many did, and they placed a massive burden on the city's resources. The 1860s saw the creation of tenements in an effort to fit more people into small areas—five- or six-story buildings where an entire family would sometimes occupy a single windowless room. These tenements earned the nickname "lung blocks" for the high incidence of tuberculosis among their inhabitants. Inadequate drainage and sewage systems made diseases such as yellow fever and cholera a constant threat.

In a city of immigrants, a mix of guile, initiative, and extremely hard work in appalling conditions usually bore rewards, and the major ethnic groups became assimilated and began climbing the city's social ladder comparatively swiftly (particularly as child immigrants reached adulthood fully conversant with the ways of the New World).

The northward spread of Manhattan's grid-style streets was matched by a steady northward flow of wealth. As the city's rich occupied the newest, most northerly homes, their previous dwellings were occupied by prospering ethnic groups while the poor—the latest immigrants—were housed in the south, usually in the tenements of the Lower East Side.

Anti-immigration laws Established and powerful groups campaigned for tighter immigration controls. They feared loss of jobs, the spread of disease and the decline of Anglo-Saxon supremacy (after the Revolution, 60 percent of Americans had been of English origin).

In 1882, the Chinese Exclusion Act banned further Chinese immigration into the U.S. The Act reflected the anti-Chinese feeling that also led to the creation of New York's Chinatown. The U.S. entered the 20th century as the world's richest industrial power, and calls for protecting its economic well-being grew stronger.

The outbreak of World War I encouraged the isolationist stance that paved the way for the immigration curbs of the 1920s (although the granting of U.S. citizenship to Puerto Ricans in 1917 was an exception). Mass immigration as seen in earlier decades came to an end.

❏   Immigration into New York is by no means a thing of the past. Easing of immigration restrictions in the 1960s caused a dramatic expansion of Chinatown (where many inhabitants are now actually Vietnamese or Cambodian). Indians, Koreans, West Indians, Filipinos, Latinos, Middle Eastern nationals, and Eastern Europeans from the former Iron Curtain countries are among the 90,000 people who still settle in New York every year. ❏

■ **Seldom has the entrepreneur (or the rogue) had such opportunities to make a name and a fortune for himself as in 19th-century New York. At that time the city, rapidly evolving from an outpost to a great metropolis, was alive with speculation, sharp dealing and money-making. From those heady times, a handful of names are remembered—fondly or otherwise—in the present day. ■**

John Jacob Astor (1763–1848) A fur-trade millionaire, John Jacob Astor switched his attentions to property in 1834, buying New York land while currying favor with city politicians and ingratiating himself into New York high society. Profits from slum housing helped Astor become the country's richest man by the time he died in 1848. In a rare act of generosity, however, Astor bequeathed $400,000 for the creation of the U.S.'s first public library, now the Public Theater in the East Village.

Andrew Carnegie (1835–1919) Andrew Carnegie started in industry as a cotton-factory worker and rose to become a magnate with interests spanning iron, coal, steel, ships, and railroads. Believing in the motto "a man who dies rich, dies disgraced," Carnegie financed numerous trusts, some 2,000 libraries, and gave $2 million for the building of Carnegie Hall—yet still had $23 million when he died in 1919. The Carnegie mansion on Fifth Avenue is now the home of the Cooper-Hewitt Museum, (see page 95).

From mill-worker to multimillionaire: Andrew Carnegie

❑ When Caroline Schermerhorn married into the Astor family in 1853, she became the fabled "Mrs. Astor," a New York high-society legend for her annual balls, regarded as the city's definitive social barometer. The 400 people invited (400 being the number of people in New York who, it was thought, fit into her ballroom) could consider themselves "in"; those not invited—which included anyone who worked for a living or who had made their millions through railroads—were definitely "out." ❑

Henry Clay Frick (1849–1919) A partner of Andrew Carnegie in the Carnegie Steel Company, Henry Clay Frick was credited with few redeeming qualities. He instigated the blackest event in the history of U.S. labor relations: hiring a mob to bring a steel-mill strike to a violent and murderous end. Some of Frick's fortunes went into acquiring the great stash of European art that now forms the Frick Collection, housed in his Fifth Avenue mansion (see page 110).

Jay Gould (1836–1892) Robber baron, dealer, and socialite, Jay Gould made his first fortune at the age of 21. He would bet on the outcome of Civil War battles, having learned the result by tapping telegraph lines. In 1869 he manipulated the price of gold, made himself a profit of $11 million on the gold market, and inciden-

36

tally brought about the calamitous "Black Friday" financial crash.

John Pierpont Morgan (1837–1913)

Much of the European money invested in the U.S. during the 19th century was channeled through banker and financier John Pierpont Morgan. Able to wield influence on every new project that needed money, Morgan gained considerable wealth and importance. He had a finger in every entrepreneurial pie and oversaw the creation of the U.S. Steel Corporation, which became the world's first billion-dollar business in 1901.

Morgan spent $25 million buying gold to help save New York—and the nation—from bankruptcy in 1907. He also founded the Pierpont Morgan Library (see page 169).

Cornelius Vanderbilt (1794–1877)

Beginning with a ferry service between Staten Island and Manhattan in the early 1800s, Cornelius Vanderbilt built a steamship empire that dominated transportation across New York Bay and plied routes as far afield as Latin America and—at the height of the Gold Rush—to California.

In 1864, Vanderbilt diverted some of his $20 million into railroads, laying the tracks that linked the steel-producing factories of Pittsburgh and the dairy farms of rural New York state to the city's docks—where his cargo ships awaited loading.

When he died in 1877, Vanderbilt was worth $105 million.

❏ J.P. Morgan fully deserved his reputation as a hard-headed businessman, but he regularly consulted society astrologist Evangeline Adams before making decisions. Evidence of the banker's interest in astrology is easy to find at the Pierpont Morgan Library, where symbols of the zodiac are incorporated into the lavish decoration. ❏

37

An early wheeler-dealer: investment banker John Pierpont Morgan

■ **Unusually for a major city, the pattern of New York's expansion is easy to trace. The city's growth was a simple case of the long, narrow island of Manhattan being smothered with urban development, starting at one end and working systematically toward the other.** ■

38

The European settlement of Manhattan began at the island's southern tip, the easiest place for ships to berth. Here the first businesses and homes became established. As the settlement grew, it could only expand northward. In the process, it acquired the haphazard street pattern which remains largely intact in today's Financial District.

The grid plan In 1811, the city's Board of Commissioners ratified a rectangular, grid-style street plan formulated by a surveyor, John Randel. Ignoring all existing streets except for Broadway—a track that followed an ancient Native American route northward—the design called for numbered streets (intended for residence) running east–west and numbered avenues (intended for commerce) running north–south.

The new Brooklyn Bridge must have seemed a miracle in its day

The grid plan provided a much-needed blueprint for Manhattan's development. In 1820, with a population of 123,000, New York was already the U.S.'s largest city, despite barely extending beyond Canal Street. North of Canal Street, a few villages had taken root in what are now Chelsea and Greenwich Village, and the areas now comprising the Upper East Side and the Upper West Side were a mixture of farms, wasteland, and squatters' camps.

When the Erie Canal opened in 1825, it linked New York to the Great Lakes and the agriculturally productive Midwest, and left the city unchallenged as the major American seaport—the gateway to lucrative international trade. This, coupled with the waves of mass immigration which began in the 1840s, set the scene for New York's rapid expansion throughout the 19th century.

élite. By the 1860s, several hundred millionaires were calling Manhattan home. Many of them occupied the luxury apartment houses recently erected along Fifth Avenue, facing the newly created Central Park—and the Upper East Side became the lasting domain of the rich.

A metropolis is born Steadily, the city gained an infrastructure worthy of the metropolis it was becoming. In 1868, the first "El" (or Elevated) train went into service. Two years later the first subway line was drilled. Work on the Brooklyn Bridge—the engineering miracle of its day—began in 1870 and was completed in 1883. Thomas Edison's company began the electrification of the city, opening its first generating station in 1882.

In 1898, the creation of Greater New York linked the five boroughs—Manhattan, Brooklyn, the Bronx, Queens, and Staten Island—under a single municipal government. New York City's population was now 3.8 million, making it the second largest city in the world.

Harlem was speedily developed by 19th-century speculators

Money moves north Property developers wasted little time in moving northward through Manhattan, flattening hilly land and erecting new buildings. Around the mid-1800s, the first of the city's handsome brownstones appeared, providing comfortable accommodation for New York's expanding moneyed classes on the city's northerly fringes.

In the Lower East Side, meanwhile, the first tenement houses arose, sheltering penniless immigrants and swiftly maturing into desperate slums.

As its poor toiled in sweatshops, New York generated incredible wealth for its already well-heeled

❏ When work began on New York's City Hall in 1803, the building stood on what was then the city's northern edge. Marble was used for the building's front and sides, but the north-facing rear was made from cheap red sandstone in the expectation that nobody would ever see it. Such was the rate of New York's expansion, however, that by the time of its completion in 1812, City Hall was already ringed by new buildings. ❏

■ **The U.S.'s early years were colored by frequent financial uncertainties, but none of the early banking troubles quite prepared the city for "Black Tuesday," the Wall Street crash of 1929, which dragged the country—and the world—into the Depression.** ■

New York lasted only a year as the capital of the U.S., but the financial institutions on and around Wall Street—most notably the Stock Exchange, which began as a trading place for the $80 million-worth of bonds created to pay Revolutionary War debts—remained at the heart of the nation's monetary system.

As unscrupulous investors played on the insecurities and inexperience inherent in the new nation's financial systems, crashes were numerous. The panic of 1837 wiped $60 billion dollars off the value of shares and left 50,000 people without jobs; 20 years later, another crash put 40,000 out of work. A further stock-market tumble occurred in 1873, and in 1907 New York's banks had to be saved from insolvency by the wealthy financier J.P. Morgan.

The roaring twenties As the federal government replaced independent financiers and the U.S. emerged from World War I as a rich and powerful nation, financial uncertainties seemed very much a thing of the past.

The economy boomed, and rumors of fortunes being made overnight caused the stock market to trade faster than ever before, its ticker-tape machines struggling to keep up with developments.

Even economically irrelevant events, such as Charles Lindbergh's successful first solo flight across the Atlantic in 1927, were enough to quicken dealing. Trading levels regularly broke new records during 1928.

The crash of 1929 Although warning signals had been observed—industrial production was declining and the economy was beginning to stagnate—few people paid any heed until the

third week of October 1929 when everyone began selling at once. Millions of shares were traded at a loss, causing 11 dealers to kill themselves and October 29, 1929, to go down in history as "Black Tuesday"— the day the Depression began.

> ❏ "Sooner or later a crash is coming, and it may be terrific"— financial expert Roger W. Babson, speaking in September 1929. ❏

By 1932, the Depression's bleakest year, more than a third of New York's 29,000 manufacturing firms had closed down, leaving a quarter of the city's work force idle. Many people unable to afford rent, were living in the shanty towns that appeared in Central Park (dubbed "Hoovervilles" after the incumbent president, Herbert Hoover) and lining up for free food provided by soup kitchens set up in Times Square.

Many of the city's most enduring skyscrapers had appeared through the buoyant 1920s, but now the building boom ground to a halt. The Empire State Building, opened in 1931, had to pay for its upkeep on the proceeds of tourist visits rather than office rents.

La Guardia leads recovery For New Yorkers, the woes of the Depression were made worse by the incompetence of their mayor, Jimmy Walker, better known for his songwriting skills than for his political abilities. Not the first—nor the last—city mayor to be embroiled in a corruption scandal, Walker departed from office in 1932 and fled to Europe. His replacement was Fiorello La Guardia, a young, credible politician pledged to ending corruption and leading the city out of the Depression. While La Guardia engineered the social policies which did indeed lift New York from the Depression, it was Robert Moses who oversaw city planning and development from the 1930s to the 1960s, and gave New York a new look. Old neighborhoods were razed to make way for the Moses-inspired expressways, tunnels, and bridges of the modern city, as well as for specific projects that included the creation of the Lincoln Center and Battery Park City.

Below: the drama of the Wall Street crash, as illustrated by an Italian magazine of the day

Staged in Queens, the 1939 World's Fair was intended to symbolize New York's emergence from the Depression, but it was the country's entry into World War II in 1941 that really restored the city's finances, as tens of thousands of soldiers and streams of tanks, trucks, and planes passed through New York bound for the European theater.

❏ In 1940, the capital budget of New York City was $1. ❏

■ **Police being paid off by criminals and the mayor using public funds for private gain are enduring images of New York—and with good reason. Corruption was part and parcel of New York life from the city's earliest days and has proved a hard vice to shake off, even in recent times.** ■

The Tweed Ring A former volunteer fireman and street-gang member, William Marcy "Boss" Tweed got himself elected in 1851, age 21, as assistant alderman to a council body popularly nicknamed "the 40 Thieves."

Tweed quickly rose to the top of the thuggish faction of New York's Democratic Party (called Tammany after a Native American chief) by promising (and delivering) jobs and money to people—often freshly arrived immigrants—in return for votes. The city's administration was soon under the thumb of the "Tweed Ring," a coterie of corrupt officials who, during their brief reign, are estimated to have helped themselves to $300 million of public money.

As commissioner of public works, Tweed was able to extract fat commissions from construction companies as a reward for giving them lucrative contracts, and to extort large sums from businesses in return for providing essential services. A share of the ill-gotten gains was earmarked for bribes to police, bureaucrats and others, to dissuade them from speaking up.

Tweed's most spectacular swindle involved the construction of the New York County Courthouse (now known informally as the Tweed Courthouse). Started in 1862 with a budget of $250,000, the courthouse eventually cost New York taxpayers $14 million, of which the Tweed Ring creamed off around $12 million.

Eventually, an angry City Hall clerk (said to have been offered a $500,000 bribe to keep quiet) passed incriminating documents to *The New York Times*. In jail, Tweed was allowed out each day for lunch and escaped to Chile before being recaptured. Again imprisoned, he died in 1878 in a jail which his corrupt regime had commissioned.

THE "BRAINS"

The secret of success: one 1871 cartoonist's view

42

❏ Since most of the people who voted for him were illiterate, Tweed claimed to have little interest in what newspapers wrote. He considered the satirical cartoons published in *Harper's Weekly*—which he called "them damn pictures"—to be more damaging to his career than reports on his dirty dealings documented in words. ❏

Mayor William O'Dwyer at his desk in City Hall (below)

Mayors Quaker Fernando Wood was viewed as the man to end corruption at City Hall in 1844, despite previous accusations of fraud and the fact that he was elected mayor with more votes than there were voters. In fact, Wood sold the job of city commissioner for $50,000 and provided guarantees of naturalization to immigrants in return for their electoral favors.

A symbol of the booming 1920s, songwriter and playboy Jimmy Walker was elected mayor in 1925. Walker dressed in white suits, frequented nightclubs, and never arrived for work until the afternoon. After raising his own salary from $25,000 to $40,000, Walker skipped town in 1932 as the news broke that he had taken $1 million in payoffs for city contracts.

After the term of the admired mayor Fiorello La Guardia, it was dirty business as usual at City Hall. The subsequent incumbent, William O'Dwyer, made a swift exit to Mexico in 1951 as his links with organized crime were about to be exposed.

The police In a city corrupt from head to toe, it was little surprise that 19th-century New York police similarly veered off the straight and narrow. Patrolmen routinely acted as paid

lookouts for illegal gambling dens and brothels, while higher ranks improved their salaries with bribes and the proceeds of bank robberies. Crimes were liable to "disappear" in return for payments, and many robberies were investigated only if a reward was offered.

Actual arrests were usually intended to improve the appearance of the city for its affluent classes, removing any "lewd women," beggars, or homeless people from well-to-do areas.

Within the force, payments secured a popular beat and would bring promotion. According to a newspaper report of 1892, a fee of $300 was required to become a patrolman, while $14,000 was the asking price for a precinct captain's job.

■ It may be a bastion of big business, high finance, the media, and the arts, but New York's lofty position in the hierarchy of world cities is largely due to the simple matter of possessing an outstanding natural harbor. This stroke of geographical good fortune made possible its rise from an obscure colonial trading post to the world's greatest port. ■

Early days New York's discovery by Europeans stemmed from the search for the North West Passage, a shortcut to the spice islands of the Pacific. Early explorers did not find the shortcut, but they did record that New York Bay provided a safe, sheltered anchorage in an area that enjoyed a comparatively mild climate and was relatively free of fog. With the Hudson River, the bay also provided access to a navigable route inland.

Even so, New York was but one of several moderately busy ports on the continent's east coast and was fortunate when the British—then ruling over the American colonies—chose it in preference to Boston as the main recipient of their exports.

The Erie Canal The trigger of New York's phenomenal rise as a seaport—and its subsequent emergence as a major world city—was the building of the Erie Canal. The Hudson River provided a transportation route between the city and the upstate farms (and the important

❑ New York's waterside streets were traditionally among the dirtiest, most dangerous, and crime-ridden in the city. The glamour accorded to Fifth Avenue partially derived from its geographical position: plumb in the center of Manhattan and as far from the rivers as it was possible to be. ❑

towns of New England), but the Erie Canal—begun in 1817 and completed in 1825 at a cost of $7 million—connected the Hudson to Lake Erie and thereby opened a swift, direct line of communication between New York and, via the Great Lakes, the newly settled farmlands of the Midwest.

Using the canal, the 500-mile journey between Buffalo (on Lake Erie's shores) and the city could be completed in 10 days. With the American

Manhattan and several of its numerous busy piers in the 1860s

The 20th-century port: South Street Seaport today (above) and (right) the Queen Mary *at 51st Street Pier*

heartland opened up, ships from almost every nation converged on New York bearing products destined for the interior.

The port expands By the turn of the 20th century, the southern end of Manhattan was lined by 22 miles of docks, with 270 piers extending along the East River and the Hudson River.

The advent of the railroads did more to improve New York's transportation links. Many freight lines ran directly to the docks, while Grand Central Station (now Grand Central Terminal) became the country's foremost rail passenger station.

By the 1930s, "the freighter, the river boat, the ferry and the soot-faced tug" plied the city's rivers—making the Hudson River itself barely viewable below 23rd Street. They were among the 3,500 vessels that berthed in New York each month.

Ocean-going luxury Cargo may have been the bread and butter of the New York docks, but the city's place among the world's great ports was symbolized by the graceful ocean liners of the 1910s to the 1940s. Greeted by low-flying planes and water jets, the *Queen Mary* arrived in New York for the first time in 1936 and was just one of several

vessels regularly ferrying the rich and famous between Europe and the U.S., where New York welcomed them in a blaze of publicity.

Gradual decline Changing patterns in international trade caused New York's port to lose its commercial importance. Simultaneously, the rising popularity of air travel reduced the demand for ocean-going liners. One by one, the great passenger ships made their final farewells to New York, although the *Q.E.2* (as well as modern cruise ships) is still a regular visitor. Nonetheless, the port of New York is the third busiest in the U.S. (after New Orleans and Houston) and annually handles 116.7 million tons of freight. Meanwhile, the fall in passenger routes failed to deter the construction, at a cost of $40 million, of a new passenger ship terminal on the Hudson River in 1974.

■ **Three centuries of almost constant growth had made it one of the world's most affluent cities, so nobody could quite believe the news in 1975 that New York was on the verge of bankruptcy. Years of poor economic management, however, had left city finances in tatters.** ■

The 1960s was a decade of turmoil and change throughout the country. In New York, violence erupted in the black ghettos of Brooklyn and Harlem, tens of thousands of Puerto Rican immigrants settled in East Harlem and the Lower East Side, and the so-called "White Flight"—the movement of around a million white middle-class families, and many businesses, out of New York—was in full swing.

Strained resources The exodus of the affluent white-collar workers and of many profitable companies (600,000 jobs disappeared in the six years from 1969) eroded one of the city's main sources of revenue at a time when the cost of its welfare policies, then among the most liberal in the country, was spiraling upward.

The incumbent mayor, John Lindsay, insisted that there would be no cuts in welfare services. Through Lindsay's intransigence, a strike by 34,000 transit workers, which brought the city to a standstill in 1966, ended up costing the city $70 million and gave the

❏ "Saving New York is like making love with a gorilla—you don't stop when you're tired, you stop when the gorilla's tired"—Felix Rohatyn, Chairman of M.A.C. ❏

green light to other unions to demand high pay increases.

Meanwhile, the number of people employed by the city had grown by nearly a third in five years, and their wages—plus increased pensions and other benefits—put further strain on the city's finances. The city administration resorted to ever more creative accounting in order to maintain its levels of expenditure, at one stage even creating a 364-day year to enable debts to be passed on to the next 12-month period. This short-term planning had the effect of increasing interest levels on money borrowed by the city—and simply postponed an inevitable crisis.

Brink of disaster This state of financial disorder was inherited by Abe Beame, elected mayor in 1974. An accountant by profession, Beame was nonetheless unable to balance the city's books, and in 1975 New York was $2 billion in the red.

NEWSPAPER GUILD OF NEW YORK ON STRIKE

❏ "Ford to City: Drop Dead!"— *Daily News* headline encapsulating President Ford's attitude to New York's financial crisis. ❏

Strikes dogged 1960s New York

Lines at Grand Central Terminal in the 1966 transit workers' strike

As Wall Street financiers warned that municipal bonds would soon be worthless, Beame made cuts in public expenditure on a scale not seen since the Depression and labor unions agreed to wage freezes.

With no money to pay for garbage collection or water supplies—and with President Ford refusing federal aid—New York's entire infrastructure seemed about to collapse.

Rescue The governor of New York injected state funds into the city and set up the Municipal Assistance Corporation (popularly known as the Big M.A.C.) to control expenditure at City Hall, but it took an eleventh-hour loan from the city's sanitation workers' union to finally pull New York back from the brink. Being advised that the future of the world economic system depended on New York's survival, the White House eventually agreed to a $2.3 billion federal loan.

In effect, the city came under the control of the M.A.C., whose primary concern was to retain the confidence of bankers. New York's underfunded services continued to decline, and welfare benefit levels were frozen for seven years.

Recovery and Ed Koch Elected in 1978, Ed Koch had a larger-than-life style that made him a popular mayor, and he presided over years of steady recovery. Money was saved by laying off approximately 65,000 city workers, while others accepted wage freezes lasting several years, making further reductions in social services. A tight grip on public expenditure helped make Koch popular with big business and encouraged a Manhattan office building boom. Symbolically, in 1976 the World Trade Center leased all its office space after three years of being largely empty and, by the mid-1980s, the stock market was booming.

Yet, as Wall Street buzzed, a 1985 survey found that more than 23 percent of New Yorkers were living below the poverty line.

Ed Koch

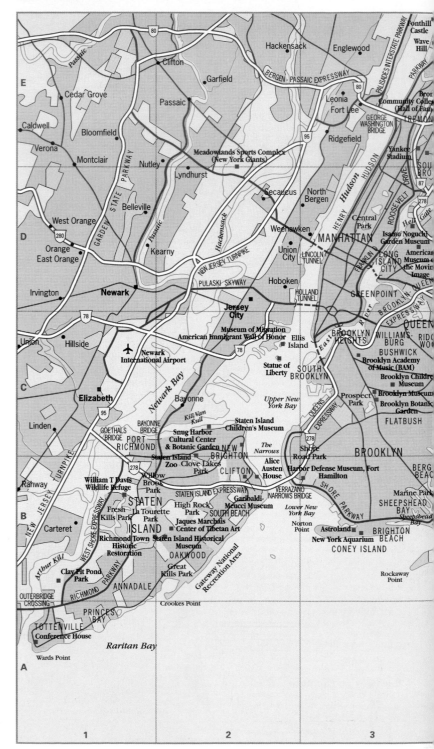

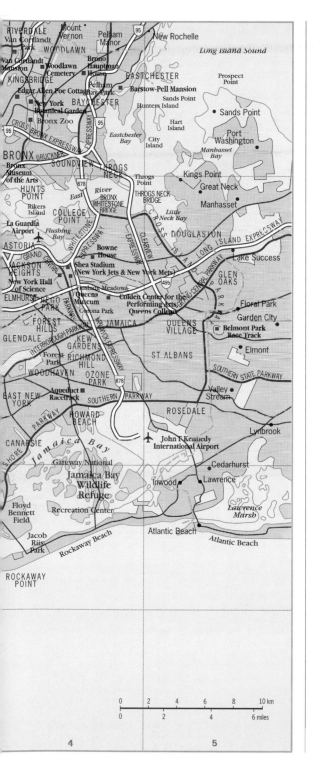

Browsing in Greenwich Village makes good entertainment: stores here range from the mildly quirky to the completely outlandish

Not for nothing did they name New York twice. What most people think of as being New York is really Manhattan, a long, narrow island squeezed between two rivers. Manhattan is the kernel of New York life, home to much of the city's affluence and élan. Most New Yorkers live in the so-called Outer Boroughs which form the remainder of New York City: Brooklyn, the Bronx, Queens, and Staten Island.

Manhattan As far as the rest of the world is concerned, the island of Manhattan is everything that defines New York, with its towering skyscrapers, teeming streets, ceaseless noise, and giant neon advertisements that turn night into day. However, strangely enough, only a fraction of Manhattan—just over 12 miles long and for the most part 2½ miles wide—actually fits this image. The island is divided into a number of separate areas, and each has its own distinctive history, looks, atmosphere, and residents.

Lower Manhattan At Manhattan's southern extremity, the modern high-rise towers of the **Financial District** rise above the oldest part of New York. It was here that the first Dutch settlement took root and, while few markers of the colonial days remain, the entrepreneurial spirit with which the colony was founded remains very much alive—from the floor of the New York Stock Exchange to the street-side foodstands dispensing all kinds of ethnic food to power-dressed brokers.

Pressed hard against the Financial District's northern edge, the short busy streets of **Chinatown** make up one of New York's longest-established ethnic areas. Lately, Chinatown's banks, bakeries, and dim sum houses have spread across the traditional boundaries into **Little Italy**— a tiny area where freshly made cappuccino and creamy pastries can still be consumed at sidewalk tables.

To the west, the ethnic atmosphere gives way to arti-ness in compact **SoHo** and **TriBeCa**, trendy locations that, not long ago, were derelict industrial areas—prime examples of the neighborhood transformations that are a New York specialty.

By contrast, the elbow of land jutting towards the East River is consumed by the **Lower East Side**, a long-time first base of newly arrived immigrants, and now home of cut-rate shops and street markets where the work-hard-and-prosper ethos that built the city stays strongly in evidence.

Some New Yorkers never venture deeper into Manhattan than **Greenwich Village**, an area packed with restaurants, cafés, bars, and clubs. Greenwich Village also has some fine houses, intriguing narrow streets, and even today, a knack for attracting the writers and artists who, historically, have shaped American culture.

Across Broadway—which runs the length of Manhat-tan—the **East Village** is a gritty counterpart to Greenwich Village: its clubs and bars are fewer and less polished, while quirky shops and offbeat cafés serve the area's modern-day Bohemians, lured by comparatively inexpen-sive rents and the earthy, uncommercialized nature of the area.

H.G. Wells on New York
"To Europe, she was America, to America she was the gateway of the earth. But to tell the story of New York would be to write a social history of the world."

Choose from a few skyscraper viewing galleries to contem-plate the almost unbelievable panorama of Manhattan and beyond

51

The W.P.A. Guide to New York City (1939)
The guide—commissioned during the Depression to create jobs for writers—gave this description of the scene around the Hudson River docks: "A surging mass of back-firing, horn-blowing, gear-grinding trucks and taxis."

Ogden Nash on the Bronx
"The Bronx? No thonx," wrote Ogden Nash in 1931, his four words summing up many a New Yorker's attitude to this particular Outer Borough. Nash later offered an apologetic update: "The Bronx? God Bless Them."
Unfortunately for the Bronx, few remember latter verse as well as the former, which is usually the one to be quoted.

Leon Trotsky on New York
"New York impressed me tremendously because, more than any other city in the world, it is the fullest expression of our modern age."

Little Italy—one of several ethnic areas that make up New York's complex cosmopolitan patchwork

Midtown Manhattan Unlike Lower Manhattan, where the streets tend to have names and to be short and crooked, Midtown Manhattan is all numbered streets and avenues that fortunately make the visitor's life a simple one.

With the exception of the Statue of Liberty (which holds its flame aloft off Manhattan's southern tip), Midtown Manhattan includes almost all of New York's main attractions: the Empire State Building, the United Nations complex, Rockefeller Center, St. Patrick's Cathedral, the Chrysler Building, Grand Central Terminal, the Broadway theater district, and department stores such as Macy's and Bloomingdale's, as well as broad, busy thoroughfares packed with people and reverberating to the wail of police sirens.

Midtown Manhattan's northern border is defined by the southern perimeter of **Central Park**, an imposing and precisely rectangular chunk of greenery which re-creates a piece of the country in the heart of the city. At this, Central Park succeeds admirably.

Upper Manhattan To the east of Central Park, gaining much of its long-lasting prestige from the mansions and apartment houses erected to face the bucolic expanse, the **Upper East Side** is far and away Manhattan's wealthiest neighborhood, a fact borne out by its exclusive clothes stores, gourmet restaurants and sizable gathering of upscale art galleries.

Three of the city's major art museums are located here: the Metropolitan Museum of Art, the Guggenheim Museum, and the Whitney Museum of American Art. To enjoy art in a luxurious setting, it is hard to beat the Frick Collection, still housed in Henry Clay Frick's 19th-century mansion.

Across Central Park, the **Upper West Side** offers Lincoln Center, the American Museum of Natural History, and the Cathedral of St. John the Divine as its major attractions. The neighborhood's tall apartment houses—among them the Dakota, which has been home to celebrities ranging from Judy Garland to Leonard

The Wollman Memorial Rink in Central Park

Bernstein and John Lennon—were the height of luxury living at the turn of the century and are still coveted addresses in what has grown into a vibrant bastion of the upper middle class.

Stretching across the northern reaches of Upper Manhattan, **Harlem** has played a key role in the history and culture of black America from the turn of the century, though in recent decades it has unfortunately been plagued by the poverty and crime common to deprived inner city areas. **East Harlem**, above the Upper East Side, is the center of the city's enormous Puerto Rican population; it, too, has sadly had more than its share of social problems.

The Outer Boroughs Locals would quickly disagree but, unless your time is limitless, the Outer Boroughs probably merit no more than day-trip excursions from Manhattan.

Brooklyn, with the exceptional Brooklyn Museum and the enjoyable Brooklyn Heights neighborhood, has most in its favor. On the coast, Brooklyn also has Coney Island. Its glory days are long gone but the amusement area and boardwalk remain a curious piece of Americana. The latter leads to the New York Aquarium and to the lively Russian community of Brighton Beach.

Surprisingly large, **Staten Island** is also worth a visit, partly for the fun of the ferry ride to reach it, but also to enjoy the refreshingly pastoral pace and the scattering of low-key museums.

In the **Bronx**, the Bronx Zoo (now called the Wildlife Conservation Park) is wonderful, as is the excellent New York Botanical Garden which is next door. A more somber relic is the cottage in which neglected author Edgar Allan Poe resided for two troubled years.

In suburban **Queens** (named to honor the wife of England's King Charles II), worthwhile features tend to be far-flung and unrewarding. Exceptions are the thriving ethnic communities, and the American Museum of the Moving Image.

Le Corbusier on New York
"A hundred times I have thought New York is a catastrophe and fifty times: It is a beautiful catastrophe."

ADMISSION TICKET

Richmondtown Restoration

New York City's Historic Village

■ You may hear—or fear—that New York is a dangerous place. But for every New York visitor who gets mugged (or worse), there are many hundreds more who leave the Big Apple with nothing but good memories—and millions have lived there for years without becoming crime victims. Unless you are very unlucky, surviving New York simply means being prepared. ■

Nighttime no-go areas
Wherever you go in Manhattan at night, you will need to be more cautious than by day. Several areas that you might visit with comparative nonchalance in daylight (most of which are described in the A to Z section of this book) should be regarded as off-limits at night: Alphabet City past Avenue C (Avenues A and B are fine), Central Park, the western edge of Greenwich Village along the Hudson River, Harlem, and most of Midtown Manhattan west of the theater district.
A native's rule of thumb: if the street is busy, you're okay; if deserted, make a beeline for the nearest avenue, or hail the first yellow cab you see.

Arriving Airports are comparatively safe havens, but be sure to check transportation routes into the city *before* leaving the terminal building.

If you take a taxi from the airport, look for the uniformed guide who will show you to the official taxi dispatch lines. Stick to official yellow-cab operators, and always check that the cab meter is on and make sure the driver is not quoting a price he has decided on. Official fares are those on the meter, with a few permitted exceptions which are clearly posted on the back of the front seat. (There's an extra 50¢ charge after 8 PM, for instance.)

Arriving at Manhattan's train and bus terminals can be more problematic, especially late at night. Although taxis can usually be hailed immediately outside, it is worth taking the trouble to plan your route from the terminal in advance. Do not let a stranger carry your bags for you. If you are planning to walk to your hotel, make sure you know the route, and be aware of the seediness of some streets west of Ninth Avenue in Midtown Manhattan.

Walking in the city Stash your valuables in the hotel safe and carry only enough cash to get you through the day. Never carry a wad of cash. If you are embarking on a major shopping expedition, take credit cards or traveler's checks to pay for your purchases.

Walking is much the best way to explore Manhattan, but you should exercise common sense when doing so. Stick

The city's self-styled (and controversial) "Guardian Angels" aim to keep the streets and subways free from crime and violence

with the crowds, avoid deserted alleys, and do not flash expensive jewelry—even costume jewelry, since it might not be recognized as such. Women should not hang bags on the backs of chairs in restaurants, and men should carry their wallets in their front pockets.

Plan your route before setting out. Manhattan's grid system makes navigation easy (though Lower Manhattan can be confusing). Even for lifelong New Yorkers, no street is perfectly safe, so never carry anything that can be easily snatched. Do not be taken in by anyone who approaches you with a hard luck story, and beware that if you buy watches or jewelry in the street, they are likely to be fakes. Videotapes bought on the street are likely to be defective or blank.

At night, again stick to the crowds on the major north-south thoroughfares, such as Broadway and Fifth Avenue, and on the main streets of Greenwich Village. If you need to walk east–west, go along a major traffic-bearing street rather than risk a short cut along a quiet one. Walk near the curb.

Riding the subway While some people still regard going down into New York's subway system as akin to a descent into hell, the system is by no means the Dante's Inferno that it may have been a few years ago. Certainly there is no speedier way to get around.

By day your biggest problem is figuring out the subway system (see pages 252–253 for how to do this). If you find yourself at the wrong station in an unsavory neighborhood, simply take the next train back as soon as you can.

Late at night in the subway, you may well find a cheerful crowd in a partying mood along with people on the night shift headed to or from their jobs—or you may find the train empty. To be on the safe side, always board the middle cars, where one of the conductors usually sits, or look for occupied cars. If you are waiting on a near-deserted platform, look for the supervised "off-hours" waiting area. Once on board, stay alert and get off at the station you intend to.

Faster than walking, driving or taking the bus, the New York subway is usually crowded only during rush-hour periods

Ready cash
The odds are astronomical against your being mugged in New York, but should a figure leap from the shadows and demand money, it is a good idea to have some cash ready to hand over. Many New Yorkers have got into the habit of carrying a small sum (sometimes contained in a spare wallet), usually around $20, partly to avoid losing a larger amount and partly to save time. The longer a mugger has to wait, the more unstable he may become.

Itineraries

You could spend your entire life in New York and never
feel you had seen the whole city. Nonetheless, these suggested itineraries will provide as balanced a view of New
York as is possible within limited time periods.

Weekend itinerary
Day one In the morning, visit the Empire State Building
and continue on foot to the New York Public Library,
Rockefeller Center, and St. Patrick's Cathedral. Have
lunch in Midtown Manhattan and spend the afternoon at
the Museum of Modern Art.
Day two Take an early-morning ferry from Battery Park to
the Statue of Liberty and Ellis Island. After returning, have
lunch at the World Financial Center and spend the afternoon exploring Greenwich Village.

56

*More than 20 years
after losing its world-
record status, the
Empire State
Building is still a
magnet for visitors*

One-week itinerary
Day one As day one of weekend itinerary.
Day two Take an early-morning ferry from Battery Park to
the Statue of Liberty and Ellis Island. After returning, have
lunch at the World Trade Center and spend the afternoon
exploring the Financial District and South Street Seaport.
Day three Spend the whole day at the Metropolitan
Museum of Art. If a whole day seems too long, spend
part of it shopping for clothes in Midtown and along
Madison Avenue, or in the discount outlets of Lower
Manhattan.
Day four In the morning, explore Central Park. Travel to
Greenwich Village for lunch and spend the afternoon
exploring Greenwich Village, SoHo, Little Italy, and
Chinatown.
Day five On the Upper East Side, tour the Frick Collection
or the Cooper-Hewitt Museum. After lunch, continue to
the Guggenheim Museum or the Whitney Museum of
American Art.
Day six Travel by subway to the Brooklyn Museum.
Spend the day at the museum, pausing to eat a picnic
lunch in the Brooklyn Botanic Garden. Alternatively,
spend the day exploring Brooklyn Heights, dropping into
the Brooklyn Historical Society and continuing to the New
York Transit Museum.
Day seven Tour the Lower East Side and the East Village.
After lunch, explore the Gramercy Park area and conclude
at the Pierpont Morgan Library.

SIGHTSEEING TOURS
N.Y. APPLE TOURS
SIGHTSEEING
ADULT $ 15 ⁰⁰
Hop-on Hop-off
Service

Two-week itinerary

Day one As day one of weekend itinerary.

Day two As day two of week itinerary.

Day three As day three of week itinerary.

Day four In the morning, explore Central Park. Have lunch on the Upper West Side before visiting the American Museum of Natural History.

Day five Spend the whole day on Staten Island, visiting the Snug Harbor Cultural Center, the Richmondtown Historic Restoration, and the Jacques Marchais Center of Tibetan Art.

Day six Tour the Lower East Side and Chinatown. Have lunch in Chinatown and spend the afternoon exploring Greenwich Village.

Day seven As day six of week itinerary.

Day eight On the Upper East Side, zip through the Frick Collection or the Cooper-Hewitt Museum. After a late lunch, continue to the Museum of the City of New York.

Day nine Visit the Forbes Galleries and idle away the rest of the morning in Washington Square Park. Have lunch at a café in Greenwich Village and then continue to the East Village, or explore the Gramercy Park area, and conclude your sightseeing at the Pierpont Morgan Library on 36th Street.

Day ten Explore Harlem and the museums of the Audubon complex on West 155th Street. After lunch, tour the Columbia University campus and the Cathedral of St. John the Divine.

Day eleven Visit Bronx Zoo and the New York Botanical Garden.

Day twelve Divide the day between the Whitney Museum of American Art and the Guggenheim Museum.

Day thirteen Travel by subway to Coney Island, tour the New York Aquarium and continue to Brighton Beach.

Day fourteen Spend the morning at the Cloisters, returning to Midtown Manhattan for lunch and to visit the Museum of T.V. and Radio, or the American Craft Museum—and any landmark building you have yet to view at close quarters.

The Statue of Liberty is essential viewing, even if you're on a flying visit to the Big Apple

Guided tours of Harlem
Harlem is one of New York's most celebrated areas but can be intimidating for the first-time visitor. One way to see Harlem without worries is with a guided tour. Harlem Spirituals, Inc (tel: 757–0425) offers a choice of three: a Sunday tour that combines a gospel church service with a tour of historic Harlem, a weekday tour that offers a soulfood lunch and a local history commentary, and an evening fling based around several hours of jazz at the Cotton Club.

■ **From the top of the World Trade Center or the decks of the Staten Island Ferry, New York has views that no other city comes close to matching. Public observation decks are a feature of a few Manhattan skyscrapers—a couple of which, in their day, were the tallest buildings in the world. The Empire State Building and the Woolworth Building are two that can now be viewed from the top of even taller towers—an angle their architects never imagined possible.**

If heights are not your strong point, then leave Manhattan to view it from afar. And do not give up on New York views as night falls; a panorama of Manhattan by night is a sight you will remember for years. ■

H.G. Wells on New York views, 1906
"Suddenly as I looked back at the skyscrapers of lower New York a queer fancy sprang into my head. They reminded me quite irresistibly of piled-up packing cases outside a warehouse. I was amazed I had not seen the resemblance before."

Empire State Building This is the star of virtually every Manhattan view except those from its own 86th-floor observation level. On a clear day, the eagle-eyed can see through the wire mesh into Massachusetts and Pennsylvania and peer down at jets swooping into New York's airports. Come after dusk to see nighttime Manhattan: the building is open until midnight.

World Trade Center The twin towers are only eight stories taller than the Empire State Building, but their sheer sides make them seem far higher. From the southernmost tower's observation level, the long-distance views are not significantly different from those of the Empire State Building. From the open-air rooftop level, however, the experience is quite different as a simple turn of the head brings a near-360 degree sweep of the New York area and beyond.

Rockefeller Center Look out from the 65th-floor windows of the Rainbow Room restaurant complex in the G.E. (formerly R.C.A.) Building and the Empire State Building rises regally to the south as the World Trade Center looms to its rear. Look north, and the green rectangle of Central Park cuts between the stately apartment buildings of the Upper East Side and the Upper West Side toward Harlem.

Above the East River From its terminal at the junction of Second Avenue and 60th Street, the cable car that crosses the East River to Roosevelt Island gives clear views of the island's former lunatic asylums and hospitals. The memorable views, though, are in the other direction, taking in a lengthy swath of riverside Manhattan from Midtown's United Nations complex northward, far into the Upper East Side. A bonus is a bird's-eye view of any passing river traffic.

Fort Tryon Park Close to the northern tip of Manhattan, Fort Tryon Park offers not only the unexpected sight of a reassembled medieval European monastery (the

Cloisters) but also, from the hilltop site of the fort itself, views across the Hudson River to New Jersey's Palisades Park and, on the other side of Manhattan, the Harlem River.

Brooklyn Some of the most rewarding views of Manhattan are found by leaving it. From Brooklyn Heights Promenade, the eastern edge of the Financial District—the so-called Water Street corridor, a heady mix of glass, steel, limestone, and marble—walls the East River. In the foreground are the tall ships of South Street Seaport. Behind Water Street's forest of high-rises, you should be able to pick out two of the world's one-time highest buildings, the Woolworth Building and the World Trade Center, while two more, the Chrysler Building and the Empire State Building, are visible in the cluster of skyscrapers marking Midtown Manhattan.

Brooklyn Bridge Be sure not to use up all your film on the Promenade: returning to Manhattan on foot across the Brooklyn Bridge reveals the same scenes from continually shifting perspectives behind the struts of the bridge, providing endless scope for inventive photographers.

Staten Island Ferry Look across the harbor from Brooklyn Heights to see the green hills of Staten Island rising to the south. You might also spot the Staten Island Ferry as it plies between the island and the southern tip of the Financial District.

Riding the ferry is much more interesting than looking at it, however. From the vessel are dramatic views of Manhattan's skyline (best on the return leg, when the skyscrapers appear to grow bigger and bigger) and slightly less dramatic ones of Governors Island (occupied by the U.S. Coast Guard), the Statue of Liberty, and the world's longest suspension bridge, the Verrazano-Narrows Bridge, which links Staten Island (itself a place of attractive views) to Brooklyn.

Statue of Liberty views
At the Statue of Liberty, which sits on an island between Manhattan and New Jersey, the outlook is stirring. Across the Hudson River, Battery Park City and the World Trade Center are prominent. In the foreground, scores of yachts, tugs and pleasure boats skim by on the water, while helicopters zip past overhead.

The Tompkins Square Park riot

In the heart of Alphabet City, Tompkins Square Park was the scene of a heavy-handed police operation on a steamy August night in 1988, when 12 mounted police, soon joined by 400 reinforcements, battled for four hours to clear the 16-acre park of the homeless people who were occupying it.

The incident was recorded on video by a local artist and the police brutality that the playback showed triggered outrage across the city, and nightly violence at the park. Mayor Dinkins closed the park for major renovations, posting police guards to keep out anyone but dog-walkers and basketball players. Reopened, the park is now fairly peaceful during the day.

Tompkins Square Park, in Alphabet City, has seen its share of problems, but it is now a fairly safe and peaceful place in daylight

▶ Abigail Adams Smith Museum 151D3

61st Street at York Avenue
Subway: N, R, 4, 6; 59th Street

Neither Abigail Adams, daughter of John Adams, the second president of the U.S., nor her husband, William Stephens Smith, an aide to George Washington, ever lived in what is now the Abigail Adams Smith Museum. Instead, the ashlar stone building—a characterful structure enclosed by less distinguished modern buildings—was the carriage house of their intended 23-acre country estate on the banks of the East River.

Financial decline caused the couple to move on in 1799, however. The stables were converted first to an inn and then to a private residence before being purchased in 1924 by the Colonial Dames of America, an organization pledged to preserving the history of the revolutionary period. The building was gradually equipped with the Federal-period furnishings and objects which now fill nine of its rooms, making for an entertaining half-hour's viewing.

Alphabet City IFCC3

Subway: subway lines Second Avenue

The process of gentrification that spread through Greenwich Village in the 1970s continued into the East Village. By the mid-1980s it had reached Alphabet City (so-called for having lettered rather than numbered avenues), which lies east of First Avenue between Houston and 14th streets. With its restaurants offering cuisines from Asia to Eastern Europe, the area draws mainstream New Yorkers in search of new dining experiences. Among its resident population are those wealthy enough to inhabit a classy, if usually small, renovated apartment in one of the many former tenement blocks.

Most of Alphabet City's population, however, are Puerto Ricans who have informally dubbed the area

The Abigail Adams Smith Museum occupies an elegant 18th-century carriage house

"loisaida" (pronounced "low-ees-SIDE-ah"), a phrase reputedly first used by a local poet and playwright. The neighborhood suffered from urban blight into the early 1980s, but the efforts of the local community and a major police initiative—and the rising interest of property developers—all contributed to regeneration. Much poverty remains though, and the area east of Avenue B can seem intimidating to outsiders.

▶ American Academy and Institute of Arts & Letters   *IBCD2*

Broadway at 155th Street
Subway: C, D, 1; 155th or 157th streets
Two august cultural bodies—the National Institute of Arts, founded in 1898, and the American Academy, founded in 1904—unified in 1977 and jointly honor American achievements in art, writing, and music.

Although much of its activity may appear to be little more than mutual backslapping, the organization also administers grants to deserving artistic causes and stages temporary seasonal exhibitions highlighting the work of individual members. If your favorite author, painter, or composer is being featured, it could be worth a visit. For details, tel: 368–5900.

▶ American Bible Society   *151D1*
Broadway at 61st Street
Subway: A, B, C, D, 1, 2, 3, 9; 59th Street
A 1960s cast-in-place concrete structure a bagel's throw from busy Columbus Circle makes an unlikely home for the American Bible Society, founded in 1816 in order to circulate the Bible "without note or comment."

The bibles the society has distributed are less notable than the bibles that it has gathered, however. Over the years, historic bibles from near and far have been collected to form the society's extensive library and archive. It includes an illustrated Armenian account of the Four Gospels dated to the early 1400s and a 16th-century bible translated by a New England preacher into Massachusetts (an Algonquin Native American dialect).

A few changing selections are displayed on the second-floor level, alongside a reconstruction of a Gutenberg printing press and a feature on the Dead Sea Scrolls.

Audubon Terrace
The American Academy and Institute of Arts & Letters occupies one section of Audubon Terrace, a Renaissance Revival complex planned in 1908 and intended to provide a suitably imposing setting for several venerable national institutions—others among them including the American Numismatic Society (see page 65) and the Hispanic Society of America (see page 126).

Situated between Riverside Drive and Broadway and 155th and 156th streets, the scheme was never entirely successful: not only a poor architectural job, it also left its tenants in a humdrum residential area far removed from the ebb and flow of New York life.

The terrace was built on a part of the estate of John James Audubon, the eminent American naturalist of the early 1800s.

Changing exhibitions of pottery, textiles, furniture, and other artifacts can be viewed in spacious surroundings at the American Craft Museum, which showcases the work of contemporary craftspeople

Museum of American Illustration

Within a few steps of the American Federation of the Arts, the Society of Illustrators (63rd Street between Lexington and Park avenues), established in 1875, holds the small but interesting Museum of American Illustration. Through lively temporary exhibitions, the museum highlights the contribution made to Americans' self-image through cartoons, advertising, book and magazine drawings, and much more. The museum is free; for the latest exhibition details, tel: 838–2560.

▶▶ **American Craft Museum**   *151C2*

53rd Street between Fifth and Sixth avenues
Subway: E, F; Fifth Avenue

From teapots and tapestries to baskets and brooches, the exhibits of the American Craft Museum are always stimulating. Chosen from the museum's own vast collection or using loaned pieces, the displays illustrate design trends and techniques and often feature the work of the most artistic and skillful 20th-century American craftsmen and women.

The museum is run by the American Craft Council, whose purchase of a brownstone house on this site in 1959 turned out to be a wise investment. A 1980s property speculator eager to erect a high-rise here agreed to give the museum a spacious chunk of the new building's first floor, enabling the displays to be mounted around a lovely three-story atrium—and partially viewed for free through the museum's huge front window.

▶ **American Federation of the Arts**   *151D2*

65th Street between Park and Madison avenues
Subway: 6; 68th Street

The American Federation of the Arts collects and arranges traveling exhibitions for the small museums of the U.S., often finding time to display some of them in its own galleries. It is pot luck what might be on display, but a look inside also reveals the building's lavishly decorated interior, a 1960s restoration of what was originally the home of a successful stockbroker, built around 1910.

▶▶ **American Museum of Natural History** *IFCF2*

Central Park West and 79th Street

Subway. 1, 9, B, C, 79th Street or 81st Street

With 36 million exhibits, this is one of the world's best-stocked museums. Whether you are gazing at a stuffed saber-toothed tiger or an ancient inscription from Guatemala, there is every chance it will be among the foremost examples of its kind on show anywhere in the world.

Darwin's theory of evolution and Mendel's law of heredity were two of the natural science breakthroughs that provided the stimulus for the museum's founding in 1869. Within a decade, the collections had acquired a specially built home, a stately Romanesque structure beside Central Park intended to be the "largest building on the continent."

The sheer size of the collections of the American Museum of Natural History makes it a daunting prospect even for the most enthusiastic visitor. One way to discover the best of the museum without wearing yourself into the ground is to join a free hour long guided Highlights Tour. These depart several times daily; details from any of the museum's information desks (tel: 769–5100). Greatly improved by a $30 million restructuring, the museum's fossil collection—already among the best in the world—now forms part of a six room, state-of-the-art complex revealing the intricacies of the evolutionary relationships as far back as the Jurassic period (180–120 million years ago). The climax of this section are the two Dinosaur Halls, which feature magnificent skeletons of Tyrannosaurus Rex and Apatosaurus.

Carl Akeley

The Akeley Gallery at the American Museum of Natural History is named after Carl Akeley, a naturalist, explorer and inventor. Akeley twice narrowly escaped death by dangerous animal. In 1911, he was gored by an elephant but saved himself by swinging beneath the creature's body; on another occasion, he ran out of bullets while confronted by an angry leopard but saved himself by strangling it. Among his many technical innovations was a new taxidermy technique, which he employed on the seven elephants that stand in the gallery. Ironically, Akeley died in 1926 from complications arising from a gnat bite.

Massive exhibit in a massive museum— the Barosaurus at the Museum of Natural History

Hayden Planetarium
Adjacent to the American Museum of Natural History is the copper-domed Hayden Planetarium, which holds astronomy exhibitions and excellent hourlong "Sky Shows," taking visitors on voyages through the cosmos using state-of-the-art technology. For details, tel: 769-5100.

The gorilla diorama at the American Museum of Natural History. Few aspects of the world's wildlife are left untouched by the museum's vast collections

Native American life and the evolution of North American animal and bird species are outlined by comprehensive but fairly dreary habitat dioramas.

More enjoyable are the excellently arranged anthropological collections on Africa, Asia, and Central and South America. This last section is particularly strong, including thousands of curious religious, ceremonial, and everyday objects. Look for the Aztec musical instruments made from human bones, the 17th-century sheet-metal ornamental llamas from the Andes, and shrunken heads from the Amazon rainforest—and be ready for intriguing insights into Mayan astronomy.

The museum unveiled a new permanent exhibition in 1993, the Hall of Human Biology and Evolution. It studies the workings of the human body, traces ancestors over the centuries, and features a computerized archeological dig and an electronic newspaper with information on human evolution.

Measuring 94 feet in length and weighing 10 tons, what is thought to be the world's largest museum exhibit replicates the world's largest mammal—the blue whale—above the Hall of Ocean Life and Biology of Fishes. The fiberglass whale steals the show, although the room's dioramas and fish skeletons do a commendable job in unraveling the mysteries of reproduction, feeding, and self-defense far beneath the ocean's waves.

Moving on, even the mindbogglingly priced gems of Midtown Manhattan's jewelry stores pale into insignificance when compared with the contents of the

museum's Hall of Minerals and Gems, a collection valued at $80 million. A great chunk of crystal-impregnated copper and scores of darkened display cases filled with sparkling, spellbinding stones are just part of a cleverly planned exhibition focusing on the natural forces that create the world's most prized pieces of rock. Some of the stones are the size of a pinhead, others are as big as your fist; the 21,000-carat Brazilian Princess Topaz weighs a quarter of a ton and is the world's largest uncut gem.

Entered directly from the museum, the **Nature Max Cinema** has screenings on natural history themes using the giant-screen IMAX system. If you have ever wanted to inspect a lion's teeth at close quarters, this is the safest way to do it. Adjacent is the museum in the Hayden Planetarium (see panel).

▶ **American Numismatic Society** *IBCD2*

Broadway at 156th Street
Subway: C, D, 1; 155th or 157th streets

A vast hoard of coins and medals that is unsurpassed anywhere in the world, the collections of the American Numismatic Society are primarily intended to aid the research of devoted coin collectors and academics. There are, however, two surprisingly engaging first-floor exhibitions open to the public. The first is a spirited documentation—using maps, photographs, and many remarkable specimens of very ancient money—of the origins of, and the spread of, coins throughout the world.

After viewing the coins, you may not have sufficient energy left to do justice to the extensive display of medals housed in the second exhibition. Upstairs, there is a public information desk where you can find out whether the foreign coin you have just found in your change is likely to improve your lifestyle dramatically.

▶▶ **Asia Society** *151D3*

Park Avenue at 70th Street
Subway: 6; 68th Street

Founded in 1956 and pledged to improving understanding between Asia and America, the Asia Society hosts conferences, concerts, workshops, and film shows, and mounts stunning temporary exhibitions of Asian art drawn from the world's foremost collections. Also on display are selections from the society's own collections, which include Chinese ceramics from the 11th century BC, some very fine pre-Angkor Cambodian sculpture, and wonderful Japanese Edo-period prints, all donated by John D. Rockefeller III. The decorative lion above the entrance to the eight-story red granite gallery building (by Edward Larabee Barnes Associates) is based on an 18th-century bronze of a Nepalese guardian lion.

St. James Church
The Sunday services at St. James Episcopal Church (861–863 Madison Avenue), a short walk from the Asia Society, draw many of New York's most wealthy believers from their Upper East Side homes. Drop in during the week to admire the church's impressive stained glass and reredos.

65

The bright interior of St. James Church on Madison Avenue—one of several notable places of worship on the Upper East Side

BATTERY PARK

St. Elizabeth Ann Seton
The well-preserved Federal-style building at 7 State Street—its columns said to be cut from ship's masts—was erected in 1783 for the prominent Watson family but has found longer-lasting fame as the shrine of Elizabeth Ann Seton. She founded the Sisters of Charity, the first order of nuns in the U.S., in 1812 and in 1975 she became the first native-born American woman to be canonized by the Roman Catholic Church. This was her home from 1801 to 1803.

▶ **Battery Park** 104B1

Subway: 4; Bowling Green

A welcome open space on the edge of the Financial District, Battery Park provides 22 acres of greenery with outstanding harbor views. Historical texts are pinned to its lamp posts, leaving you with no excuse for not discovering something of early New York simply by strolling the tree-lined pathways.

The park took its name from the row of cannons that the British stored during the 17th century along State Street, which now borders the park but which then marked the Manhattan shoreline. The park attained its present form as a result of mid-1800s landfill.

If you are taking the ferry to the Statue of Liberty and Ellis Island, you will enter Battery Park's most interesting structure to reach the ticket booth, which is situated on the one-time parade ground of **Castle Clinton**. This circular fortification, finished in 1811, was built to repulse British attack.

Though there is little evidence of the fact today, Castle Clinton—which originally stood some 300 feet offshore and was linked to land by a causeway—has enjoyed a prominent place in New York life. As its defensive importance waned, the fort was planted with floral gardens and became the scene of well-attended concerts (some presented by 19th-century showman P. T. Barnum) and exhibitions; later it predated Ellis Island as a landing and processing point for immigrants, almost 8 million of whom came ashore here between 1855 and 1889. The castle also served a 46-year stint as the city aquarium.

The rest of Battery Park is dotted with statues and memorials of minor interest—not to be confused with the concrete slabs shielding the air vents of the Brooklyn-Battery Tunnel (which runs beneath the park). Giovanni da Verrazano, the first European known to sail into New York harbor, is one notable honored, while the pint-sized Peter Minuit Plaza is named after the Dutchman who bought Manhattan from its Native American inhabitants for the equivalent of $24 paid in the form of a few tools and trinkets. For Battery Park City, see page 18.

Above and right: Battery Park, the gateway to the Statue of Liberty, combines history and small-time commerce

■ On manic streets beneath the towering skyscrapers, it is easy to forget that Manhattan is a small island. One of the best ways to get a grasp of its size and shape is from the water that surrounds it, on a guided boat trip. ■

Most boat-tour operators seem to be offering much the same thing—a sightseeing trip along the Hudson River and the East River that includes a stop at the Statue of Liberty and a view of any New York landmarks visible from the water (though only one circles Manhattan). There are variations, however, so consider all the options to find the trip that suits you best.

In-depth sightseeing The most comprehensive sightseeing cruise is run by **Circle Line** (tel: 563–3200), whose vessels are converted World War II landing craft. This comprises a three-hour narrated circumnavigation of Manhattan Island, passing beneath 20 bridges on the

Even on a short stay, sightseeing by boat can make a pleasant change from hot sidewalks and traffic jams

way. The same company operates a two-hour cruise after dark (Manhattan at night is not a sight to be easily forgotten) and periodic "celebrity cruises," which feature notable New Yorkers giving their own view of the city.

Other options Typical of other operators is **Spirit Cruises** (tel: 727–7735), which offers a more condensed sightseeing tour, concentrating on Lower and Midtown Manhattan landmarks (and the Statue of Liberty) on a two-hour trip; there are also brunch cruises on Saturdays and Sundays and a Moonlight Party Cruise on Fridays and Saturdays, which casts off at 1:30 AM for drinking, dancing, and moonlit Manhattan views lasting into the small hours.

The catamaran of **Express Sightseeing Cruises** (tel: 800/BOAT RIDE) has the swiftest tours, zipping from the Statue of Liberty to the United Nations in 75 minutes. By contrast, **Seaport Liberty Cruises** (to book, tel: 638–8888) uses a replica 19th-century river boat for 90-minute sightseeing trips, with two-hour lunch cruises and one-hour evening cocktail spins as other options.

Eat as you go
Visitors love to sightsee but New Yorkers love to eat, and they are the people most in evidence on the lunch, brunch, and dinner cruises offered by World Yacht (tel: 630–8100). These are not calorie-counting affairs: lunch and brunch are lavish buffets, and dinner is a four-course treat followed by dancing.

BROADWAY

Broadway's first bend

Broadway's angular scythe through Manhattan's otherwise largely grid-style street plan gave rise to squares such as Union, Madison, and Times. Its first bend—after traveling for 3 ruler-straight miles north from Bowling Green—was due to the refusal of a Dutch landowner, Jacob Brevoort, to allow it to cross his property, a site now occupied by Greenwich Village's Grace Church.

Broadway's nerve center: the theater district near Times Square

Times Square Tours

Call into the Times Square Visitors Center, inside the Harris Theater, 226 W 42nd Street, for the story of Times Square, told with posters and assorted memorabilia. Each Friday at noon, the center is the starting point of a free two-hour walking tour of the neighborhood, pointing out places of interest.

▶▶ **Broadway** *151C2*

The story of Broadway is the story of New York. This is the city's oldest and longest thoroughfare—in one guise or another, Broadway not only runs north-south through Manhattan but continues for 140 miles to Albany. It has witnessed every good, bad, and indifferent phase in the city's growth, while its internationally famous theater district of Times Square and adjacent streets is, for many, what New York is all about.

Originally part of a Native American trail, Broadway was known to early Dutch settlers as De Heere Straat, or Main Street. It has remained New York's major (and perhaps most famous) artery ever since.

Broadway acquired the city's first numbered housing in 1793 and was also the first New York street to see its residential properties put to commercial uses. The commerce came in contrasting forms, with seedy bars, brothels, and gambling dens alongside the city's finest retail outlets. In the 1880s, a popular saying held that if you fired a shotgun in any direction at the junction of Broadway and Houston Street, you would not hit an honest man.

In the days before traffic lights and one-way streets, Broadway was bedlam. Holding the city's major businesses and being the main route north, Broadway's sidewalks were thronged with pedestrians and its center was a crush of handcarts and horse-drawn wagons. At times, police had to physically intervene to prevent the thoroughfare becoming completely blocked.

Walkers took their lives in their hands when attempting to cross Broadway. The junction with Fulton Street was so infamously hazardous that, in 1867, the authorities erected a footbridge—only for it to be torn down at the insistence of shop owners fearful of losing their side's share of captive pedestrians.

What evolved into New York's theater district began in Broadway's southern reaches and steadily moved north, one of the first theaters opening in 1798 at the junction with present-day Park Row. Broadway's theaters quickly forged a reputation for entertaining the city's well-to-do classes with productions of artistic merit and were considered a cut above their Bowery counterparts, popularly regarded as offering low-brow titillation for the consumption of the masses.

By the 1880s, the heyday of vaudeville and the age of stars such as Lillie Langtry, the Broadway theaters had pushed north to Union Square. Around this time, however, the Metropolitan Opera House opened on an unlikely site 26 blocks north and began drawing the city's élite to an area then dominated by livery shops and stables. Broadway crossed this area at Longacre Square.

Ten years passed before a theater opened at Longacre but by then a section of Broadway around 34th Street had famously been labeled "the Great White Way" on account of its giant advertising billboards lit by hundreds of electric light bulbs.

Soon, **Times Square**—as Longacre Square was renamed after the publisher of *The New York Times* got permission to build an office tower above it—was similarly illuminated. Once joined to the subway system, it quickly became the heart of the city's theater district.

Broadway continued north but the theater district

stayed put. By the 1920s many of the theaters were showing movies and, 50 years on, the oldest of them were demolished in a spate of office building.

As if to echo the sleaziness of an earlier Broadway, Times Square degenerated into porno shops, prostitution and drug dealing, though the sheer gaudiness of the place and the many genuine theaters still operating in its vicinity continued to attract a tide of tourists.

With the help of several billion dollars, a different Times Square began to appear through the 1990s: numerous new commercial developments, and considerable improvements in appearance and safety have utterly transformed the area (see page 18).

The nighttime neon of Broadway—less stunning than in its heyday perhaps, but still dazzling visitors a century after the first electrically lit sign was switched on

Above and opposite: riding above it on the Skyfari aerial tramway is a good way to get an impression of the re-created habitats found at the Bronx Zoo

Bronx Zoo practicalities
The closest subway stop to the Bronx Zoo is Pelham Parkway, which leaves a short walk to the zoo's Bronxdale entrance. An alternative route from Manhattan is with the Liberty Lines Express Bus (BxM11), which runs from Madison Avenue to the Bronxdale entrance (for details, tel: 718/652–8400).

Summer is the best time to visit. During the winter (November to April) many of the zoo's open-air sections are closed and the animals moved indoors. Admission is free on Wednesday. There is a charge for using the monorails. For general information on the zoo, tel: 718/367–1010.

► **The Bronx** 49D4

That the Bronx has had a worse press than any other New York borough is largely because one section, the South Bronx, became an international symbol of the most extreme forms of urban decay. Since the 1970s, abandoned buildings stripped clean of their fittings and regularly targeted by arsonists have littered the area. A major injection of funds for the building of affordable housing for the predominately low-income population and widespread community initiatives are steadily, if slowly, having an impact, but the South Bronx's image as a place depressed is a hard one to lose.

The rest of the Bronx is quite different. Off **Grand Concourse**, a stately thoroughfare laid out in 1892 and still (though no longer deserving of its title) cutting south-north through the borough, lie safe and tidy residential areas, immense parks, and the **Bronx Zoo.**

In the South Bronx, **Yankee Stadium** (161st Street and River Avenue) has been the home of the New York Yankees since its completion in 1923. A $100-million renovation program carried out in the mid-1970s was intended to improve the stadium as much as the building. If you visit the stadium, continue to the **Bronx Museum of the Arts** (1040 Grand Concourse). Opened in 1971, the museum has exhibitions of local art and Bronx-related cultural topics.

If they are not fans of the Yankees, most New Yorkers visit the Bronx for just one thing: the **Bronx Zoo►** (now officially called the Wildlife Conservation Park), the largest city zoo in the nation. Spanning 265 acres, the zoo puts its emphasis on herds and flocks rather than single animals and on re-created natural habitats rather than cages. The indoor rain forest of JungleWorld, for example, finds gibbons and monkeys leering at their human visitors from across artificial rivers. You should also spot a few Indian gharials, a type of alligator whose ancestry goes back 180 million years. Rare snow leopards are the highlight of the Himalayan Highlands, while World of Darkness—where day is transformed into night—allows glimpses of foxes, aardvarks, bushbabies, and bats (including the vampire variety, which receive a daily ration of blood).

The animals of the zoo's principal open space, Wild Asia, can be viewed only on a 25-minute narrated monorail ride. The open-sided cars glide above a plain roamed by antelopes, elephants, rhinoceroses, and sika deer—a species now extinct in its native habitat.

More traditional exhibits include the ape and reptile houses, and the MouseHouse, its cages inhabited by innumerable tiny furry things. There is also a separate Children's Zoo, intended to provide young minds with an insight into animal behavior and offering plenty of cute and cuddly creatures for stroking.

Beginning across Fordham Road from the zoo, the **New York Botanical Garden▶** is a wonderful mixture of formal gardens, rock gardens, and rugged woodlands—including a 40-acre hemlock forest. In the northwest corner, the Enid A. Haupt Conservatory is filled by a glorious array of banana plants, palm trees, cacti, and other vegetation and stages seasonal flower shows. After enjoying the vegetation, stop for refreshment at the Snuff

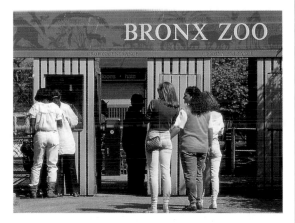

Mill terrace Café (*Open* summer only), invitingly shaded by trees and overlooking the Bronx River.

The **Edgar Allen Poe Cottage▶** (off Grand Concourse at East Kingsbridge Road) is where the writer lived for two years during the 1840s, in the hope that the country air would improve his wife's health. In the unheated dwelling, however, Poe's tubercular spouse resorted to hugging the cat for warmth and died during the first winter. Holding a few of the Poes' sparse furnishings, the cottage is an aptly bleak memorial to a man whose short life was seldom a happy one.

In the grounds of the **Bronx Community College▶** (181st Avenue and University Avenue) is the **Hall of Fame for Great Americans**. Here the bronze busts of around 100 prominent Americans are lined up along an

The Bruno Hauptman house
The house at 1279 East 222nd Street, east of the Bronx's Woodlawn Cemetery, looks like any other but it was here in 1934 that police arrested Bruno Hauptman on the charges of abducting and holding to ransom (and subsequently murdering) the baby of flying-ace Charles Lindbergh.

The celebrated case galvanized the media and popularized the term "kidnapping." Hauptman was found guilty and executed, but doubts over the verdict rose with the discovery that the police had kept vital pieces of evidence from the jury.

The site where the $50,000 ransom was paid is also in the Bronx: St. Raymond's Cemetery, between East Tremont Avenue and Eastern Boulevard, just south of Throg's Neck.

Yankee's Stadium's first game
Financed by brewery magnate and then Yankees owner Colonel Jacob Ruppert, Yankee Stadium staged its first game in front of 60,000 people in April 1923. The legendary Babe Ruth hit three home runs, a major contribution to the Yankees 4–1 win over Ruth's former team, the Boston Red Sox. That same year, Ruth helped the Yankees win their first World Series.

THE BRONX

Riverdale

When New Yorkers mention the Bronx, they are not usually thinking of Riverdale, part of which is the site of enviable homes and which reaches from the eastern edge of Van Cortlandt Park to the Hudson River.

One place worthy of a visit is the 1846 Fonthill Castle, a Gothic Revival structure modeled on an English folly and originally the home of actor Edwin Forrest. It now serves as the admissions office for the College of Mount St. Vincent, at Riverdale Avenue and 263rd Street. Another is Wave Hill (675 W 252nd Street; tel: 718/549–3200), 28 acres above the Hudson River holding two 19th-century mansions with gardens and greenhouses. It is the site of horticultural exhibitions and summer concerts.

The New York Botanical Garden

open-air colonnade. Though the Hall of Fame is every bit as pompous as it sounds, its neoclassical style is noteworthy and is replicated across the campus, much of which is credited to the prominent turn-of-the-century New York architect Stanford White (of the firm McKim, Mead & White).

Predating the college, and most other buildings in the Bronx, the **Van Cortlandt Mansion▶** (off Broadway between 240th and 242nd streets) was built in 1748 for a family prominent in politics and farming, their land holdings consuming what are now the wild expanses of **Van Cortlandt Park**. The mansion, built from rubble stone masonry in Georgian style with Dutch adornments, also provided a part-time base for George Washington, who marched from here into Manhattan to celebrate the signing of the Paris Peace Treaty in 1783, ending the Revolutionary War. The mansion shows off its English, Dutch, and Colonial furniture, and a few other 18th-century odds and ends. Periodically, there are demonstrations of brick making and open-hearth cookery.

Strange as it may sound, a more intriguing stop than the mansion is **Woodlawn Cemetery▶** (East 223rd Street and Webster Avenue). Rather than raid the art collections of Europe or finance Manhattan skyscrapers, some ultra-rich early New Yorkers chose to spend their fortunes on extravagant mausoleums. Among those buried here in ostentatious style are merchants Richard H. Macy, J. C. Penney, and F. W. Woolworth—whose sphinx-guarded, pseudo-Egyptian palace defies belief. Other more discreet tombs commemorate cultural figures such as writer Herman Melville and jazz giant Duke Ellington.

■ **New York's first black immigrants were slaves who arrived with the Dutch, by whom they were treated with comparative benevolence. However, a change for the worse occurred during the British era, when the colony's new rulers showed no respect for people, whom they regarded merely as chattel. They responded to slave uprisings with public hangings and burnings. Since then, the struggle for civil rights has unfortunately been a long, uphill battle.** ■

Early racism After the Revolutionary War, a few freed slaves attained respectable social positions but others were illegally transported to the Deep South. All were subject to racial hostility.

By the early 1800s, New York's African Americans encountered segregation in public places and were prevented from obtaining the necessary work skills to be employed as anything other than laborers and servants.

The rise and fall of Harlem In response, the first black churches and mutual aid societies were formed and, after years of enduring racism in the city's slums, it was amid the stylish brownstones of Harlem (originally built for wealthy whites) that New York's blacks first felt they had found a secure and self-supporting enclave.

Harlem's population doubled during the 1920s, a period when its art, music and literature flowered into the "Harlem Renaissance." Swiftly, however, the Depression made Harlem a ghetto, and its problems, along with those of African-American communities in other boroughs, were never tackled by the authorities. The Civil Rights Movement—and the Harlem speeches of Malcolm X—brought racial issues into the public spotlight during the 1960s.

Modern times David Dinkins became New York's first black mayor in 1990, as Harlem was evolving into one of Manhattan's newest areas of tourist interest. Meanwhile, Harlem institutions such as the Schomburg Center of Research in Black Culture have earned widespread recognition.

The raising of black consciousness in the 1960s was helped by public campaigners such as Malcolm X, seen here addressing a Muslim meeting in Harlem. He was assassinated in 1965

Green-Wood Cemetery

Henry Pierrepont, the man who developed Brooklyn Heights, was not only concerned with providing homes for the living. With Green-Wood Cemetery (main entrance at Fifth Avenue and 25th Street), he created a 478-acre landscaped plot to be enjoyed by some of the most prominent New Yorkers on their earthly demise. The cemetery drew 100,000 visitors a year in its Victorian heyday to wander its 20 miles of footpaths, take in the views over New York harbor, and contemplate the many richly decorated tombs. Richard Upjohn's remarkable Gothic Revival gate and gatehouse, at the Fort Hamilton Parkway entrance, is just the start. Among the 500,000 interred are Henry Ward Beecher, William Marcy "Boss" Tweed, Peter Cooper, and Samuel Morse.

Absorbed into New York City in 1898, fiercely independent Brooklyn at least has its own view of the Statue of Liberty

▶▶▶ Brooklyn   48C3

Brooklyn was once a full-fledged city in its own right, with an affluent population and revered cultural institutions. In 1898, buoyed by the opening of the Brooklyn Bridge spanning the East River, it decided (by a narrow majority) to become part of New York City.

The decision has been cursed by Brooklynites ever since. Post-independence humiliations have been many: the Depression and a huge influx of immigrants turned many of Brooklyn's stylish neighborhoods into slums and created breeding grounds for organized crime; the naval shipyards were closed down; Brooklyn's award-winning *Daily Eagle* newspaper bit the dust after a strike. Perhaps most galling of all, the Brooklyn Dodgers moved to Los Angeles in 1955.

Despite these setbacks, Brooklyn remains the most distinctive and enjoyable of the Outer Boroughs, with its own unique personality. The moderate tempo of its streets comes as a welcome relief after the bustle of Manhattan.

If it were still a city, Brooklyn would be the sixth most populous in the U.S. Within its metropolitan sprawl are four pockets of special interest. Downtown Brooklyn and the historic Brooklyn Heights lie closest to Manhattan. Just to the north, Fort Greene is gaining a reputation as the home of the new black artistic community. South of downtown, the elegant Eastern Parkway leads past the massive Brooklyn Museum and the Botanic Garden; farther south, on the coast, is the fabled but faded Coney Island amusement park and Russian-dominated Brighton Beach.

From the Brooklyn Bridge, any turning to the right leads into the short leafy streets of **Brooklyn Heights▶▶▶**. The 1814 invention of the steam-powered ferry made this district, set on bluffs above the East River, a residential area coveted by the bankers and speculators active in Manhattan's Financial District, just across the water.

Continued on page 76.

■ **Where Brooklyn meets the Atlantic Ocean you will find not only a coastline but two contrasting images of New York life: Coney Island amusement park, world-famous but now a pale shadow of its former self, and Brighton Beach, a declining seaside resort energized and transformed since the 1970s by a massive influx of Russian émigrés.** ■

Coney Island Up until the mid-1940s, this was many New Yorkers' idea of heaven. For a nickel subway fare they could swap their overcrowded, over-heated city streets for a day of fun beside the ocean, munching cotton candy and making themselves dizzy on the roller coasters, or lurking around the peep shows. Coney Island is undoubtedly a legend but today it is also—in every sense—history. In the amusement park area between Surf Avenue and the Boardwalk and West 8th and West 16th streets, little more than run-of-the-mill fairground rides suggest the old days, though a 1927 roller-coaster, the fearsome Cyclone, is still in business, as is the even older wooden Wonder Wheel.

Coney Island's name
The most plausible of many theories as to how Coney Island acquired its name is that it derives from the Dutch *Konijn Eiland*—Rabbit Island.

On summer days, Coney Island's beach still gets plenty of users, while remaining surprisingly clean, and the Boardwalk beside it is as atmospheric as ever—windswept, breezy, and with an exhilarating polyglot flavor.

New York Aquarium Five species of shark, beluga whales, dolphins, and sea lions are among the inhabitants of the New York Aquarium, accessed from the boardwalk. Aquarium visitors will also find the Sea Cliffs exhibition, a sophisticated re-creation of a rocky coastal habitat populated by walrus, seals, penguins, and sea otters.

Brighton Beach Continue east along the Boardwalk to reach this revitalized area where between 10,000 and 20,000 ex-Soviet immigrants form the largest Russian community in the U.S., beneficiaries of the U.S.S.R.'s relaxing of restrictions in the years before its collapse. With caviar and ice-cold vodka advertised in Cyrillic script, and the riotous restaurants along Brighton Beach Avenue known to round off the evening with frenzied dancing and the occasional drunken brawl, so-called Little Odessa (many settlers arrived from the Black Sea port) is fast becoming one of the most celebrated areas of New York City. Bakeries and restaurants here offer the culinary specialties of former regions of the Soviet Union.

Maxim Gorky on Coney Island, 1906
"Fabulous and beyond conceiving, ineffably beautiful, is this fiery scintillation."

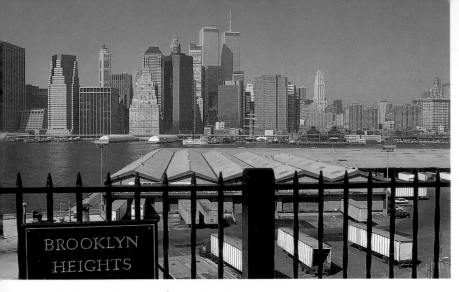

BROOKLYN HEIGHTS

Stroll along the Brooklyn Heights Promenade for classic views of Manhattan. At the base of the sky-scrapers is the South Street Seaport

Continued from page 74.

Brooklyn Heights subsequently became covered with brownstone dwellings—Gothic, Greek, or Romanesque in style—which largely survive intact in an area that became a National Historical Landmark in 1965.

Structure your explorations sufficiently to include Orange Street and its **Plymouth Church of the Pilgrims►**. It was here during the 1800s that abolitionist minister Henry Ward Beecher (see panel on page 78) delivered eloquent and impassioned sermons against slavery and made the church a platform for the leading abolitionists. He is remembered by a statue in the adjoining garden. Another worthwhile stop is at 128 Pierrepont Street, where **Brooklyn's Historical Museum►** mounts exhibitions of local memorabilia.

Below the Heights, downtown Brooklyn spills along Fulton Street, which bends around Borough Hall, an unappealing Greek Revival building erected in 1848. Of far greater interest, the **New York Transit Museum►►►** occupies a former subway station at the junction of Boerum Place and Schermerhorn Street. Inside, art deco air-vent coverings and mosaic-tiled station name plates recall the care that went into the early years of what became the world's second-largest mass transit system.

Downstairs along the one-time platforms stand subway carriages built from 1904 to 1964: step aboard and wonder how passengers avoided being scalped by the vicious-looking fans that preceded air conditioning.

Between Downtown Brooklyn and the former naval dockyards, **Fort Greene►** is another district well endowed with leafy streets and elegant brownstones, now owned by Brooklyn's more affluent blacks among others. Many became rooming houses during the Depression, causing the area to fall into neglect.

Though signs of inner-city poverty remain apparent, Fort Greene is very much on the rise. African-Americans still make up 70 percent of the district's population, a significant number of them being successful in the arts. Jazz singer Betty Carter and artist Ernest Critchlow are long-

Stroll: Brooklyn Heights
An enjoyable way to walk off a good lunch is with a stroll along the Brooklyn Heights Promenade. Also called the Esplanade, this wide pathway overlooks the East River, and has views of Manhattan strong enough to draw Brooklyn office workers with picnic lunches and to push the prices of west-facing pent-house apartments along nearby Columbia Heights into the realms of the phantasmagoric.

established locals; another is film-maker Spike Lee, who resisted the lure of Hollywood and located his production company here. Lee grew up in Fort Greene and his 1986 movie, *She's Gotta Have It*, made use of a local landmark: **Fort Greene Park**, designed in 1860 by Olmsted and Vaux (better known for Manhattan's Central Park). The Doric column was added later in memory of the 12,000 American patriots who died on British prison ships during the Revolutionary War and lie buried beneath the park.

Fort Greene sees comparatively few tourists. It is sensible to keep to the area south of the park, where you will find the most impressive of the brownstones and several churches (visit on Sunday morning for the atmosphere).

There are many more brownstones located in the residential streets between Flatbush Avenue and Sixth Avenue, an upscale section of the Park Slope neighborhood. A much more spectacular sight in this area, however, stands at the center of Grand Army Plaza (on Flatbush Avenue by the main entrance to Prospect Park,

Brooklyn

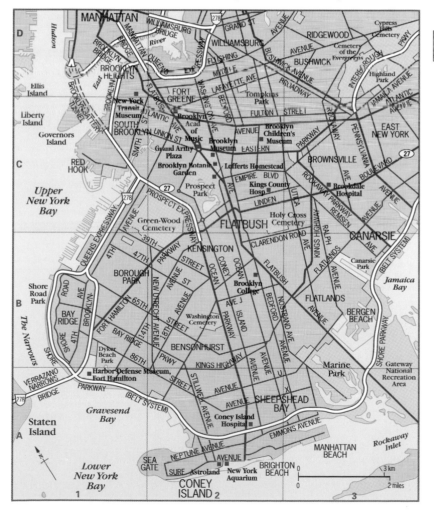

The Hasidic Jews

Since the 1940s, Brooklyn's Williamsburg district (north of Downtown) has been a base of the ultrastrict Hasidic community. Men wear beards, side curls and dark frock coats and hats; the heads of married women are shaven and covered by a wig. The Hasidim adhere rigidly to kosher diet, and some eschew T.V. and radio. Another sizable Orthodox Jewish community in Brooklyn is the Lubavitchers, adherents to a Hasidic sect that originated in 18th-century Russia.

Henry Ward Beecher

Clergyman at the Plymouth Church of the Pilgrims for some 40 years in the latter half of the 19th century, Henry Ward Beecher spoke out against slavery and in favor of women's suffrage. Equally controversial for the time, Beecher's writings supported Darwin's theory of evolution. His later years were dogged by allegations of adultery, charges of which he was cleared only after his death in 1887.

described below): the oversized Soldiers' and Sailors' Memorial Arch, raised in 1892 to commemorate the Union forces who died during the Civil War.

This Brooklyn version of an imperial Roman arch was designed by John H. Duncan, who was also responsible for the similarly grandiose General Grant Memorial (see pages 110–111). The memorial's sheer size makes it much more of an architectural curiosity than a fitting shrine to the dead. The sense of pomposity is compounded by the heroic sculptures added to the memorial in 1898, though some amends are made by the finely detailed bas-reliefs that decorate the walls on the inside of the arch. **Prospect Park▶** itself is a broad and bucolic open space completed in 1874. With none of the restraints that were imposed with Central Park (such as incorporating major traffic arteries) architects Olmsted and Vaux gave their imaginations free rein here and considered Prospect Park their finest work.

The grand streets and landscaped open spaces—as well as the triumphal monuments—that Brooklyn acquired during the late 19th century were the hallmarks of a city very much on the rise. In keeping with the optimism of the times—and in an effort to create a symbol of Brooklyn's cultural superiority over Manhattan—the

Brooklyn Heights. Not all of the city's best skyscrapers are in Manhattan

Brooklyn Museum▶▶▶ (200 Eastern Parkway) was founded in 1897 with the intention of becoming the largest museum in the world. Such great ambitions were never fulfilled, however, and this fine museum has undeservedly been playing second fiddle to the better-known museums of Manhattan for decades. It is probably most renowned as the resting place for the world's third largest stock of ancient Egyptian artifacts, a remarkable collection dating from predynastic times to the Roman conquest.

The museum's sixth floor reveals an exceptional collection of 19th-century American portraiture, including Gilbert Stuart's iconographic image of George Washington. Elsewhere, Francis Guy's light and airy *Winter Scene in Brooklyn* of 1817 stands out, and a quality selection from the Hudson River School culminates in Albert Bierstadt's *Storm in the Rocky Mountains, Mt. Rosalie*, an intense landscape of rugged, exposed granite beneath brooding storm clouds.

The fifth floor of the museum has colonial-period ceramics, and interiors ranging from 17th-century farmhouses to 1920s art-deco lounges. Note the Moorish Room: a dreamy conglomeration of patterned tiles, gold-brocaded walls, oak panels and thick velvet drapes, which once graced John D. Rockefeller's Manhattan mansion.

Other stories are filled by comprehensive Asian art collections, while the first floor holds pottery, figurines and votive objects from Africa, Oceania, and Central and South America. Most striking among the latter is perhaps the Paracas Textile, a 2,000-year-old Peruvian burial cloth.

The Native American collections, on the same floor, feature diverse tribes and exhibits ranging from buckskin jackets to totem poles.

If you are feeling drained after exploring the museum, head for the 52 divinely landscaped acres of the **Brooklyn Botanic Garden**▶▶, just to the rear, where soft colors and wondrous fragrances will revive your senses.

The quiet charm still to be found in parts of Brooklyn Heights contrasts with the frenetic streets of Manhattan, just across the East River

Literary Brooklyn Heights
Brooklyn Heights has strong literary associations. Poet Hart Crane and novelist John Dos Passos both lived at 110 Columbia Heights during the 1920s (Crane also resided briefly at 77 Willow Street). Henry Miller spent a short time at 91 Remsen Street during the 1920s, and Truman Capote wrote *Breakfast at Tiffany's* in the basement of 70 Willow Street. Norman Mailer wrote *The Naked and the Dead* while living with his parents at 102 Pierrepont Street (he now lives elsewhere in Brooklyn Heights). At the same address Arthur Miller wrote his play *All My Sons*, before moving to 155 Willow Street, where he is remembered by a plaque though he wrote *Death of a Salesman* at 31 Grace Court.

Bad luck and the Brooklyn Bridge

In its early years, the Brooklyn Bridge saw more than its share of tragedy. Its designer, John A. Roebling, died following an accident before his bridge was complete. His son, Washington, took over, but became paralyzed as a result of "the bends," and had to supervise the construction work from his sick bed. Twenty of the 600-strong work force died during the construction. Six days after the bridge opened, the screams of a woman who tripped on the approach caused a panic in which 12 people lost their lives, mistakenly believing the bridge was about to collapse. In 1884, however, circus-owner P. T. Barnum led 21 elephants across it; since then there have been few doubts as to the bridge's strength.

The pedestrian walkway on the Brooklyn Bridge. The towers of Manhattan's Financial District gleam behind the intricate web of suspension cables

▶▶ Brooklyn Bridge 77D1

Subway: Brooklyn Bridge

Completed in 1883, the Brooklyn Bridge was the world's first steel suspension bridge, and, for 20 years, the longest. It formed the first fixed link between the then separate cities of Brooklyn and Manhattan.

Enhanced immeasurably by its two Gothic 272ft-high stone arches (when they were finished, only the spire of Trinity Church rose higher into the New York sky), the bridge is an aesthetic as well as an engineering masterpiece. It has inspired many writers, including Brooklyn-based Walt Whitman, to wax lyrical over its beauty.

Bike riders, skaters, joggers, and (occasionally) muggers—and high winds (sometimes)—can be a hazard to walkers on the bridge's pedestrian path, easily the best way to appreciate the structure. From Manhattan, the views used to be of Brooklyn's busy shipyards, a scene re-created by a display beside the footpath, while another recounts the bridge's origins.

▶ Carnegie Hall 151C2

57th Street at Seventh Avenue
Subway: D, E, N, R; Seventh Avenue or 57th Street

Financed by a $2-million gift from steel magnate Andrew Carnegie, Carnegie Hall opened to the public in 1891 and quickly gained an international reputation for its outstanding acoustics. Its horseshoe-shaped auditorium is modeled on those of Italian opera houses. Refurbishment has restored the hall to the sumptuous appearance of its younger days, something best appreciated by attending a concert—a must if you have time.

Even if you fail to see inside the hall, look around the **Carnegie Hall Museum** which records the hall's origins and the long list of famous names that have graced its boards. Besides Benny Goodman's clarinet and Arturo Toscanini's baton, the museum exhibits a 1964 bookings diary with a handwritten entry recording the first New York appearance of "The Beetles."

Gothic vaulting (left) and (below) a sculptural detail of what will, if and when it is completed, be the world's biggest cathedral

►► Cathedral of St. John the Divine   *IBCB2*

Amsterdam Avenue at 112th Street
Subway: 1; Cathedral Parkway (110th Street)

The cornerstone of the Cathedral of St. John the Divine was laid in 1892, marking the beginning of what is now an immense Episcopalian edifice spread across 11 acres—the largest church in the U.S., and the largest Gothic church in the world, yet still years short of completion more than a century later.

The original plans were for a church of Byzantine/Romanesque design, but delays caused by engineering problems and lack of finance meant that only the choir and four stone arches were completed in the first 25 years. Changing tastes (and the death of the project's original architect) saw the structure remodeled in French Gothic form, and it was given a façade reminiscent of Notre-Dame in Paris.

The nave, covering a staggering 32,000 square feet, was completed in a comparatively swift 10 years but the U.S.'s entry into World War II again halted progress, as did a decision during the 1960s to divert building money to the needs of the community. Another building program got under way in 1978, when funds were available to import a master stonemason from England to cut the Indiana limestone used in the towers and to train a small army of local apprentices.

As its towers still rise, enclosed by scaffolding, the cathedral's exterior takes on a surreal appearance. Inside, the scale is breathtaking. The clash of Gothic and Romanesque/Byzantine styles is most apparent from the unfinished crossing, where the structure's anatomy is revealed and above which the red-tiled dome, installed as a "temporary" shelter during 1909, remains in place.

Foremost among the cathedral's decorations are two sets of religious tapestries: the Mortlake Tapestries, woven in England during 1623 from cartoons by Raphael, and the 17th-century Barberini tapestries, which were woven on papal looms.

New York Public Library: 115th Street branch
The main branch of the New York Public Library on Fifth Avenue (see page 168) is one of the city's greatest architectural delights, and the 115th Street branch (between Seventh and Eighth avenues) is no mere pile either. Dating from 1908, the library was the work of the firm of McKim, Mead and White, and its imposing Renaissance style was intended to match the grandeur of early Harlem.

CENTRAL PARK

▶▶▶ **Central Park**   *IFCF2*

From almost any high point in Manhattan, what holds the eye longest is not the Empire State Building or the World Trade Center but the great rectangle of greenery in the heart of the dense urban clutter. Central Park fills 843 acres and runs for 50 city blocks between the Upper East and Upper West sides.

The candidates in New York's mayoral campaign of 1850 were agreed on just one issue: the need for a large public park of the kind civic leaders and journalists had been advocating since poet and newspaper editor William Cullen Bryant raised the idea in 1844. At that time, property developers were breaking all records in their northward streak across Manhattan.

In 1856, the city paid $5½ million for a tract of land—an area well to the north of the city as then established, dotted with pig farms and squatter camps and mostly used as a garbage dump. Two years later work began on the park, to the plans of Frederick Olmsted (a farmer-turned-engineer-turned-journalist-turned-landscape architect) and English architect Calvert Vaux.

The park's design called for a major earth-moving project as glades, copses, and rock outcrops were created, and some 5 million trees planted. Bridges linked the park's internal thoroughfares and—a revolutionary concept at the time—cross-park traffic was carried by sunken roads to keep the pastoral view intact.

With tree-lined driveways for the wealthy to parade in horse-drawn carriages, and footpaths for the working classes (who typically at the time toiled in sweatshops and lived in filthy tenements) to experience, as Olmsted expressed it, "a specimen of God's handiwork," the park was an instant success.

Though now fully enclosed by buildings and with far more monuments than Olmsted would have liked, Central Park is still a great escape from the city streets. The Fifth Avenue and Upper West Side apartment buildings that appear above the treetops simply add to the park's country-in-the-city effect.

Getting lost temporarily in Central Park is surprisingly easy. Be sure to pick up a map from one of the information kiosks before you enter.

From the south, the first place to make for is the **Dairy**. In pursuit of a romantic rural vision, the Gothic-style Dairy was built here in 1870 as a place where traditionally attired milkmaids would serve fresh milk (a luxury at the time) to mothers and young children. The quaint building now holds the park's main Visitor Center, with displays and several leaflets describing park walks.

North of the Dairy, across the 65th Transverse, the 22-acre **Sheep Meadow** did indeed hold sheep during the park's earliest years, the resident flock being led across the park's West Drive twice a day to the Sheepfold, which occupied the site of the present Tavern on the Green. Oddly enough, given Olmsted and Vaux's obsession with re-creating the country in the city, the Sheep Meadow was originally intended as a military parade ground.

Just east of the Sheep Meadow begins the **Mall**, one of the first completed sections of the park and its only formal area. Many 19th-century New Yorkers got their first taste of European-style promenading along its tree-lined esplanade, and some also gained their first experience of donkey- and goat-cart riding, both of which were offered to visitors here.

Olmsted initially resisted attempts to have statuary in the park but eventually agreed to the memorials of writers—Shakespeare, Robert Burns, and Sir Walter Raleigh among them—which are grouped around the Mall's southern end to form the **Literary Walk**.

Continuing north, the Mall leads into the **Concert Ground** and the **Naumberg Bandshell**, the scene of free live music on most summer weekends.

Cross the 72nd Street Transverse and you enter **Bethesda Terrace**. At its heart is the Bethesda Fountain and the elegant *Angel of the Waters* statue. One of the few pieces commissioned especially for the park, the statue, inspired by the biblical story of the Bethesda Pool in Jerusalem, was unveiled in 1873 to commemorate the opening of the aqueduct that gave New York its first regular supply of fresh water.

There is more water directly north of Bethesda Terrace, in the form of the **Lake**. A leisurely paddle along this imposingly calm body of water is a fine way to round off a park visit. Boats can be hired from the Loeb Boathouse, on the eastern banks of the lake.

Stroll: Strawberry Fields
From the Upper West Side, entering Central Park on 72nd Street leads into Strawberry Fields, a 3-acre section maintained by an endowment from Yoko Ono, as a memorial to her late husband John Lennon.

Overlooked by the Dakota apartment building, where the Lennons lived (see page 96), Strawberry Fields is planted with 161 species of plant, representing 161 nations of the world. The authorities were not unanimous in agreeing to the tribute: conservative elements wanted a memorial to Bing Crosby.

New York's "green lung" and the Plaza Hotel

CENTRAL PARK

Central Park in style
One way of seeing the park is as the city swells of the 1880s did: by horse and carriage. Buy a ticket from the stand at Grand Army Plaza (at the junction of 59th Street and Fifth Avenue) and climb aboard. Prices have risen over the last hundred years, however: expect to pay around $15 per person for a half-hour trot.

If you are determined to do something more energetic, cross the lake on foot by way of the Bow Bridge—one of Central Park's seven original cast-iron bridges—to **The Ramble**. Comprising 33 acres of painstakingly re-created rurality, complete with rustic birdhouses and beehives, The Ramble is ripe for exploration and is also an excellent location for birdwatching. It is not advisable to ramble alone, however, as this is an isolated and dangerous area.

Across the 79th Street Transverse from The Ramble, a replica Scottish castle, **Belvedere Castle**, was erected in 1869 for no reason other than fun. Occupied for many years by a weather station, the castle no longer fulfills a meteorological role but its stone terraces provide excellent views across the park and beyond.

To the left, a path leads to the **Shakespeare Garden**, planted with trees and plants mentioned in the bard's works, and continues to the **Great Lawn**, occupied by softball fields that have worn the grass into bare dirt. The Great Lawn attracted half a million people to hear a Simon & Garfunkel concert in 1981. Free open-air concerts are given here each year during the summer by the New York Philharmonic.

The northerly section of the park (north of the reservoir) is the least visited and consequently the most dangerous. If you do want to explore here—the lure is a landscape far rockier and much more hilly than that to the south—it is wisest to enter and leave the park at its Fifth Avenue and 105th Street entrance. Doing this will lead directly into the park's **Conservatory Garden** and allow you to pass through the lavish wrought-iron gates that once fronted the mansion of Cornelius Vanderbilt.

Central Park has had its share of well-publicized crimes, and the occasional mugging happens from time to time. In spite of this, you will find that most of the park is no more dangerous than the average New York street, though there are isolated areas where a person wandering alone may be viewed as an easy target. Never visit the park after dark.

Top: a sedate tour or (above) the more energetic pastime of rollerblading

The Chelsea Hotel

■ When the Chelsea opened in 1888 at 222 West 23rd Street, it was the first apartment building in New York to be topped by a penthouse. Its fancy façade featured wrought-iron balconies decorated with sunflower motifs. Converted to a hotel in 1905, the Chelsea did not become famous through its architecture, however, but as a haunt of writers, painters, and composers, who gave it a Bohemian ambience unmatched by any other hotel in the world. ■

Painter John Sloan and writers Mark Twain and O. Henry (the pen name of William Sydney Porter) were among the Chelsea's early guests, but the hotel hit its artistic stride during the 1930s, after poet Edgar Lee Masters eulogized it in verse and novelist Thomas Wolfe took up residence.

Impressed by the size of his suite, Wolfe dubbed his bathroom the "Throne Room" and kept 4,000 loose pages of prose strewn across his floor. Selections from these would be assembled and supplied to his publisher as finished works.

The 1950s and 1960s Its literary links were already established by the time Dylan Thomas made the Chelsea his New York base during the early 1950s. His last conscious hours, after he had claimed to have downed 18 whiskeys in a Greenwich Village bar, were spent in room 205, and he died in the hospital a few days later of suspected alcohol poisoning.

A decade later, Brendan Behan took shelter at the Chelsea and begged to be commemorated by a plaque—as he now is. Besides Behan, Beat writers William Burroughs and Gregory Corso, expatriate Russian novelist Vladimir Nabokov, and abstract expressionist painter Jackson Pollock were among the renegades who gathered at the Chelsea's bar (which is now a Spanish restaurant).

Pop and punk The hotel provided a backdrop for Andy Warhol's rambling split-screen film *Chelsea Girls* (which starred Warhol acolyte Edie Sedgwick, a Chelsea resident) and through the 1960s its guests included many pop-music icons—among them Bob Dylan, who wrote his epic song "Sad Eyed Lady of the Lowlands" in one of its rooms. The hotel's most ignominious night came in 1978, when punk rocker Sid Vicious allegedly stabbed his girlfriend to death in their suite—the film *Sid and Nancy* actually featured the hotel.

Step into the Chelsea's lobby and you will find plaques commemorating its most illustrious residents and many works donated by artist guests. The Chelsea's rooms vary greatly in style, size and price, and some of them are occupied by eccentric long-term guests.

Its decorative design may once have been ahead of its time, but the Chelsea has long been known not as an architectural landmark, but as a cultural one

CHINATOWN

Pre-Chinatown remnants
On St. James Place you can find the First Shearith Israel graveyard, predecessor of the cemeteries of Greenwich Village and Chelsea. The first Jewish cemetery in the United States, the site was consecrated in 1656, when it was considered to be well outside town.

On nearby James Street, St. James Church is an 1837 Greek Revival edifice. Al Smith, once an altar boy at the church, rose from this poor then-Irish neighborhood to become New York's governor and a 1928 Democratic presidential candidate.

Frenetic but fascinating, Chinatown's streetlife never takes a break

▶▶▶ Chinatown   *IFCB3*

New York streetlife enters a new dimension on the tightly clustered, densely crowded sidewalks of Chinatown, which lies between the courthouses, Little Italy, and the Lower East Side. Stalls are laden with seafood, vegetables, or fruit; herbalist shops dispense wondrous remedies; bakeries concoct sweet cakes; and rows of gaudy neon signs advertise (in English and Chinese) the noodle shops, tea parlors, and dim sum houses that bring most non-Chinese New Yorkers to the area.

There has been a Chinese presence here since the 1850s, but only with the relaxing of immigration laws in 1965 did Chinatown really begin to expand. Spilling beyond its traditional boundaries, Chinatown now holds around half of New York's 300,000 Chinese population and still grows, swelled by arrivals from Vietnam and other parts of Southeast Asia.

The handover of Hong Kong to Beijing has also been felt. Hong Kong banks have opened here, and brightly lit shopping malls stuffed with jewelry and electrical goods have spread along Canal Street.

Tumultuous they may be, but Chinatown's streets are some of the safest in New York. Local businesses—including more than 300 restaurants—depend on New Yorkers in search of food and visitors in search of the exotic, so they play their part in keeping things quiet. Chinatown's crime is not on the streets but behind closed doors: the feuds between rival gangs, or the fresh arrivals who toil for subsistence wages in Canal Street's garment factories, are facets of Chinatown outsiders never see.

In fact, beyond business and people, there is not a lot for visitors to see in Chinatown. A few places of interest are noted in the Chinatown Walk opposite, but the neighborhood cries out for a decent historical collection.

約 ... 界慶祝中華民國八十一年雙十國慶
THE CHINESE COMMUNITY OF NEW YORK CELEBRATES
THE 81ST "DOUBLE TEN" ANNIVERSARY OF THE FOUNDING OF REPUBLIC OF CHINA

CHINATOWN

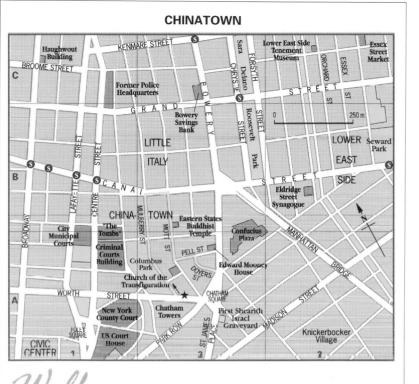

Haughwout Building
KENMARE STREET
Lower East Side Tenement Museum
Essex Street Market
BROOME STREET
Sara Delano Roosevelt
FORSYTH STREET
CHRYSTIE STREET
ORCHARD STREET
ESSEX STREET
C
Former Police Headquarters
BOWERY
GRAND
STREET
Bowery Savings Bank
0   250 m
LAFAYETTE STREET
CENTRE STREET
LITTLE
ITALY
STREET
Roosevelt Park
LOWER EAST SIDE
Seward Park
B
CANAL
BROADWAY
Eldridge Street Synagogue
STREET
CHINA-TOWN
MULBERRY ST
MOTT ST
Eastern States Buddhist Temple
Confucius Plaza
MANHATTAN BRIDGE
City Municipal Courts
"The Tombs"
Criminal Courts Building
PELL ST
Columbus Park
DOYERS ST
Edward Mooney House
Church of the Transfiguration
CHATHAM SQUARE
STREET
A
WORTH   STREET
New York County Court
Chatham Towers
PARK ROW
ST JAMES PLACE
First Shearith Israel Graveyard
MADISON STREET
Knickerbocker Village
FOLEY SQUARE
US Court House
CIVIC CENTER

𝒲𝒶𝓁𝓀 Chinatown streetlife

Effervescent streetlife is the main attraction of Chinatown, which holds few specific sights. This walk covers the main ones and captures the atmosphere of the area—leaving scope for independent meandering.

Begin at **Columbus Park**, which replaced a notorious slum and red-light area of the mid-1800s. Today, noisy ball games and the rumble of traffic along Mulberry Street rob the park of any peacefulness. Walk up to **Canal Street** and you will pass Chinatown's biggest and brightest shopping emporiums before reaching Mott Street.

At 64 Mott Street, the **Eastern States Buddhist Temple** is a genuine temple but also sells souvenir Buddha figures, arranged in eye-catching rows. Built in 1801, the Georgian **Church of the Transfiguration**, at 25 Mott Street, predates Chinatown. Close by, **Doyers Street** was once

the domain of opium dealers and prostitutes, and its bend was used as an ambush point during 19th- and early 20th-century Tong Wars, when rival Chinese gangs fought over the control of drug-trafficking, prostitution, and gambling. Nowadays perfectly safe, Doyers Street is lined by restaurants.

■ **Chinese faces were few and far between in early 19th-century New York, but nowadays the Chinese community is expanding fast in both size and importance. Whether in academia or business, Chinese-Americans are frequently among the city's most spectacular achievers.** ■

Chinese in the U.S.

Although only a few Chinese were present in New York prior to the late 1800s, they were already established in California where 25,000 had arrived in 1852. Most of them worked in the California gold mines and, subsequently, on the transcontinental railroad that linked the West Coast to the rest of the country. The Chinese gained a reputation as dependable laborers, but in the economic depression that followed the Gold Rush, they found themselves prevented from opening businesses or owning land. Banding together, the Chinese settled in what became the "Chinatown" districts of many California communities, some making the cross-country trip to the less hostile atmosphere of New York.

The 75 Chinese immigrants estimated to be living in New York in 1870 were mostly individuals who had jumped ship and assimilated themselves as best they could into established ethnic groups. By 1890, however, New York's Chinese population had rocketed to 12,000. Many of the new arrivals came here from California, where they had provided labor for the transcontinental railroad.

With their language and culture at odds with European New York, the lone Chinese males (denied the company of their relatives by an anti-immigration law of 1896) rarely strayed from Chinatown. Aided by family-based self-help organizations, they toiled in stores and laundries, sending any spare money back home.

The seamy side The popular imagination saw Chinatown as a neighborhood of incredible exotica. Rich tourists were given guided tours by opportunistic locals, failing, of course, to see the ax murders, the slavery, the gambling, and the opium dens described in lurid press accounts.

Gambling, prostitution (provided by white women), and opium dens did in fact exist, but usually in upstairs rooms or basements. These activities were overseen by the Tongs—an American term for a Chinese-American secret society. Many Tongs claimed long histories to impress recruits.

Acceptance and expansion The Japanese invasion of China in 1937 helped unite warring factions in the Chinese community, and the subsequent U.S.-Sino military alliance reduced anti-Chinese feeling among New Yorkers. A bigger change came in 1965, when limitations on Chinese immigration were lifted and waves of new arrivals from Taiwan and Hong Kong came to Chinatown.

The new Chinese were eager to embrace American ways. They quickly made their presence felt in mainstream New York life—though some younger elements embraced briefly notorious criminal gangs such as the Ghost Shadows and the Flying Dragons—and many left the inner city for suburbia as soon as they could.

Chinese food to go. Chinatown's eateries cover a vast range of styles and regional cuisines

The unmistakable Chrysler Building—New York art deco at its finest, and everyone's favorite skyscraper

The cheating spire
The Chrysler Building's "world's tallest" title was acquired through some slightly devious behavior by its architect, William Van Alen. The needle-like spire that tops its 77 stories was secretly assembled inside the tower and pushed through the roof. In this way Van Alen outwitted his former partner, H. Craig Severance, whose contemporaneously completed Bank of Manhattan Building (40 Wall Street) would otherwise have earned the accolade.

Police riots
In 1857, City Hall Park was the scene of violence between New York's two rival police forces, the discredited Municipal and the newly formed Metropolitan. Their battles continued into City Hall and ended only when National Guardsmen drew their bayonets.

In September 1992, New York's finest again disgraced themselves in the park, when a poorly planned demonstration against Mayor Dinkins culminated in officers (some of them clearly the worse for drink) stepping over the barricades and blockading the entrance to City Hall.

▶▶ **Chrysler Building**   *151B3*
42nd Street at Lexington Avenue
Subway: 4, 6, 7; 42nd Street/Grand Central
The definitive symbol of New York art deco and briefly the world's tallest building, the 1,045-foot Chrysler Building was completed in 1930. Its tower is still among the city's most recognizable landmarks. More impressive than the exterior view, however, is the lobby, retaining its walls of red-veined African marble and a mural by Edward Trumbull depicting the glories of world transportation. The elevators, too, still have their original decor of laminated woods, and the entire 77-story building is studded by automobile motifs.

▶ **City Hall**   *104C2*
Subway: N, R; City Hall
A cluster of municipal buildings stands near the foot of the Brooklyn Bridge. The oldest among them, the **City Hall**, a mix of Federal and French Renaissance styles dating from 1811, is still in use for its original purpose. The barriers that line the front of the building are intended to prevent the frequent demonstrations in City Hall Park from blocking councilors' access to the building. Inside, a circular staircase winds beneath the eye-catching rotunda to the second floor, where the **Governor's Room** is lined by portraits of early New York notables and items of furniture mostly contemporaneous with the building. Included in the collection is a writing table used by George Washington.

Immediately north stands the **Old New York County Courthouse**, intended as a shrine to justice but a building whose financing was one of the biggest swindles in New York history (see page 42). It is now used as municipal offices. Across Centre Street, the present **New York County Courthouse** has a hexagonal shape and a magnificent Corinthian portico.

■ City dwellers love to root for the home team, and New Yorkers—with their city represented by two professional teams in football, hockey, and baseball—are no exception. Loyalties and rivalries run deep, even though the closest most people get to actual games is the couch facing the T.V. in their living rooms: tickets, especially for football games; or for playoff games in other sports, tend to be hard to get hold of and expensive. ■

The New York Marathon

What began in 1970 with 127 runners making four laps around Central Park is now the world's largest urban marathon. Its 26-mile course is contested by some 22,000 runners and watched by over 2 million spectators. Held on the third or fourth Sunday in October (or occasionally on the first Sunday in November), the Marathon begins on Staten Island at the Verrazano-Narrows Bridge and passes through each of the city's five boroughs on the way to the finishing line at Central Park's Tavern on the Green.

Baseball Until recently, the more successful of the city's two teams has been the New York Mets, who play at Shea Stadium in Queens (tel: 718/507–8499). Ticket prices range from around $8 for the bleachers, where you will hear the New York crowd at its most witty but also get the worst view, to around $17 as you move up into the tiered seating.

Beset by off-the-field problems through the early 1990s, the New York Yankees are now putting their troubles behind them and returning to their glory days. The Yankees play at Yankee Stadium in the Bronx (tel: 718/293–6000), and ticket prices are similar to those for the Mets.

The season runs from April to October.

Basketball From fall to spring, basketball fans can watch the New York Knicks (short for "Knickerbockers") playing at Madison Square Garden (tel: 465–JUMP). The Knicks had an all-win "dream" season in the early 1970s, but

One of the great events of New York's sporting year

their record has been off and on since. Tickets cost upwards of $17 and are difficult to get only if the Knicks have qualified for the end-of-season play-offs. College basketball should not be underestimated. Many collegiate players are embryonic professionals and most of the best appear at the inter-college tournaments staged at Madison Square Garden during November and March.

Hockey The incredible lack of success of the city's New York Rangers was dramatically ended by their winning of the Stanley Cup in 1994. The Rangers face off at Madison Square Garden (tel: 308–NYRS) in a season lasting from late fall to spring. New Yorkers who want to see a local hockey team win are more inclined to travel to Uniondale on Long Island, where the New York Islanders play at the Nassau Coliseum (tel: 516/794–4100).

Football Both of New York's two professional football teams play outside the city's boundaries, at Giants Stadium, the Meadowlands, East Rutherford, New Jersey (tel: 201/935–8222). In recent years, the Giants have been much more successful than New York's A.F.C. team, Jets. The football season runs from August to December and tickets for the Jets start at around $25. Particularly for Giants games, however, tickets are virtually impossible to obtain without booking many months (if not years) in advance.

Horse-racing At daily races held from May to July and from September to mid-October, thoroughbreds can be seen stampeding along the turf at Belmont Park, Elmont, Long Island (tel: 516/488–6000), and from late October to May at the Aqueduct Racetrack, Ozone Park, Queens (phone number as for Belmont Park). During August, the state's horse lovers move upstate to the Saratoga Raceway (tel: 518/584–6200) for a month-long series of meetings.

Betting on horse races If your interest in horses extends only as far as betting on them, aim for one of the many branches of New York City Off-track Betting, where bets can be placed and races watched on T.V. simulcast. Other venues for a wager are The Inside Track, Second Avenue between 53rd and 54th streets (tel: 752–1940), a sports bar in the style of an English pub with two giant screens and 15 T.V. monitors, or the elegant Select Club, 165 Water Street (tel: 425–0052).

Tennis Early in September, one of the big events in the international tennis calendar, the U.S. Open, takes place at Flushing Meadows, Queens (tel: 718/271–5100). Tickets for the later stages of the Open have traditionally been snapped up many moons in advance, though it has always been possible to see international stars play at short notice—there are often people with extra tickets trying to sell them on the boardwalk leading to the stadium area. With the completion of new, enlarged quarters, the ticket situation has loosened up considerably, though. The springtime Tournament of Champions draws many top players to the West Side Tennis Club in Forest Hills, Queens (tel: 718/27–5100).

Scalpers
Scalpers offering tickets for all major sporting events are usually found on the approach routes to the venue. Be wary of forged tickets and that prices, which can start well in excess of the ticket's face value, will drop as game time approaches.

Sports bars
The city's many sports bars provide alcohol and T.V. screens tuned to every sports event anyone could possibly want. If a New York team is involved, you can also be sure of loud and frequent partisan comments and suggestions.

Informal basketball

The George Washington Bridge

Look southward from any high point in or around the Cloisters and you will be able to admire the elegant form of the George Washington Bridge, spanning the Hudson River from 178th Street and once described by famed modernist architect Le Corbusier as "the most beautiful bridge in the world."

Altarpieces and chapel furnishings at the Cloisters

▶▶ The Cloisters   IBCF1

Fort Tryon Park, Washington Heights
Subway: A; 190th Street

Manhattan and medieval European monasteries may seem an unlikely partnership, but venture to **Fort Tryon Park**, close to Manhattan's northern tip, and you will find—perched on a spectacular site above the Hudson River—parts of five 12th- to 15th-century monastic buildings from France and Spain brought together to form the Cloisters, a fitting home for a large portion of the Metropolitan Museum of Art's medieval collection.

Although much of the Cloisters' architecture is new disguised as old, the genuinely historic parts—assorted columns, cloisters, chapels, apses and much more—were gathered by sculptor George Gray Bernard as he roamed the back roads of Europe during the early 1900s. Bernard grabbed all the forgotten religious art and architecture he could lay his hands on. Some of his pieces were discovered lying in pigsties and ditches near old churches, others were being used as garden ornaments. Bernard put the rather haphazard collection on show in

Manhattan and it was brought to the Met in 1925 with funds provided by John D. Rockefeller, who subsequently commissioned the construction of the Cloisters to put it on permanent show.

The exceedingly wealthy Rockefellar also owned the land that became Fort Tryon Park (see panel page 93) and donated to the Cloisters its most memorable exhibit—the Unicorn Tapestries (see below).

Each section of the Cloisters is arranged more or less chronologically, and highlights particular aspects of medieval creativity. The Romanesque Hall, for example, is entered through one of three sculptured church doorways, demonstrating the stylistic shift from 12th-century Romanesque to 13th-century Gothic. Most impressive of the three is the latest: a High Gothic masterpiece from Burgundy which shows Christ crowning the Virgin, flanked by Clovis, first Christian ruler of France, and his son, Clothaire. The two men are so realistically sculpted they seem ready to reach forward and shake your hand.

Two for the price of one

If you visit the Metropolitan Museum of Art and the Cloisters on the same day, a single ticket is valid at both. During the summer there is also a direct bus link between the two museums, which is quicker though more expensive than public transportation.

Off the Romanesque Hall you will find the apse of the 12th-century Fuentiduena Chapel, which survived as its church crumbled around it: note the frescoes and the statues of St Martin and the Annunciation of the Virgin, both of which remain highly impressive despite the ravages of age.

Next door, stroll around the cloisters of the Benedictine Saint-Guilhem Monastery admiring the 12th-century carved capitals before passing through the Romanesque room for the Langon Chapel. During the 12th century, few places produced better wood sculpture than Autun, in Burgundy. Gaze long enough at the chapel's major piece—an Enthroned Virgin and Child—and its many subtleties of form and texture gradually become clear.

Beyond the Langon Chapel are several Gothic rooms and the Cuxa Cloister, its pink arches and columns built in 1188 for a Pyrenean monastery. Across the cloister are the amazing Unicorn Tapestries, probably 16th-century and of Flemish origin. Depicting the hunt for the mythical unicorn as an allegory for Christ's Incarnation, the Unicorn Tapestries are vivid in color and rich in detail. Pick out the images of love and fertility (within the flora and fauna), which mingle with the Christian symbols and suggest that the series may have been commissioned to celebrate a wedding.

The beauty and glowing color of the tapestries tend to outshine everything else in the Cloisters, except for the six glorious stained-glass lancet windows in the adjoining Boppard Room. Produced during the 1400s, the panels originally stood in the Carmelite Church of St. Severinus in Boppard-on-Rhine in Germany. With stunning artistry and craftsmanship, the glass shows several saints occupying canopied niches around the central figure of the Virgin.

Another important exhibit is a few steps away: Robert Campin's *Annunciation* altarpiece, an early Flemish triptych pioneering the use of oils on wood panels and also breaking new ground by using a contemporary domestic setting.

A "medieval" home for medieval treasures: the Cloisters

Fort Tryon Park
This park, in which the Cloisters stands, was the site of the Battle of Washington Heights during the Revolutionary War. The fort that stood here then was renamed Tryon by the victorious British, after the last British governor of New York. Subsequently, its 66 acres were divided into private estates which, one by one, were later purchased by John D. Rockefeller. Rockefeller gave the land to the city in 1930, and the Olmsted Brothers (descendants of Frederick Olmsted, architect of Central Park) were commissioned to landscape the lawns, terraces and picnic grounds that stand here now.

COLUMBIA UNIVERSITY

Riverside Church

Just south of the Columbia University campus, the Cathedral of St. John the Divine rises in its monumental and still unfinished form (see page 81). Another substantial example of religious architecture sits just to the north, between 120th and 122nd streets off Riverside Drive, in the very imposing French Gothic form of Riverside Church.

Since its inception, the church—now interdenominational—has championed the underprivileged, and radical liberal views have frequently been aired from its pulpit. An elevator runs to the tower's 20th-story observation level for blustery views across the Hudson River and over Upper Manhattan. Go after the Sunday morning service for an earful of the world's largest carillon, housed in the tower.

Alma Mater, *Daniel Chester French's statue, outside Columbia University's Low Library*

▶ **Columbia University**   IBCB2
114th–120th streets between Amsterdam Avenue and Broadway
Subway: 1; 116th Street

Founded in 1754 with a charter from the British king George II (it was originally named King's College) on a site in Lower Manhattan, Columbia University was intended to raise New York's cultural profile at a time when the fast-growing city was regarded as an uncouth, money-crazed upstart by the comparatively refined communities of Boston and New Haven, where the universities of Harvard and Yale were well established.

The campus occupied various locations in Manhattan. Through its steady movement northward, Columbia acquired ownership of the land that was later occupied by Rockefeller Center; it sold the prized plot during the mid-1980s for $400 million. The university arrived at its present location in 1897.

The specially designed campus (on the grounds of a former lunatic asylum) placed the academic buildings around a series of fountain-dotted plazas at the heart of which stands the majestic **Low Library**, based on Rome's Pantheon. This was the gift of Seth Low, university president and briefly, starting in 1902, mayor of New York.

An elegant three-tiered stairway leads up to the library's colonnaded entrance. Inside, you will see 16 green marble columns supporting an impressive octagonal rotunda. What you will not see is students poring over weighty tomes: the library is used only for ceremonies and exhibitions. On the second floor, the Columbiana Collection charts the history of the university with a mass of drawings, documents, paintings and assorted paraphernalia.

On the library's steps you will pass Daniel Chester French's symbolic sculpture, *Alma Mater*, which was covered in gold leaf until 1962 and which formed an

unlikely rallying point for the anti-Vietnam War demonstrations that spread across the campus in 1968. Just east of the library is the Italian Renaissance St. Paul's Chapel, which has a masterly vaulted interior.

Free guided tours of the campus operate most weekdays; tel: 857–1754.

▶▶ Cooper-Hewitt Museum   187C1

91st Street at Fifth Avenue
Subway: 4, 6; 86th or 96th streets
Inspired by their 1897 visit to London's Victoria and Albert Museum, the three Hewitt sisters set about creating a visual library of design that would inspire new ideas.

From their motley assortment of wallpaper, keys and unusual jewelry, the Cooper-Hewitt Museum has grown into a collection of more than 250,000 items. It includes ceramics, wall coverings, textiles, decorative arts, drawings and prints, plus encyclopedic reference and picture libraries devoted to design matters.

Selections from the eclectic stocks make up the museum's thematic shows. Whether they feature 17th-century French needlework, contemporary Italian typewriters, Middle Eastern embroidery, American hatboxes or three centuries' worth of maps (to mention a few past shows), here you will find New York's most imaginative, and sometimes most controversial, exhibitions.

The status of the museum rose greatly in 1967 when its collections, previously displayed in Lower Manhattan, were put into the care of the prestigious Smithsonian Institution and later moved to their present home, the former residence of industrialist Andrew Carnegie.

Carnegie was one of the world's richest men by the time he announced his intention to have built the "most modest, plainest, and roomiest house in New York." Not exactly plain, the 1901 Georgian mansion, in red brick and limestone, sits amid extensive gardens and has 64 rooms—intended for Carnegie, his wife and daughter, and their 19 servants.

As you wend your way around the exhibitions, notice the vaulted ceilings, the Tiffany glass windows, and the Louis XVI music room furnished with French antiques and with a set of bagpipes molded into the decorations—a reminder of Carnegie's Scottish origins. A major renovation of the building was undertaken in the mid 1990s.

▶ Daily News Building   151B3

220 East 42nd Street
Subway: 4, 6, 7; Grand Central Terminal/42nd Street
Created by Raymond Hood, who with it established his credentials as the father of New York skyscraper architecture, the 1930 Daily News Building (now properly called the News Building) is a landmark, a no-frills structure of thrusting verticality. Inside the largely original lobby, a frieze recounts the rise and rise (though a question mark hangs over its immediate prospects) of the New York newspaper that became a legend for its punchy headlines and salacious stories. An immense revolving globe sits at the center of displays on meteorological themes. If the building seems familiar, you may be remembering the 1980s *Superman* films, in which it starred as the offices of the *Daily Planet*.

Columbia University riots
By 1968, the student activism that had begun a few years earlier with the Free Speech Movement at the University of California at Berkeley had escalated into nationwide campus demonstrations protesting against U.S. involvement in Vietnam and inept academic administrations. In April, Columbia University saw marches, sit-ins, and the taking of five university officials hostage for 26 hours. The besieged university president eventually asked city police to clear the campus, in the course of which they arrested 698 students and injured 100—and united the student body and university staff in allegations of police brutality.

95

Peter Cooper
The fortunes of inventor and philanthropist Peter Cooper, grandfather of museum founders Sarah, Amy and Eleanor Hewitt, were built on glue and iron. The Cooper foundry, in New Jersey, was where the tracks of the U.S.'s first great railroads were forged. Recognizing that his riches stemmed from the "cooperation of the masses," Cooper founded the first free college, the Cooper Union, which still stands in what is now the East Village (see pages 98–99).

DAKOTA APARTMENTS

The Dakota in movies and books

Plenty of the Dakota's residents have had leading roles in films. So, too, has the building. With its turrets, towers and gables, the Dakota provided a suitably unsettling location for Roman Polanski's 1968 story of demonic possession, *Rosemary's Baby*. It also played a part in the 1970 time-travel novel, *Time and Again*, by Jack Finney.

The Dakota Apartments—home of the stars, and a screen star itself

▶ **Dakota Apartments**

1 West 72nd Street
Subway: 1, 2, 3; 72nd Street

Wealthy New York house owners of the 1880s had yet to be convinced that apartment living was the lifestyle of the future when Edward S. Clark, heir to the Singer sewing machine fortunes, commissioned a luxury apartment house in what is now the Upper West Side but was then wild, open land dotted by shanty dwellings and not even linked to the city's power supplies.

So far out was the site that critics suggested it might as well be in the Dakota territories—which is how the building got its name and the ears of corn, arrowheads and the Native American head that decorate its entrance.

As the city spread northward and Midtown Manhattan house prices rocketed, there were suddenly lots of takers for the Dakota's marble floors and oak- and mahogany-paneled dwellings. The building quickly became—and continues to be—a prestigious address, with a roll call of rich and famous residents that has included Leonard Bernstein, Lauren Bacall, Judy Garland, and John Lennon—who was murdered while entering the building in 1980. Lennon's widow, Yoko Ono, still lives here.

■ **More inspired by Manhattan's celebrity-filled soirées than by its art museums, the ever-quotable Andy Warhol might be the one world-famous artist New York can truly call its own.** ■

Born Andrew Warhola to Czech immigrant parents in Pittsburgh, Andy Warhol moved to New York in 1949 and within seven years was among the city's most sought-after commercial artists, much of his work appearing in high society magazines.

Fame in a soup can Warhol loved the party-going life of New York but found his own fame—and artistic vocation—after a trip to a supermarket in 1962. As the artists of the pop art explosion created collages of consumerist images, Warhol began painting soup cans, according the gravity of serious portraiture to each one.

Be it depictions of dollar bills, electric chairs, or Brillo boxes, Warhol relished the publicity that his work aroused. A reviewer wrote that Warhol's silk-screened images of Marilyn Monroe were "as sentimental as Fords coming off the production line." In reply, Warhol declared "I want to be a machine" and named his studio the Factory.

In the mid-1960s, Warhol's Factory became filled by every oddball character in New York, many of whom starred in the underground movies that the artist began making, including *Chelsea Girls*, described by one critic as "an image of the total degeneration of American society."

Getting rich The Factory's excesses ended in 1968, when Warhol narrowly survived an assassination attempt and found his financial affairs under scrutiny. Feeling he should be earning more money, the guru of pop art became a society portrait painter, charging $25,000 a time, while his revamped *Interview* magazine began providing lucrative advertising alongside its celebrity gossip.

Warhol's wealth and fame became greater than his creativity. After moving to an expensive Upper East Side house in 1975, he squandered time and money on several ill-fated projects and appeared happiest during his daily shopping expeditions.

Shortly before his death in 1987, Warhol opined "getting rich isn't as much fun as it used to be."

Andy Warhol said
"In the future, everybody will be famous for 15 minutes."
"I don't think my art has any lasting value."
"I never wanted to be a painter. I wanted to be a tap dancer."

THE EAST VILLAGE

Little Ukraine
In an area of the East Village around Second Avenue between 4th and 14th streets is New York's Little Ukraine. Ukrainians began settling here in the late 1800s and, though their numbers have been greatly depleted, are still much in evidence among the neighborhood's many Slavic restaurants and shops selling traditional Ukrainian crafts—such as painted Easter eggs. The tiny Ukrainian Museum, 203 Second Avenue, has changing exhibitions on past and present Ukrainian life in New York and in the homeland.

▶ The East Village *IFCC3*

In the 1950s, rising rents in Greenwich Village began pushing New York's more radical artists and writers across Broadway into the East Village. Here they took cheap apartments in tenement buildings otherwise inhabited by hard-up eastern European immigrants, many of them from the Ukraine.

The heart of New York hippiedom in the 1960s and the epicenter of its 1970s punk rock scene, the East Village is regularly in the vanguard of alternative culture—despite increasing signs of gentrification, expect to see at least one person dressed head-to-toe in leather and sporting bright green hair. Bizarre one-of-a-kind stores, ethnic eateries and a vibrant street scene are the things the East Village does best, although a handful of historical sights are also worthy of attention.

Astor Place carries the name of John Jacob Astor, one of early 19th-century New York's wealthiest men. Like the similarly extremely affluent Cornelius Vanderbilt, Astor owned one of the series of marble-fronted houses that became known as **Colonnade Row**. Once the grandest residences in New York, those that survive, now looking rather shabby, are on Lafayette Street (numbers 428 to 434).

Across Lafayette Street, Astor financed the city's first free public library in a brownstone building which, since the 1960s, has been the **Public Theater** (originally Joseph Papp Public Theater), a venue for varied theatrical, cinematic and other arts events.

Another 19th-century remnant is the **Cooper Union Building**, just south of Astor Place. Founded in 1859 by millionaire railroad tycoon Peter Cooper to provide free education for all, the college was the first of its kind in the U.S. and also became an airing place for political views: Abraham Lincoln was among the famous orators who spoke here.

East of Astor Place is St. Mark's Place, where the unprepossessing building at number 77 was home to Anglo-American poet W.H. Auden from 1953. This was also where, four decades earlier in the basement, Leon Trotsky had plotted the Russian Revolution.

Nearby, the church of **St. Mark's-in-the-Bowery** arose on the estate of New York's Dutch governor, Peter Stuyvesant, in 1799. Its original body was later topped by a spire and fronted by a cast-iron portico. The church serves its eccentric East Village congregation with episcopal services, poetry readings and performance art. On the church's eastern side, Stuyvesant and six generations of his descendants lie buried.

The Public Theater

s Films Du Losange

REGULAR 7.00
Little GA 007

AKESPEARE FESTIVAL PRODUCTION

THE JOSEPH PAPP PUBLIC THEATER
425 Lafayette Street
N.Y.C. 10003

NEW YORK SHAKESPEARE FESTIVAL

Walk The East Village stores and sights

This walk touches historical sites and also highlights the contemporary flavor of the East Village.

Begin at the 1799 church of **St. Mark's-in-the-Bowery** and continue along Stuyvesant Street to the **Cooper Union Building** (1859), the U.S.'s first free college.

Directly ahead, the Astor Place subway station is marked by a fetching beaux-arts-style booth. Just across Fourth Avenue is the local branch of Barnes and Noble, a massive bookstore with a popular café.

Along East 6th Street you will find a variety of intriguing stores selling unusual clothing, antiques and ornaments. On East 7th Street, **Caffè della Pace**, number 48, draws the East Village's fashionable faces for espresso and snacks. **McSorley's Old Ale House**, at number 15, has been a local landmark since 1854.

Unusual store in the East Village

THE EAST VILLAGE

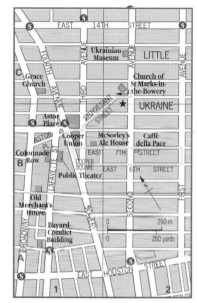

ELLIS ISLAND

Ellis Island: the future of many a would-be American was determined in these buildings. Museum displays now bring to life the hopes, fears, and disappointments of those newly arrived immigrants

▶▶▶ Ellis Island   48C2

Around 100 million present-day Americans have ancestors who passed through Ellis Island, a modest speck of land in the shadow of the Statue of Liberty in New York's Upper Bay. From 1892 to 1924 this was the country's busiest immigration center.

Later serving as an army hospital and as an enemy alien detention center, Ellis Island was closed in 1954 and suffered total neglect until a $160-million restoration project reopened its major building as the Ellis Island Immigration Museum in 1990.

Those who arrived at Ellis Island hoping to become Americans were drawn from Europe's underclasses (immigrants of means were processed elsewhere and allowed immediate entry into the U.S.). The elation they experienced on seeing the Statue of Liberty quickly dissipated as they reached the place nicknamed the "Island of Tears" and faced the bureaucracy that stood between them and American citizenship.

Would-be Americans were screened for contagious diseases and signs of insanity and questioned about their relatives and their work skills. Any sign of sickness, or giving the wrong answers, could mean being detained and perhaps deported (as two percent of the new arrivals were). Some also got their first taste of American corruption at Ellis Island: among the many scams were bribes for immigration officers and overpriced train tickets for onward travel in the U.S.

From statistics projecting the country's future ethnic make-up to trunks and string bags that carried treasured possessions, the museum has many eye-opening exhibits. The jail-like dormitories where detainees were kept are singularly depressing, but the taped oral histories of former arrivals do most to suggest the hopes, the fears, and the sheer sense of bewilderment that most of the would-be immigrants experienced as they stepped into this building.

▶▶▶ Empire State Building   151B2

34th Street at Fifth Avenue
Subway: B, D, F, N, R; 34th Street
The World Trade Center may be taller and the Statue of Liberty a more potent national symbol, but New York's best-loved and most enduring emblem is the Empire State Building, over 60 years old and still rising above Midtown Manhattan with a gracious, ageless aplomb. As construction mania swept through New York during the booming

Empire State Building facts
Height: 1472ft.
Weight: 365,000 tons.
Number of bricks: 10 million.
Budget: $60 million.
Actual cost: $40,948,900.
Tallest visitor: King Kong, 1933
Greatest tragedy: Plane crashing into the 79th story in 1945, killing 14.

The lobby of the Empire State Building

New York Skyride
If the views from the observation levels of the Empire State Building fail to satisfy, get an aerial view of the city on the New York Skyride—a flight simulator tour of the city at dizzying speed aboard a "spacecoptor." The Skyride is on the Empire State Building's second floor.

1920s, the Empire State Building was the winner in the financiers' race to create the world's tallest building, snatching the title in 1931 from the Chrysler Building and holding it until the first World Trade Center tower was finished in 1973.

Although the building rose to 1,250 feet (gaining a further 222 feet with a T.V. mast in 1951), it was constructed within only two years. The zoning laws (see page 24) of the time resulted in the tiered design that tempers the

At Federal Hall National Memorial, the statue of George Washington commemorates his inauguration as president, which took place in an earlier building on the site

The original Federal Hall
The historic significance of the present Federal Hall is eclipsed by that of its predecessor, which housed the first U.S. government and which was where, in April 1789, George Washington was sworn in as the country's first president.

Despite its role in U.S. history, the original building reached such a dilapidated state that it was sold for scrap in 1812.

impact of the structure's bulk and contributes greatly to its elegant profile.

Conceived in an economic boom, the building was completed amid the gloom of the Depression, the Wall Street crash occurring as the 2-acre site—which held the original Waldorf-Astoria Hotel—was being cleared. Consequently, much of the office space remained unrented for years, and most of the building's early income was from tourists visiting for the views.

Admire the art deco fittings of the lobby before descending to the concourse for a ticket and the express elevator to the 86th-floor observation level (the enclosed 102nd-floor level hardly justifies the additional elevator ride to reach it). On a clear day you see for 80 miles.

▶　　**Federal Hall National Memorial**　　*104B2*
Wall and Nassau streets
Subway: 2, 3, 4, 5; Wall Street
Its finely proportioned flight of steps and smart Doric columns impose themselves grandly in the heart of the Financial District, but a sense of history is disappointingly missing from the echoey interior of the 19th-century Federal Hall. Built as the first U.S. Custom House, it later served as a bank before being declared a national memorial in 1939.

If you are exploring the Financial District, Federal Hall ought to be on your itinerary but do not expect anything spectacular. Inside, only a short film and a rather tame collection of exhibits record events that took place on the site: a glass-encased section of balcony railing, on which Washington leaned when addressing the crowds after his inauguration and a pair of the great man's belt-buckles form the highlights.

▶　　**Film Center Building**　　*151C1*
Ninth Avenue between 44th and 45th streets
Subway: A, C, E; 42nd Street
You may not want to visit any of the 75 film companies that have offices here, but the Film Center Building justifies a call for one of the city's most stunning art-deco interiors: its lobby, vestibule and entrance hall—the work of Ely Jacques Kahn. Already an outstanding modernist architect, by the late 1920s Kahn also had a reputation for his distinctive interior decoration based on interlinked geometric forms—employed here to wonderful effect.

▶▶　　**Financial District**　　*IFCA2*
The nation's monetary institutions took root in Lower Manhattan from the early 1800s, and as the city grew, so did its Financial District, quickly becoming a global center of trade and commerce. Side by side in this compact area stand grandiose neoclassical buildings, whose form signified their status as repositories of wealth, and the highrise glass and steel blocks that are the contemporary towers of mammon.

The exuberant 1980s saw Wall Street (just one of several thoroughfares here, but internationally synonymous with the highest of high finance) yield millions and give birth to the yuppie. But the party was over by the end of the decade, when a succession of scandals put the greedy behind bars and heralded the economic uncertainties of the early 1990s. By 1996, however, stock prices were again breaking records on a seemingly daily basis and million-dollar bonuses were once again energizing the city's economy.

Facing Wall Street from Broadway, the striking neo-Gothic form of **Trinity Church** has, since the 1840s, been reminding the Financial District's power brokers of a force greater than money. Note the bronze doors and the reredos, and continue into the small church museum to look at drawings showing a Manhattan skyline dominated by church spires rather than high-rise towers. In the graveyard, which has been receiving the dead since 1681, lies Alexander Hamilton, the first U.S. treasurer.

Predating Trinity Church by almost a century is Manhattan's only surviving prerevolutionary church, **St. Paul's Chapel**, which faces Fulton Street from Broadway. Laid out in a graceful Georgian style with a surprisingly bright interior, the chapel was regularly visited by George Washington, and dutifully maintains the Washington Pew, where the first president sat during the service marking his inauguration in 1789.

Wall Street's name
An oaken barricade erected by Dutch governor Peter Stuyvesant in 1653 to mark the northern boundary of New Amsterdam and deter British invaders was the "wall" that gave the world-famous street its name. The wall never quite fulfilled its promise, because its planks were steadily removed to build and repair the wooden homes of settlers. In 1699 its remains were finally demolished by the then well-entrenched British.

Now dwarfed by skyscrapers several times as high, Trinity Church began life as the city's tallest building, at 264 feet high

The Federal Reserve
Many Financial District buildings house major financial corporations where every day millions of dollars are traded and transferred in paper and electronic transactions. One of the few that actually holds money—in the form of gold—is the Manhattan branch of the Federal Reserve (33 Liberty Street), formally known as the Federal Reserve Bank of New York. Nationally, the Federal Reserve acts as banker to major banks and to the U.S. government, regulates monetary policy, and sets interest rates. The high security of the fortress-like building can be lawfully penetrated on guided tours, but tickets must be acquired well in advance (tel: 720–6130).

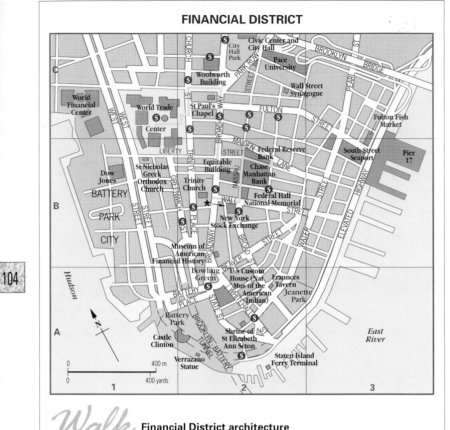

FINANCIAL DISTRICT

Walk **Financial District architecture**

Encompassing historic churches and financial and architectural landmarks, this walk is a good way to explore the varied facets of the Financial District.

Begin at **Trinity Church** (page 103) and continue along Wall Street, stopping at **Federal Hall** and detouring along Broad Street for the **Stock Exchange** (page 182). Continue along

Nassau Street for **Chase Manhattan Bank**, the first international-style structure in Lower Manhattan.

Across Maiden Lane, you can gaze (advance reservations essential, tel: 720–6130) at over 11,000 tons of gold—the wealth of many nations—stored below ground at the **Federal Reserve Bank**. Otherwise, examine the richly decorative ironwork of the enormous building's facade.

On the corner of Broadway, the much-detested 1915 **Equitable Building** rises for 40 sheer stories; this was New York's first high-rise office building and the first to plunge its neighboring buildings—and much of the street—into darkness.

Continue along Broadway for **St. Paul's Chapel** (page 103) and finish the walk at the **World Trade Center** (page 193).

■ **Tussles during the 19th century among Eastern Europe's Slavic peoples—Poles, Ukrainians, and Russians—and the totalitarian suppression of more recent times helped create two of New York's most stridently nationalistic communities: the Poles and the Ukrainians, who now coexist peaceably alongside their former foes, the Russians.** ■

Polish-Americans Struggles against colonial oppression in their own country made New York's Poles natural allies of the Americans in the revolutionary battles with the British. Later, New York offered refuge to those who had led an unsuccessful Polish republican uprising in 1830. The 234 who arrived were among Poland's finest minds, and were to give New York its first Polish cultural institutions.

Later Polish arrivals tended to be peasants who found factory jobs in the Greenpoint area of Brooklyn, though some opened the stores and bookshops that would become community focal points. Soviet control of postwar Poland brought exiled intellectuals, while the collapse of Communism in the 1990s led to new arrivals.

The Ukrainians Enforced military service in the czar's army caused many Ukrainians to flee their Russian-dominated homeland during the 1800s. Arriving in New York with their families, they turned a section of what is now the East Village into the world's largest urban Ukrainian community by 1919.

Russian immigrants The bulk of Russian immigrants were Jewish refugees who had fled persecution under the tsar (see page 139). More symbolic of the effect of European political upheavals, though, were the Russian aristocrats who arrived in New York as Leon Trotsky (here since the abortive 1905 revolution) left for Moscow to help the Bolsheviks seize power. Another arrival was ground-breaking choreographer George Balanchine. These newly arrived Russians quickly became integrated into New York society—a far cry from the former Soviet Russians who settled in Brighton Beach (see page 75).

The Pulaski and Kosciuszko bridges
Two of the bridges—the Pulaski and the Kosciuszko—linking Brooklyn and Queens bear the names of Poles who aided the American cause in the Revolutionary War. Cavalry expert Casimar Pulaski was noted for his bravery in battle (he died in an attack on the British); the engineering skills of Thaddeus Kosciuszko were crucial in preparing the anti-British fortifications at West Point and Saratoga.

105

The first taste of America for European immigrants: Ellis Island

FLATIRON BUILDING

The Flatiron Building—an unmistakable Fifth Avenue landmark

23 Skidoo

A story goes that in the days when well-dressed ladies had skirts to their ankles, high winds would find voyeurs lingering outside the Flatiron Building on 23rd Street hoping to spot female legs exposed by the breeze. The shouts of the police when moving the gentlemen on are thought to be the origin of the term "23 skidoo."

Daniel H. Burnham

The architect of the Flatiron Building, Daniel H. Burnham, made his name in Chicago in the 1880s, where, in partnership with John Root, he pioneered the modern skyscraper by making the first use of a steel frame to support a high-rise structure. Burnham's design ideas became a fundamental element in the highly influential "Chicago School" of architecture. Burnham's Chicago work was made possible partly because of a devastating fire that required the entire downtown area to be rebuilt. He also played an important role in the reshaping of San Francisco, wrecked by the earthquake of 1906, for which he planned a new Civic Center.

▶ **Flatiron Building**   *151A2*

Broadway and Fifth Avenue at 23rd Street
Subway: N, R; 23rd Street

Architect Daniel H. Burnham solved the problem of fitting a building into the triangular plot of land where Broadway crosses Fifth Avenue with the most logical solution: a triangular building. It was the world's tallest (285 feet) on its completion in 1902 and was one of·the first to be erected around a steel frame—the basic support of every subsequent skyscraper.

Nowadays, it is not height or building techniques that make the Flatiron Building one of New York's most-loved structures but its pretty French Renaissance features and the fact that its limestone body tapers to an impossibly slender 6-foot-wide corner curve on 23rd Street. In recent years, the building has provided a convenient sobriquet for the immediate area, now known locally as the "Flatiron District."

▶ **The Forbes Galleries**   *113C2*

Fifth Avenue between 12th and 13th streets
Subway: L, N, R 4, 6; 14th Street/Union Square
Even in New York, few magazine publishers have broken the speed record for ballooning across the country or have hurtled along Fifth Avenue on a motorcycle. Malcolm S. Forbes did both of those things, and more, in a career that began by accident and left him with wealth estimated, at his death in 1990, to be in excess of $700 million.

Born in 1919, two years after his father had founded *Forbes*, a ground-breaking magazine of investigative financial journalism, Forbes had turned the ailing title into a thriving concern by the time he took it over in 1964. One of the secrets of his success was a genius for garnering maximum publicity for himself and the magazine. Through the 1970s the media doted on Forbes and his colorful activities, which ranged from lavish parties and his mania for motorbikes and balloons to his offbeat collecting interests.

The Forbes Galleries bear the fruits of Forbes' quirky collecting passion. They occupy the first floor of the Forbes Magazine building. Among the displays are 500 model boats and submarines (some of them in bathtubs) viewed to the accompaniment of what purports to be the sound of the Battle of Jutland. Some 12,000 model soldiers are arranged in battle-ready poses, and there is an amazing room of trophies awarded for achievements such as having the best pure-bred bull of 1878 and the best 5 acres of turnips grown with Bradburn's manure.

The Presidential Papers room holds less eccentric material, drawn from the Forbes collection of 3,000 historical documents, while another special room displays gem-encrusted Easter eggs—and scores of other priceless objets d'art—made by master jeweler-goldsmith Peter Carl Fabergé for the last two czars of Russia.

▶▶ **Fraunces Tavern**   *104A2*

54 Pearl Street
Subway: 1, 4, 9; Bowling Green, South Ferry or Broad Street
This Federal-style brick building, which looks like a dollhouse beneath the glass-and-steel high-rises of the Financial District, stands on the site of the original Fraunces Tavern, a hotbed of subversion during the 18th century, when its customers included George Washington and his fellow revolutionaries.

At the successful completion of the Revolutionary War, Washington made a famously emotional farewell to his officers here after a meal in the Long Room—a scene recreated with period furniture on the tavern's third floor, while other objects and paintings from the revolutionary period are displayed on the fourth floor.

It may seem strange today, but the tavern became the unofficial seat of several government bodies during the earliest days of nationhood and spent three years as the recognized base of the Department of Foreign Affairs, the War Department and the Treasury, before being unceremoniously sold to a Brooklyn butcher.

Visit the tavern around lunchtime, when the atmosphere is enhanced by the smell of food wafting up from the first-floor restaurant, a cozy niche favored by Financial District types.

The Salmagundi Club
At 47 Fifth Avenue, opposite the Forbes Magazine Galleries, an 1853 Italianate brownstone mansion built for a coral magnate provides a home for the Salmagundi Club. Founded in 1871 (but moving here in 1917), the Salmagundi Club is the oldest artists' club in the United States and numbered Stanford White and Louis Comfort Tiffany among its early members. Occasional exhibitions provide a chance to peek at the building's extravagantly appointed interior.

The word "salmagundi" describes a mixed salad dish popular in the 18th century, but was presumably adopted from a series of pamphlets, the *Salmagundi Papers*, written and published in the early 1800s by author Washington Irving and friends. The *Salmagundi Papers* satirized New York life and, among other things, first coined the word Gotham as an alternative name for the city.

107

A bomb at the Fraunces Tavern
George Washington was not the last revolutionary to make a point at the Fraunces Tavern. In January 1975, the building was rocked by a bomb that killed four Wall Street businessmen and left 55 people injured. Responsibility was claimed by an underground group called the F.A.L.N., in revenge for the U.S. Government's resistance to Puerto Rican independence.

■ **For those with money and preferably a well-known face (or name) to go with it, New York can easily become the ultimate playground. What follows is a very selective Manhattan list for the well-heeled person about town. For those visitors who need to budget carefully for every cab ride, a peek inside one or two of these establishments offers a glance at the luxurious end of New York's wide spectrum of lifestyles.** ■

Café des Artistes (67th Street at Central Park West, tel: 877–3500). A mural of frolicking nymphs, painted in 1934 by Howard Chandler Christy, contributes to the Café des Artistes' reputation as New York's most romantic dining spot. The nymphs have yet to lose their allure, and the café's Continental cuisine is divine. Expect to spend around $150 for a dinner for two with wine. This is only one of many restaurants in that price category, but is probably the loveliest. A less costly alternative is the café's bar, the scene of much refined chitchat and cocktail imbibing.

Afternoon tea at the Pierre (Fifth Avenue at 61st Street, tel: 838–8000). Even if they are lodging elsewhere, discriminating visitors to New York seeking a taste of the high life should try afternoon tea at the Pierre hotel. This long-established ritual takes place beneath the Pierre's striking rotunda, its two-story-high walls decorated by Edward Melcarth's remarkable mural, which appears to be a microcosmic documentation of mankind's history. The hotel's doting staff offer you a choice from a dozen or so fine teas and bear plates of melt-in-the-mouth scones. This slightly decadent treat costs around $20.

Four Seasons (East 52nd Street between Park and Lexington avenues, tel: 754–9494). The serious trade here is power-lunching corporate executives—plus a sprinkling of lawyers, politicians, and publishers. On the ground floor of Mies van der Rohe's landmark Seagram Building, this Philip Johnson-designed restaurant features a large Picasso tapestry and other noted modern pieces. The lunch menu is designed to be good but simple, so it does not detract from the deals being struck across the tables. At dinner, the chef presents exceptional contemporary American creations, some of which are prepared at your table. A full dinner here is liable to cost $100 per person; lunch should be a comparatively modest $40.

The 21 Club (West 52nd Street between Fifth and Sixth avenues, tel: 582–7200). A row of cast-iron model jockeys stand to attention along the façade of the 21 Club, which opened on New Year's Eve 1929 and was—in those Prohibition times—just one of scores of speakeasies lining 52nd Street. The others quickly disappeared but the 21 Club endured, maturing into a favorite watering hole of the New York establishment. Despite a complete

Getting around luxury New York
When money is no object, travel between expensive stores in a chauffeur-driven stretch limousine. Equipped with V.C.R.s, telephones, and bars—and other features that make Manhattan's traffic-stopping gridlock almost seem attractive—stretch limos can be rented from around $50 per hour. Carey Limousines (tel: 599–1122) and Imperial Limousines (tel: 229–9292) are among the operators awaiting your call.

refurbishment in the 1980s, the 21 Club's dark, wood-paneled walls and deep-pile carpets offer a picture of old-style luxury New York that is rarely found today. Although appearances suggest otherwise, it is not an exclusive club, but you should not show up without a reservation. Many regulars come here to confirm their place in the New York social pecking order as much as to dine: the food may be fine but tends to vary in quality, depending on who's in charge in the kitchen. You might try the "21 Burger," or the pretheater prix-fixe dinner, but you probably won't have change from $30 and $50 respectively.

Rainbow Room (30 Rockefeller Plaza, 50th Street between Fifth and Sixth avenues, tel: 632 5100). With a big band playing the music of Gershwin and Cole Porter and a 65th-floor view of the Manhattan skyline, you will experience New York's romantic side when you spend an evening at the Rainbow Room.

When it opened in 1934, the Rainbow Room was a glamorous crown atop the new Rockefeller Center. A $20-million face-lift in the 1980s has brought back some of the grandeur, although it's unabashedly touristy.

Perhaps the best order of doing things at the Rainbow Room is to have drinks, dinner, a turn on the revolving dance-floor, and finally return to your table for a baked Alaska for dessert. Reservations need to be made six weeks in advance.

Sightseeing by helicopter
One way to beat the crowds at the Statue of Liberty or the World Trade Center is to view such attractions, and the rest of Manhattan, from a helicopter. Sightseeing helicopter flights are operated day and night by Island Helicopter Sightseeing (tel: 683–4575) and Liberty Helicopter Tours (tel: 800/542–9933 or 967–6464).

109

Specialty grocers
Manhattan's avid foodies are willing to pay high prices for superior quality and variety at fancy food emporiums such as **Balducci's** (6th Ave. at 9th St.) in Greenwich Village, where food is displayed like art, and the huge Soho trendsetter, **Dean and Deluca** (560 Broadway at Prince St.). On the Upper West Side, there's **Zabar's** (2245 Broadway at 80th St.), which sells fine foods on the street level and kitchenware upstairs

The luxurious Plaza Hotel: evocative of Old World elegance

Having made his fortune in Pittsburgh, industrialist Henry Clay Frick moved to New York, where he had this elaborate mansion built to house his superb collection of European art

▶▶ Frick Collection   151D2
70th Street at Fifth Avenue
Subway: 6; 68th Street

Henry Clay Frick made a fortune through coke and steel, and was little loved in his day for his mean-spirited business practices. Ironically, the Frick Collection of 14th- to 19th-century European art, housed on the first floor of the French-style mansion in which Frick spent the last five years of his life (he died in 1919), is perhaps the most loved of New York's many art collections.

The absence of ropes, descriptive texts, and other museum trappings is intended to make seeing the collection akin to visiting a private house, though guards hover in every nook and cranny. The collection is a triumph of quality over quantity, and there is not a single painting in the 19 rooms that does not deserve its wall space.

Highlights are many and naturally vary according to individual taste. Few could fail to be impressed, however, by Gainsborough's *The Mall in St. James's Park*, a refined vision of privileged promenaders that stands out in a dining room lined by 18th-century English portraiture.

The living hall has two particularly potent canvases: Titian's *Portrait of a Man in a Red Cap* and El Greco's *St. Jerome*. But it is on the walls of the west gallery that the cream of the collection is hung: two of Turner's studies of northern European ports resonate on facing walls, close to Rembrandt's 1658 *Portrait of a Young Artist—Self-Portrait* and the same artist's much debated (its authenticity is disputed) *Polish Rider*.

After leaving the final room, take a break in the garden court before starting through the collections once again, this time concentrating on the outstanding sculptures, tapestries, and decorative arts exhibits.

▶ Fulton Fish Market   104C3
South and Fulton streets
Subway: 2, 3, 4; Fulton Street

If you are an insomniac or a very early riser, be at the Fulton Fish Market (tel: 732–7678) at 6 AM on the first or third Thursday of each month (Apr–Oct) for an odoriferous behind-the-scenes tour of the daily market. Here truckloads of squirming fish and creeping crustaceans are unloaded and prepared for sale to the city's classiest restaurants.

In 1995, the market was temporarily closed following a dispute between the city authorities, who own it, and the allegedly mafia-linked parties that had run it for years.

▶ General Grant Memorial   IBCB2
Riverside Drive at 122nd Street
Subway: 1; 116th Street

The largest mausoleum in the U.S., its gray granite form rising 150 feet beside the Hudson and its entrance fronted by six Doric columns, the General Grant Memorial (commonly known as Grant's Tomb) holds the remains—in 9-ton marble sarcophagi—of Ulysses S. Grant and his wife Julia. As commander-in-chief of the Union forces in the Civil War, Grant achieved enormous fame: an estimated million people lined the route of his funeral procession in 1885. Inside, a chilled atmosphere prevails, and your footsteps echo as you walk around reading the

Moving pictures
Each summer, Henry Frick had his fantastic art collection packed into crates and transported in a special railroad car so he could enjoy it while staying at his estate in Massachusetts. Asked if he was worried about losing the priceless canvases through an accident in transit, Frick allegedly replied, "No, they're insured."

brief accounts of Grant's distinguished military service and his much less successful eight-year tenure as 18th U.S. President. Outside, the mosaic-decorated benches result from a community arts project.

▶ Gracie Mansion 187C2

East End Avenue at 88th Street
Subway: 4, 6; 86th Street
Guided tours: Apr–Oct, Wed

The official residence of the mayor of New York since 1942, Gracie Mansion was built in 1799 as a country retreat for shipping magnate Archibald Gracie. Following the collapse of his business, Gracie sold the mansion, and it spent an ignominious period as a refreshment stand before being purchased by the city. Despite the numerous modifications made over the years, recent renovations have made the mansion a finer example of Federal architecture (the first architectural style considered distinctly American) than it ever was in its infancy. The house can be fully appreciated only on guided tours (reservations necessary; tel: 570–4751).

Grant's military career
Following an unremarkable graduation (21st in a class of 39) from West Point Academy, Ulysses S. Grant distinguished himself in service, but resigned from the army in 1854 while stationed in California. Grant failed as a farmer (his subsequent occupation), and was working as a clerk in his father's store in Illinois at the outbreak of the Civil War. His military experience led to his appointment as brigadier of the Illinois Volunteers. A series of battle successes followed, showing a strategic brilliance that culminated in Grant's capture of the Confederate stronghold of Vicksburg after a 47-day siege in 1863. the following year, Grant was made commander of all Union armies. As president, Grant faced the postwar Reconstruction period and difficulties that would have tested the skills of the most experienced politician—his battle planning skills proving no match for the chicanery of Washington DC.

Henderson Place
In a cul-de-sac on the north side of 86th Street, close to Gracie Mansion, stands the lovely row of 24 Queen Anne-style houses that constitute the Henderson Place Historic District. The houses were commissioned during the 1880s by fur-hat manufacturer John C. Henderson to provide homes for "persons of moderate means."

The grandiose mausoleum of Civil War general Ulysses S. Grant was inspired by Napoleon's tomb in Paris

Greenwich Village secondhand stores may not offer such good bargains as less fashionable areas of the city, but they are hard to beat for sheer variety

Grace Church

One of the few things in Greenwich Village likely to bring to mind the European Middle Ages is the 1846 Grace Church, on Broadway between 10th and 11th streets. The church's finely proportioned Gothic Revival design—among the earliest examples of the style in the U.S.—helped its architect, James Renwick, win the commission for the larger, grander St. Patrick's Cathedral in Midtown Manhattan. Set on Broadway's first curve, the church's spire could originally be seen from as far south as what is now Battery Park.

▶▶▶ Greenwich Village   IFCC2

No place in New York has a greater cultural aura than Greenwich Village. For almost 100 years this has been a breeding ground and rallying point for the nation's most inventive and imaginative minds.

From its earliest days, Greenwich Village has kept its distance from mainstream New York life. Its first homes were built to enable the wealthy to escape the outbreaks of disease that were common in the 1790s, pushing back the boundaries of the city that, until then, had been contained within present-day Lower Manhattan.

By the late 1800s, the rich were moving north again, and their Greenwich Village town houses were being converted into stores, factories and boarding houses for foreign immigrants. By the turn of the 20th century, Greenwich Village's diverse ethnic mix had fostered an atmosphere of tolerance that, coupled with low rents, attracted the unconventional elements that gave birth to the country's first, and eventually its most celebrated, enclave of Bohemianism.

Over three decades, writers and artists from Walt Whitman to Edward Hopper were to turn American culture upside down from their Greenwich Village bases. During the 1950s, the earliest Beat writers began taking Greenwich Village still farther away from the materialist values of middle America, but rents were soon on the rise as new transit links made Greenwich Village the target of moneyed professionals in search of a well-placed neighborhood full of character.

Living in Greenwich Village today certainly requires financial security, but the lawyers and investment bankers who have flocked here have certainly not dampened the community spirit or Greenwich Village's rebellious streak. A Bohemian mood still percolates through its innumerable Italian cafés and restaurants, even though today most Greenwich Village visitors are not impoverished souls at creativity's cutting edge.

Continued on page 116.

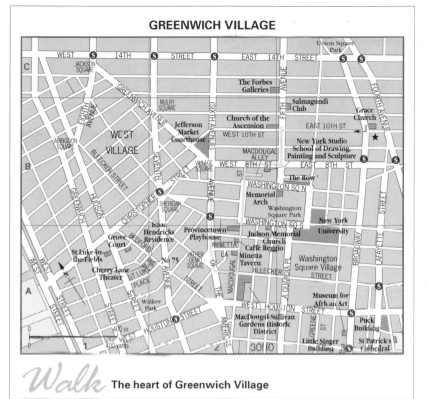

GREENWICH VILLAGE

Walk   **The heart of Greenwich Village**

From Grace Church in the east, this walk passes through the heart of Greenwich Village, concluding at the foot of Christopher Street.

Leaving Grace Church, walk along 10th Street to the 1840 **Church of the Ascension**, a Gothic brownstone designed by English architect Richard Upjohn, also responsible for Trinity Church in the Financial District.

8th Street holds many stores and the New York Studio School of Drawing, Painting and Sculpture, first home of the Whitney Museum. This was founded in 1931 by Gertrude Vanderbilt Whitney; her own studio was a converted stable at 17½ MacDougal Alley (a private street).

In business since 1785, **Caffè Reggio** is the oldest of many cafés lining MacDougal Street; its dark interior has been seen in films such as *Godfather II* and *Serpico*.

On Sixth Avenue, Village Square is dominated by the gables, turrets, and towers of the 1877 **Jefferson Market Courthouse**, now a library. Across Sixth Avenue is **Balducci's**, a long-established purveyor of groceries and very fine foods.

Washington Square Park

■ **Like delis and subway stations, bars are among the stock images of New York life. From rough-and-ready Bohemian hangouts to elegant hotel cocktail lounges, New York bars come in all shapes, sizes and forms. Miss them and you are missing New York. (For guidance on New York bar-going etiquette, see pages 224–225.)** ■

Cigar bars

Cigarette smoking may be widely abhorred, but cigar smoking is rising in popularity in New York bars, several of which set aside a particular night of the week for cigar smokers to enjoy a drink and a smoke at the same time. Although cigar smoking might be seen as a traditionally male pursuit, as many New York women as men have adopted the habit. One place always heavy with cigar smoke is the Havana Tea Room (265 E 78th Street), which also offers Cuban music.

New York's oldest bar

In business since 1854, McSorley's Old Ale House (15 East 7th Street) is justified in its claim to be New York's oldest surviving bar. For years a men-only establishment patronized by career drinkers from the Bowery's Skid Row, McSorley's began admitting women in 1970 and now attracts a young, mainly student crowd.

Writers, artists, and bars Greenwich Village is littered with bars where major names of art and literature have gathered to eat, drink and (not infrequently) be carried home very much the worse for wear.

On his New York stays, Welsh poet Dylan Thomas held court at the **White Horse Tavern** (567 Hudson Street). One night in 1953, a drunken Thomas spluttered "I've had my 18th whisky, and I think that's the record." Within a few days he was dead. The literary associations might seem all but buried beneath the throng of customers, but cuttings on the wall remind drinkers at **Pete's Tavern** (129 E 18th Street) that this was once a lair of O. Henry, the pen name of William Sydney Porter, short-story writer and a trenchant New York observer in the early 1900s. To sample the East Village's Bohemian ambience, slip into something black and then into **d.b.a.** (41 First Avenue), a popular local hangout with minimalist decor and good variety of beers.

No longer in its original location, the **Cedar Tavern** (82 University Place) was a meeting place for the painters of what became the New York School of Abstract Expressionism. As Jackson Pollock and others loudly lamented the state of art, Beat writers such as the late Allen Ginsberg and William Burroughs eavesdropped from neighboring tables.

Bars for beer-drinkers Beer connoisseurs will welcome the 200 imported varieties sold at the **Peculier Pub** (145 Bleecker Street). The wooden bench tables here often overflow with New York University students. For New York's best brewed-on-the-premises beer, head for the **SoHo Brewery** (42 Thompson Street), which boasts a fine selection of invigorating ales.

Bars with a view The Manhattan skyline looks better than ever when viewed with a cocktail in your hand. At the **Greatest Bar on Earth**, on the 107th floor of the World Trade Center, a pianist tickles the ivories, and the views stretch for miles. In Midtown Manhattan, try the 39th-floor **Top of the Sixes** (666 Fifth Avenue), where the drinks are accompanied by free snacks and a splendid panorama, or the now refurbished **Top of the Tower**, at the Beckham Tower Hotel (3 Mitchell Place, off 49th Street), for a splendid outlook across the East River.

Bars for the good-looking The **Coffee Shop** (29 Union Square West) is a favorite stamping ground of the young and beautiful, with a long, snaking bar, Brazilian food, and loud music. Alternatively, try the equally hip **Fez** (downstairs from the Time Café on Lafayette at Great Jones Street), with its good jazz and basement dance floor. Mingle among fashionable faces at **Live Bait** (14 East 23rd Street), a bar and southern-food eatery decked out as a fishing shack. Another promising spot is **Bar Six** (502 Sixth Avenue) attached to a French-Moroccan bistro.

Real bars Costello's (225 East 44th Street), the best of several Midtown Irish bars. On the Upper West Side, the **All State Café** (250 West 72nd Street) is a dimly lit, wood-paneled saloon with few equals as a place for a long evening's drinking in the New York style.

Hotel bars It is by no means only guests who like to drink in hotel bars. Many are favored by locals for their elegant surroundings and the fact that you do not have to shout over loud music to hold a conversation. The **King Cole Bar**, at the St. Regis Hotel (2 E 55th Street) serves drinks in front of an impressive Maxfield Parrish mural. For a private tryst, try the Vodka Bar of the **Royalton** (44th Street between Fifth and Sixth avenues—you can also celebrity-spot in the lobby bar), the Conservatory Bar at the **Mayflower Hotel** (Central Park West at 61st Street) or **Fifty Seven Fifty Seven**, at the Four Seasons Hotel (57 E 57th Street), which draws publishing and media bigwigs.

Marie's Crisis Café
Few places symbolize changing New York better than Marie's Crisis Café (59 Grove Street). Nowadays, do not be surprised to find this lively bar packed by gay men singing hit songs from famous Broadway shows. Two centuries ago it was a home of Thomas Paine, whose publication, *Crisis*, helped fuel the American Revolution.

The photos and flags that adorn the walls of McSorley's Old Ale House suggest a time when New York bars provided informal employment centers and enabled many new immigrants to land their first jobs in the United States

115

GREENWICH VILLAGE

Greenwich Village writers
James Agee, James Baldwin, Willa Cather, James Fenimore Cooper, Hart Crane, Theodore Dreiser, e. e. cummings, Henry James, Ruth McKenney, Herman Melville, Edna St. Vincent Millay, Eugene O'Neill, Anaïs Nin, John Dos Passos, Edgar Allan Poe, John Reed, William Styron, Mark Twain, Tennessee Williams, Edmund Wilson, Thomas Wolfe.

Washington Square Memorial Arch

Continued from page 112.

There is no better place to begin exploring Greenwich Village than **Washington Square Park**►►► where jugglers, thespians, unicyclists and chess-players put on a show for the families, visitors and street urchins who promenade along the park's pathways.

On the park's northern side, the triumphal **Washington Memorial Arch**►► stands at the foot of Fifth Avenue, 77 feet high and erected by Stanford White in 1892 on a spot where he had earlier raised a wooden marker to celebrate the centenary of Washington's inauguration.

What the white marble arch does not commemorate, however, are the 22,000 people who were buried beneath the park when it served as a mass cemetery during epidemics. There is also no reminder of the fact that during the early 1800s some of the park's trees were used for public hangings.

Inside the Memorial Arch
In 1916, maverick artist Marcel Duchamp and friends forced their way through the locked door of Washington Square Park's Memorial Arch and climbed the 110 steps to the top. Once there, they hung balloons, Chinese lanterns and banners proclaiming Greenwich Village as the independent republic of New Bohemia. After having a picnic, Duchamp and company were forced down by militiamen.

With somewhat less spectacle, a man is thought to have lived in the arch for seven months during World War II. He was noticed only when he hung his wash out to dry.

Besides ending hangings and covering over the burial ground, the creation of the park in 1827 greatly increased the social cachet of the immediate area. Fashionable town houses rose around it, the only survivors being **The Row**►► on the north side: note their porticos, shuttered windows and elongated stoops—emphasizing the distinction between the owner's entrance and the servants' entrance at ground level.

To the park's south and east are a few of the buildings of New York University. With 14 separate schools scattered throughout Greenwich Village, the university is one of the city's major landowners.

Continued on page 118.

FOCUS ON *Gay life*

■ **New York City is home to one of the most vibrant gay and lesbian communities in the United States, centred around Chelsea and Greenwich Village. The contributions of its members help to make New York what it is in publishing, advertising, art and design, theater, dance, restaurants, law, business, and many other fields.** ■

The census of 1880 found five men in prison for "unspeakable crimes against nature"—a euphemism of the time for homosexual activity. By the 1930s, a small network of gay rendezvous points had spread across Manhattan; places where discretion was uppermost and which remained invisible to the heterosexual world.

In the period following World War II, when the values of family life were extolled to the hilt, gays and lesbians increasingly felt the backlash. Sexual minorities were pilloried in the press, and the police were urged to clamp down on behavior that was feared and perceived as a menace to society.

Gay Pride The two days of rioting that followed a police raid on Greenwich Village's Stonewall Inn became a turning point in gay history: for the first time, the community had risen up to defend itself, and its newfound solidarity led to the founding of the Gay Pride movement. The movement's many achievements are celebrated annually by the Gay Pride Parade along Fifth Avenue and through Greenwich Village (see page 27).

Gays have steadily become established and largely accepted throughout the city, not least because gay spending power has a significant and highly beneficial effect on local economies. Gay issues are widely debated in mainstream media, while legal breakthroughs include the formal recognition of gay couples in 1993. Gays have also featured prominently in the rejuvenation of the Chelsea neighborhood.

Information
For general information and the latest on gay and lesbian events, nightclubs and more, contact the Gay and Lesbian Switchboard (tel: 777–1800). Although homophobia is much less a feature of New York than it may be in some cities, such crimes do occur and can be traumatizing. An emergency telephone number is available for support and advice for victims, tel: 807–0197.

Specialty stores aimed at the gay community find a ready market in New York. This gay clothing store is in Greenwich Village

Its subway station may have preserved its original handsome blue tiles (above), but Bleecker Street today (right) has little to recall its importance in the 1950s and 1960s. At that time its cafés and folk clubs reverberated with the pioneering ideas and developing sounds of a whole new postwar subculture, kicking off with the Beat writers and later including folk singers who were to become household names all over the world

Continued from page 116.

Not content with his Memorial Arch, Stanford White also erected the **Judson Memorial Church►**, on the park's south side, in largely Romanesque style. More noteworthy than the architecture are the church's stained-glass windows, the work of Hudson River artist John LaFarge.

A block away, on MacDougal Street, the unremarkable exterior of the **Provincetown Playhouse** does nothing to suggest that the group based here forged new ground in American drama in the 1910s, helped in no small measure by the talents of Eugene O'Neill. Just south, on the corner of Minetta Lane, the **Minetta Tavern►** displays photos and mementos from the dawn of Greenwich Village Bohemia.

Running across MacDougal Street, **Bleecker Street►►►** holds the best of Greenwich Village's bars and clubs, though nothing these days matches the stirrings of the early 1960s when local folk clubs spawned talents such as Bob Dylan, Judy Collins, and Arlo Guthrie. A decade earlier, the Bleecker Street cafés had reverberated to the performance poetry and drunken debates of embryonic Beat writers: Gregory Corso, Jack Kerouac, Allen Ginsberg, and William Burroughs (see page 119).

More restaurants, bakeries, and cafés line Bleecker Street as it continues westward across Sixth Avenue into the West Village, the main artery of which, Christopher Street, cuts westward from Village Square and the extraordinary **Jefferson Market Courthouse** (see page 113), toward the Hudson River; on Sixth Avenue is Balducci's (see page 113).

At 53 Christopher Street was the **Stonewall Inn**. It gave its name to the "Stonewall Riots," which united the local gay community in 1969 and led to the founding of Gay Pride (see page 117).

The Beats

■ A small group of interesting characters frequenting the bars around New York's Columbia University and Greenwich Village in the 1940s evolved into what became the Beat Generation, the country's first postwar subculture and one that used drugs, jazz, and Eastern religion to inspire the new forms of writing that, for a brief time in the 1950s, seemed set to tear American society to pieces. ■

If the Beat Generation had a starting point, it was the West End Café (on Broadway between 113th and 114th streets) in the mid 1940s. Here teenaged student Allen Ginsberg, 30-year-old William Burroughs and 22-year-old Jack Kerouac swapped ideas, later adjourning to an apartment at 421 West 118th Street to hold animated discussions to the sound of the newly emerged bebop jazz.

Beat writing Ginsberg began writing "serious" poetry, Kerouac worked on his breathless prose style, and Burroughs steadily assembled the pieces that would evolve into his novels. By the end of the 1940s, the chief hangouts were the San Remo (189 Bleecker Street) and the Cedar Tavern (then at 24 University Place).

Success and notoriety Ginsberg was living in San Francisco in 1956 when, besides working for an advertising agency and studying Buddhism, he wrote his epic poem, *Howl*, describing characters and ideas from the past few years. The poem was published to enthusiastic reviews—and an obscenity trial that greatly increased the notoriety of "the Beats," as did *On the Road*, Kerouac's novel published the next year.

When Ginsberg and Kerouac returned to New York, the *Village Voice* proclaimed "Witless Madcaps Come Home to Roost," and the events of a decade earlier quickly became, and continue to be, a source of legend.

Why "Beat Generation"?
Ginsberg and another writer, John Clellon Holmes, conceived the term "Beat Generation," partly from the "Lost Generation" of the 1920s and partly from a Times Square junkie who always described himself as "beat." When Holmes's novel *Go* was published in 1952, the New York Times reviewer seized on the handy phrase, but this did not help Ginsberg, Burroughs, or Kerouac find publishers for their work.

119

The late Allen Ginsberg (left) listens to a speaker at a 1960s anti-Vietnam War rally near Tompkins Square Park

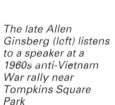

■ For every major religious edifice such as St. Patrick's Cathedral or the Cathedral Church of St. John the Divine, New York has dozens more places of worship that seldom receive a visit from passing travelers. Many of these are mentioned in the A to Z section of this book, but those described below are especially notable for illustrating the city's many forms of ecclesiastical architecture or for highlighting New York's endless diversity. ■

Same church, different religion
Indicative of the changing ethnic makeup of the Lower East Side, the 1895 Russian Orthodox Cathedral at 4th Street between Avenues C and D is now San Isidro y San Leandro Orthodox Catholic Church of the Hispanic Rite, serving the Lower East Side's now predominantly Puerto Rican population.

The statue of Shinran-Shonin outside the New York Buddhist Church

Greek Orthodox Just one of many churches in the Financial District that predate the high-rise glass towers and provide a striking contrast of style, the **St. Nicholas Greek Orthodox Church** (155 Cedar Street) is New York's earliest Greek church. The compact interior is decorated with brass chandeliers, icons, and the model ships that are reminders of its original seafaring congregation (St. Nicholas being the patron saint of sailors). As the Greek community prospered and moved northwards, the **Greek Orthodox Cathedral of the Holy Trinity** (74th Street near First Avenue) became its religious focal point, in 1931. The interior of the stylish Romanesque church holds more icons.

Jewish Also in what is now the Financial District, New York's first Jewish residents established the city's earliest synagogue some 300 years ago on what became William Street. A replica of the 20-seat shrine can be seen on the fifth floor of the **Wall Street Synagogue** (47 Beekman Street). Later, the city's first Jewish architect raised the **Central Synagogue** (Lexington Avenue at 55th Street). Its rough-hewn Moorish facade, complete with onion domes and banded arches, was intended to reflect the Jewish experience in Moorish Spain. With a colorful interior decorated in shades of red, blue, and ocher, the synagogue was completed in 1872.

Roman Catholic In 1918, just north of the Central Synagogue, architect Bertram Goodhue produced an accomplished and imposing facade for the **Church of St. Vincent Ferrer** (Lexington Avenue at 66th Street), but he saved his best touches for the expansive interior. Note the reredos and Charles Connick's exceptional stained-glass windows.

Russian Orthodox The seat of the Russian Orthodox Church in North America is on New York's Upper East Side, where the **St. Nicholas Orthodox Cathedral** (97th Street near Fifth Avenue) was erected at the turn of the century, financed by donations collected across the tsarist Russian empire. The cathedral's splendidly ornate style—red brick patterned with blue and yellow tiles and five bulging onion domes—is based on the church architecture of 17th-century Moscow.

An embarrassed architect
With Grace Church (see page 112) and St. Patrick's Cathedral (page 150), church architect James Renwick made his name. Among his less acclaimed works, however, was the 1846 **Calvary Church** (Park Avenue at 21st Street). The church still stands but without its steeples.

Muslim The design of St. Nicholas is strikingly different from the drab buildings around it, as is that of the **Mosque of the Islamic Culture Center** (Third Avenue at 96th Street), which also deviates from the usual grid-style alignment of Manhattan buildings by being pointed towards Mecca. The first permanent place of worship for New York Muslims, the $12-million mosque was largely financed by the government of Kuwait.

Buddhist On the other side of Central Park, you might easily go right past the **New York Buddhist Church** (Riverside Drive between 105th and 106th streets) without realizing the fact—were it not for the unmistakable bronze statue of Shinran-Shonin, the 13th-century founder of a Buddhist sect, that stands outside.

Abyssinian Baptist Harlem's **Abyssinian Baptist Church** (138th Street near Lenox Avenue) was founded in 1808 by, and to serve, New York's black community and quickly acquired the largest black congregation of any church in the U.S. Past ministers include Harlem's first black member of congress, Adam Clayton Powell. His struggles to end racial discrimination and raise African-American living standards made him a nationally controversial, but locally revered, figure in the 1940s. The present Gothic-style church dates from 1923 and has a display recording Powell's achievements.

From Greek Orthodox (above left) to Buddhist (above): New York's places of worship mirror its diverse ethnic makeup

Sarabeth's Kitchen

It may sound like a coffee shop, but Sarabeth's Kitchen's prestigious addresses (Madison Avenue and 92nd Street) can mean only one thing: food to delight the palate and lighten the wallet. It all began with marmalade, made from a recipe passed down through eight generations of Sarabeth's family. Now Sarabeth's Kitchen (with another branch on the Upper West Side; see page 281) is where many locals start their day, breakfasting on homemade muffins, waffles, and pancakes. Lunch and dinner are also served.

▶▶▶ **Guggenheim Museum** 187C1

Fifth Avenue between 88th and 89th streets
Subway: 86th Street

A member of an ultrawealthy New York family whose fortunes were founded on copper and silver mines, Solomon R. Guggenheim followed the usual track of an Upper East Side millionaire with more money than he knew what to do with by dabbling in art. Guggenheim's first purchases were unremarkable Old Masters, but his tastes and his acquisitions were changed radically in 1927 when he met Baroness Hilla Rebay von Ehrenwiesen, an outspoken and energetic enthusiast of the European abstract art scene.

Through the baroness, Guggenheim met artists such as Robert Delaunay, Fernand Léger, and Albert Gleizes and quickly amassed a superb stock of their work and works by other contemporary artists, particularly Wassily Kandinsky, hanging them on the walls of the rooms he occupied with his wife at New York's Plaza Hotel. At the suggestion of the baroness, Guggenheim commissioned architect Frank Lloyd Wright to design and build a museum to be called (with an ideological correctness insisted on by the baroness) the Museum of Non-Objective Painting.

Guggenheim had been dead for 10 years by the time Wright's extraordinary achievement opened in 1959, its name changed to the Solomon R. Guggenheim Museum. It proved to be the architect's only New York building, and he referred to it as his "Pantheon." By this time, Guggenheim's initial collection of abstracts had been enlarged and greatly broadened in scope by purchases and bequests, particularly the Thannhauser Collection of impressionist and post-impressionist paintings which were bequeathed by a prominent dealer and collector.

The best way to see the collection is to take the elevator to the top level and slowly work your way down the museum's remarkable spiral ramp. In this way you can study the exhibits, look over the parapet to the lobby below, and finish up where you began without ever getting lost. Precisely what will be on show when you visit has been scheduled years in advance; the museum stages several special exhibitions each year, often focusing on the work of an individual artist. What you can be fairly certain of seeing, however, is the permanently displayed Thannhauser Collection, hung in comparatively orthodox fashion in several galleries reached off the second level of the ramp.

Highlights of the Guggenheim's permanent collections include works by Kandinsky, Modigliani, Klee, Mondrian, Braque, Chagall, Gleizes, and Malevich, though if your favorites are not on display, you might concentrate your energies instead on the quality selections of the Thannhauser Collection.

Among these, Van Gogh's *Mountains at Saint-Rémy* is outstanding, its vibrant swirls of color painted in 1899 as the artist recovered from one of his bouts of mental illness. Works by Cézanne include *Still Life: Flask, Glass, and Jug* and *Bibémus*, a shimmering preabstract landscape, and the slightly mystifying *Man With Crossed Arms*, described as a "proto-Cubist" piece, whose figure has been thought to embody the spirit of quiet resignation that the artist himself possessed during the last years of his life.

A couple of paintings by the enigmatic Henri Rousseau (also known as "Le Douanier"—the Customs Man) are amusing and defiantly odd. In *The Football Players*, five handlebar-moustached and ludicrously attired figures strike up absurd poses while frolicking with a ball in a forest; similarly handlebar-moustached but more correctly attired soldiers form the core of *The Artillery Men*.

The earliest of several canvases by Picasso, *Le Moulin de Galette*, was painted in 1900 when the artist was 19 and was inspired by his first visit to Paris. The gloomy but angular figure of 1904's *Woman Ironing* is a product of the latter stages of Picasso's Blue Period; from a year or two later, *Fernand with a Black Fortilla* marks a change of style—and perhaps the first step toward Cubism.

The most striking piece in the Thannhauser Collection is also the earliest: *The Hermitage at Pontoise*, an 1867 landscape by Camille Pissarro. The artist later became a leading impressionist (Gauguin and Cézanne were among Pissaarro's students and associates) but here uses a realist style that goes hard against the grain of traditional French landscape painting—and seems to make the idyllic rural scene radiate from the canvas.

The vertiginous interior of the Guggenheim

123

■ **It has been called a doughnut, a snail, and an insult to art, but Frank Lloyd Wright's Guggenheim Museum is one of the outstanding contributions to New York architecture—even though there is plenty of truth in the accusation that it often steals the show from the art that it exhibits. Wright inserted the inscription "let every man practice the art he knows" in bronze on the entrance floor—intended perhaps as a lasting riposte to the building's critics.** ■

The Guggenheim in the 1990s

Renovation work completed in 1992 has left the Guggenheim looking almost as good as new. The following year's completion of Gwathmey/Siegel's 11-story tower, welded to the rotunda, has provided much-needed extra office and exhibition space. Despite being widely criticized for its failure to blend with Wright's original building, the tower leaves the museum core uncluttered by the trappings of gallery administration.

More than 30 years after it opened, the Guggenheim remains a unique feature of the New York landscape

"Organic architecture" The originator of the "Prairie style," Wright in his best architecture blended buildings into the organic, natural forms around them. The Guggenheim's predominantly curving exterior is totally out of step with the vertical lines of the neighboring Upper East Side apartment houses but has plenty in common with the trees and shrubbery of Central Park, directly across Fifth Avenue.

With the Guggenheim Museum, his only major New York commission, Wright also made a radical departure from the traditional room-by-room gallery style. The exhibits here occupy partitioned spaces off a quarter-mile-long spiral walkway that rises six stories high, steadily growing wider as it climbs.

Controversy The architect persistently battled with the city authorities and disagreed with the museum's director over the structure's supposed failure to meet the practical needs of an art museum. All this contributed to delays, and 16 years elapsed between Wright's finished plans and the Guggenheim's opening in 1959, the year of his death. The aesthetic debate has raged ever since, though the museum is now very much part of the Upper East Side landscape.

► **Harlem** *IBCC2*

Increasingly part of the city's tourist circuit and long a vital and distinct component in New York's character, Harlem begins north of 110th Street and splits into two sections.

Above the Upper West Side, West Harlem (or Harlem proper) is the longest-established home of the city's African-American population. Above the Upper East Side is East Harlem—or **El Barrio** ("the Neighborhood") —which has become New York's largest Spanish-speaking area, the majority of its residents having Puerto Rican origins.

During the 1890s, eager to repeat the success they had had on the Upper West Side, property speculators covered West Harlem with brown-stones and elegant apartment blocks. The anticipated rush of buyers never materialized, however, and Harlem's homes were rented out largely to black tenants. Rents were inflated because of housing pressure at the time—thousands of African-Americans were arriving in New York, and the competition for housing was great. Tens of thousands of the nation's blacks fled the Deep South for Harlem, seen at the time as a promised land. By the 1920s, the Harlem Renaissance was in full swing: a flowering of African-American culture through art and literature as jazz and blues percolated through Harlem nightclubs such as the Cotton Club and Smalls' Paradise. Although Harlem has endured many inner-city problems, the past few years have seen a new spirit in the neighborhood.

125

Fidel Castro in Harlem
Arriving to address the United Nations in 1960, Cuban leader Fidel Castro and his entourage spent several nights in a Midtown Manhattan hotel, reputedly running up a $10,000 bill for damage before being asked to leave. No other hotel was eager for Castro's patronage, but Harlem's Teresa Hotel (272 West 125th Street), long known as a radicals' meeting place, filled the breach. During its weeklong stay, the Cuban contingent was cheered by locals and was visited by Soviet leader Khrushchev. In 1971, the Teresa became an office building.

Not many people visit Harlem for its architecture, but the buildings can be just as lively as the atmosphere

HARLEM

Marcus Garvey in Harlem

Arriving in Harlem from Jamaica in 1914, Marcus Garvey predated the Black Panthers in the 1960s in encouraging black pride and assertiveness. Winning many followers through his brilliant powers of oration, Garvey founded the Universal Negro Improvement Foundation, published the *Negro World* newspaper and purchased two ocean liners to carry out his promised repatriation of America's blacks to Africa.

Eventually, Garvey was arrested on trumped-up charges and deported. He died in London in 1940. Garvey's doctrines became crucial elements in Rastafarianism, and in 1973 the Harlem park that straddles Fifth Avenue between 120th and 124th streets was renamed in his honor.

Unfortunately, the park, which holds a curious fire-watch tower dating from 1856, is a drug-users' hangout and is best left unvisited.

Harlem gospel choir

With leafy boulevards neighboring its low-rent housing projects, it is quite safe if you stick to daylight hours and main thoroughfares.

Along the main commercial strip, West 125th Street, you will find the **Apollo Theater** (number 253), legendary for its amateur talent nights and for showcasing every African-American jazz, blues and soul act, from Billie Holliday in the 1930s to James Brown in the 1960s. Brown's *Live at the Apollo* album was recorded here in 1962 and captures some of the venue's raw excitement. You will also find the temporary exhibitions and photographic archive of the **Studio Museum in Harlem** on West 125th Street (number 144) and more soul-food restaurants than anyone could wish for.

For the best of early Harlem architecture, explore the **St. Nicholas Historic District** on 139th Street. The stylish 1890s town houses between Seventh and Eighth avenues were occupied by successful blacks from 1919 and hence earned their lasting nickname "Striver's Row."

Upbeat Sunday gospel services have become one of the major points of visitor interest in Harlem, although the tour group numbers at some churches have led to complaints that local congregations are being snubbed. One of Harlem's most celebrated churches for its outstanding choir and history of community involvement, is the **Abyssinian Baptist Church** (see page 121).

Always shabbier than its westerly counterpart, **East Harlem** was first settled by working-class Italian and Irish families but, from the 1920s on, it steadily evolved into the city's major Puerto Rican neighborhood. The **Museum of the City of New York** and **El Museo del Barrio** (see pages 156–157) stand on its fringes, but the place to make for is **La Marqueta**, found under the Park Avenue viaduct between 110th and 116th streets, where salsa music resounds among the market stalls and food stands.

► **Hispanic Society of America**
Broadway at 155th Street
Subway: 1; 157th Street

Paintings by Velázquez, El Greco and Goya are among the most prized possessions of the Hispanic Society of America, founded in 1904 by Archer M. Huntington, aesthete son of transportation magnate Collis P. Huntington. However, this substantial gathering of Spanish and Portuguese art, archaeology, tilework, and tomb decorations is overall less impressive than its setting: a sumptuous two-story Spanish Renaissance interior, decorated with ruby-red terra cotta.

Puerto Ricans

Early 19th-century New York drew Puerto Ricans active in the sugar and coffee trade. Others, inspired by the American Revolution, came here hoping to use the city as a base to plot the overthrow of their Spanish colonial masters.

The U.S. in Puerto Rico In 1898, Puerto Rico was deeded by Spain to the United States, which established a military government on the Caribbean island and allowed American interests to rule its economy. In return, Puerto Ricans were made United States citizens (although not until 1917) and so were able to settle freely in the United States.

The profiteering of American companies encouraged Puerto Rican migration and, by 1930, around 45,000 Puerto Ricans had settled in New York. Many were employed in jobs formerly held by upwardly mobile Jews and Italians; others worked in traditional trades such as cigar-making.

El Barrio Although there were Puerto Rican neighborhoods across Manhattan, the area around the low-rent apartments of East Harlem became *El Barrio*, base of Puerto Rican cultural institutions and Spanish-language cinemas and publications. Over a period of time, Fiorello La Guardia (who took office in 1933) recognized the political power of the Puerto Ricans by encouraging them to register to vote.

In the 1950s, when inexpensive flights began operating between New York and San Juan—the Puerto Rican capital—the Puerto Rican population in New York soared to 600,000, some spilling from El Barrio into the Bronx. The majority of the new arrivals had been rural-dwelling farm laborers, who subsequently found it difficult to adjust to big city life.

Americans of Puerto Rican descent are now a major part of the city's ethnic jigsaw puzzle. While the area is celebrated among trendy New Yorkers for its spicy foods and for its salsa music, El Barrio unfortunately continues to struggle with every contemporary inner-city problem.

Rum, produced from Puerto Rican sugar cane, is one of the better-known ethnic specialties

127

At an exhibition in Los Angeles in 1956, the phrase "the New York School" was first coined. It became the lasting appellation for the group of artists who, in New York a decade or so earlier, had spearheaded the country's first modern art movement—and one that was to create a worldwide audience for American art—abstract expressionism.

The Cedar Tavern

Rare is the major art movement that was not influenced to some degree by drunken debate. Abstract expressionism was no exception. The favored gathering place of many of the artists who became the New York School was the Cedar Tavern, then at 24 University Place. Here, discussions would rage into the night and sometimes culminate in an inebriated rearrangement of the furniture.

Fans of abstract expressionism who also like a drink may be pleased to know that the Cedar Tavern still exists (though it has moved to 82 University Place). These days, however, it is plain and rather uninteresting.

The Armory Show of 1913 (see page 149) not only brought modern European art to the U.S. for the first time, but also made it plain that the country had no modern style to call its own. Dadaist Marcel Duchamp summed up America's contribution to world art as "her plumbing and her bridges."

Even if they viewed it only as a stop on the way to Paris, however, New York was still a magnet for young American artists. They arrived to escape humdrum rural towns, to take classes at the city's Art Students League, and to paint in spacious light-filled loft studios available for cheap rents.

European influences As Europe moved toward war, many of the continent's most innovative and influential artistic minds fled across the Atlantic. When the Nazis marched down the Champs-Elysées, New York eclipsed Paris as the nerve center of international art.

In the late 1940s, as the conclusion of the war seemed to present a world free of the shackles of traditionalism and filled with new possibilities, the abstract expressionists emerged.

Jackson Pollock A farmer's son from Wyoming, Jackson Pollock had arrived in New York in the 1920s and was later employed briefly at the embryonic Guggenheim Museum.

In 1947, Pollock seized one of his paintings from its easel, fixed it to the floor, and started applying paint directly from the can in great sweeping arcs across the canvas. Soon after, Pollock dispensed with easels and brushes entirely, pouring paint onto the flat canvas and manipulating it with "sticks, trowels, or knives."

As the final product depended entirely on the act of Pollock dripping and throwing paint (compared to a western cowboy's lasso skills), the technique gave rise to the term "action painting" (also called "gestural painting").

De Kooning, Gottlieb, and Rothko Another key abstract expressionist was Willem de Kooning. While de Kooning used figures much more than Pollock—often formed by white contours on black—he was every inch the action painter, attacking his canvas with an energy that sent specks of paint flying in every direction.

A major influence on the abstract expressionists was the *Pictographs*, a series of paintings by Adolph Gottlieb, each of which was divided into compartments holding a mythological figure or symbol.

The abstract expressionists sought to transmit primal emotional states through their work—a goal that went beyond what was possible within traditional painting and which the horrors of the war had helped awaken.

Mark Rothko, an associate of Gottlieb's, became the foremost figure of what was termed the "color field" branch of abstract expressionism. As the full terrors of the Nazi concentration camps emerged, there was a special poignancy when Rothko, the Latvian-born son of Russian Jewish émigrés, asserted that "human incommunicability" had rendered figurative painting obsolete. Rothko's work evolved into floating rectangles of color, which, he said, provided "a spiritual basis for communion."

Barnett Newman and after Barnett Newman likened the color field artists' work to that of "primitive" cultures, keen to reach a "metaphysical understanding." In the late 1940s, Newman produced the first of his "zip paintings," their flat field of color split by a narrow vertical line.

Ironically, it was a misinterpretation of Newman's work that influenced later artists such as Jasper Johns. These later artists paved the way for the break from the mentally wrought canvases of abstract expressionism to the recasting of familiar images practiced by the 1960s pop art movement.

Perhaps in keeping with the anguished soul-searching of their work, the lives of abstract expressionism's two major figures both ended prematurely: Jackson Pollock died after driving his car into a tree in 1956, and Mark Rothko committed suicide in 1970.

Abstract expressionism on display
The Museum of Modern Art (see pages 158–160) has an excellent collection of abstract expressionist works and, besides those mentioned on these pages, also features work by other highly influential members of the movement such as Robert Motherwell, Franz Kline, and Arshile Gorky.

The Guggenheim Museum (pages 122–124) has a fair number of abstract expressionist canvases in its possession (sometimes on display in temporary exhibitions), and important works by Pollock, de Kooning, and Rothko usually turn up in the Highlights Gallery of the Whitney Museum (page 191).

One, *a huge canvas of 1950 by Jackson Pollock, now in MoMA*

Passenger Ship Terminal
Great ocean liners such as the *Queen Mary* and the *U.S.S. United States* would berth at the piers at the western ends of 48th, 50th, and 52nd streets (just north of the Intrepid Sea-Air-Space Museum) in the days before air travel made them uneconomic. To make the docking area as luxurious as the ships, the swanky New York Passenger Ship Terminal was completed in 1976. Unfortunately, most scheduled services had been abolished by the time, although modern luxury cruise ships can sometimes be seen docked here.

Photography House
One of the most handsome neo-Georgian mansions on the Upper East Side is home to the International Center of Photography. The four-story red-brick building was completed in 1914 by the firm of Delano & Aldrich for Willard Straight, a wealthy ex-diplomat who founded the influential *New Republic* magazine. The International Center of Photography also has a Midtown branch, called simply I.C.P. Midtown, at 1133 Sixth Avenue at 43rd Street.

▶▶ International Center of Photography 187D1
Fifth Avenue at 94th Street
Subway: 6; 96th Street
One of the world's few museums entirely devoted to photography, the International Center of Photography (ICP) has four galleries mounting changing exhibitions of both internationally established names and lesser-knowns beginning to make their mark.

One gallery is usually filled with selections from the center's permanent collection, which holds prints by almost every notable photographer you can think of: Henri Cartier-Bresson, Ernst Haas, Weegee, and Robert Capa to name a few.

▶ Intrepid Sea-Air-Space Museum 151C1
West end of 46th Street
Subway: A, C, E; 42nd Street
The flight deck of the *Intrepid*, a Navy aircraft carrier, is the core of this entirely militaristic museum. Permanently moored on the Hudson River, the *Intrepid* saw action in the Pacific during World War II and served in an antisubmarine role during the Vietnam War.

Now decommissioned, the vessel is stuffed with exhibits from its own wartime adventures—its aircraft shot down 650 enemy planes and destroyed 289 ships—and from its peacetime role of retrieving Mercury and Gemini space capsules. There is a plethora of armed forces' hardware, not least the fighter and bomber planes that sit on the flight deck with their cockpits open for inspection.

Temporary exhibitions explore diverse aspects of warfare, although they tend to highlight technical achievements rather than human experience. The staging of fund-raising rock concerts and dance nights at the museum in 1997, as well as alleged poor maintenance of planes, caused a rift between the museum and the military, particularly the U.S. Navy, which owns many of the exhibits and which threatened to withdraw them.

▶ Isaacs-Hendricks Residence 113A2
77 Bedford Street, Greenwich Village
Subway: 1; Christopher Street
You could be forgiven for walking right past the Isaacs-Hendricks Residence without noticing it. Alterations in 1836 and 1928 have detracted from its Federal style, of which it is one of the earliest surviving examples, having been erected in 1799. The clapboard wall on the side with Commerce Street is the main clue to the house's pedigree.

▶ Jan Hus Presbyterian Church 187B2
74th Street between First and Second avenues
Subway: 6; 77th Street
Named for the Czech martyr of the Reformation, the Jan Hus Presbyterian Church was founded in 1914 to serve Czech settlers in an area that was known as Little Bohemia into the 1930s. The church, with a bell tower modeled on the Powder Tower in Prague, is more popular for its secular activities than for its services. Musical and dramatic events are regularly staged at the church's hall.

Only a fraction of New York's Czech-American population now lives in Little Bohemia and, besides the church, there are only a couple of notable reminders of the Czech presence, such as the run-down Bohemian National Hall, on 73rd Street between First and Second avenues, raised in 1895.

▶ **Jewish Museum**   *187D1*

Fifth Avenue at 92nd Street
Subway: 6; 96th Street

An imitation French Gothic *château* might seem a strange home for the largest stock of Judaic ceremonial art and historical objects in the U.S., but the fine collections of New York's Jewish Museum have been housed in just such a place since 1944. It was then that the premises were bequeathed to the museum by the widow of their original owner, banker Felix M. Warburg.

The museum's permanent collection contains, perhaps, exactly what you might expect. Some of the tremendous stash of coins, household objects, and religious pieces dates back to Roman times; much more is representative of Jewish life from medieval times into the present century. One exemplary feature is the re-created turn-of-the-century café in which visitors can select oral histories of Jewish lives in European cities of the time, and of early Jewish arrivals to the United States.

The Jewish Museum also stages lively and sometimes provocative temporary exhibitions—exploring the Jewish experience from new and challenging perspectives—that are presented so as to excite even the most jaded New York museum-goer, and there is also a children's "hands-on" area.

The Intrepid Sea-Air-Space Museum

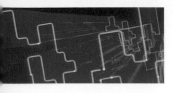

■ **From the major T.V. networks to the loony public-access channels and from the venerable *New York Times* to free magazines packed with ads for tarot readers, media is a big part of New York life, and information oozes from every pore of the city.** ■

Television All New York's daily newspapers carry full listings of T.V. programs. A full week's listings is also included as a separate magazine with the many sections of the Sunday *New York Times*. With so many channels to choose from (most of which operate around the clock), it may be best to stick to the highlights in *Village Voice*. While all hotel rooms will have T.V.s, budget-priced rooms rarely come equipped with cable channels, and even medium-priced options tend to be skimpy on the cable selections available. One perk of more costly hotels is a fuller range of viewing options, sometimes including Manhattan's public-access channels on which people—crazed astrologers and self-styled sex therapists alike—pay to make a half-hour show.

Radio New York's radio stations are numerous, and your best bet is to turn the dial until you find what you'd like to hear. FM frequencies offer an ear-boggling choice of stations, each with its own specialty, from round-the-clock hip-hop, soul, funk, jazz, country, or heavy rock, or classical sounds. Stations on the AM wavebands are primarily spoken word, and include phone-ins of the kind that launched pioneering shock-jock Howard Stern. Whatever

Radio stations give up-to-date traffic news

feelings they invoke, such shows soon acquaint out-of-town listeners with the intricacies of the New York accent.

Newspapers Of New York City's daily newspapers, *The New York Times*—now with color—is unmatched for in-depth coverage of international and national affairs, while its Metro section delivers the New York news that matters. The special features of the *Times* provide intriguing insights into city life, and the Friday edition is invaluable for its listings of weekend events and activities.

While the *Times* is regarded as politically liberal, the tabloid *New York Post* is the home of conservative reaction, despite having some sharp columnists. New Yorkers who hate the *Post's* politics but love tabloid headlines turn instead to the *Daily News*. Once the best-selling newspaper in the country but now experiencing a sharply declining circulation, the *Daily News* has built its reputation on well-written racy stories which match its famously racy headlines. It can be relied upon to reveal the most heinous of crimes and the juiciest of scandals.

The weekly *Village Voice* (it comes out every Wednesday) began in the mid-1950s as an alternative paper (author Norman Mailer was one of its cofounders) and is now as much a part of the city as the Empire State Building. It explores city politics and fringe issues with relish and carries comprehensive arts and entertainment listings.

However, stiff competition from newer and free weekly papers such as the entertaining, easier-to-read, and better presented *New York Press*, forced the *Village Voice* to abolish its cover charge (at least when sold in Manhattan) and rethink its style. Also weekly, but not free, is the relatively glossy *Time Out New York*, its thorough listings complemented by celebrity interviews and features.

Magazines Appearing in weekly editions, *New York* is a glossy celebration of the New York lifestyle and has a strong events-listing section. The *New Yorker*, which is also published weekly, has become more lively and colorful since the arrival of British editor Tina Brown in 1992.

Noted for long, detailed articles written by literary heavyweights, the *New Yorker* is hardly light reading, although there are many who buy it solely for its thoughtful film reviews and its cartoons.

Free publications All manner of free publications are to be found in New York's shops, restaurants, bars, and hotel lobbies, and in special bins around the city. Whether they specialize in pet care, advancing your career, or the beliefs of the New Age, many such publications are simply vehicles for advertising. Others, such as *Resident*, and the various neighborhood newspapers such as *Tribeca Trib* are also packed with advertising, but are worth reading for gossip and local news.

133

A sense of occasion is never lacking at the Metropolitan Opera House: the crystal chandeliers above the auditorium are sucked into the gold-leafed ceiling before a performance

Guided tours of Lincoln Center
Hour-long guided tours depart from Lincoln Center's concourse level fairly frequently between 10 AM and 5 PM on most weekdays. The anecdote-packed tours weave their way through all the complex's major buildings (except the Metropolitan Opera House; see below), visiting the backstage areas and often catching rehearsals in progress. For details, tel: 875–5350. Tours of the Metropolitan Opera House leave from the entrance foyer of the Met from Monday to Friday at 3:45 PM and on Saturday at 10:30 AM (tel: 769–7020).

► **Lincoln Center for the Performing Arts**   *151D1*

62nd to 66th streets between Columbus and Amsterdam avenues
Subway: 1, 66th Street/Lincoln Center

The buildings and plaza of the Lincoln Center for the Performing Arts are looking somewhat dated, but what takes place inside is impressive.

The complex arose in the 1960s as part of a Utopian plan to give New York a single cultural rendezvous point. One element in Lincoln Center's genesis was the decision of the New York Philharmonic, faced with what seemed likely to be the imminent destruction of Carnegie Hall, to seek a home of its own. Philharmonic Hall was completed here in 1962, changing its name in 1973 to Avery Fisher Hall in honor of the man who parted with $10 million to improve its atrocious acoustics (not completely brought up to snuff until the 1980s).

The Philharmonic's search for new premises coincided with that of the Metropolitan Opera; the 10-story **Metropolitan Opera House** now rises boldly above the plaza, two enormous Marc Chagall murals visible through its windows.

The New York State Theater, designed by architect Philip Johnson, is the permanent home of the New York City Opera and New York City Ballet.

Eero Saarinen's **Vivian Beaumont Theater** ironically has until recently endured poor reviews for its cultural offerings. Next door, the **New York Public Library for the Performing Arts** holds 50,000 tomes and finds room for three separate galleries hosting temporary exhibitions.

On the north side of the complex is the world-famous **Juilliard School,** which numbers violinist Itzhak Perlman and actor William Hurt among its alumni. Beside the school, **Alice Tully Hall** provides a refreshingly intimate and acoustically brilliant home for the Lincoln Center Chamber Music Society—and for free concerts given by students, usually on Wednesday lunchtimes.

▶▶ **Little Italy**   87B2

Both Italian and little, Little Italy has had its boundaries steadily eroded by the expansion of Chinatown and by the drift of its original inhabitants to Italian enclaves in the Outer Boroughs. Between 1890 and 1924, however, 145,000 migrants from Sicily and southern mainland Italy settled here, in an area between Houston and Canal streets.

After years of decline (the area's tenement buildings are just beginning to show signs of gentrification), only a few thousand Italians remain in the neighborhood. Many of them are employed in the restaurants, cafés and bakeries along Grand and Mulberry streets, which provide Little Italy's main appeal. The food is good but far from cheap, and the cost-wise way to take in Little Italy's atmosphere is with a cappuccino at an outdoor table.

The closest the district comes to a genuine Italian landmark is **Umberto's Clam House** (129 Mulberry Street), which acquired fame for all the wrong reasons in 1972, when, in settlement of a gangland feud, "Crazy" Joe Gallo was shot while dining on a seafood supper.

The local Irish, who predated the Italians, had their spiritual needs fulfilled by what is now **"Old" St. Patrick's Cathedral** at 264 Mulberry Street. The city's earliest Gothic-style building, the cathedral lost its original facade in an 1866 fire and was demoted to a parish church when a new St. Patrick's Cathedral was consecrated in Midtown Manhattan in 1879.

On the fringes of Little Italy, take a look at the **Old Police Headquarters** at 240 Centre Street. This Renaissance palace, topped by a green dome, was an immeasurably imposing symbol of law and order when it arose in the midst of one of the city's most crime-ridden districts in 1909.

Walk on to the **Puck Building** at 295–307 Lafayette Street. This was completed in 1886 to house the *Puck* satirical magazine and, with its deliriously complex red brickwork, was instantly revered as a prime example of New York commercial design.

Festival of St. Gennaro
Each September, Little Italy's Mulberry Street is lined by makeshift stalls selling homemade sausage, calzone and other Italian specialties (plus an increasing number of Chinese ones) and jumps to the sound of marching bands in a two-week celebration of the Feast of St. Gennaro. The religious aspect of the festival, honoring the patron saint of Naples, is evident as a likeness of the saint is carried along the streets and showered with dollar bills. In 1995, the festival was almost canceled following allegations that most of the estimated $10 million raised by the event went to one of New York's Italian crime families. Mayor Giuliani refused to issue licenses for stallholders until guarantees were made that the proceeds would reach charities.

135

The tenements of Little Italy. Many of them have a restaurant or a café at street level—worth a stop at any time for a cappuccino, an ice cream, or a pizza

■ **No ethnic group has had a greater impact on New York than the Italians, who first arrived in large numbers during the 1880s. Through a combination of hard work, traditional values, and business acumen, the Italian community had prospered enough to take the helm of the city by the 1940s.** ■

A refuge for Italian liberals and revolutionaries through the 19th century, New York's first Italian neighborhood was on Bleecker Street during the 1860s. Its population was chiefly made up of sophisticated northerners. By contrast, the grinding poverty of rural southern Italy triggered the massive influx of the late 1800s, and 145,000 people were soon packed into the tenements of what became, and still is, Little Italy.

136

Many Italians work in the restaurant industry, providing New Yorkers and visitors alike with pasta, pizza, and other universally popular specialties

Exploitation of immigrants
Speaking little or no English, these new arrivals were exploited, not least by their fellow countrymen who had been in the U.S. long enough to learn the language yet who still knew enough about traditional Italian values to overwork and underpay the immigrants.

Little Italy's men built New York's sewers and subways and its women worked in garment industry sweatshops. Any spare money was sent home to their villages. Many Italians had escaped Little Italy for East Harlem by the 1910s, and by the 1940s were wealthy enough to move to suburban areas in the Outer Boroughs.

Rising fortunes
It was from East Harlem that Fiorello La Guardia emerged. This Protestant Italian son of a Jewish mother was destined to be remembered as the best mayor New York ever had. La Guardia's rise was a symbol of the assimilation of Italian-Americans into city politics, a sphere where they replaced the Irish as the dominant ethnic group.

With descendants of the first Italian-Americans excelling in every walk of New York life, a new wave of immigrants appeared almost unnoticed during the prosperous 1980s. In contrast to the Italian arrivals of a century or more earlier, these Italians were affluent and stylish. They moved into the Upper East Side and opened the upscale boutiques and wonderful Italian restaurants that won the hearts and wallets of New Yorkers who could afford to eat there.

▶▶▶ Lower East Side   IFCB3

Don't come to the Lower East Side expecting epoch-making architecture, fashionable faces, glamorous boutiques or expense-account restaurants. This is downbeat New York and has no pretensions. It is traditionally the first stop for newly arrived immigrants from around the world whose priority is to work hard and earn enough money to move on.

The first to arrive in the Lower East Side were the Irish, fleeing their homeland's famine in the mid-1800s. They were followed by successive waves of German and Eastern European immigrants, including the 2 million Jews who turned the Lower East Side into the world's largest Jewish community.

Living in windowless rooms in overcrowded tenements and often working in sweatshops for breadline wages, the immigrants nonetheless founded cultural institutions and places of worship and established the educational organizations that were to make their children's lives easier than their own.

The 1924 tightening of immigration laws slowed the European influx into the Lower East Side, although by then its more successful inhabitants had moved on and established ethnic pockets elsewhere, and it was to these new districts that new arrivals headed.

With land here yet to become valuable, many Lower East Side tenements remain, as do the delis, garment and jewelry stores on which the first locals made their money. Nowadays, the owners are likely to be Indian or Korean, representing the latest waves of immigration from foreign shores.

Less immediately obvious to outsiders are the Lower East Side's Caribbean immigrants, including the many Puerto Ricans who dominate a broad area east of Essex Street and spill north across Houston Street into Alphabet City (see page 60).

It is the stores and their heavily discounted prices that bring most visitors to the Lower East Side. The area is at its busiest on Sundays when bargain-hunting New Yorkers descend on the narrow streets off Delancey

Tenement life: the annual move
Few Lower East Siders ever stayed in a particular tenement for longer than they had to, and the offer of a free month's rent in return for a year's tenancy was usually sufficient inducement for tenement dwellers to up stakes and move every 12 months. It also became common for entire families to move back and forth across the same street, often moving in and out of the same tenements many times over at yearly intervals.

137

For vast stocks of cut-price clothing, the stores and stalls of Orchard Street, at the heart of Jewish New York on the Lower East Side, are hard to beat

LOWER EAST SIDE

How the other half lived
Photographs and text by
Jacob Riis, published as
How the Other Half Lives in
1894, focused attention on
the grim realities of everyday life in the Lower East
Side and were instrumen-
tal in bringing about laws
improving housing and
working conditions.
Nonetheless, for most
Lower East Side residents,
the only real escape was
to save enough money for
a move to Brooklyn, the
Bronx, or Queens.

Walking tours
The Lower East Side
Tenement Museum orga-
nizes various walking
tours, each concentrating
on a specific facet of
Lower East Side life—such
as ethnic heritage, the
lives of women, tenement
architecture, and the
exploits of New York's earliest street gangs. The
walks are not cheap but
they are enjoyable and
informative. They leave on
Sunday afternoons from
outside the museum. For
details and reservations,
tel: 431–0233.

*Typical Lower East
Side tenements on
Delancey Street.
Buildings like these
sprang up in the 19th
century to house
newly arrived immi-
grants—often in very
overcrowded and
unhealthy conditions*

Street for some of the biggest clothing discounts to
be found in the city. The crush is fiercest outside the
garment stores lining **Orchard Street►**. When the
crowds become overwhelming, explore the marginally
less busy neighboring streets such as Allen, Grand, and
Essex.

The tumult of Sundays is not repeated during the week,
when the streets are much quieter—and actually rather
dull. An exception to this is the **Essex Street Market►**,
where Lower East Siders buy their fresh meat, vegetables, and fruit.

The current ethnic mix of the area is evident in the con-
versations carried out here in Yiddish, Spanish, and
Chinese—and in the plantains and bean sprouts sitting
alongside the Jewish staples. The market is closed on
Sundays. It is useful to bear in mind also that many stores
are closed on Saturdays in observance of the Jewish
Sabbath.

Beyond shopping, the atmosphere and the sampling
fresh-made knishes (doughy pastries that are filled with
meat or potatoes) from one of several dozen Jewish
bakeries, the Lower East Side has little to hold your attention. Before leaving, however, be sure to visit the **Lower
East Side Tenement Museum►►►** at 97 Orchard
Street (*Closed* Sat). It is housed in a six-story tenement
that was built in 1863 and housed 11,000 people over a
70-year period.

The museum provides a fascinating background to
Lower East Side life and reveals countless illuminating
facts about the deprivations of tenement living. The
upper floors have been re-created to show the conditions
that the house's tenants endured.

■ **Since 1654, when 23 Sephardic Jews deported from Brazil landed in New York and resisted the Dutch governor's attempts to remove them, the Jewish community has shaped the character of New York life. The city's Jewish population has given the world everything from bagels to Irving Berlin.** ■

Established and respected in the commercial life of colonial America, the Sephardic community—which traces its origins back to Moorish Spain—continued to flourish after the American Revolution. In the 1830s, arrivals from Germany, the Ashkenazy—who had a different set of Jewish traditions—began looking for new opportunities in the city.

Germans and Russians Assisted by mutual aid societies, the Germans settled in the Lower East Side and were soon establishing the area's jewelry and garment industries. Such businesses employed other Ashkenazy: Russian Jews who arrived during the late 1800s, fleeing the pogroms of Tsar Alexander III. For the most part, these Russians shunned the charity offered by the German Jewish aid societies and formed their own self-help organizations. In the garment industry sweatshops, the Russians formed powerful labor unions.

The Ashkenazy immigrants also brought a rich cultural life to the Lower East Side, particularly with the Yiddish theaters in an area which became known as the "Yiddish Rialto." Although the Yiddish theater began with vaudeville and farce, the arrival of Jacob Gordin, a leading Russian playwright, helped it develop serious drama and stage works by the likes of Henrik Ibsen and Maxim Gorky. Future stars such as Walter Matthau and Edward G. Robinson cut their teeth before the lively Yiddish theater audiences. Meanwhile, the smoke-filled Lower East Side cafés became centers of political and literary debate, as well as the venues for closely fought chess matches.

Some anti-Semitism was encountered, but New York immigrants never suffered the hostilities that had been their fate in Europe, and Jewish culture soon became deeply embedded in New York life.

Later arrivals The Lower East Side was still the first area of settlement for poor Sephardic arrivals from Turkey, Greece, and Syria during the Balkan Wars of the 1910s. By the 1930s, however, Europeans fleeing the rise of Nazism were able to move directly into comfortable Jewish enclaves established in the Upper West Side and the Outer Boroughs.

In the 1970s, a few Soviet Jews began settling in Brooklyn's Brighton Beach. Today, the most conspicuous aspects of New York's Jewish community are seen in areas dominated by ultra-orthodox sects, such as the Satmarers and Lubavitchers.

139

Black hats (fur trimming denotes a rabbi) and matching long coats make men belonging to the rigidly orthodox Satmar sect instantly recognizable

■ **Many visitors come to New York for no reason other than to shop. Once the designer outlets and the big-name department stores have been exhausted, however, the attention of the serious shopper turns to the city's flea markets and secondhand stores—where the quest for that elusive item at a giveaway price can bring hours of sheer pleasure.** ■

Thrift stores

The intrepid bargain-hunter might not want to leave New York without delving into at least a few of its thrift stores. Often linked to a church and run by volunteer labor with the proceeds going to charity, thrift stores are filled with cast-off clothing, household objects, books, and other items. For a full list, consult the Yellow Pages.

140

Flea markets Wherever the New York sidewalk is wide enough you are likely to find an impromptu flea market. The merchandise will probably range from out-and-out junk to stolen goods (often with fake designer labels). Resist temptation and instead visit one of the city's four main official flea markets, where better fare turns up.

On weekends, the **Canal Street Flea Market** (western end of Canal Street) offers a very large choice of cheap and often ugly and useless objects, though some handy clothing accessories might be unearthed.

Every weekend between March and December, the **Annex Antiques Fair and Flea Market** (Sixth Avenue between 24th and 26th streets) features a varied stash of bric-a-brac, clothing and jewelry. The quality tends to be low, but a browse can be worthwhile.

Prices are higher at the Saturday **Greenwich Village Flea Market** (Greenwich Street at Charles Street), though this small market merits a visit if you are exploring the neighborhood.

On Sunday, the **Green Flea Indoor/Outdoor Market** (Columbus Avenue between 76th and 77th streets) is a larger and classier affair, with clothing, jewelry, ornaments, and furniture. On Saturday, the market is at 67th Street, between First and York avenues.

Books Not only do they love bargains, New Yorkers also love to read. Spend a whole day browsing in the **Strand Book Store** (Broadway at 12th Street) and you will barely make an impression on its 8 miles of shelves; the stocks range from dog-eared paperback best-sellers to discarded review copies of pristine hardbacks—all sold for a fraction of their original price.

Much smaller but equally interesting, the intimate **Bleecker Street Books** (350 Bleecker Street) carries general-interest subjects. By contrast, a massive, unclassified clutter of paperbacks fills **Ruby's Book Sale** (119 Chambers Street), where you might also be tempted by piles of vintage magazines.

Clothing The city's more affluent elements may shop for clothes among the designer-name stores that proliferate in Midtown Manhattan, but the sartorially adventurous—and those in search of a bargain—hit the vintage clothing stores downtown in Greenwich Village and Soho.

The enormous stocks of **Antique Boutique** (712–714 Broadway) have plenty to keep the vintage-clothes fanatic engaged, although dedicated bargain-hunters might be

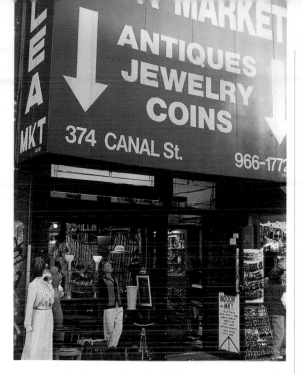

The Post Office Auction
Once a month, the General Post Office (33rd Street between Eighth and Ninth avenues) auctions off the contents of packages that have been undelivered and unclaimed for a year. Even if you do not intend to buy anything, it is worth turning up for the viewing to see the sometimes weird and wonderful (but mostly mundane) objects that pass through the New York postal system. For details, tel: 330–2932.

Left: you will find plenty of junk (and, just possibly, a bargain or two) on sale in Canal Street

It is hard not to be overwhelmed by the sheer volume of print at the Strand Book Store, which claims to be the world's largest secondhand bookstore

better served by a search through the racks at **Stella Dallas** (218 Thompson Street) or **Cheap Jack's** (Broadway between 13th and 14th streets).

Clothes of the 1950s are the specialties—though far from the total extent—of the reasonably priced stock at **Love Saves the Day** (Second Avenue at East 7th Street) and meanwhile, **The Family Jewels** (832 Sixth Avenue) carries everything from 1920s evening gowns to 1960s miniskirts, along with an eclectic assortment of hats, purses, and shoes. **Church Street Surplus** (Church Street at Canal Street) also stocks a broad range of vintage clothing, as does **The Quilted Corner** (Fourth Avenue at Twelfth Street), alongside curtains and fabrics.

Another happy hunting-ground is **Alice Underground** (Broadway between Broome and Grand streets). Here you will find great collections of very classy—but attractively priced—clothes.

C.D.s and Records New York has a massive audience for all kinds of music, but predominant on the second hand racks are indie rock and classical rarities.

Underground rock music and hot dance cuts are found at **St. Mark's Sounds** (20 St. Mark's Place). Seekers after obscure jazz, reggae, African, gospel, and rock music could pass many hours browsing the racks of **The Golden Disc** (239 Bleecker Street) where rare vinyl nestles alongside CDs and tapes. **Footlight Records** (113 E Twelfth Street) is the city's prime source of show music, big band records, and film soundtracks, and also has a strong jazz selection.

Fans of classical music should explore the used records section of **Academy Records** (10 West 18th Street) and seek out the many rarities sold for princely sums at **Gryphon Records** (251 West 72nd Street).

METROPOLITAN MUSEUM OF ART

The Met's imposing neoclassical entrance

▶▶▶ Metropolitan Museum of Art 187C1

Fifth Avenue and 82nd Street
Subway: 4, 6; 86th Street

Founded in 1870, the Metropolitan Museum of Art is now among the world's most important art museums. Over the years, the collection has been greatly swelled by donations from some of America's richest people. The Met will exhaust you long before you exhaust it. The best way is to think of it as a dozen or so separate museums.

The original building
Few New York facades are as overwhelming in their grandeur as that of the Metropolitan Museum of Art, even though the exuberant neoclassical features that greet visitors to the Met's Fifth Avenue entrance are but one of many additions made to the museum's original body.

In 1880, in an effort to blend the planned museum into its setting on the edge of Central Park, its original architects Jacob Wrey Mould and Calvert Vaux (one of the park's co-designers) devised a High Gothic form for the main facade, which then faced the park.

As its collections grew, so too did the museum building. In 1902 it gained the Fifth Avenue entrance that remains in place today. Only a segment of Mould and Vaux's work can still be seen, inside the much more recent Robert Lehman Wing.

It is essential to plan your visit. Bear in mind that some galleries close in rotation. Schedules are available from the desk, or for recorded information tel: 535–7710.

If you cannot decide where to begin, aim first for the European paintings on the third floor. Rows of aristocratic English portraits line most of the first room, where works by Reynolds, Gainsborough, and Lawrence provide much to admire in their technical virtuosity. Of the Met's English paintings, it is two landscapes that are most likely to hold your gaze: Turner's *Grand Canal, Venice*, capturing the artist at the height of his powers, and Constable's radiant *Salisbury Cathedral*.

Moving on, the French rooms reveal choice works spanning three centuries. Among many striking pieces, George de la Tour's *The Penitent Magdalen* has a rare ability to draw the viewer into its dark corners, and Rousseau's *The Forest in Winter at Sunset* seems to resonate with the primeval forces of nature.

The galleries of French impressionists and post-impressionists include wonderful contributions from Manet, Monet, Cézanne, Gauguin, and Renoir, but winning the day are the canvases of Van Gogh, among them *Self-Portrait with a Straw Hat* and the stunning *Cypresses*.

The Dutch galleries include almost a whole room of Rembrandts and five of Vermeer's 40 extant paintings.

Continued on page 144.

■ **Detailed explanatory labels are an essential aid to comprehending the Met's Egyptian collections, an otherwise overwhelming stash of 40,000 objects that stretch from predynastic times to the arrival of the Romans.** ■

You don't need to be a scholar to enjoy the collections or the lasting impression they provide of one of the world's greatest civilizations. Some of this colossal stock of treasures were donated by individuals but many come from the Met's own 30-year excavation program. The single biggest exhibit, the Temple of Dendur (see panel), was a gift from the government of Egypt to the United States in the 1960s.

Although the walk-through Tomb of Perneb—a structure that draws attention as soon as you enter the Egyptian galleries—is a reconstruction, most of the objects on display are originals in such excellent states of preservation that they seem far younger than they really are; their imagery, and their often extravagant use of color are surprisingly forceful.

The trappings of death The most powerful examples are the numerous brightly decorated coffins, that of the 12th-dynasty (1097–1843 BC) Khnumnakht being particularly notable for its painted eyes—intended to allow the dead to look intensely into the land of the living.

The smaller items, too, can be striking. From the Ptolemaic period (332–30 BC) are a sculptured Anubis, the jackal-headed god of embalming who watched over the dead, and the erect and disconcertingly alert bronze likeness of a cat, used as a coffin for the animal regarded by some ancient Egyptians as sacred. Look also for the detailed 11th-century (2009–1998 BC) house and garden models from the tomb of Mekutra, used to show the layout of the deceased's property.

The Temple of Dendur
Destined to be submerged following the construction of the Aswan Dam, this 2,000-year-old temple was packed up and transported to the museum from its original site on the banks of the Nile. The sandstone temple, a monument to Isis and two Egyptian brothers who drowned in the Nile, was constructed around 15 BC in an effort by the Roman emperor Augustus to win the hearts of the conquered locals. It manages to be both spectacular and disappointing, overwhelmed by the modern gallery that was built to contain it and overlooked, through a vast glass wall, by the trees of Central Park and the penthouses of Fifth Avenue.

143

The Temple of Dendur stands in its own huge gallery

METROPOLITAN MUSEUM OF ART

Continued from page 142.

Among the Spanish contributions, focus on El Greco's *View of Toledo*, a striking depiction of the 16th century religious center beneath menacing storm clouds.

The American Wing holds an outstanding collection, defining the development of art and design in the U.S. as European traditions were by stages mimicked, absorbed and finally submerged, as American styles developed.

Foremost among the paintings are the finely detailed landscapes of the Hudson River artists, many of which captured the continent's natural breadth and diversity as white settlers steadily forged westwards. A series of period rooms shows the progress of the decorative arts, from Queen Anne armchairs and Philadelphia Chippendale chests of drawers to the unique art nouveau glasswork of Louis Comfort Tiffany, who worked in Long Island, and a large living room that brilliantly expresses the vision of Frank Lloyd Wright's Prairie-style architecture, intended to replicate the wide open spaces of the American heartland in a domestic setting.

Compared with their American counterparts, the European period rooms seem vulgarly stuffed with finery—they include Venetian bedrooms, English interiors by Robert Adam, and a Louis XIV state bedchamber. The phenomenal collection of clocks, mirrors, and objets d'art lining the adjacent passageways is enough to bring tears to the eyes of any passing antique dealer.

Just a few steps away, a flamboyantly decorated 16th-century Spanish patio leads to the stairwell and the main entrance to the museum's cache of medieval art. Should medieval art be your abiding interest, make this your first call. Only with a clear head are the 4,000-odd exhibits—from the fall of Rome to the dawn of the Renaissance and

Continued on page 146.

More medieval art
After a thorough rummage through the Met's main collections, true medievalists might consider forsaking the remainder of the museum for New York's second batch of medieval treasures, displayed at the Met's Cloisters wing (see pages 92–93). Admission tickets are valid at both locations on their day of issue.

One of the less well-known and more restful corners of the labyrinthine Met: the Petrie Sculpture Court

■ Documenting the origins and spread of Islam through the highly skilled and often beautiful art and craft works that it inspired, the Met's Islamic Art collections fill 10 richly laden galleries on the third floor. Though these are among the Met's lesser-known exhibits, they make up one of the finest such displays in the world. ■

After a bright introductory room describing the founding of Islam by Muhammad in 622 and the religion's steady outward spread from Mecca, the initial galleries are lined with dozens of well-stocked display cases revealing a wonderful assortment of gold and silver pieces such as beads, pendants and plaques from the craftsmen of Egypt, Iran and Syria during the 9th, 10th, and 11th centuries.

A side room is even more copiously stocked, holding the enormous collection of ceramics unearthed during the Met's own excavations in Nishapur during the 1930s and 1940s. The Iranian town was a 10th-century center of Islamic creativity.

Calligraphy and ceramics Flanked by exquisite mosque lamps and perfume sprinklers, another gallery holds a series of leaves from the Koran, demonstrating the development of calligraphy from angular kufic scripts on parchment from 9th-century Egypt to the final refinement of cursive scripts achieved by the oblique cutting of the pen nib in 13th-century Iraq. (Chairs are thoughtfully provided for close scrutiny.) In the same room stands a 14th-century prayer niche (Mihrab), each of its tiny ceramic tiles individually fired to maximize the glaze and heighten the floral decoration. Since it showed the direction of Mecca, the Mihrab was (and still is) the most important item in a Muslim place of worship.

Small is beautiful Many exquisite examples of 14th-century miniature painting, used in text illustration and characterized by pure and harmonious colors and a strong sense of patterning, are displayed in rotation. The influence of miniature artwork was carried over into Islamic carpet design through later years, and carpets and prayer rugs are the prize exhibits of subsequent galleries. Look especially for the lavish textiles—some decorated with gold leaf—with which Mogul emperors lined their tents. Finally, peer into the Nur ad-Din Room, a reassembled winter reception room typical of a wealthy Syrian home of the early 1700s: heavily decorated wood-paneled walls rise from a patterned marble floor and reach up to stained-glass windows and a sumptuous beamed ceiling.

A 14th-century gilded and enameled glass mosque lamp

METROPOLITAN MUSEUM OF ART

Prints and photographs
As comprehensive and as engrossing as any other section of the museum, the Met's collections of prints and photography includes everything from Rembrandt etchings to Russian constructivist photography. Every print-maker and shutter-clicker that you have ever heard of—and many less familiar—are represented.

Continued from page 144.

from a tiny 3rd-century Alexandrian medallion to a three-story-high wrought-iron choir screen from 17th-century Spain—likely to fall into a comprehensible pattern.

Unlike the tightly packed rooms of the main museum, the newer Lila Acheson Wallace Wing holds spacious, light-soaked galleries and makes an excellent setting for the museum's 20th-century art.

Picasso's portrait of Gertrude Stein is a piece that stands out, though the bulk of the collection is provided by Americans—de Kooning, Lichtenstein, Pollock, and O'Keeffe among them. This is not the greatest collection of modern art in New York (for that, see the Museum of Modern Art, pages 158–160), but the side room holding selections from the Berggruen collection of Paul Klee

Changing exhibitions of sculpture and sweeping views over Central Park are two good reasons to visit the Met's rooftop

drawings is a definite plus. So, too, is the rooftop sculpture garden, reached by elevator. Its views across Central Park tend to draw your attention away from the sculpture, which is taken from the permanent stock in the museum and exhibited on a rotating basis.

Another recent addition to the museum is the Michael C. Rockefeller Wing, named after the collector who disappeared (presumed drowned) on a trip to Papua New Guinea in 1961. This wing now houses the art of Africa, Oceania, and the Americas. Of a large, wide-ranging, and constantly intriguing assemblage, items from the Asmat tribe of Irian Jaya (the region of Indonesia adjoining Papua New Guinea) are perhaps the most absorbing. The Asmat people believe that death is never natural but caused by an enemy; when too many deaths occur, it is necessary to seek vengeance. The Asmat *mbis* ceremony culminated in enemies being tracked down and killed; their heads were then placed on the *mbis* poles, covered with carved ancestral figures and other symbols. Several 20-foot-high examples tower over visitors.

Continued on page 148.

■ **Bequeathed by a millionaire banker who allegedly spent his youth roaming Europe tracking down masterpieces and telegramming his father for the money to buy them, the Robert Lehman Collection—housed in a modern pavilion attached to the main building—makes a relaxing break from the museum's more crowded rooms.** ■

The Lehman Collection's more important paintings, chiefly 14th- and 15th-century Italian works, are hung on the second floor in reassembled period rooms from the Lehman house at West 54th Street. Other paintings vie for attention with the temporary exhibitions of drawings at first-floor level, including work by Dürer and Rembrandt.

Botticelli Modest in size but immense in its importance, the highlight of the collection is perhaps Botticelli's *Annunciation*, revealing the achievements of late 15th-century Florentine art in the use of perspective. The painting sets a row of classical pillars between a resonant Virgin and the Archangel Gabriel. God's message arrives as light through a doorway, the rays cutting a diagonal path, splitting the painting's horizontal and vertical lines and linking the two figures.

Venetian painters The Bellini family is represented with a Madonna and Child by Jacopo Bellini and an early work by his more famous son, Giovanni, placed at around 1460 and depicting the Madonna and Child in intense poses before an eerily still landscape. From a few years later, another Venetian, Jacometto Veneziano, contributes two portraits: *Alvise Contarini* and *Nun of San Secondo*, intriguing works prefiguring the Venetian portrait style that came to prominence during the 1500s.

Giovanni da Paolo Among a strong complement of Sienese works, da Paolo's *Expulsion from Paradise* stands out, not least for its lively use of color. The painting shows God soaring above an intensely vibrant constellation, pointing a finger at a barren Earth—the destination for a spindly Adam and Eve who are being shooed out of Eden by a nervous angel.

Another interesting Sienese contribution in the Lehman pavilion is *Temptation of Saint Anthony Abbot*, credited to the Osservanza Master.

French works
The collection's 19th-century French paintings are less inspired despite bearing famous names: Monet's unusually airy *Landscape near Zaandam* is worth a look, as are *Promenade among the Olive Trees* (above) by Matisse, and Cézanne's *House behind the Trees on the Road to Tholonet* and *Girl Bathing*.

Jacopo Bellini's **Madonna and Child**

147

Eating and drinking at the Met

A thorough exploration of the Met calls for great stamina, and even if you have consumed a hearty breakfast before arriving, you will be in need of further nourishment well before it is time to leave.

On the museum's first floor, near the entrance to the Michael C. Rockefeller Wing, a spacious atrium holds a self-service cafeteria, with a choice of hot and cold dishes at reasonable prices, and a slightly more expensive waiter-service restaurant.

If you are only pretending to visit the museum—or its size simply becomes too much to bear—you could while away the day over a glass or two of something at the atrium's bar.

Figures and figurative art: visitors and exhibits at the Metropolitan Museum of Art

Continued from page 146.

The Met has a couple of offbeat departments that—though not designed for the purpose—might well come as a godsend if you have young minds to keep occupied.

The Musical Instruments galleries house 4,000 weird, wonderful, and sometimes priceless tune-making devices. Among the displays, look for the remarkably unattractive legs of the world's oldest existing piano—dated 1720 and a product of the workshops of Bartolommeo Cristofori—and a Stradivari violin made in 1691 and restored to its original appearance.

Strange instruments are plentiful, such as the 19th-century Indian mayuri, a kind of bowed sitar in the shape of a peacock, and a Native American shaman rattle, its carved animal emblem intended to symbolize the transfer of magical power from the spirits to the shaman.

Though it gets comparatively scant attention from the public, the Met's Arms and Armor collection is, predictably, among the best of its kind to be found. Close study of the massed rows of suits of armor, from the 15th century onwards, reveals the high level of artistic flair and craftsmanship that went into the creation of battle apparel.

One example, thought to have been worn by Sir George Clifford in the late 1500s, shows a mass of interwoven Tudor Roses and fleurs-de-lis. Some of the weapons are no less ornate, be they engraved flintlock pistols or shortswords, or an emerald- and diamond-decorated saber.

Explore just a few of the sections mentioned above and you will easily have filled a day without even touching on the Met's Greek and Roman art (including part of a villa once buried beneath lava at Pompeii and endless rows of immeasurably valuable Greek vases), the Chinese and Japanese galleries (which feature a dazzling display of painted scrolls and Astor Court, a traditional Chinese garden created by Chinese crafts people and modeled on a 12th-century original), the Indian and Southeast Asian art, or the arts of the Ancient Near East.

▶▶▶ Midtown Manhattan   IFCD2

Midtown Manhattan is the New York of popular imagination: a place where battalions of power-dressed office-workers march along packed sidewalks to the sounds of wailing police sirens and bumper-to-bumper traffic, as street vendors dispense hot dogs and pretzels in the shadows of the world's most striking high-rise architecture.

In reality, such scenes unfold only between 42nd and 59th streets, an area with many highlights, most of which are detailed elsewhere in this book and explored by the walks on page 150. To New Yorkers, Midtown is usually the section bounded on the north by 59th Streeet and on the south by 34th Street. The Midtown map on page 151, however, extends the area south to 14th Street.

Where Broadway crosses 14th Street, busy Union Square▶ was ringed by elegant homes and became the center of the city's theater district in the late 1800s. By the early decades of the 20th century, the social life had moved north, and Union Square had become a left-wing rallying point. In 1927, police hoisted machine guns onto nearby rooftops during a demonstration. Three years later, a 35,000-strong protest against unemployment ended in pitched battles between police and protesters.

Now, Union Square is home to two new art deco subway entrances and the **Farmers' Market,** where fruit, cheeses, vegetables, and homemade bread are sold from stalls on Wednesdays, Fridays, and Saturdays.

Just east along 14th Street, the offices of Consolidated Edison—the firm responsible for providing New York's power supply—fill a building notable at night for its illuminated facade and clock tower and by day for its **Energy Museum▶**, which records the triumph of Thomas Edison in electrifying the city. Audiovisual displays explain the vine-like entwinements of pipes and cables beneath a typical New York street.

Continued on page 152.

The Venetian-style Metropolitan Life Insurance tower, once the world's tallest building, dominates the Midtown skyline near Madison Square Park

The Armory Show
The 69th Regiment Armory, on Lexington Avenue between 25th and 26th streets, is not the only National Guard barracks to be modeled on a medieval fortress, but it is the only one to have staged the legendary Armory Show of 1913, the first exhibition of modern European art in a country then still obsessed with traditional landscapes and portraiture. The work of Marcel Duchamp and others shocked critics and public alike and the Armory Show's effect on American art was profound. A small plaque on the Armory's facade notes the historic event.

Walk Midtown Manhattan landmarks

Beginning at the Empire State Building and finishing at the United Nations complex, this walk passes seven decades worth of landmark New York architecture.

After visiting the **Empire State Building** (pages 100–102), continue north along Fifth Avenue to the **New York Public Library** (page 168), its entrance set back from the street and guarded by sculptured lions. Walk east along 42nd Street to Grand Central Terminal (pages 166–167) and the **Philip Morris Headquarters**, on Park Avenue, a modern building with

a gallery holding exhibits from the Whitney Museum of American Art.

Farther east on 42nd Street, pass through the cast bronze doors of the 1923 **Bowery Savings Bank** (now the Home Savings Bank of America) to see the lavish Romanesque interior. Close by, note the stunning art deco bas-reliefs by Edward Trumbull on the exterior of the **Chanin Building**. Ahead are the unmistakable **Chrysler Building** (page 89) and **Daily News Building** (page 95), while turning north on First Avenue reveals the **United Nations** complex (page 184).

Walk Midtown churches and museums

View of St. Patrick's Cathedral and the Olympic Tower

Beginning and ending at Rockefeller Center, this walk includes several Midtown churches, the **Museum of Modern Art** (pages 158–160), and the **American Craft Museum** (page 62).

Facing **Rockefeller Center** (pages 173–174) across Fifth Avenue, the twin-spired **St. Patrick's Cathedral** was completed in 1878 in richly carved Gothic form. Inside, the chapels and shrines glow with candlelight.

On East 50th Street, the art deco **Waldorf-Astoria Hotel** has accommodated royalty and every U.S. president since its opening in 1931: if the President is in town during your visit, join the throngs outside and you may catch a glimpse of his motorcade. Nearby, the slim octagonal brick tower of the **General Electric Building** is another art deco landmark. Byzantine-style **St. Bartholomew's Church** boasts a splendid triple-arched entrance portal.

Back on Fifth Avenue, a single corner tower gives **St. Thomas' Episcopal Church** a disjointed look, but don't miss the striking reredos inside.

MIDTOWN MANHATTAN

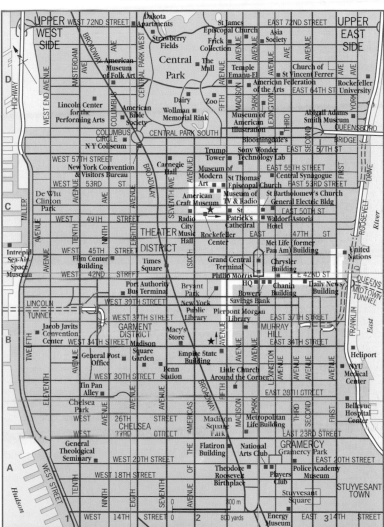

UPPER WEST SIDE

WEST 72ND STREET

Dakota Apartments

Strawberry Fields

Central Park

St James Episcopal Church

Frick Collection

The Mall

EAST 72ND STREET

Asia Society

UPPER EAST SIDE

American Museum of Folk Art

Temple Emanu-El

American Federation of the Arts

Church of St Vincent Ferrer

EAST 64TH ST

Rockefeller University

Lincoln Center for the Performing Arts

Dairy

Wollman Memorial Rink

Zoo

Museum of American Illustration

Abigail Adams Smith Museum

QUEENSBORO BRIDGE

American Bible Society

COLUMBUS CIRCLE

CENTRAL PARK SOUTH

Bloomingdale's

N Y Coliseum

Trump Tower

Sony Wonder Technology Lab

EAST 57TH ST

WEST 57TH STREET

Carnegie Hall

Museum of Modern Art

St Thomas Episcopal Church

EAST 55TH STREET

Central Synagogue

EAST 53RD ST

New York Convention & Visitors Bureau

WEST 53RD ST

De Witt Clinton Park

American Craft Museum

Museum of TV & Radio

St Bartholomew's Church

General Electric Bldg

EAST 50TH ST

Radio City Music Hall

Rockefeller Center

St Patrick's Cathedral

Waldorf-Astoria Hotel

WEST 49TH STREET

THEATER DISTRICT

EAST 47TH ST

Intrepid Sea-Air-Space Museum

WEST 45TH STREET

Film Center Building

Times Square

Grand Central Terminal

Mel Life (former Pan Am) Building

Chrysler Building

United Nations

WEST 42ND STREET

Phillip Morris

E 42ND ST

Port Authority Bus Terminal

Bryant Park

HQ

Chanin Building

Daily News Building

QUEENS MIDTOWN TUNNEL

Bowery Savings Bank

LINCOLN TUNNEL

WEST 39TH STREET

New York Public Library

Pierpont Morgan Library

EAST 37TH STREET

WEST 37TH STREET

GARMENT DISTRICT

MURRAY HILL

Jacob Javits Convention Center

WEST 34TH STREET

Macy's Store

EAST 34TH STREET

Heliport

General Post Office

Madison Square Garden

Empire State Building

NYU Medical Center

WEST 30TH STREET

Penn Station

Little Church Around the Corner

Tin Pan Alley

EAST 28TH STREET

Bellevue Hospital Center

Chelsea Park

WEST 26TH STREET

Madison Square Park

Metropolitan Life Building

CHELSEA

WEST 23RD STREET

EAST 23RD STREET

General Theological Seminary

WEST 20TH STREET

Flatiron Building

National Arts Club

GRAMERCY

Gramercy Park

EAST 20TH STREET

WEST 18TH STREET

Theodore Roosevelt Birthplace

Players Club

Police Academy Museum

Stuyvesant Square

STUYVESANT TOWN

WEST 14TH STREET

0   2   800 yards

0   300 m

Energy Museum

EAST 14TH STREET

AMSTERDAM AVENUE
BROADWAY
WEST END AVENUE
COLUMBUS AVENUE
CENTRAL PARK WEST
FIFTH AVENUE
MADISON AVENUE
PARK AVENUE
LEXINGTON AVENUE
THIRD AVENUE
SECOND AVENUE
FIRST AVENUE
YORK AVENUE
ROOSEVELT DRIVE
East River
HIGHWAY
MILLER HIGHWAY
TENTH AVENUE
NINTH AVENUE
EIGHTH AVENUE
SEVENTH AVENUE
AVENUE OF THE AMERICAS (SIXTH)
FRANKLIN
TWELFTH AVENUE
ELEVENTH AVENUE
WEST STREET
Hudson

151

Madison Square Park: the square holds several tributes to notable figures in U.S. history

Continued from page 149.

During the mid-1800s, the city's elite relocated from Greenwich Village into the new areas of **Gramercy Park►** and **Murray Hill►**. Favored by more prominent citizens were the brownstone town houses around **Gramercy Park►►**, between 20th and 21st streets, part of a residential area laid out in imitation of the grand squares of London. An aura of wealth and understated elegance still lures well-heeled but publicity-shy New Yorkers to Gramercy, where Gramercy Park is the city's only private park: local residents get keys. Look through the park's high railings and you will see statues that include a likeness of actor Edwin Booth in the role of Hamlet. In 1888, Booth founded the influential **Players Club►** in an 1845 building at 16 Gramercy Park South. Two ornamental theatrical masks decorate its entrance, which was designed by Stanford White.

The codesigner of Central Park, Calvert Vaux, added the Ruskin-influenced Gothic features to the building next door, now the **National Arts Club** but earlier occupied by Samuel Tilden, governor of New York from 1874. Tilden's stand against corruption in New York public life did not alleviate his fears of public insurrection: he had a secret passageway set under the house to hasten his escape if angry mobs barricaded the entrance.

A few blocks east, at 235 East 20th Street, the **Police Academy Museum►►** has many intriguing exhibits, among them Al Capone's machine-gun and a stash of terrifying weaponry collected during amnesties.

Heading west, 20th Street holds the **Theodore Roosevelt Birthplace** (see page 182), while 23rd Street leads into **Madison Square Park**. On the south side of the park is the **Flatiron Building** (see page 106) and, on the east side is the 1893 **Metropolitan Life Building**, which gained its tower in 1909.

Baseball's birthplace
Baseball was introduced to the U.S. in 1842, but not until 1845 did a group of enthusiasts—who had been playing the game regularly at what later became Madison Square Park—band together to create a fixed set of rules and the first baseball club, the Knickerbocker Club. As baseball spread in popularity across the country, it was known at first as the "New York Game."

When asked to provide a funeral for an actor in 1870, one Murray Hill church representative said "we don't accept actors but there's a little church around the corner that does." From then on, the 1849 Church of the Transfiguration, on 29th Street just off Fifth Avenue, became better known as the **Little Church Around the Corner►►**, serving New York thespians in spiritual need. A picturesque garden fronts the church, and the intimate interior holds several memorials to actors.

Chelsea►, west of Fifth Avenue, is thriving; a bastion of local gay culture as well as the long-time home of the **General Theological Seminary►**, between Ninth and Tenth avenues and 20th and 21st streets. This is among the city's earliest examples of Gothic Revival architecture. The oldest sections date from the 1830s and they overlook a placid wooded square in the heart of the **Chelsea Historical District►**, an easily strolled area revealing the diverse residential styles of 19th-century New York.

Moving north, McKim, Mead & White's monumental 1913 **Post Office►**, on Ninth Avenue at 33rd Street, stands between Chelsea and the **Garment District**—powerhouse of the city's fashion industry. It dissolves into the **Theater District**, near Times Square.

The Algonquin Hotel
In the Oak Room of the Algonquin Hotel at 59 West 44th Street stands a round table that, from 1919, became *the* Round Table. Around it a legendary coterie of critics, playwrights, and journalists engaged in sparkling wit and repartee. The exchanges were reported in Franklin P. Adams' widely read column in the *New York World* magazine.

Cheek-by-jowl Midtown skyscrapers —with a view!

The Irish

■ It was an Irishman, Thomas Dongan, who gave his name to the charter of 1686 that created New York's modern system of administration. As governor of a British colony, however, Dongan probably never expected that in years to come his countrymen would flock to New York to free themselves of British oppression and take a controlling grip on New York life. ■

154

The unwelcome Irish
Most of the large numbers of penniless Irish that arrived in the city during the 1800s were forced to occupy the worst areas, and some turned to petty crime to make a living. In so doing, they incurred the wrath of many long-established New Yorkers. Some turned against Irish immigrants as a whole. The auctioneer and one-time city mayor Philip Hone wrote of New York's Irish: "they increase our taxes, eat our bread and encumber our streets, and not one in twenty is competent to keep himself."

Under British rule, Protestant and Catholic Irish were established in professional life in New York, but—mindful of British treatment of the Irish at home—both groups embraced the American Revolution and saw their chance to build a truly democratic, self-governing society.

Fall and rise The potato famines brought tens of thousands of Irish into New York during the 1800s. They arrived on the "Irish berths": cramped, airless sections of ships where disease was rife, and once ashore, the penniless Irish—faced with growing anti-Catholic feeling—were forced to occupy crowded rooms, often in atrocious conditions.

By 1860, Irish Catholics made up a quarter of the city's population and were the backbone of the police force, fire-fighting teams and building trades. Irish organizational skills created powerful unions and paved the way for Irish domination of New York's entire administrative machine from the 1870s to the 1940s.

Church and tavern One symbol of the Irish Catholic ascendancy in New York was the building of St. Patrick's Cathedral in 1878. But while the church was important in Irish immigrant life, so too was the tavern. A first stop for new arrivals, taverns were informal clearinghouses for jobs. Some served free lunches to Irish workmen.

Irish-Americans are still strongly represented in New York public office. New York's last outpost of authentic Irish culture is Bainbridge, in the Bronx. First settled in the 1840s by Irishmen who saw its enticing greenery while working on the Harlem Railroad, Bainbridge's bars are the genuine article, without an ornamental leprechaun or bottle of green beer in sight.

St. Patrick's Day (March 17) sees the city's biggest street parade, along Fifth Avenue

► Museum for African Art

113A3

Broadway between Houston and Prince streets
Subway: N, R; 6 Prince Street or Spring Street
Arts and crafts from sub-Saharan Africa form the core of the temporary exhibitions staged in this highly respected museum, one of the U.S.'s major spaces for African art, along with the Smithsonian Institution. Far from being static displays, the shows frequently take provocative directions. In 1995, for example, a display titled "Exhibitionism" studied the approach taken to African art by Western museums.

► Museum of American Financial History

104B2

Broadway at Bowling Green
Subway: 4; Bowling Green
This one-room collection need not detain you long, but it is an appropriate stop when touring the Financial

Visitor Information Center
On the first floor of what looks vaguely like a Middle Eastern mosque facing Columbus Circle (the main junction between Midtown Manhattan and the Upper West Side, and a short distance from the Museum of American Folk Art), the Visitor Information Center provides free maps and information to New York visitors and has many shelves of free leaflets describing the city's attractions.

District. Inside the former Standard Oil Building, once presided over by multimillionaire John D. Rockefeller, the changing exhibitions explore diverse historical avenues in the U.S. economy.

► Museum of American Folk Art

151D1

Lincoln Square
Subway: 1; Subway line 66th Street
From toys and weather vanes to carved walking sticks and gravestone rubbings, the collections of the Museum of American Folk Art are drawn from the output of artists and craftspeople—many of them revered figures within their own communities—from all over the Americas. Be it Mexican wooden animal figures or Navajo blankets, the work on display is frequently of an exceptionally high standard and decorated with symbolic detail that only becomes apparent with close inspection.

In a city that falls over itself to honor the art of Europe, these exhibitions of indigenous American culture—a mix of permanently shown items and various pieces chosen to form special temporary shows—are very welcome.

Woven hangings at the Museum of American Folk Art—a showcase for the talents of craftspeople from all over the Americas

MUSEUM OF THE CITY OF NEW YORK

The Museum of the City of New York, whose dignified grand entrance on Fifth Avenue is the gateway to a mixed collection charting aspects of the Big Apple through the ages

The New York Academy of Medicine

A short walk from the Museum of the City of New York is the New York Academy of Medicine (2 E 103rd Street), which occupies a 1926 building raised with Byzantine, Italian, and Romanesque features. Inside, the academy's library is open to the public. One reason to drop in, might be to view the collection of 4,000 cookbooks (many of them rare), donated by a physician who believed that the key to good health was a nutritious diet.

Special events

The Museum of the City of New York organizes numerous special events, including puppet shows for children and classical concerts and lectures for adults. During the spring and fall, the museum also runs four-hour guided walking tours through different sections of the city. For details on any or all of these events, tel: 534–1672.

▶ **Museum of the City of New York**　　IBCA3

Fifth Avenue at 103rd Street
Subway: 6; 96th Street

Chronicling the rise and rise of one of the world's most diverse and colorful cities is no easy task, and while the Museum of the City of New York has its share of interesting bits and pieces from the formative years of the great metropolis, it struggles to bring them together with any cohesion. Many of the museum's exhibits seem lost in the spacious innards of the neo-Georgian building that houses them.

The devoted history buff will find plenty here to mull over, however. Chronologically, things begin on the third floor with staid dioramas of Native American life in the years leading up to European discovery. Far more intriguing are the first maps of the New York area and drawings and paintings from the mid-1600s, thought to be the earliest depictions of what was then the Dutch trading post of Nieuw Amsterdam.

Six undistinguished period interiors give a very general impression of the furnishings—from simple Dutch tables to ornate English colonial cabinets—that stood in New York drawing rooms from the 17th to the early 20th century. Close by, several cases hold a glittering array of New York-made silver tea caddies, tankards, and cutlery that graced the kitchens of the city's most illustrious residents from the late 1700s.

A few figureheads and many model ships and boats are the principal pieces in a forgettable room intended to document the city's growth into a major seaport. Take care, though, to look at the paintings—such as Alonzo Chappel's simple but expressive *Bowery on a Rainy Day*, painted in 1849, and another that shows ice-skaters in Central Park during 1865—that hang on nearby walls and do more to evoke the New York of their period than many of the more valuable exhibits around them.

The museum enjoys its finest moment on the fourth floor, where a glorious collection of toys (some dating to the mid-1700s) includes a room filled by elaborate three- and four-story dollhouses. The dolls, too, are as impressive as the houses and include a specimen of almost every type produced in the U.S. from the late 18th to the mid-19th centuries. The oldest doll is a French-made import dating from 1724.

The Rockefeller Rooms on the museum's sixth floor comprise the master bedroom and dressing room from the mansion purchased in 1884 by John D. Rockefeller at West 54th Street—a site which is now consumed by the garden of the Museum of Modern Art. A wealth of intricately carved woodwork with mother-of-pearl inlays inspired by English designer Charles Eastlake, the rooms were the height of fashion in Victorian New York. What you will not see here is the mansion's wonderful Moorish room, which is now held in the Brooklyn Museum (see page 79).

Temporary exhibitions fill the first-floor rooms, while the museum's basement is occupied by poorly arranged memorabilia from New York's earliest fire-fighters. The centerpiece is a well-maintained hose-carriage of 1865, but smaller and more revealing pieces fill the surrounding display cases. Among the helmets, lamps, model fire-appliances, and press clippings detailing New York's most famous fires and the men who put them out, look for the fire-fighters' ear trumpet a device intended to improve communication in blazing buildings. When plugged at one end, it also served as a beer-drinking vessel and a handy weapon for when the "fire laddies" (as they were known) gathered for an evening in a tavern.

El Museo del Barrio
A few strides across 104th Street from the Museum of the City of New York, El Museo del Barrio is very much a product of its East Harlem environment, evolving from a local school classroom into a museum devoted to the cultures of Latin America, particularly that of Puerto Rico. The small permanent collection of pre-Columbian objects is regularly eclipsed by temporary exhibitions that span paintings, sculpture, video, and more, reflecting diverse aspects of Latin American life, past and present.

157

Times change: one of the museum's dioramas shows what New York's East River waterfront looked like in the 1850s

On line for a special MoMA exhibition

The MoMA building
In 1939, MoMA acquired not only its current home but also what would, on completion, be one of the first international-style buildings in the U.S. Architects Philip Goodwin and Edward Durrell Stone interrupted West 53rd Street's row of brownstones with a façade of marble, tile, and glass. The very term "international style" had been coined at a MoMA exhibition in 1932, by Philip Johnson, who was later to oversee several additions to the building, most notably the Sculpture Garden

Van Gogh's Starry Night

53rd Street between Fifth and Sixth avenues
Subway: E, F; Fifth Avenue

This really is *the* Museum of Modern Art. Nowhere in the world will you find a museum so well stocked, so aptly designed to illustrate the principal movements and trends, and showing so many of the major works of the past 150 years of artistic achievement.

Paintings and sculpture form the core of the museum's permanent stock, but there are also excellent collections of photography, drawings, prints, and illustrated books, a section on architecture and design and an encyclopedic film and video archive.

It may seem hard to imagine today, but when MoMA (as it is known) staged its first exhibition in 1929, the artists it featured—Cézanne, Gauguin, Seurat, and van Gogh—were not represented in any other New York museum. The otherwise all-encompassing Metropolitan Museum of Art was just one that considered such names to be too much of a risk. Nonetheless, 47,000 people visited the MoMA exhibition in a single month.

A decade later, MoMA acquired its present site (a gift of the Rockefeller family) and through the energy of its young director, Alfred H. Barr, Jr., and the benevolence of a host of millionaire benefactors, it steadily became the world's primary repository for modern art's most influential works, acquiring a prestige all of its own.

The museum itself is a stimulating place, with escalators linking the multilevel galleries and natural light in abundance, enabling visitors to enjoy its contents without suffering exhaustion or eye strain. The painting and sculpture galleries are arranged broadly in chronological sequence across the third and fourth floors, starting with a room of post-impressionists richly hung with canvases by Cézanne, Toulouse-

Lautrec, Seurat, and notable others. It is van Gogh's mighty *Starry Night*, however, that stands out, arguably the museum's most celebrated possession.

Given a corner of its own just outside the post-impressionist galleries, Monet's *Water Lilies*, painted in 1920, is a remarkable study of the subtleties of light and shadow on water and land, the ripples of color appearing to undulate before your eyes.

The next sequence of galleries picks out some of the seminal works of cubism—pioneering pieces like Picasso's *Three Women* and Braque's *Man With a Guitar*, which can be contrasted with offerings from the genre's other leading proponents, such as Gris and Léger.

Moving on, you will pass prime examples of expressionism and futurism, before entering a room dominated by Mondrian's colorful geometric grids—the New York-influenced *Broadway Boogie-Woogie* being prominent.

In a later gallery, you will find the pick of MoMA's extensive Matisse holdings (where *Dance* holds center stage). Beyond it, a single room is devoted to Klee paintings and drawings. Finally, you will reach an entire wall covered by

The Sculpture Garden
Directly opposite the lobby, and a great place to pass an hour on a sunny afternoon after viewing the interior exhibits, is MoMA's Abby Aldrich Rockefeller Sculpture Garden, filled with an excellent and diverse collection of sculpture. Highlights include Henry Moore's *Family Group*, Picasso's *She Goat*—and Rodin's striking *Memorial to Balzac*, a towering bronze that was rejected by its Parisian commissioning committee in the 1890s.

works by Picasso. Dating from the 1930s, some of these arresting images show the impact on Picasso of Europe's slide into war. They include the hauntingly grim *Charnel House*.

A wealth of works by Miró—who had tremendous influence on New York artists in the 1940s—dominates the surrealist rooms, though it is the arguably less accomplished pieces by Dali (*The Persistence of Memory*) and Magritte (*The False Mirror*) that provide instantly familiar, if no less surreal, images.

Also on the third floor are temporary photographic exhibitions, drawn from a permanent stock that ranges from Cartier-Bresson to Diane Arbus.

The fourth floor is detailed on page 160. Taking the escalator to the fifth floor, you will pass beneath an aluminum-bodied Pinin Farina sports car and a 1945 Bell helicopter as you enter the architecture and design exhibitions. These feature architectural models and drawings from Frank Lloyd Wright, Le Corbusier and others. The permanent design collection covers everything from Tiffany lamps to state-of-the-art Italian saucepans.

Inside the MoMA building—New York's earliest piece of architecture in the international style and a fitting home for some of the most famous paintings and sculptures of the 20th century. Clever design, using plenty of natural light and with space to stand back and relax, allows unhurried appreciation of the exhibits

MoMA's fourth floor

■ **The Museum of Modern Art's fourth-floor galleries hold some of the most influential works in modern American art, from seminal abstract expressionist canvases to the latest mixed-media experiments.** ■

Temporary exhibitions at MoMA
It hardly need be said that a museum of MoMA's standing has no trouble in attracting temporary exhibitions of international repute. This is great news for art-loving New Yorkers, but not so good for visitors who may have traveled to New York only to find that their favorite artworks have been stored away to make room for a blockbusting temporary show. To avoid this, contact the museum (tel: 708–9480) or the New York Convention & Visitors' Bureau (tel: 800/NYC–VISIT or 397–8222) before making travel plans.

European influences Many items here reveal the influence of Europeans such as Matisse and Miró, both of whom have later works displayed here. An entire room, in fact, is devoted to Matisse's wonderful *The Swimming Pool*, a large-scale paper mural that originally decorated a wall of his home.

The New York School The most important galleries chart the development of abstract expressionism and the New York School (see pages 128–129). The influence of the surrealists' concern with the subconscious and universal myths is seen in early works by Jackson Pollock (*The She-Wolf* and *Gothic*) and Willem de Kooning.

Similar themes are explored by the so-called gesture artists, among them Franz Kline and Robert Motherwell, who used large blocks of black and white. By contrast, the color field artists such as Barnett Newman and Mark Rothko used shimmering bands of luminous color to evoke emotional states.

Move through the chronologically arranged galleries and the abstract expressionist canvases grow steadily bigger and bolder, reaching their apotheosis in Pollock's monumental *One*.

Recent works After the draining and intense works of the abstract expressionists, it comes almost as light relief to enter the galleries of contemporary art, including Jasper Johns' *Target with Four Faces*; Robert Rauschenberg's study in mutating forms, *Bed*; the comic-strip paintings of Lichtenstein; and Claes Oldenburg's enjoyable oversized papier-mâché models of America's favorite foods.

Painting from one of the Museum of Modern Art's excellent fourth-floor galleries

▶▶ **Museum of Television and Radio**   *151C2*

25 West 52nd Street
Subway: E, F; Fifth Avenue

For serious media students and couch-potatoes alike, the Museum of Television and Radio is the stuff that dreams are made of. For almost anyone else, a visit will be a highly entertaining experience—and a perfect antidote to the more run-of-the-mill forms of sightseeing. More than 40,000 American television and radio broadcasts from the 1920s to the present are stored here, all of them available to the public at little more than a flick of a switch. Several thousand new programs are added to the extraordinary collection every year.

Each day, several small screening rooms show selections from the museum's televisual archive (schedules are available from the lobby, or tel: 621–6800), while the headphones in the cozy radio listening room can be switched to one of five separate channels, each exploring a different area of broadcasting history—anything from a landmark Metropolitan Opera transmission to a wartime comedy show.

A T.V. addict's dream come true—the Museum of Television and Radio offers your own choice of viewing at one of around 100 individual video consoles

More demanding visitors can riffle through the library's computerized cataloguing system and make their own selections from the entire collection. Not only listing television program titles, the database also carries details of the personnel involved in each production—a handy resource if you have forgotten who played Thing in *The Addams Family* or want to discover the real-life identity of your favorite *Batman* villain.

Once you have made your choice (restricted to two hours of viewing time), leave the library for the viewing room, where your selection will be made ready almost immediately (though there may be a three-day wait for particularly obscure items) for watching at a video console.

Commercials—of which the museum has 10,000 in stock—also feature among the daily screenings, as do television shows from other countries, from heavyweight documentaries to vintage episodes of *Monty Python's Flying Circus*.

The museum building
You may be too eager to renew your acquaintanceship with Perry Mason or Lou Grant to notice, but the building that houses the Museum of Television and Radio is a curious blend of classical and modern styles from architects Philip Johnson and John Burgee. With its 16-story limestone-clad tower, the structure has been described as the world's first vertical museum.

■ **The advent of art deco coincided with the skyscraper boom that gripped New York during the 1920s, and the new decorative style was seen as the natural accompaniment to the world's most adventurous architecture. Walk around the city and you will find the art-deco influence everywhere, from world-famous buildings to fine details of decoration.** ■

Zoning laws

In 1915, when the Financial District's Equitable Building rose straight up in the air, robbing adjacent streets and buildings of their sunlight and breezes, the city authorities responded with the U.S.'s first set of building regulations—or zoning laws.

The Zoning Law of 1916 divided New York into commercial and residential plots and insisted that future high-rise buildings were constructed with cutbacks as they rose above the street. This greatly affected the architecture of the city for the next 50 years.

Art deco first emerged in 1925 at the Paris Exposition Internationale des Arts Décoratifs, a show intended to highlight the fine skills of French craftsmen at a time when the German Bauhaus was revolutionizing the world of the decorative arts.

New York was already aware of art deco, however, as the Metropolitan Museum of Art had amassed a collection of the finest European work and inadvertently aided the creation of an American art deco style dubbed "moderne." With the emphasis on overall effect rather than individual craftsmanship, art moderne was tailor-made to the needs of the American market. Mass-produced terracotta and bronze friezes covered with geometric and floral designs, available by mail order, soon began appearing on buildings all over the country.

The new style began to affect interiors, too. Some of New York's finest art deco entranceways and lobbies, such as the Film Center Building (see page 102), are the work of the talented architect Ely Jacques Kahn.

One of the many fine art deco sculptures in Rockefeller Center

New York Telephone Company One of the city's earliest art-deco buildings was the New York Telephone Company (also called the Barclay-Vesey Building, 140 West Street), described by one critic as "Mayan art deco." To get around the constraints imposed by the narrow street, designer Ralph Walker gave the building a series of pedestrian arcades decorated by a cast-concrete frieze cluttered with depictions of bunches of grapes, rabbits, elephant heads, bells, and much more.

Chrysler Building The single most spectacular and lastingly impressive art-deco building in New York, the Chrysler Building (see page 89) was one of the first buildings to use exposed metal. It rises in a series of cutbacks with each new level marked by a different type of decoration—a brickwork frieze of car wheels or immense winged radiator caps. Its most distinctive feature, however, is the seven-story dome, which takes the form of a tiered arch with triangular dormer windows encased in chrome steel.

Empire State Building The Chrysler Building was soon eclipsed as the world's tallest building by the Empire State Building. Built purely for commercial renting, every inch of the Empire State Building was critical, and consequently the decoration was kept to a minimum—allowing the structure to emerge as a specimen of skyscraper art deco at its most restrained and dignified.

Chanin Building Sculptor René Chambellan's façade for the Chanin Building (122 East 42nd Street), which draws the eye away from the nearby Chrysler Building, depicts swooping birds on a bronze band that winds around the building below a terracotta frieze of geometric animal forms. Inside the bronze- and marble-dominated lobby, further bas-reliefs depict the "City of Opportunity"—or New York as it was for the building's owner, Irwin Chanin, a property developer who struck it lucky.

Raymond Hood Destined to become one of the leading architects of Rockefeller Center, Hood used black brick and gold terracotta to emphasize the upright form of the **American Radiator Building** (40th Street between Fifth and Sixth avenues). He later developed this idea with vertical columns of windows and spandrels for the **Daily News Building** (see page 95). In the former **McGraw-Hill Building** (42nd Street between Eighth and Ninth avenues), with its green and gold terracotta, Hood continued his move towards the international style, but the building's lobby retains its impressive art-deco interior.

With **Rockefeller Center** (pages 173–174), New York art deco had its greatest day. Raymond Hood had a large hand in the center's showpiece R.C.A. (now G.E.) Building. At the building's foot, Paul Manship's *Prometheus* is the first of scores of art-deco items decorating the entire complex. Meanwhile, Rockefeller Center's **Radio City Music Hall** takes art-deco into another dimension. Its vast and theatrical interior is intended to be as much a part of the evening's entertainment as the performers appearing on stage.

The Chrysler Building, resplendent with eagle gargoyles

Temporary exhibitions at the National Academy
Short-term exhibitions at the National Academy of Design feature work from its affiliated art societies and from the School of Fine Arts students. Often far more interesting, however, are the academy's shows featuring new or rediscovered European and American artists, usually long before they are exhibited by the city's more prestigious museums.

Our Lady of Lourdes Church
Sections from the Gothic-influenced 1865 home of the National Academy of Design (which stood at 23rd Street and Park Avenue South), together with pieces of other buildings, were incorporated into the very bizarre facade of Harlem's Our Lady of Lourdes Church, on 142nd Street between Amsterdam and Convent avenues.

▶ **National Academy of Design**   187C1
Fifth Avenue at 89th Street
Subway: 4, 6, 86th Street
Founded in 1825 by a group of accomplished artists, architects, sculptors, and engravers—including the artist/inventor Samuel Morse and the creator of Washington Square's handsome town houses, Ithiel Town—the National Academy of Design was established with the intention of becoming an artist-run school and museum to encourage "the highest standards in the arts."

Selections from the permanent collections are shown in the upstairs galleries, but one piece you can be certain of seeing is the sculptured figure of Diana by Anna Hyatt Huntington, which pivots at the foot of an elegant staircase leading up the Academy's galleries.

▶▶ **National Museum of the American Indian**   104A2
US Custom House, Bowling Green
Subway: 4; Bowling Green
For many years, the U.S.'s major collection of Native American artifacts was housed in the Audubon Terrace complex in Harlem, where its geographical distance from most of the city's major museums caused it to be neglected by the majority of New York visitors. In the early 1990s, much of the collection was moved to the Smithsonian Institution in Washington, D.C., but the city retained enough to fill several floors of the architecturally distinguished U.S. Custom House (see page 190).

As the rights of indigenous peoples are slowly being recognized by the powers that be, some items formerly

A focal point at the National Academy of Design: Anna Hyatt Huntington's statue of Diana

Early equipment on display at the Fire Museum

in the museum's possession have been returned to the Native American tribes that produced or owned them. Nonetheless, the museum retains a colossal collection. Baskets, quilts, and pottery drawn from the many and extremely diverse cultures of North, South, and Central America are among some of the objects displayed. Other fascinating exhibits include some of the infamous treaties that paved the way for European colonization of Native American lands.

▶   New York City Fire Museum   IrCB2
278 Spring Street, SoHo
Subway: 6; Spring Street
It may not be at the top of every New York visitor's itinerary, but the New York City Fire Museum fills three floors with the buckets, hand-pumps, and horse-drawn fire-appliances that saved the city from near-total destruction on more than one occasion.

The antiquated carriages are the most spectacular exhibits, but the bulk of the museum is made up of a mind-boggling collection of hose-pipe nozzles, ladders, axes, tools, fire alarms, extinguishers, uniforms, and helmets.

▶▶   New-York Historical Society   IFCF2
Central Park West at 77th Street
Subway: 1; 79th Street
Predating all the city's other museums, the New-York Historical Society was founded in 1804 (its hyphen dates from that time) and was uniquely placed to receive the bequests of wealthy New Yorkers. Consequently, the society is able to boast a substantial collection of works that range from early portraits of significant New Yorkers to important canvases from the country's first home-grown art movement, the Hudson River School. The society also holds a substantial collection of glassworks by Louis Comfort Tiffany and all extant watercolors in John James Audubon's *Birds of America* series.

The Great Fire of 1835
The temperature in New York City on December 16 and 17, 1835, was well below freezing, but that did not stop one of the most destructive fires in the city's history from razing 674 buildings on a 13-acre site in and around the Financial District.

Crowds arriving from the notorious Five Points slums looted the burned-out buildings and helped the flames engulf many more. With insurance companies enduring the same losses as many of their clients, many of the city's banks and financial institutions were unable to reopen and as a result New York endured galloping inflation for the next two years.

■ **In the 1930s, passengers boarding the New York–Chicago early evening service from Grand Central Terminal were, quite literally, given the red carpet treatment. Few who trod the venerated carpet, however, would have thought that just a few decades later the terminal—an architectural tour de force that was dubbed "the gateway to the nation"—would be threatened by cheap air travel and by the rising value of the land on which it stands.** ■

Grand Central Station?
Many people, including lifelong New Yorkers, often erroneously refer to Grand Central Terminal as "Grand Central Station." In fact, as trains can only begin or end their journeys there, "terminal" is the correct word to use. The confusion was not helped by an enormously popular radio drama series which began in 1937, set in New York and titled *Grand Central Station*.

In the 1960s, the Penn Central Railroad (the company in charge of Grand Central Terminal and previously responsible for the demolition of the original and much-loved Pennsylvania Station) proposed to raise a 55-story office tower above the terminal, but these shortsighted plans were luckily thwarted by public pressure, and the building eventually became an official New York City landmark (in 1978), gaining lasting protection.

Grand Central Terminal was completed in 1913 on a plot of land that then marked New York's northern edge. The land had been purchased by transportation magnate Cornelius Vanderbilt (see page 37), who had gained control of all rail routes into New York. After a 10-year period of construction, the station was unveiled to wide public acclaim both as an engineering marvel and as a delight to the eye. It remains one of the world's great railroad stations: an enduring symbol of the city.

Architectural elegance The terminal's construction was a joint effort. The engineer William Wilgus and the architects Reed & Stem devised the innovative split-level design that allowed for a smooth flow of traffic—either train, subway, or pedestrian—into and through the station; Whitney Warren focused on creating the terminal's graceful Beaux-Arts style. Since it was the arrival and departure point for millions of travelers (by 1939, as many people were passing through Grand Central Terminal each year as lived in the entire U.S.), stores, hotels, restaurants, and offices opened up in close proximity to the terminal, making the site a prime Midtown Manhattan plot.

Many side entrances and maze-like tunnels link the terminal with its surrounding streets and adjacent office towers such as the former Pan Am Building (now the Metropolitan Life Building, see panel on page 183), immediately to the north.

On the terminal's southern facade you will first see Jules-Félix Coutan's 48-foot-high figures of Mercury, Hercules, and Minerva, draping themselves around an American eagle. There is also a bronze likeness of Cornelius Vanderbilt—seemingly counting potential railway passengers as they pass.

The interior Once inside, head for the terminal's second story and look upwards. On the 150-foot-high vaulted

ceiling, French artist Paul Helleu used 2,500 electric lights to replicate the zodiacal constellations. The design is based on a medieval manuscript illustration, and the debate continues as to whether or not Helleu was aware that medieval illustrators commonly depicted the heavens reversed—giving God's view

If you lower your gaze slightly, you will see the glass-walled catwalks along which pedestrians pass swiftly through and high above the heart of the terminal (these provide the best views of the concourse). Most trains from here today are used by commuters.

The grandeur of the **Main Concourse** is often obliterated by the pounding of half a million pairs of commuters' feet each day. Nonetheless, try to find a slow moment to descend the marble flight of steps onto its floor and seek out a quiet corner to contemplate its 75 foot windows, its claim to be the world's largest room (it is 470 feet long), and the once serious suggestion to develop the concourse into three separate bowling alleys. (At the time of writing, the Grand Central Terminal is undergoing a massive renovation: this is due for completion in the fall of 1998.)

A pearl of a restaurant The terminal's lower levels provide access to the subway system and also to a number of restaurants, including the legendary **Oyster Bar**.

The restaurant is known not only for its diverse selection of oysters and other seafood, but also for its low ceiling, covered by tan-colored Guastavino tiles. In a vaulted area just outside the restaurant, a whisper into one corner can be distinctly heard in the other corner. However, the restaurant proper has no such magical acoustics, being one of the noisiest in the city (at the time of writing, the restaurant is also being refurbished—it is still possible to eat there, however).

Still, there are few better places in the city for listening in on the lunchtime gossip of New York executives, although the suggestions that fortunes have been made on the Stock Exchange by inspired eavesdropping are apocryphal at best.

The huge scale and grand style of the Main Concourse (said to be the largest room in the world) affirm Grand Central Terminal as a monument to the halcyon days of train travel

Guided tours
For a more detailed exploration of Grand Central Terminal, join the guided tour run by the Municipal Art Society (tel: 935–3960), which begins at 12:30 PM each Wednesday from outside the branch of Chemical Bank on the Main Concourse.

The imposing main entrance to the New York Public Library on Fifth Avenue

▶▶▶ New York Public Library 151B2

Fifth Avenue and 42nd Street
Subway: B, D, F; 42nd Street

You cannot borrow a book at this branch, the Central Branch of the New York Public Library (the 3 million or so tomes are for reference only), but you can explore one of the city's finest expressions of architecture, a Beaux-Arts temple created by the legendary firm of Carrère & Hastings and opened in 1911. Just approaching the building is a treat. Its terrace and elegant steps are decorated by twin sculptured lions, fountains fronting statues symbolizing Truth and Beauty, and bronze flagpole bases cast at Long Island. The triple-arched portico entrance leads into the exquisitely proportioned Astor Hall—named after John Jacob Astor, founder of the nation's first library (one of the three that combined to create the present library's original holdings). The information desk here dispenses floor plans and marks the starting point for the free tours (*Guided tours* Mon–Sat 11 AM and 2 PM).

Immediately ahead, Gottesman Hall stages some of the library's temporary exhibitions. Turn left for the De Witt Wallace Periodical Room at the end of the corridor. Publisher De Witt Wallace spent many hours in this room scanning periodicals and abridging their contents for his fledgling venture, the *Reader's Digest*. His profits financed the room's 1983 restoration: its brass lamps and walnut chairs regained their original glory and were joined by Richard Haas' murals of New York magazine and newspaper offices. Climb the marble stairway to the fourth floor, noting the original lamps and the lions'-head drinking fountains along the corridors on the way to the vaulted McGraw Rotunda, decorated in 1940 by Edward Laning's murals. This marks the entrance to the public catalog room, where researchers hunt through computer databases. Beyond the catalog room lie the main reading rooms—the most beautiful part of the library. Across the corridor from the catalog room is the Edna Barnes Salomon Room, which displays the library's paintings and selections from its stock of printed treasures.

The library's treasures
The New York Public library has an extraordinary stock of rare and valuable books and prints, some of which may be on display. These include a Gutenberg bible; a 1493 folio edition of a Christopher Columbus letter describing his American discoveries; the first full folio edition of Shakespeare, from 1623; the 1640 Bay Psalm Book (the first English book published in America); a handwritten copy of George Washington's farewell address; and an early draft of Jefferson's Declaration of Independence.

▶▶▶ **Pierpont Morgan Library** 151B2

36th Street at Madison Avenue
Subway: 6, 33rd Street

Born into wealth and educated in Europe, J. Pierpont Morgan had become one of New York's leading financiers by the closing decades of the 19th century. But, unlike his nouveau riche contemporaries, he trusted his own taste and judgment as he lavished a fortune on European cultural treasures, acquiring rare books, manuscripts, and drawings that by 1890 had become one of the finest private collections in the country.

In 1902, Morgan commissioned the leading architect of the day, Charles F. McKim, to create the Renaissance-style Pierpont Morgan Library. The Palladian porch that marks the library's original entrance on 36th Street merits a special look, though the present entrance is on the Madison Avenue side and enters a 1928 annex on the site of Morgan's son's brownstone residence.

The temporary exhibitions filling the immediate rooms could hold your attention for hours, but look first around the library itself, starting at the West Room, where Morgan's study is preserved as it was on the fabled financier's death in 1913. Once described as "the most beautiful room in America," the study is lined by Italian Renaissance paintings and dominated by Morgan's immense wooden desk.

From the study, free-standing columns of green-veined marble mark the way to the imposing rotunda and the East Room. In a nutshell, the East Room is one of the plushest reading rooms you are ever likely to see. Three tiers of bookcases, fashioned from bronze and inlaid walnut, rise to a ceiling covered by colorful murals of artists and scholars (and signs of the zodiac), while above the fireplace hangs a 16th-century Flemish tapestry.

Sumptuous though it certainly is, the East Room is never overbearing, and you could spend a long time here, poring over priceless letters and manuscripts.

The Pierpont Morgan collections

The following are just a few items from the vast collections of the Pierpont Morgan Library: three Gutenberg bibles; a Shakespeare first folio; an autographed manuscript of Milton's *Paradise Lost*; manuscripts and early editions of Rudyard Kipling, Oscar Wilde, and Gertrude Stein bearing the authors' doodles and changes; musical scores from the hands of Bach, Brahms, and Beethoven; etchings and prints by Rembrandt, Rubens, and Degas; and a huge selection of pre-19th century paintings and *objets d'art*.

169

Space for the studious: the reading room of New York Public Library. Choose your tome from the library's many miles of shelving and consult it here

QUEENS

Street numbering in Queens
Anyone who has spent several days mastering the Manhattan street-numbering system will find the streets of Queens even more of a challenge. Part of the price for Queens affiliating itself to New York City in 1898 was the loss of its named streets for a numbering system imposed by the civic powers in Manhattan.

The system, it seems, is still having teething troubles. Usually streets and avenues run at right angles to each other, and an address such as 10–35 14th Street will be located on 14th Street near the junction with 10th Avenue. This is not always the case, however, and most problems occur when neighborhoods run into each other at something other than a perfect right angle. If you get lost, the solution might be to ask a local. But then again it might not: Queens residents are often as baffled by the system as everyone else.

The interior of Bowne House, the oldest building in Queens

▶ **Queens** 48C3

An almighty slab of land holding 2 million people and spreading across 119 square miles of western Long Island, Queens is completely incomprehensible unless you think of it as its residents do: a network of separate and self-contained communities, many of which are ethnically distinct and have nothing except geography in common with the neighborhood that happens to be found next door.

While much of Queens fits the sprawling-house-and-two-car-garage image of the typical American big-city bedroom community, many portions reflect New York's immigration patterns. Large communities of Koreans, Indians, and Japanese nestle beside other areas long dominated by Greeks or Puerto Ricans.

Even though you probably failed to realize it at the time, if your arrival point in New York was **La Guardia** or **JFK** airport, you have already had a brief taste of Queens. Both airports are sited in the borough. Planes into JFK swoop above the 20 square miles of marshlands comprising the **Jamaica Bay Wildlife Refuge**, a place much more interesting to migrating birdlife than to all but the most ornithologically obsessed humans.

You will need a car and a very detailed map to explore all of Queens but the main points of interest—which will also give a broad flavor of the borough's ethnic mix—are slotted into a handful of key areas, easily reached by public transportation from Manhattan.

Take the subway from Manhattan to **Flushing**, for example, and you will soon see why the route is unofficially dubbed the "Orient Express." What Flushing's Japanese supermarkets, Korean restaurants, and Chinese dim sum houses do not suggest, however, are the town's 17th-century links with Quakers.

At 137–16 Main Street, a Friends' Meeting House has stood since 1694 and, on a nearby corner, the 1661 **Bowne House▶▶** one of the city's oldest houses has further connections with the Society of Friends. The house's owner, John Bowne, was exiled for defying the ban imposed by Peter Stuyvesant—New York's iron-fisted Dutch governor—on Quaker meetings. However, he persuaded the Dutch West India Company—who did not want to risk losing any would-be settlers—to insist that all religious groups would be tolerated in the new colony: a step toward the religious freedoms later enshrined in the Constitution.

The house holds some of Bowne's colonial furnishings, plus those of his descendants, who lived here until the 1940s. Tours of the small modest dwelling wend their way into the kitchen, where the clandestine Quaker meetings took place.

A short walk from the Bowne House, the 1774 **Kingsland Homestead** is an example of the Dutch and English architectural mix that was typical of Long Island farmhouses of the period.

A mile east of Flushing, **Flushing Meadows-Corona Park▶▶** began life as a swamp and garbage dump, but by 1939 it was drawing millions to the World's Fair, which symbolized New York's emergence from the Depression. A few relics from the 1939–1940 fair remain, as do many more from a second World's Fair held here in 1964–1965.

The United Nations In Queens
The City Building, which houses the Queens Museum in Flushing Meadows-Corona Park, was used by the United Nations as the organization awaited the completion of its site in Manhattan. Among the motions carried here was the 1947 one that paved the way for the creation of the state of Israel.

Among these are Philip Johnson's **New York State Pavilion Building**—the architectural highlight of the 1960s show, but these days in a much crumbled condition that reflects poorly on the construction ideas of the time—and the 140-foot high **Unisphere**, intended to represent the Earth and its satellites.

Another 1960s survivor, the **New York Hall of Science►**, is these days crammed with hands-on computer exhibits designed to explain the rudiments of science to children.

More modest sized memorabilia from both world fairs is displayed inside the **Queens Museum►**, housed in a structure that dates from the 1939–1940 fair. What fascinates most here is the Panorama: a scale model of New York City that covers 18,000 square feet and includes every building in the city. Created for the 1960s fair, the Panorama is updated regularly.

The park is also home to the **Queens Wildlife Conservation Center**, a small zoo featuring North American animals in their natural habitat, as well as the **National Tennis Center**—where the annual U.S. Open is held.

A busy street in Queens

Roosevelt Avenue, in the Jackson Heights neighborhood of Queens, is known for its bakeries and restaurants

Steinway

Just east of Astoria is the town of Steinway, created by William Steinway when he moved his piano factory here—partly to escape the power of unions—from Manhattan in 1872. The factory still stands at 19th Avenue and 39th Street. Steinway himself, meanwhile, moved into a stonework Italianate villa overlooking the East River at 18–33 41st Street. The slightly spooky villa has certainly seen better days, as has the now entirely unsalubrious neighborhood that surrounds it.

Baseball fans and devotees of the Fab Four might care to note that **Shea Stadium**, home of the New York Mets and the venue of a now legendary concert by the Beatles in 1965, stands in the northerly section of the park.

On the borough's northern side, facing the Bronx across the East River, **Astoria▶** is one of the world's largest Greek communities. Lining 31st Street and Ditmars Boulevard are countless Greek bakeries, cafés and restaurants, and even the graffiti on the walls is in Greek.

Not remotely Greek, though, and failing to live up to its grand title, is Astoria's **American Museum of the Moving Image▶**, 36–11 35th Avenue, which occupies part of a working studio complex. During the 1920s, Paramount shot silent movies here with legendary figures such as Rudolph Valentino, Clara Bow, Gloria Swanson, and the Marx Brothers before they—along with the rest of the American film industry—relocated to Hollywood.

The museum presents selected cinematic classics and carries temporary exhibitions on various aspects of movie history. On permanent display is a large but only mildly interesting collection of props, costumes, filmmaking equipment, fan magazines, and vintage movie posters.

Heading back toward Manhattan is the heavily industrialized **Long Island City**, which is forging a reputation as an artists' enclave. In its early days, the area of Long Island City known as Hunters Point was linked by ferry to Manhattan, encouraging business development here. Some of the old warehouses and factories, now unused, have been redeveloped into artists' studios.

A showpiece of artistic Long Island City is the riverfront **Isamu Noguchi Garden Museum▶▶**, 32–37 Vernon Boulevard. This is devoted to the work of the accomplished and acclaimed sculptor. The son of a Japanese poet who emigrated to California, Noguchi's unconventional ideas were derided by his first instructor, but his imagination and creativity is clear enough throughout the 12 indoor galleries that chart his long career (Noguchi died in 1988, age 84), and in the gardens that hold still more of his enigmatic creations.

▶▶ Rockefeller Center 151C2

47th–52nd streets between Fifth and Sixth avenues
Subway: B, D, F, 1; 47th Street—Rockefeller Center

This is the world's largest commercial and entertainment complex, through which a quarter of a million people pass each day. The project changed the face of American urban planning from the 1940s on.

The center is named after multimillionaire John D. Rockefeller, Jr., who was approached in 1928 by the Metropolitan Opera with a view to his developing a down-at-the-heels Midtown site, on land rented from Columbia University, as a new Opera House. Rockefeller agreed, but the Wall Street crash led to the shelving of the plans and left him with 11 acres of land and a very large debt.

In the country's first major pooled architectural project, Rockefeller commissioned several firms to erect 14 buildings on the site with the provisos that the structures form an aesthetically unified entity and that the complex should be a pleasing environment for working, eating, shopping, and relaxing.

As a result, the art-deco buildings themselves take a secondary role to the numerous cafés, restaurants, underground walkways, and shopping plazas secreted in and around them, allowing a flow of light and easy movement of people. This became the blueprint for city-center renewal initiatives throughout the country.

To reach the heart of the complex, enter from Fifth Avenue along the short Channel Gardens to the sunken Plaza▶, which holds an open-air restaurant and a wintertime ice rink and is presided over by Paul Manship's 1934 figure of *Prometheus*.

Rising above Prometheus' head, the 70-story **G.E. Building** (better known by its original title, the R.C.A.

Rockefeller Center Facts
Number employed in construction 1931–40: 75,000.
Number of telephones: 100,000.
Number of elevators: 488.
Cost of buying Columbia University's leasehold in 1985: $400 million.

Gertrude Stein on the R.C.A. Building, 1935
"The most beautiful thing I have seen."

173

Summertime brings bright umbrellas and a holiday atmosphere to the sunken plaza amid the office buildings of Rockefeller Center

Building is the heart of Rockefeller Center. Enter the lobby and note the murals by José Maria Sert—replacements for those of Diego Rivera, who refused to appease the anticommunist Rockefellers by removing a handsome likeness of Lenin.

Take the elevator to the **Rainbow Room** restaurant complex, in whose **Rainbow Promenade Bar**, for the price of a drink, you can gaze out over Manhattan. Return to the lobby to collect a free map from the information desk, essential as you begin weaving deeper into Rockefeller Center's impressive labyrinth.

Simple wanderings will reveal much of interest but one place not to be missed is **Radio City Music Hall**. The hall's 1932 gala opening was attended by the likes of Charlie Chaplin and Clark Gable, and it instantly became one of the great American entertainment palaces. More recently a favored location for live concerts and the occasional film premiere, the 6,000-seat hall is still an art deco delight and can be seen on guided tours (tel: 632–4041).

Less glamorous but still in the realms of the showbiz world, the offices and studios of **N.B.C. Television** can be viewed on hour-long guided tours (tel: 664–7174).

174

Getting to Roosevelt Island
A road bridge crosses from Queens to Roosevelt Island, but to reach the island from Manhattan, use either the subway (lines B or Q) or (much the best choice) the cable car, which makes a 3-minute jaunt over the East River from a terminal at Second Avenue and 60th Street.

The Roosevelt Island cable car

►   **Roosevelt Island**   *187A2*

Once given over to 27 hospitals that kept the incurably sick and insane (and the simply scandalous, such as Mae West) segregated from the rest of New York society, Roosevelt Island is today regarded as one of the most successful attempts at integrated mixed-income housing. Would-be residents now have to wait several years to get an apartment in the area. Besides near-total absence of crime, Roosevelt Island dwellers also enjoy automobile-free streets and a sight of the Midtown Manhattan skyline unsurpassed in few other locations in the city. For visitors, the peacefulness and the views (and the cable car that crosses to the island) are the only attractions, though the ruins of the old hospitals, shielded by fences at the island's southern end, add a distinctly eerie note.

► **SoHo** _113A2_

Named for being SOuth of HOuston Street (and bordered also by Canal, Lafayette, and Sullivan streets), SoHo is dominated by large cast-iron buildings put up in the mid-19th century to house factories—the notorious sweatshops.

When these were outlawed in 1962 (the innumerable fires and fatalities that resulted from unsafe working practices earned SoHo the nickname "Hell's Hundred Acres"), SoHo industries moved away, and the district suffered a decade of neglect.

The determined efforts of conservationists saved the area and its unique buildings from demolition and, after 10 years of colonization by up-and-coming artists who were attracted by spacious rooms lit by immense windows, SoHo entered a period of swift gentrification. Its loft-style apartments found favor with the city's rich and trendy—and with the art dealers who made the area internationally synonymous with contemporary art. With chic clothing stores and fashionable restaurants alongside scores of art galleries, SoHo is now transformed—but it is the dozens of remaining cast-iron buildings that shape its character.

Available through mail-order catalogues and assembled cheaply and quickly on site, prefabricated cast-iron structures represented a revolution in urban design in the mid-1800s. Their ersatz European decoration—based on classical Rome or the French Renaissance—also aped the then fashionable look of the U.S.'s new business buildings, the classically themed "temples of commerce."

Among the earliest examples of the cast-iron form, the **Haughwout Building** (488–492 Broadway) dates from 1857 and still imposes its harmony on the surrounding streets, rising in four tiers of arched windows and Corinthian columns—a design said to be based on the Sansovino Library in Venice.

On Greene Street, numbers 28–30 and 72–76 show the artistry that later ironwork facades acquired, while the **Little Singer Building** (561–563 Broadway) suggests the next great architectural step: replacing cast-iron floor supports with steel—the basis of the modern skyscraper.

You need never look far for signs of creative endeavor in SoHo

Richard Haas' SoHo mural Since 1973, at the junction of SoHo's Prince and Greene streets, the neighborhood's bringing together of contemporary art and historic cast-iron buildings has been celebrated in a witty trompe l'oeil by Richard Haas, which cleverly confuses the actual features of the buildings with painted representations.

■ **You do not have to be an art dealer or critic to find New York's 500 or more art galleries fascinating. Most of the galleries are clustered close together in SoHo—very much the international nerve center of contemporary art—though others are well established on the Upper East Side and along 57th Street. Take the time to see the nonprofit galleries, too, showcasing the work considered too risky by the commercial galleries. ■**

The Gallery Guide

The *New York Times*, the *Village Voice,* and many special art publications carry art gallery listings, but the most comprehensive details are provided by *Gallery Guide*. A publication listing over 500 galleries and providing maps to help locate them, the *Gallery Guide* is published monthly and distributed free in galleries and a few selected bookstores. Be warned that the popularity of the *Gallery Guide* makes it almost impossible to find any later than the middle of the month.

Upper East Side galleries The epitome of Upper East Side elegance and sophistication, the Paris-founded **Wildenstein & Co.** (19 East 64th Street) specializes in French impressionism, but its holdings extend from contemporary paintings to antique objets d'art.

The diverse stocks of **Hirschl & Adler** are displayed in three separate galleries. The main location (21 East 70th Street) carries a broad selection of 18th- and 19th-century European pieces; at the same address, Hirschl & Adler Folk holds American folk art, from paintings to crafts, while **Hirschl & Adler Modern** (4th floor, 420 West Broadway, in SoHo) specializes in American and European names from the mid-1950s.

Focusing on modern American painters, the **Gagosian Gallery** (Madison Avenue between 76th and 77th streets) provides a museum-like space for lesser-known works by well-known names, including Jackson Pollock, Willem de Kooning, Andy Warhol, and Cy Twombly.

57th Street galleries If you only have the opportunity to visit one 57th Street gallery, make it **Pace** (32 East 57th Street). This deserves its place among the world's leading galleries for a stock that includes virtually every European and American name of major significance from the last 30 years.

Influential in the emergence of pop art and noted for the high quality of its purchases, the **Sidney Janis Gallery** (110 West 57th Street) has been a fixture on the New York art scene for four decades and continues to present established and new names in stimulating exhibitions.

Abstract expressionists turn up in many New York galleries but one of the better places to find works by the color field artists is the **André Emmerich Gallery** (41 East 57th Street).

Some intriguing historical documents from the turbulent 1930s can be seen alongside fine examples of German expressionism at **Galerie St. Etienne** (24 West 57th Street).

First established in SoHo, the Mary Boone Gallery (745 Fifth Avenue) is what serious art watchers ignore at their peril. With a knack of latching onto developing trends before any other gallery had noticed them, through the 1980s Mary Boone helped launch some of the brightest new names in American art, such as David Salle and Julian Schnabel.

SoHo Galleries In the early 1960s, the **Leo Castelli Gallery** (2nd floor, 420 West Broadway) brought artists such as Andy Warhol, Roy Lichtenstein, Jasper Johns, and Frank Stella to wide attention and is now among the world's leading galleries. The gallery has a graphic arts annex, which can be found at 578 Broadway.

Minimalist and conceptual art is the stock-in-trade of the highly regarded **John Weber Gallery** (142 Greene Street), closely linked with established figures such as Sol Lewitt and regularly showcasing new artists with a similar outlook. Innovative and challenging sculpture, painting, and photography from Europe and the U.S. are regularly on show at **Metro Pictures** (150 Greene Street), where work by Cindy Sherman and Louise Laller is also often featured.

Guided tours of art galleries
If you want to be led through the city's art gallery labyrinth by an expert—and if you have the money (expect to spend $30–$50 per person) and the interest, this is an excellent way to get an insider's view of the world's most frenetic art scene—check out Art Horizons International (tel: 969–9410).

Nonprofit galleries Artists' Space (38 Greene Street) has an esteemed reputation as a launch pad for artists working with installations and video, and in the past has done wonders for Laurie Anderson, David Salle, and Cindy Sherman. Each September, a group of unknowns is selected from the Artists' Space files for a group exhibition—worth seeing if you are around.

Since the mid-1970s, the Dia Art Foundation has provided funds for long-term installations and environmental pieces. Among these is a notable work by Walter de Maria: the **New York Earth Room** (141 Wooster Street), which is filled with 14 tons of soil and is much more interesting than it sounds. The almost adjacent Visual Arts Gallery (137 Wooster Street) has changing selections of mostly video and photographic works from students of New York's School of Visual Arts.

SoHo has become the place to go if you are interested in contemporary art. Over the past 20 years, numerous small galleries have opened in the area, providing launch pads for many new names in the art world

*South Street Seaport
and the cargo ship
Peking*

► **South Street Seaport**　　　　*104B3*

Eastern foot of Fulton Street
Subway: 2, 3, 4; Fulton Street

A large collection of stores, seafood restaurants, bars, craft centers and galleries make up the South Street Seaport district, which transformed an abandoned area beside the East River—the place where New York's 19th-century maritime trade flourished—into a history-themed pedestrian mall, eagerly patronized by Financial District employees after work.

By day, however, most visitors come to Seaport itself to explore the vintage ships of the South Street Seaport Museum complex—which jump-started the area's gentrification some two decades ago—moored beside the South Street piers. The most interesting exhibit is the 1911 *Peking*, a four-masted cargo vessel that spent its glory days shifting nitrate from South America to the U.S. and made several roundings of Cape Horn.

Climb aboard and descend to a lower deck where a pictorial display recounts the ship's working life. Back on dry land is the **Museum Gallery**, which has a minor exhibition of maritime photos and ships-in-bottles and assorted certificates and documents attesting to New York's historical place as one of the world's great seaports.

SOUTH STREET SEAPORT MUSEUM

SEPTEMBER 11,
MUSEUM ADMISSION

TICKET VALUE: $0.00
SYSTEM IS MADE POSSIBLE BY A GENEROUS GI

Stroll: Water Street
Water Street, between Wall Street and South Street Seaport, was New York's main riverside thoroughfare in the 19th century, lined by sailors' boarding houses, bars, and brothels.

►► **Staten Island**　　　　*48B1*

A ride on the Staten Island Ferry (see the panel opposite) is reason enough to make the crossing from the Financial District to the hilly chunk of land wedged between New Jersey and Brooklyn, but Staten Island has much more than a ferry to call its own. Settled by Dutch and French farmers in 1661 and an important British base during the Revolutionary War, the island has evolved into leafy suburbia with a tranquil mood that makes it seem a million miles from the hurly-burly of the rest of New York City. It also has some surprising collections among its museums.

The ferry docks at St. George, the island's least enthralling community (even the Staten Island Museum here can be bypassed without worry). Two miles west (take bus S40 from the ferry terminal), Sailors' Snug Harbor is a better first stop. Founded in the 1800s as an institution for "decrepit and worn-out sailors," it is now better known as **Snug Harbor Cultural Center▶**. Restoration has kept a number of its imposing 19th-century buildings intact.

It is farther south that Staten Island's real treasures are to be found (take bus S74). Visiting in 1991, the Dalai Lama himself described as "accurate" the stone cottage on Lighthouse Hill intended to replicate a Tibetan mountain temple and provide an apt home for the **Jacques Marchais Center of Tibetan Art▶▶▶**, a wondrous stock of sculptured deities, ritual objects, incense burners, and many other items from the world's various Buddhist cultures.

Now the largest private gathering of such material in the western world, the collection was inspired by the discovery in 1880 by the young Jacqueline Norman Klauber (who later renamed herself Jacques Marchais) of 12 Tibetan figurines that her great-grandfather had brought back from a trip to India and stored in the family attic. This stimulated a lifelong fascination with Buddhism and its

The Conference House
Students of international summitry visiting Staten Island might consider making a trip to the Conference House. In September 1776, the stone-built house became the venue of the only peace talks attempted between the British forces and the American revolutionaries. The house served as a rat-poison factory before becoming a museum in 1926. The interior has period furniture and numerous items recording the revolutionary conflict—and the failed attempt to broker a peace.

The Staten Island Ferry terminal

sacraments, and no opportunity was missed to expand the collection.

Whether you are looking at the Buddhist Wheel of Life or a yak butter burner, informative explanatory texts make sense of the exhibits, and illuminate their complex symbolism. Visits are by appointment only (tel: 718/987–3478 or 718/987–3500).

A mile south is the 100-acre **Richmondtown Historic Restoration▶▶**, which shows the fruits of half a century of gathering and restoring buildings dating from the 17th to the 19th centuries and equipping them with (usually) the original occupants' possessions. Local history buffs, dressed in period costume and keen to pass on their knowledge, help with tours around the old homes. These range from a sparsely furnished Dutch building which doubled as local church and schoolhouse to a general store packed with 1840s consumer goods—all providing a fascinating insight into forgotten ways of life and a time when the island was still rural.

Also within the complex, the Island Historical Museum presents a chronological record of Staten Island's growth, with many enjoyable exhibits from some of its early industries, which over the years have ranged from brewing to oyster harvesting.

The Staten Island Ferry
The actual vessel is entirely ordinary, but the views from the Staten Island Ferry can be wonderful. The Statue of Liberty, Governor's Island, and the Verrazano-Narrows Bridge all appear as the skyscrapers of Lower Manhattan shrink into the distance and the green hills of Staten Island draw nearer. The ferry (pedestrians only) takes half an hour to make the 5-mile crossing, and the amazingly cheap round-trip fare is payable before departure only from the Staten Island terminal, at the end of Whitehall Street.

STATUE OF LIBERTY

Wild Staten Island
The hilly, bucolic interior of Staten Island holds many acres of unspoiled land, parts of which can be explored on marked walking trails. The Greenbelt (tel: 718/667–2165) spans wetlands, woodlands, streams, rivers, and parks; organized weekend activities include horseback -riding and guided nature hikes. The one-time mining of clay on Staten Island's southwest shore has helped create the 250-acre Clay Pit Ponds Preserve (tel: 718/967–1976), with pine woods and many man-made ponds that now provide wildlife habitats.

Statue of Liberty Facts
Height: 151ft. 1in.
Weight: 450,000lbs.
Length of hand: 16ft. 5in.
Length of index finger: 8ft.
Length of nose: 4ft. 6in.
Thickness of waist: 35ft.
Best movie role: in Alfred Hitchcock's *Saboteur*.
Biggest fictional blunder: Liberty's torch is described as a sword in Franz Kafka's *America*.

If you have time to spare, visit the **Alice Austen House►**, a bayside home on Staten Island's eastern edge, dating from 1710 and filled by some of the 8,000 photographs taken by the untrained Alice over a 50-year period to 1934. In 1951, *Life* magazine discovered and published some of her work. Her talents were soon recognized far afield, yet at the time her fame was growing, Alice was spending her poverty-stricken old age toiling in a public workhouse.

Another small and equally unexpected collection is the **Garibaldi Meucci Museum►**, where Giuseppe Garibaldi—one of the founders of unified Italy—spent two years in the 1850s in the home of American-Italian Antonio Meucci, both of them working in a local candle factory. Garibaldi's place in history is assured, but fate was unkinder to Meucci, an inventor who developed a prototype telephone but failed to patent the idea. To reach both this and the Alice Austen House, take bus S51 from the ferry terminal.

►► Statue of Liberty   48C2

There is no greater symbol of the nation and its promise of freedom and opportunity for all than the Statue of Liberty, which has held the flame of liberty above New York harbor since 1886. From Manhattan, a visit to the statue begins with a ferry ride from Battery Park Pier. Boats to the statue also stop at the excellent Ellis Island (see page 100).

At the statue, there are two options. If you have the time and energy, begin an assault on the 354 steps that lead up to the crown—but be warned that the staircase is narrow and that you can only climb as fast as the person in front (the ascent can take three hours). Alternatively, take the elevator to the pedestal level, from which the views are only marginally less impressive than those from the crown. On the way down, visit the intriguing museum, which records the creation of the statue and the effect it had on newly arrived immigrants when seeing it for the first time.

Liberty Island is in fact closer to New Jersey than to New York, but its statue is universally regarded as a fundamental part of the city

■ **Originally intended to stand in Egypt, partly funded by a French lottery, and at first regarded in the U.S. as a waste of money, the Statue of Liberty may be America's most famous landmark, but the story of its construction is much less straightforward than most people may realize.** ■

Liberty in Egypt? A sculptor with a taste for monuments on the grand scale, Frenchman Frédéric Auguste Bartholdi visited Egypt and presented to the Egyptian sultan his plans for a gigantic figure of a robed female peasant holding a torch, to be sited at the entrance to the Suez canal.

The sultan rejected the scheme, but Bartholdi, on a trip to the U.S. in 1871, found the perfect spot for his torch-carrying lady at the entrance to New York's harbor, 4,000 miles from her original intended location.

French friendship The idea of a gift from France to the U.S. to mark the nations' shared belief in democracy had been around for some time, and Bartholdi's statue idea was taken on board by France's new Third Republic, busy modeling its constitution along U.S. lines.

As a sign of friendship, both governments agreed that the work would be shared, Bartholdi producing the statue while its pedestal was made in New York. In France, a popular lottery raised 250,000 francs toward the project, but in the U.S., the idea was greeted with apathy.

As *Liberty Enlightening the World* (as the statue is officially titled) took shape outside Bartholdi's Paris studio—being too large to fit inside—the pedestal had barely left the drawing board, and the American press was full of satirical cartoons and articles condemning its expense.

Raising the money After Congress rejected a bill allocating $100,000 to the work, and the mayor of New York vetoed a plan for the city to donate $50,000, newspaper publisher Joseph Pulitzer attacked the miserliness of the nation's rich, and appealed for contributions—no matter how small—from ordinary Americans.

Packed into 214 crates, the finished statue arrived in New York in June 1885. Two months later, Pulitzer announced that the goal of raising the necessary sum of $100,000 had been reached.

The statue was hoisted onto its pedestal in May, 1886, and officially unveiled in October. The response, as Pulitzer's newspaper recorded, was "one long cheer."

Liberty Enlightening the World—*a powerful symbol of welcome to generations of new arrivals in New York Harbor*

181

Stock Exchange *104B2*

Broad Street near Wall Street
Subway: 4; Wall Street
Housed in a 1903 neoclassical building, the New York Stock Exchange might be expected to form the highlight of a tour around the Financial District. Unless you have a vested interest in the ups and downs of the Dow Jones average, however, the exchange's 37,000-square-foot litter-strewn dealing floor—populated by color-jacketed brokers, reporters, and pages—looks no more interesting from behind the glass of the public viewing gallery than it does on T.V.

The exhibits on the exchange's history, and on share dealing in general, do nothing to lessen the sense of anticlimax. Nonetheless, if you want to view the spot where the crash of 1929 plunged the nation into the Great Depression, it is best to pick up your ticket, free and time-stamped for the half-hourly tours, from the entrance soon after 9 AM.

▶ **Theodore Roosevelt Birthplace** *151A2*
20th Street between Broadway and Park Avenue
Subway: 6; 23rd Street
The nation's future 26th president, Theodore Roosevelt, entered the world in 1858 in a Midtown Manhattan brownstone, a building subsequently demolished but precisely reconstructed on its original site in 1923 to house a museum honoring the only president to have been a New York native.

The lower floor carries an absorbing exhibition on Roosevelt's life, from his childhood struggles with asthma and the tragedy of the deaths of his mother and his wife on the same day, to his entry into politics on a ticket of ending the corruption endemic in New York affairs and his rise to become the nation's youngest ever president in 1901, aged 42.

Upstairs, more than half the furnishings in the period rooms come from the original house of the Roosevelt family. Best capturing the personality of Roosevelt himself is the room stuffed with his hunting trophies and outdoor memorabilia.

▶ **TriBeCa** *IFCB2*
Subway: 1; Franklin Street
TriBeCa—the TRIangle BElow CAnal Street (bordered on the east by Broadway and continuing west to the Hudson River)—became the stamping ground of the artists who were priced out of their SoHo lofts (see page 175) as that district's property values soared throughout the 1970s.

Like SoHo, TriBeCa's old warehouses—formerly at the center of New York's dairy and poultry trade—offer apartments with ample space and natural light, making perfect studios. Also like SoHo, however, TriBeCa is increasingly taking the fancy of upscale residents in search of stylish Lower Manhattan living and sound property investment, so prices have risen here too.

Besides providing as good a picture of New York-style urban regeneration as you are likely to find, a walk through TriBeCa uncovers something of note at almost every turn. Art galleries, much less slick than their SoHo counterparts, occupy many of the former industrial

The Stock Exchange

182

A radical exorcism at the Stock Exchange
The bulletproof glass screen that shields the trading floor of the Stock Exchange from the public gallery has been in place since 1967, the year when yippie (a twist on the term "hippie") Abbie Hoffman and friends tossed 300 one-dollar bills on to the trading floor. Traders went scurrying for the cash and one of Hoffman's co-activists described the incident as "exorcising the evil spirits of the Stock Exchange."

buildings. A notable example is the **Clocktower** at 108 Leonard Street. Dozens of pricey restaurants nourish fashionable faces while, at 37–41 Harrison Street, a primly restored row of early-1800s Federal-style town houses makes a wholly incongruous appearance.

Trump Tower   151C2

Fifth Avenue at 56th Street
Subway: E, F; Fifth Avenue

High-profile property tycoon Donald Trump was brave enough to put his name to this horrid glass tower—a monument to the booming economy of the early 1980s and the frenzied building that it financed. He also became one of the people actually to live in one of the 263 plush apartments that fill the tower's upper levels.

Although the façade is among the city's least inviting, it is worth stepping inside Trump Tower for some serious window-shopping. Serenaded by the tinkling of a five-story waterfall, you can explore a host of designer-name boutiques here—though the pink marble surfaces and the obsessively manicured shrubbery might have you running for the exit surprisingly quickly. Just next door at 727 Fifth Avenue are the classy baubles of **Tiffany & Co**, the renowned jewelry store.

The former Pan Am Building
Bauhaus architect Walter Gropius was among the team that designed the Pan Am Building on Park Avenue, adjoining Grand Central Terminal. The largest commercial office building ever constructed, it is also possibly the only one so closely resembling an aircraft wing. Following the demise of Pan Am, the Metropolitan Life Insurance company purchased the building in 1992 and set about removing its much-photographed Pan Am logo. The building itself remains as familiar a sight as ever, though, still blocking the view along Park Avenue.

183

Stroll: Duane Park
By day, the streets around TriBeCa's Duane Park provide fruitful territory for a stroll. Head northwards along Hudson Street, and turn off to explore Harrison and Leonard Streets.

Inside or out, nothing is understated at Trump Tower

UNITED NATIONS

▶ United Nations

First Avenue between 42nd and 46th streets
Subway: 4, 6, 7; 42nd Street—Grand Central

Given the problems blamed on its huge and infamously cumbersome bureaucracy, it might seem apt that the main building of the United Nations—the organization of world states formed in San Francisco in 1945 and operating on this plot since 1947—should be the Secretariat Building. This enormously unappealing building houses the U.N.'s 16,000 pen-pushers and rises for 39 marble-and-glass stories above the East River.

The U.N.'s public entrance is through the General Assembly Building. The lobby carries temporary exhibitions on international themes, and from here a stairway leads down to the souvenir shop, post office (selling United Nations postage stamps, which are valid only on mail that is posted here), and also to a rather gloomy cafeteria. (The Delegates' Dining Room has a great East River view, and a splendid lunch buffet. This and the gardens outside are the best parts of the U.N.)

To see any more of the U.N., you need to buy a ticket for a guided tour. Departing every 15 minutes or so from the lobby, the tours last around an hour and sweep through the various U.N. buildings, pausing on the way at displays on the work of the U.N. and at artworks donated by member states. None of these matches the emotional impact of the half-melted items culled from the ruins of Hiroshima and Nagasaki, which are also on display. Assuming no meetings are in session, the tour stops by the Security Council chamber—where the calmness imposed by the empty chairs and desks belies the fact that this is the only U.N. body with any teeth, able to impose economic sanctions and instigate military actions—and the General Assembly room, the very size of which suggests it can never be anything more than a debating chamber.

The U.N. in session
During its September to December sitting, the General Assembly of the U.N. can be witnessed in session from the public gallery. Free tickets are issued from the information desk in the lobby on a first-come, first-served basis. In theory, the tickets are handed out at 10:30 AM and 3:30 PM. In practice there are liable to be long delays. Security concerns are paramount, particularly since the discovery of several letter bombs addressed to U.N. personnel in January 1997, and sometimes no tickets will be issued at all, even if you have been waiting all day.

The General Assembly in session. The immense hall can accommodate delegations from up to 179 countries, and proceedings are conducted in six official languages

■ **The gridlock that ensues whenever heads of state arrive to take their places at the United Nations now seems such an established part of New York life that it is easy to forget that the organization came within a whisker of opting for Philadelphia as its permanent home. What is more, present-day budget problems are causing the U.N. to reassess not only its expenditure but also its continued presence in the Big Apple.** ■

The United Nations Charter was signed by representatives of 50 countries in San Francisco in April 1945, but the General Assembly convened its first meeting in London in 1946, a year during which the scramble among several cities to become the organization's permanent base grew intense. San Francisco, Boston, and Philadelphia were in the running before New York's application to become the U.N.'s home was instigated by the city's most famous (some would say most infamous) planning department chief, Robert Moses, who promised that a successful bid "would make New York the center of the world."

Philadelphia or New York? Among those on the city's campaign committee was Nelson Rockefeller, of the Rockefeller banking dynasty, who was carving a political career for himself with the ambition of becoming president. Rockefeller persuaded U.N. officials to use New York as their base when sizing up the rival bids during 1946, but by December it seemed that Philadelphia would be chosen, and that city's authorities began preparing the future U.N. site. Meanwhile, property developer William Zeckendorf had been buying land alongside New York's East River for residential use. Rockefeller made Zeckendorf an offer he could not refuse for the land, presented the site to the U.N. officials and won the bid—the land being paid for with an $8½ million grant from Rockefeller's father. The complex of buildings was completed in 1963, designed by an international team of architects led by William K. Harrison.

Mixed feelings Although not all New Yorkers could see the wisdom of diverting their taxes into easing the U.N.'s arrival and providing incentives for its diplomats, the organization's presence took the city's prestige through the roof and injected millions into its economy.

Overstaffing and well-publicized expenses abuses caused streamlining to be ordered in 1992, and the U.N. Children's Fund and U.N. Development Program considered leaving bases for rent-free accommodations elsewhere. Meanwhile, in a move certain to gain the favor of New Yorkers (and encourage their support in a forthcoming election), mayor Giuliani announced in 1997 that U.N. officials would no longer be able to claim diplomatic immunity when issued with parking tickets.

Considered by many to be New York's most boring building, the U.N. Secretariat towers above the East River and is home to the organization's huge administrative machine

Gracie Mansion, official residence of the Mayor of New York, echoes the opulent feel of the Upper East Side

Museum Mile
The Upper East Side holds almost all of New York's finest museums on a stretch of Fifth Avenue that has become known as Museum Mile. From 79th Street going north, you will find the Metropolitan Museum of Art, the Guggenheim Museum, the Cooper-Hewitt Museum, the Jewish Museum, and the Museum of the City of New York. Just outside the officially defined mile are the Frick Collection on 70th Street, the Whitney Museum of American Art on Madison Avenue, and Museo del Barrio on 104th Street.

▶▶▶ **Upper East Side**   *151D3*

Manhattan is money-mad, but nowhere is the sheer pleasure of being incalculably wealthy so clearly evident as amid the mansions, high-rent apartment houses and ultrachic shops of the Upper East Side, synonymous for a century with the kind of lifestyle only a bottomless bank account can buy.

A vacant space until the creation of Central Park and Manhattan's steady northward population shift made it ripe for development, the Upper East Side's first homes were modest affairs alongside new elevated train lines that ran above Park Avenue, and the streets to its east, from the 1870s.

By the 1890s, the city's wealthiest people began eyeing the two-block corridor formed by Fifth and Madison avenues. The richest of the rich erected grand mansions in styles ranging from mock-Gothic to imitation Italian Renaissance along the former, while the merely very rich moved into the fine brownstone town houses constructed along the latter.

With a few exceptions, such as the 64-room former home of Andrew Carnegie (now the Cooper-Hewitt Museum) and that of Henry Clay Frick (site of the Frick Collection), the Fifth Avenue mansions were demolished during the 1920s to make way for the luxury apartment houses that stand here now, their windows giving priceless views over Central Park and their entrances guarded by white-gloved doormen.

Through the 1950s, the Madison Avenue brownstones were steadily converted to stores and offices, and now

Walk Art and elegance

Giving a taste of the Upper East Side's elegance and taking in several interesting but often overlooked buildings, this walk also includes a couple of important art collections.

Begin on 65th Street at **Temple Emanu-El**, a 1929 synagogue with space for 2,500 people. Its design incorporates Romanesque and Byzantine features symbolizing the mixing of East and West. Two blocks

UPPER EAST SIDE

Temple Emanu-El

east and to the north, the red-brick **Seventh Regiment Armory** was built in 1880. Its drill hall is used for shows and sales, and some rooms were decorated by Louis Comfort Tiffany.

Ahead, on Park Avenue, is the **Asia Society** building (page 65), west of which stands **St. James' Episcopal Church**, dating from 1884 but given its two tiers of stained-glass windows and impressive reredos during a 1924 rebuilding. Facing Fifth Avenue, the former mansion home of Henry Clay Frick holds the **Frick Collection**, mostly of European Old Masters (page 110). By contrast, four blocks north and to the east, the very best of modern American art is the specialty of the **Whitney Museum** (page 191).

fashionably groomed locals patronize the art galleries, antique stores and designer clothing outlets of one of the nation's most exclusive—and expensive—commercial strips.

Strolling Madison Avenue dreamily window-shopping and eavesdropping on neighborhood banter is the perfect way to acclimatize yourself to Upper East Side life.

Further reasons to come to this area are the so-called Museum Mile (see the panel), and Gracie Mansion—the official residence of New York's mayors since 1942 (see page 111).

■ **"He adored New York City. He idolized it out of all proportion."** These lines from the opening of Woody Allen's *Manhattan* could easily be applied to the director himself, whose films have regularly celebrated New York and its inhabitants—and done so more convincingly than perhaps any other filmmaker. ■

Woody Allen versus Mia Farrow
In the summer of 1992, New York was gripped by the acrimony between Allen and his long-time companion Mia Farrow, following her allegations of child abuse and the revelation that Allen had had an affair with Soon-Yi, Farrow's 21-year-old adopted daughter. In June 1993, Allen was found not guilty of abusing Dylan, the couple's 7-year-old adopted daughter, but was banned from seeing her for six months.

In 1942, the six-year-old Allen Konigsberg rode the subway from Brooklyn with his father and emerged onto 42nd Street. He would later recall that he was "in love with Manhattan from the earliest memory."

Home to New York By the mid-1950s, Konigsberg had become Woody Allen and was working as a TV gag-writer in Los Angeles when (legend has it) he proposed by phone to his Brooklyn sweetheart because he needed someone to go with to see *Casablanca* on the weekend.

Meanwhile, Lenny Bruce and Mort Sahl had reshaped stand-up comedy and paved the way for the stage-shy Allen to progress swiftly from playing tiny Greenwich Village nightspots to becoming a major figure on the national comedy circuit.

A television appearance by Allen led to his (by then ex-) wife mounting an unsuccessful $1 million lawsuit for defamation of character, but Allen's anti-wife jokes did not prevent him from remarrying, this time to an Upper East Sider through whom he claimed to have assumed "citizenship of Manhattan."

The films Allen's first film to give New York a starring role was *Annie Hall* (1977). It marked a break from his earlier pastiche movies: in it Allen cast himself as a stand-up comic and writer devoted to New York but hopelessly ill at ease in Los Angeles.

Two years later, from its George Gershwin soundtrack to its outstanding monochrome photography, *Manhattan* was as much an ode to New York as it was a tale of the "emotional alienation of the Manhattan intelligentsia." The key scenes unfolded in Central Park, the Whitney Museum of American Art, and the New York Aquarium.

In 1984, *Broadway Danny Rose* described the life of a New York theatrical agent through anecdotes recounted at the Carnegie Deli.

Allen's best New York film to date, however, was *Hannah and Her Sisters* (1986), exploring the complex relationships of a group of upper-middle-class Manhattan intellectuals. City scenes are cleverly used to underscore their dilemmas.

WOODY ALLEN'S

MANHATTAN

▶▶ The Upper West Side   151D1

Between the modernism of Lincoln Center and the turn-of-the-century mood of the Columbia University campus, the largely residential Upper West Side has remained solidly bourgeois over the past hundred years.

Still standing in a neat cluster around 72nd Street are some of the city's first luxury apartment houses. The Dakota, the earliest of them all, is described on page 96. Another one which is worth a glance is the Kenilworth Apartments, at the corner of Central Park West and 75th Street. The limestone twirls decorating its facade bring fresh meaning to the term "wedding-cake architecture." Elsewhere, gracefully aging town houses cover large sections of the area and, close to the Hudson River, several streets hold picturesque Queen Anne-style homes.

While its buildings remain, recent decades have seen marked changes in the Upper West Side's social make-up. The park-facing apartments along Central Park West have always been occupied by the well-to-do, but much of what became Lincoln Center was a slum during the 1950s, and not by accident was it chosen as the site of the 1960 film *West Side Story*.

The Nicolas Roerich Museum
Born in Russia in 1874, Nicolas Roerich's life was devoted to art, archeology, and philosophy. In 1929, his "Peace through Culture" banner, intended to indicate and safeguard cultural monuments and institutions during times of war, earned him a Nobel Peace Prize nomination.

The Nicolas Roerich Museum (319 West 107th Street) remembers this remarkable character with a few of his books and possessions and many of his enigmatic paintings, often depicting a lone figure striving to find enlightenment amid Himalayan landscapes.

Lincoln Center's arrival was followed by an influx of academics and media folk—many of them fleeing the rising rents of Greenwich Village. They have made the Upper West Side a liberal and cultured enclave boasting bookstores, cafés, and some fashionable bars. Other new arrivals are high-earning professionals with young children, taking advantage of the neighborhood's proximity to the green vistas and playgrounds of nearby Central Park and Riverside Park.

The American Museum of Natural History is one of the Upper West Side's main draws for visitors. From it you are well placed for further exploration on foot. Aim also to investigate the curious Nicolas Roerich Museum, on the northern edge of the Upper West Side (see the panel).

Central Park West from the bridge on the Lake. The Dakota and other prestigious apartment houses arrayed along here have much-prized views over the park

U.S. CUSTOM HOUSE

▶ **U.S. Custom House** *104A2*

Broadway at Bowling Green
Subway: 4; Bowling Green

On the site of Fort Amsterdam, Manhattan's first permanent European settlement, the 1907 former U.S. Custom House is an eloquent Beaux-Arts statement designed by the previously unknown Cass Gilbert.

The Custom House cost a staggering $7 million, but at the time of its construction, customs revenue was the biggest contributor to the Treasury's coffers. New York's customs—with the city established as a major seaport—were the most lucrative of all.

Heavily endowed inside and out with symbols of maritime trade, the building has at its entrance several Corinthian columns topped by the head of the Roman god of commerce and holds a frieze etched with dolphins, anchors, masts, and other nautical emblems.

Raised on pedestals on the Custom House's steps, four limestone sculptures by Daniel Chester French (best known for his statue of Abraham Lincoln in Washington, D.C.) represent the four great trading continents: Asia contemplating her navel, Europe looking to the past, Africa an unknown quantity—and America, lively enough to leap from her seat and sprint across Bowling Green.

Inside, the building is capped by an impressive rotunda and decorated by a series of 16 frescoes by Reginald Marsh, commissioned by the Works Progress Administration, a government office that created work for American artists and writers during the Depression. It shows the travels of American explorers and—much more interestingly—an ocean liner docking in New York, with Greta Garbo among the disembarking passengers.

The U.S. Custom Service moved to the World Trade Center in 1973, and the building was closed. One section, ironically in a building packed with markers to the glories of commerce, reopened as the city's bankruptcy court.

Since 1994, the U.S. Custom House has been the home of the National Museum of the American Indian (see pages 164–165).

Though no longer used by U.S. Customs, the lavishly built Custom House at Bowling Green stands as testimony to the prosperity that maritime trade once brought to New York

▶▶ **Whitney Museum of American Art**   *187B1*

Madison Avenue at 75th Street
Subway: 6; 77th Street

In one form or another, the Whitney Museum has ignored fashion, upset critics, baffled the general public, and been single-minded in its devotion to supporting emerging American artists for eight decades. It now finds itself in possession of some of the most important names—and works—of 20th-century art.

Wealthy would-be sculptor Gertrude Vanderbilt Whitney began supporting young artists in the 1910s, purchasing and displaying their output at her Greenwich Village studio. During the 1920s, she presided over the Whitney Studio Club, a celebrated art forum that displayed the output of Edward Hopper, Stuart Davis, and John Sloan.

These and other Whitney-backed artists emerged as major creative forces in contemporary American art, though they did not do much to impress the Metropolitan Museum of Art, who rejected Whitney's offer of her personal collection in 1929. The snub encouraged Whitney to found her own museum, which moved to its present home—a severe rectangular block of granite-clad reinforced concrete designed by Marcel Breuer—in 1966.

Now as much as ever, the Whitney pitches its energies towards chronicling current developments and supporting new American artists. First held in 1932 (and continuing in odd-numbered years), the Whitney Biennial continues to be a controversial, invitational exhibition of the country's latest trends—often meeting the mixed response that greeted Gertrude Whitney's earliest buys.

Throughout the year, temporary exhibitions are drawn from the extensive permanent stock, often to highlight the work of a single artist. For most visitors, however, the Highlights of the Whitney Gallery, a chronological run-through of the gems among the museum's holdings, is the big draw. Claes Oldenburg, Mark Rothko, Jasper Johns, Georgia O'Keeffe, Roy Lichtenstein, Andy Warhol, Willem de Kooning, Jackson Pollock, and Edward Hopper are just a few of many notables sure to be represented.

Most of the big names of 20th-century American art are represented at the Whitney Museum

The Whitney branch museums
In 1973, the Whitney opened its first branch museum—staging free exhibitions on special themes—in the Financial District. By the late 1980s it had four such branches elsewhere in Manhattan (and another one in Connecticut). Sadly, the effects of the recession have left just one branch museum remaining in the city: at the Philip Morris Building, 120 Park Avenue.

WOOLWORTH BUILDING

F. W. Woolworth

Rags-to-riches stories are seldom more spectacular than that of Frank Winfield Woolworth. He began his retail career as a humble clerk during the mid-1800s—an era when customers had to approach staff to ask about merchandise and, as likely as not, haggle over a price. In 1879, the first Woolworth five-and-dime store broke new ground by allowing customers to pick up and examine the stock, which was priced at either 5¢ or 10¢. By the time the Woolworth Building was commissioned, Woolworth presided over 2,000 stores and was able to uphold their no-credit credo by paying for the building in cash—a total of $13½ million.

Stroll: Battery Park area

After visiting the World Trade Center, take a stroll towards the Hudson River, stopping by the palm-tree-decorated atrium of the World Financial Center and then continuing to the riverside Esplanade of Battery Park City.

Symbol of a world-famous empire: the Woolworth Building

▶▶▶ **Woolworth Building**   *104C2*

Broadway between Barclay Street and Park Place
Subway: 2, 3; Park Place

Nowadays dwarfed—but not outshone—by the nearby towers of the World Trade Center, the Woolworth Building became the world's tallest building on its completion in 1913, when its 800-foot-high tower, with Gothic pinnacles, canopies, and gargoyles, became an instant city landmark. The Woolworth Building retained its title of "world's tallest" until it was overtaken by the Chrysler Building in 1929.

Commissioned by F.W. Woolworth as a headquarters for his ultralucrative chain of 2,000 five-and-dime stores, the building was designed by Cass Gilbert (also responsible for the U.S. Custom House, see page 190) and officially opened by President Woodrow Wilson. He flicked a switch in the White House to bathe the building—nicknamed "the Cathedral of Commerce" by a commentator of the time—in the glow of 80,000 light bulbs.

The exterior may be impressive, but the lobby—one of the richest in New York—is the real treat. Step inside to admire the blue, green, and gold mosaics on the vaulted ceiling, wonder at the grand marble staircase, and look for the sculptured caricatures of Woolworth (counting his change) and Gilbert (holding a model of the building), alongside others.

The building is still owned by the Woolworth company, which gave it a much-needed general overhaul during the 1980s.

► **World Trade Center** 104C1

Church Street between Liberty and Vesey streets
Subway: E; World Trade Center

Reaching more than a quarter-mile above Lower Manhattan, the twin towers of architect Minoru Yamasaki's World Trade Center became the world's tallest building in 1973. Although the W.T.C.'s height was topped by Chicago's Sears Tower in 1974 and it has the least aesthetic appeal of New York's better-known skyscrapers, the towers' unadorned, stainless-steel bodies expressing monotony on a massive scale and serving to make the bland TV mast, atop the southernmost tower, look positively thrilling.

The roof of the World—1,350ft. up, on the 110th floor

A curious fact
From the southern tower's rooftop observation level, the northerly tower of the World Trade Center is farther away than it is at ground level—an effect caused by the curvature of the earth.

Yet more than a million visitors come here each year—not for the architecture but for the views from the observation deck. Tickets are available from the concourse level of the southernmost tower. An unexpected bonus is the elevator that speeds to the 107th floor in 58 seconds flat: you may not feel the elevator move, but you will feel the air pressure change.

The south, west, and east sides of the enclosed observation deck give a panoramic view far beyond Manhattan; only looking north does the view encompass what you can see from the Empire State Building—Midtown skyscrapers are toy-like, not seemingly near enough to touch (as they are uptown), and Central Park is just a big patch of green. An escalator winds up farther still to the vertiginous open rooftop level (closed in bad weather).

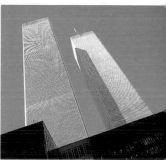

The towers are but two of the seven buildings that make up the World Trade Center, set around a 5-acre plaza that is the site of free open-air concerts in summer and holds sculptures—by Fritz Koenig, James Rosati, and Masayuki Nagare—unsuccessfully intended to humanize the scale of the complex.

A better place to escape the feelings of architecture-gone-out-of-control is on the subterranean level, where an assortment of stores and restaurants serves the practical needs of the 50,000 people who work in the World Trade Center towers—employees of the many companies who rent the center's 10 million square feet of office space. Six people died and more than 1,000 were injured when a bomb exploded in an underground parking lot in February 1993. It was believed to have been planted by Muslim fundamentalists.

Adult

World Trade Center Observation Deck

Excursions

Riverside living in the tranquil surroundings of the Hudson Valley. It is hard to believe the frenetic streets of New York City are barely 30 miles away

Their affluent forebears may have had summer residences the length and breadth of the state, but many New Yorkers today go weak at the knees at the thought of leaving the familiar confines of the great metropolis and venturing beyond the commuter belt that girdles the city.

Those who take the plunge, however, are rarely less than pleasantly surprised. Within an hour's drive of Manhattan's seething streets lies a countryside thick with placid villages and abundant in blissfully rural vistas, some of which have barely changed since the times of Dutch settlement.

The Hudson Valley North of the city, the Hudson River flows through the 140-mile-long Hudson Valley (see pages 200–205). Once the major transit route into New York from New England, the river was of great strategic importance during the Revolutionary War, and several forts were founded along its course, one of which evolved into the famous Military Academy at West Point.

Though the battle sites remain, the valley no longer echoes to the sound of musket fire: its verdant hillsides and farmlands, studded with vineyards and orchards, are the embodiment of pastoral tranquility. These are the scenes that inspired the nation's first homegrown art movement, the Hudson River School; many examples of the artists' work can be seen in the region's museums.

Within the valley's nooks and crannies are many surprises: stately American Gothic homes, millionaires' mansions, and the homes of Washington Irving (author of *Rip Van Winkle*), and Samuel F.B. Morse, the inventor of Morse code. The valley concludes with the urban jungle (relatively speaking) of Albany, capital of New York State.

The Catskill Mountains Halfway up the Hudson Valley, the Catskill Mountains loom to the west (see pages 196-199). The highest peak in the Catskills, Slide Mountain, reaches only slightly above 4,000 feet, and rather than providing scope for rock-climbers, the so-called mountains—their sides coated by pine forests and cut by tumbling streams—provide a postcard-perfect natural setting for the dozens of tiny communities enclosed in their folds. The rounded tops of the mountains are a legacy of the last ice-age, as are the deep gorges that sometimes hold spectacular waterfalls.

Photogenic views are abundant on the lanes that wind around the hills, and the Catskills' largest village, Woodstock, has a reputation for arts, crafts, and culture stretching back to the early part of the century. With streets lined by clapboard homes and dozens of galleries and craft stores displaying and selling locally produced works, Woodstock is a lovely place to succumb to the Catskills' rural pace, and its sidewalk cafés are prime vantage points for people-watching.

Long Island With its south coast bordered by the Atlantic Ocean and its north coast by the Long Island Sound, the appropriately named Long Island (see pages 206–211) runs for 125 miles east from New York City, becoming progressively less populated as it does so.

Farming and seafaring were the traditional staples of Long Island life, but New Yorkers began frequenting the south shore's fine beaches a century ago: a group of pretty seaside villages called the Hamptons became a summer retreat for the wealthy, and to this day they remain a vacation destination for affluent beach lovers.

There are more excellent beaches along the protected dune-covered sand spit of Fire Island, though many of Long Island's more intriguing stops are on the north shore, where old whaling centers and immaculately preserved farming villages nestle among mansion homes built for families such as the Roosevelts and the Vanderbilts.

Clear skies, cool temperatures, and fall colors make autumn a good time for touring the Catskills

195

Car rental and public transportation
In the following pages, the excursions are described on the assumption that you are traveling by car. Note, though, that you will save money by renting a car outside New York City. All the main towns of the Hudson Valley and Long Island are well served by public transportation and have offices of the major car-rental companies, so it makes sense to rent once you have arrived. A healthy alternative is to combine public transportation with exploration by bicycle. Bike-rental outlets are plentiful in most towns during the summer. To discover the best of the Catskill Mountains, however, you will certainly need a car.

Drive Catskill Mountains

This drive goes from Kingston to Saugerties, twice crossing the ear-popping Catskill highlands and passing some of the region's most interesting villages along the way.

The drive takes you through the popular village of Woodstock and continues through several smaller towns, skirting forested hillsides beneath high peaks.

The breathtaking scenery is found on the drive's eastward leg, on Route 23A, as it climbs from Prattsville to Hunter—famous for its winter skiing and summer festivals. An alternative route from Prattsville would take you to East Durham, worth a detour for its two museums.

The final stretch of the drive descends sharply into the Hudson Valley towards the serene village of Saugerties. A lovely, seldom crowded place, with quaint antique stores and preserved homes, Saugerties is also within easy reach of Slabsides, the log cabin of venerated local naturalist John Burroughs.

The points of interest you will pass along the route are covered in detail on pages 197–199.

196

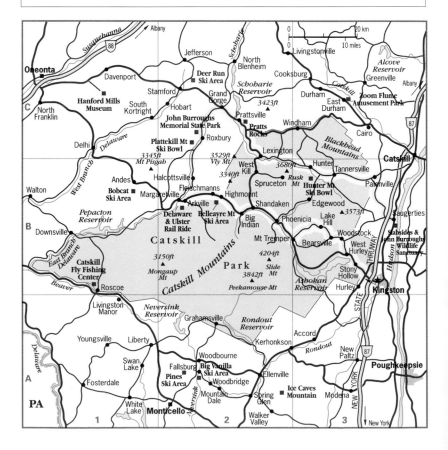

Kingston and Hurley While forest-covered hills and tiny villages secreted along winding lanes are what the Catskills are really all about, the region's largest town, Kingston▶▶, should not be overlooked. Kingston began as a Dutch trading post in 1616. By the mid-1700s it had evolved into a significant commercial base and during the Revolutionary War it became the first capital of New York state.

At 312 Fair Street is the **Senate House State Historic Site▶**, which has been restored to its 1777 style to mark Kingston's two months as the seat of statehood; the senate swiftly moved south as the British approached from the north. An adjoining building displays a selection of paintings by locally born Hudson River artist John Vanderlyn and a few by his peers.

The Senate House is one of several 17th- and 18th-century Dutch-built stone houses that occupy the Stockade District, within fortifications erected in 1658 to protect the town from Native American attack. The same area holds the **Urban Culture Park Visitor Center▶▶**, outlining Kingston's history, and stands within easy reach of the **Old Dutch Church▶**. Though built in 1852, the church was founded in 1659, and its cemetery bears Dutch tombs from that time.

Kingston's second historical area is the river-front **Rondout** district, where the indoor and outdoor exhibits of the **Hudson River Maritime Museum** chronicle the town's heyday as a boat-building and river trade center.

Like Kingston, **Hurley▶**, a few miles west, enjoyed a brief spell as the state capital during 1777 and retains more than its share of Dutch-built stone houses. Ten such dwellings stand along Main Street, whose occupants open their doors for public inspection on the second Saturday in July. If you happen to be passing through on any other summer day, the restored 18th-century **Hurley Patentee Manor** is the place to head for.

New Paltz
New Paltz, south of Kingston on Route 32, was settled in 1677 by a refugee community of French Huguenots. They were no slouches at home building, and six of their houses remain in excellent condition along the appropriately named Huguenot Street. From the 1692 Deyo House, the local historical society leads tours of the homes, furnished in period style and giving an inkling of the trials and tribulations of local 17th-century life.

On Route 42 near Shandaken

Woodstock The best-known and busiest of the Catskill villages, Woodstock▶▶▶ (8 miles west of Kingston on Highway 212) gave its name to the legendary rock festival of 1969, even though the actual gathering took place 60 miles away. Nonetheless, if the festival had taken place here, it would have been well in keeping with the village's long-established Bohemian character.

Hunter and its festivals
New Yorkers know Hunter (north of Woodstock on Route 214) best as a ski resort, but when the snow leaves the slopes of Hunter Mountain the area kicks into its summer season with a series of festivals remarkable for their diversity. Early July finds an Italian festival, closely followed by a German Alps festival, and the first part of a country music festival. August sees the National Polka Festival, a Celtic festival, the second part of the country music festival, and a Golden Oldies festival. Rounding out the season is the Mountain Eagle Native American Indian Festival, in early September.

In the early 1900s, an Englishman inspired by the Utopian ideals of John Ruskin and William Morris founded the **Byrdcliffe Arts Colony** on a 30-acre site in the hills around Woodstock (look for the signposted road off Highway 212). Artists and artisans arriving to live and work in the studios helped create a rich program of cultural events in the village, a tradition which continues into the present day.

West from Woodstock Continuing deeper into the Catskill hills, the roads weave between peaks and pass tiny villages such as **Phoenicia** and **Shandaken**, where white-water rafting and a rich sprinkling of gourmet-class French restaurants are the main sources of local income. Both appeal to well-heeled weekending New Yorkers, who regard this area as their own piece of heaven.

On the western side of the Catskills, **Arkville** offers a touch more diversity with the **Delaware & Ulster Rail Ride▶**, a 12-mile segment of a historic railroad that makes a touristy but extremely photogenic jaunt to Halcottsville and back, several times a day.

Roxbury and Prattsville North of Arkville, **Roxbury** acquired the **Jay Gould Memorial Reform Church** in 1892. This imposing structure of limestone and oak was erected by the children of the unloved robber baron Gould, who was born here in 1836.

CATSKILL MOUNTAINS

A more worthwhile call is to the **John Burroughs Memorial State Park►**, 2 miles west. Here the Catskills' foremost naturalist was born in 1837 and was buried in 1921. Burroughs accompanied the likes of Theodore Roosevelt, Thomas Edison, and Henry Ford on camping trips into the Catskills and introduced the wonders of its nature to many more in his informative writings.

Named after local tannery-owner Zadock Pratt, **Prattsville►►** claims to be the first planned community in the country and backs up this assertion with some excellently maintained 1830s houses. One of them, the home of Pratt himself, now stores the local history collections of the commendable **Zadock Pratt Museum►**.

In **East Durham** on the Catskills' northern edge, an entertaining collection of farm tools, fossils, Native American artifacts, military paraphernalia, and household furnishings makes up the **Durham Center Museum►**, inside a former schoolhouse built in 1825. The Catskills' most bizarre souvenirs are also to be found in East Durham: ornaments made from real butterflies, produced at the **Butterfly Art Museum►**. Founded by a lepidoptera-crazed German immigrant who arrived here in 1932, the museum has an extensive collection of mounted butterflies and a less exotic-looking batch of preserved beetles. In complete contrast, the watery rides of the **Zoom Flume Amusement Park►** close by on Shady Glen Road are the perfect way to keep cool on a hot day.

Not far from **Saugerties**, back in the Hudson Valley (off Route 9W near West Park) is Slabsides and the peaceful woodlands of the **John Burroughs Wildlife Park►**.

Left, right, and below: aspects of Woodstock, the classic Catskills village

Pratt Rocks
Just outside Prattsville on Route 23, are the Pratt Rocks, which carry engravings depicting Pratt and his horse. They were commissioned by Zadock Pratt during the 1860s, to enable an itinerant stone-cutter to earn the money to pay for lodgings.

199

 **Hudson Valley**

Ever-changing views of the Hudson River and its tree-studded valley will guarantee lasting memories of this drive.

See map opposite.

Take two or even three days to make the most of the route, visiting some of the valley's many unique communities and historic homes—some of which have been a feature of the Hudson Valley region since its earliest European settlement. The drive ends at Albany, New York's capital and one of the few Hudson Valley towns where modern buildings are as much in evidence as those from times long past.

The points of interest you will pass along the route are covered in detail on pages 200–205.

The Philipsburg Manor, north of Tarrytown: scenes of rural New York life during the 17th century

▶▶ **Hudson Valley**

Yonkers to Tarrytown Although it is entirely unrepresentative of the pastoral scenes farther to the north, industrial **Yonkers** should be your first stop out of New York City on the Sawmill River Parkway or via Metro North (taxis at every train stop will transport you locally for

Sunnyside, home of author Washington Irving, is one of several preserved buildings near Tarrytown

a few dollars). The evocative Hudson River School land-scapes gracing Yonkers' **Hudson River Museum►** will whet your appetite for what lies ahead.

Nearby, a taste of Hudson Valley history is provided by the stone-built **Philipse Manor►**, where Frederick Philipse III—grandson of a Dutch settler who made a fortune through shipping and slavery—led a life of ease until he was imprisoned during the Revolutionary War for supporting the British. The final insult to Philipse could well be the rows of presidential portraits that now hang above his former furnishings in the manor's museum.

Farther north on Route 9, just south of Tarrytown, a neo-Gothic castle, complete with towers, spires, and battlements, stands beside the river, screened by woodlands. Known as **Lyndhurst►►**, the exuberant structure is among the finest examples of American Gothic architecture and is the work of the genre's leading practitioner, Alexander Jackson Davis.

Built in 1838, Lyndhurst was purchased by the despised robber baron Jay Gould in 1880. To his credit, Gould maintained the building well, and his descendants lived here until 1961. A feast for the eye, the building sits in 64 acres of sumptuously landscaped grounds, and its interior is filled by a grand collection of Victoriana. As Lyndhurst was nearing completion, author Washington Irving moved into a far less ostentatious dwelling a mile away at **Sunnyside►►** adding Dutch gables and a Romanesque tower to a 17th-century farmers' cottage. Guided tours explore the 17 rooms where the creator of *Rip Van Winkle* and *The Legend of Sleepy Hollow* spent the later years of his life. Besides becoming the U.S.'s first internationally known fiction writer, Irving was also a useful plumber: the taps fixed to his bathtub and the hot water tank in his kitchen were major innovations.

A short detour on Route 9 north of Tarrytown takes in the **Philipsburg Manor►►**, where you can see a reconstruction of the 17th-century mill at the heart of the Philipse family's empire. With livestock scurrying across the yard and the gristmill and granary in operation, the tours led by guides in 1750s attire are informative and fun.

Little more than a pitchfork's throw from the manor, the **Old Dutch Church▶** was built at the direction of Frederick Philipse I in 1697. Except during services, it is rarely possible to enter the church. The cemetery is intriguing, however: alongside the tombs of numerous Dutch settlers are those of Andrew Carnegie and Washington Irving. The headless hero of Irving's *Legend of Sleepy Hollow* arose from his eternal slumbers here.

Tarrytown to West Point On the Hudson's west bank, accessible via the Tappan Zee Bridge (1-287 west) Route 9W passes close to the village of **Nyack▶**, birthplace of the great American realist artist Edward Hopper in 1882. The artist spent much of his life here, at what is now the **Hopper House Arts Center** (82 North Broadway). His finest canvases are hung in prestigious museums elsewhere, but devotees will find a few of his local landscapes here, plus a large number of souvenir prints and books.

Farther north off Route 9W is the **Stony Point Battlefield State Historic Site▶**, the remains of a British fort attacked and captured in a daredevil midnight raid by General "Mad" Anthony Wayne in 1779. A small visitors' center describes the battle and its significance: Wayne's derring-do greatly increased the prestige of the American forces and earned him a Congressional gold medal.

Beyond Stony Point, Route 9W climbs into the **Hudson Highlands**: an area of rare beauty, where the river narrows and the increasingly sheer tree-clad valley walls are studded with exposed rock.

Route 218 wends a scenic route above the river, passing through the **United States Military Academy** at **West Point▶**. Since 1802, West Point has sought to instill discipline, moral fiber, and leadership qualities into its

---

The naming of Tarrytown
According to author Washington Irving, local Dutch wives were responsible for the naming of Tarrytown. It was "due to the inveterate propensity of their husbands to linger about the village tavern on market day." Less romantically inclined sources suggest the name was a corruption of the Dutch word for wheat, *Tarwe*.

The campus of the Military Academy at West Point. Visitors here can stroll in the footsteps of many famous Americans

cadets. Numerous presidents, generals, and astronauts have graduated from here; even among the drop-outs there have been some famous names, such as 19th-century author Edgar Allan Poe and the late Timothy Leary, the LSD guru of the 1960s.

Ports of call here include the **West Point Museum**, room after room of mementos—guns, flags, uniforms, medals, and more—from every conflict that has ever involved the U.S.; the remains of the Revolutionary-era **Fort Putnam**, perched 450 feet above the Hudson; and the **Drill Ground** (known as the "**Plain**"), where some of West Point's 4,000 cadets may sometimes be seen marching with geometric precision.

West Point to Poughkeepsie At **Newburgh**, the next major settlement, George Washington occupied a stone dwelling, built by Dutch settler Jonathan Hasbrouck, at 84 Liberty Street during the 16 months between the British surrender and the signing of the peace accord in Paris. Preserved as **Washington's Headquarters/ Jonathan Hasbrouck House►**, the house is one of several 18th- and 19th-century homes that make a short stroll around the town worthwhile.

A better picture of the stresses of the Revolutionary period is provided by the **New Windsor Cantonment State Historic Site►►**, southwest of Newburgh near Vails Gate. Here, 10,000 of Washington's troops were accommodated in log cabins at the end of the war; only a speech by Washington himself quelled a mutiny in their ranks. During the summer months, local history buffs re-create bygone scenes here, some of them making loud bangs with replica Revolutionary-era weaponry.

North of Newburgh lie the foothill villages of the Catskill Mountains. In complete contrast, on the east bank of the Hudson is **Poughkeepsie**, founded by Native Americans and now struggling to keep a grip on its past as shopping malls and new housing developments swiftly turn it into quintessential suburbia. One venerable institution from Poughkeepsie's past that remains is **Vassar College►**, founded in 1881 as an all-women's college. It was the first campus to feature a museum and art gallery; in the art museum today you will find some very minor works by Rembrandt and Whistler sharing wall space with noteworthy Hudson River School landscapes.

Nothing out of place: the Plain, West Point's parade ground

Vassar College
Strange as it may seen, profits from the production of beer helped fund Vassar College—founded in 1861 by local brewer Matthew Vassar. The intention of the rich and philanthropic Vassar was to offer women the liberal arts education that was available to men. The college did begin to admit men in 1969, although its student body remains overwhelmingly female. Besides male students, another comparatively recent addition is the Frances Lehman Loeb Art Center, built by architect Cesar Pelli, to house the college's artworks. Pelli is better known for the far grander World Financial Center in Manhattan.

The Shakers
Founded in 1747, the Shakers—so named for the ecstatic trembling that followed their ritualistic dances—became one of the largest and most respected of the religious cults of the post-Revolutionary era. By the 1840s, more than 4,000 Shakers were living in twenty Shaker villages spread from Maine to Kentucky. Shaker skills and craftsmanship had enormous impact on rural America, and the sect's many inventions included the flat-headed broom, the wooden clothespin, and the circular saw. They also introduced the selling of garden seeds in sealed packets. Increasing wealth led to conflict within Shaker communities, which steadily declined from 1875. Many Shakers, however, retained their beliefs until death.

Albany's eggshell
What looks like a gigantic upturned eggshell in the center of Albany is in fact the home of E.S.I.P.A., or Empire State Institute for the Performing Arts. Inside, the eggshell has seating for 900 and a regular program of varied musical and theatrical events.

A 2-mile detour south from Poughkeepsie on Route 9 leads to **Locust Grove▶▶**. The house was bought in 1847 by inventor Samuel Morse, who enlisted the aid of Alexander Jackson Davis to transform it into a Tuscan-style villa. The handsome building remains in fine fettle, and a pile of Morse's telegraph equipment shares the interior with a diverting cache of Victorian furnishings.

Poughkeepsie to Albany Morse may be remembered by the code that bears his name, but he could not match the achievements of a latter-day local, Franklin D. Roosevelt. Destined to become the nation's longest-serving president, Roosevelt was born in a clapboard house beside the Hudson in 1882, near the hamlet of Hyde Park, on Route 9 north of Poughkeepsie.

Roosevelt converted the house into a 35-room Georgian-style mansion in 1916 and used it to treat royalty and heads of state to Hudson Valley views. It is now preserved as the **Franklin D. Roosevelt National Historic Site▶▶**, and everyone is welcome to step inside and admire the Roosevelt taste in interior design.

On the grounds is the **Franklin D. Roosevelt Library and Museum▶**, which stores the presidential archive and has an exhibition on Roosevelt's life and achievements. A shuttle bus continues to the **Eleanor Roosevelt National Historic Site▶**, the house used by Roosevelt's wife Eleanor as a summer resort and as a permanent home during her widowhood.

Compared to the Roosevelts' home, the **Vanderbilt Mansion National Historic Site▶▶**, 2 miles farther north, recalls a very shallow life. Frederick W. Vanderbilt, grandson of millionaire Cornelius Vanderbilt, spent much of his life reducing the family fortune, lavishing $2 million of it on this three-story beaux-arts mansion. Inside, the Persian rugs, Flemish tapestries, and other money-is-no-object features are on public display because Vanderbilt's niece could not find a buyer for the house in 1940, even at the knockdown price of $250,000—so she donated it to the nation.

The most imaginative home in the Hudson Valley is no multimillion-dollar mansion but **Olana▶▶**, on Route 9G southwest of Hudson. An inspired mix of Moorish and Middle Eastern building styles, Olana arose in the 1870s as the home of a leading Hudson River School artist, Frederick Church. Decorated with Islamic and Byzantine motifs, Olana's arched doors and windows frame gorgeous views—Church himself landscaped its hilltop site. The interior is packed with rugs, ornaments, and treasures from all points east.

On the final stretch toward Albany, make an eastward detour to Old Chatham, a base of the religious community of the Shakers from 1787. Living by a code of celibacy, temperance, and sharing, the Shakers' simple and superbly crafted furnishings changed the face of American applied arts. Examples are now displayed in many of the nation's museums, but the **Shaker Museum▶▶** at Old Chatham is undoubtedly the most comprehensive collection: eight buildings with numerous examples of Shaker achievements in carpentry, metalwork, and weaving. Other exhibits detail the history of the community and its beliefs.

Marking the northern end of the Hudson Valley is Albany►►, which boomed during the 18th century as a trade and transportation center, becoming New York's state capital in 1797. A thorough restoration program has kept many of Albany's 19th-century buildings in good order but what dominates the town center is the 1960s white marble modernism of **Empire State Plaza**, whose quarter-mile-long pedestrian walkway is decorated by free-form sculpture. Take the elevator to the observation gallery on the 42nd floor of the plaza's tallest building, the **Corning Tower►**, for views that reach far across the valley.

At ground level, the plaza runs out beneath the pink granite exterior of the 1898 **New York State Capitol►►►**, raised at a cost of $24 million and gaining French, Italian, and Romanesque features as tastes—and architects—changed during its 30 years of construction. No detail is any less ornate than it could be, a fact pointed out with relish on the hourly guided tours, which wind their way up the elegant marble staircase to the restored legislative chambers.

Across the plaza is the **New York State Museum►►►**, which uses copious exhibits and walk-through dioramas to pull together the region's history, shedding light on subjects as diverse as the geology of the Adirondacks and Manhattan's skyscraper architecture.

Though presented with less flair, there is more from the past on show at the **Albany Institute of History and Art►►** at 125 Washington Avenue. Much of it dates to the time of Dutch settlement—a feast of furniture, crockery, and aristocratic portraiture, alongside a commendable selection of Hudson River School paintings.

The state government of New York has its offices in Albany's Empire State Plaza

The Schuyler Mansion
If traveling through the valley has not exhausted your appetite for period homes, the pick of Albany's stately residences is the 1762 Schuyler Mansion at 32 Catherine Street. It was built for the well-connected Philip Schuyler, a successful businessman who served with distinction as an officer during the Revolutionary War.

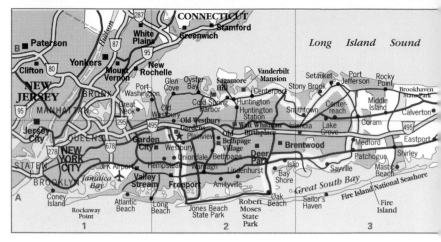

Drive Long Island

This drive takes in some of Long Island's beaches, historic homes, and atmospheric fishing ports.

From the beautifully landscaped Old Westbury Gardens, the drive continues to popular Jones Beach before passing the south-shore communities of Sayville and Patchogue. The route then passes tiny farming hamlets before reaching the picturesque villages of Setauket and Stony Brook on the north shore.

The Vanderbilt mansion can be reached down a side road off the main route, or you can continue direct to Walt Whitman's birthplace and the one-time whaling settlement of Cold Spring Harbor. The final stop is at Sagamore Hill, the stately home of Theodore Roosevelt.

The points of interest you will pass along the route, as well as other highlights of a more extended visit to Long Island, are covered in detail on pages 207–211.

The beaches on Long Island's south shore are extensive enough to absorb any number of vacationing New Yorkers

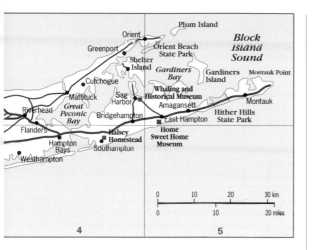

▶ **Long Island**

Old Westbury and Old Bethpage Much of western Long Island is now seamless suburbia criss crossed by freeways, but a century ago it was still charged with rural possibilities. John S Phipps, the son of Andrew Carnegie's business partner, chose a plot near Old Westbury as the site for a rambling country estate. Phipps' red brick Westbury House was completed in 1903. Today, the 100-acre grounds, known as **Old Westbury Gardens**▶▶, are the main attraction for the green-thumbed visitors who beat a path to the wrought-iron gates. Landscaped and planted to perfection, the gardens have thousands of mature trees and an aromatic rose garden in their midst.

Long Island provides not only an escape from New York City but also, in **Old Bethpage Village**▶▶, an escape from the 20th century. Crushed-oystershell lanes lead into this re-creation of an early 1800s farming village, typical of those that dotted Long Island long before the days

Amityville
A house on a hill in Amityville, in deepest Long Island suburbia, caused its occupants to flee in terror during the early 1970s. After the subsequent book and film, both called *The Amityville Horror*, describing (and apparently greatly exaggerating) the events, were released, locals found themselves spending a lot of their time directing sightseers to the scene of the grisly goings-on. Not surprisingly, the house has proved difficult to sell over the years and still casts a strange spell over this otherwise rather ordinary community.

The William Floyd Estate
Close to Mastic Beach, where the road to eastern Fire Island meets the mainland, the William Floyd Estate is what is left of the plantation owned by General William Floyd, one of the signers of the Declaration of Independence. The simple house Floyd built in 1724 remains at the center of the 600-acre estate, greatly added to by successive generations of his descendants. The last of them lived here until 1975, while many of the others lie buried within the grounds in the family cemetery. The house's 25 rooms unfurl a fascinating tale of changing family fortunes.

The north shore of Long Island has great appeal for New Yorkers seeking a place in the country

of interstate freeways and creeping suburbia. As the village's tailor, blacksmith, quilters and storeowners go about their daily tasks, explaining them to visitors, it is hard not to be impressed by the thoroughness of it all.

Jones Beach and Fire Island Most New Yorkers hitting Long Island, however, are thinking not of old farming ways but about bronzing themselves on the south shore. On any summer weekend, **Jones Beach** is a picture of New York at play. For space and solitude make the short trip east to **Fire Island State Park▶**, which has the added appeal of a 19th-century lighthouse now employed as a visitors' center.

The 1,000-acre state park consumes the western extremity of **Fire Island▶▶**, longest of the sand spits that flank the southern shore of Long Island. Though never more than half a mile wide, Fire Island runs for 32 miles and, other than the road links near both ends, can be reached only by ferries from various points on the mainland.

All of Fire Island is public land, although several sections are dominated by private resort communities, each with its distinctive social makeup. Day-trippers are not always welcomed with open arms at the more exclusive places. One welcoming day-trip spot, which can be reached by ferry from Sayville, is **Sailor's Haven▶▶**. The fine beach, the nature trails weaving around the dunes, and the hardy vegetation forming the **Sunken Forest▶** should not be missed. A visitors' center provides absorbing background material on Fire Island's subtle ecology.

The Hamptons East of Fire Island, the settlements collectively known as the Hamptons sat placidly at the center of windmill-studded farmland until the late 19th century, when wealthy New Yorkers began discovering their vacation potential and transformed them into classy seaside resorts. The Hamptons are still a getaway for the rich but retain great charm. They also have fine beaches, chic boutiques and pricey restaurants.

Southampton▶ is one of Long Island's oldest towns, and the 1648 **Halsey Homestead▶** claims to be the oldest timber-framed house in the entire state. The best-looking of the Hamptons is **East Hampton▶▶▶**, its narrow streets bordered by neatly trimmed hedges and picket-fenced cottages. Locally born actor and dramatist John Howard Payne liked the place so much that he composed the most sentimental of songs, "Home Sweet Home," here; a fact duly acknowledged by

the preservation of his house as the **Home Sweet Home Museum**▶, mostly filled with 18th-century ceramics.

There is more to see in four buildings of impressive vintage maintained by the East Hampton Historical Society along Main Street. The most engrossing is the 1784 **Clinton Academy**▶, once a revered seat of learning and now carrying exhibitions on varied facets of local life.

Sag Harbor Unless you want to make the 20-mile drive to the eastern end of Long Island (see panel), head

Cross the Robert Moses Causeway to reach the south shore

northwest from East Hampton to **Sag Harbor**▶▶. Though few people would believe it on first sight, this sleepy waterside community was once a busy port, second only to New York City in its importance. Until 1871 it boasted the world's fourth largest whaling fleet.

Perhaps even less believably, you need to pass through a whale's jawbone framing the doorway of a former Masonic Temple to enter the town's **Whaling and Historical Museum**▶▶, where the evidence of past glories is abundant: piles of scrimshaw and nautical knick-knacks stacked to the ceiling, and a more modest assortment of household paraphernalia.

The 1789 **Custom House**▶ is another survivor of Sag Harbor's seafaring heyday, as is the **Whaler's Church**▶, built in 1841 in a curious Greek-Egyptian style. As if to mark the decline of Sag Harbor's sea trade, the church's steeple—long a navigational aid to shipping—was blown down by a hurricane in 1938.

Shelter Island A quick ferry ride (pedestrians and vehicles) north from Sag Harbor, **Shelter Island** is not only a shortcut to Long Island's north fork (a second ferry crosses to Greenport) but also a place of the utmost tranquility, where narrow, weaving lanes are flanked by Victorian cottages. A picture-postcard expression of life in the middle of nowhere, Shelter Island has nonetheless enjoyed a robust past. It was a haunt of 18th-century pirates and, during Prohibition, a landing point favored by bootleggers.

Long Island's eastern tip
If you drive east from East Hampton to Montauk, you will kick yourself for not continuing a further 5 miles to Montauk Point, the last stop before the Irish coast. A lighthouse, built on the instruction of George Washington in 1797, sits at the easternmost point. The reward for braving vertigo and dizziness to climb its 138 steps are views of Rhode Island and the Connecticut coast.

Sagamore Hill was completed in 1885 for the only U.S. president to have been born in New York City, Theodore Roosevelt; cost of the 22-room house was $16,975

Riverhead
One reason to visit Riverhead, a town off the main routes between the Hamptons and the north shore, might be the Suffolk County Museum, whose exhibits range from local Native American cultures to whaling. Another reason could be the produce of the Palmer Vineyards (make a reservation first, tel: 516/722–WINE). If you are here in mid-August, Riverhead's Polish Street Fair and Festival should not be missed.

The north shore An exploration of Long Island's north shore should begin at **Sagamore Hill►►►**, a highly desirable three-story residence set in 80 green acres just east of Oyster Bay. The house was completed in 1884 as the summer home of Theodore Roosevelt.

Two floors of the main house hold roomfuls of Victorian furnishings and an extraordinary number of Roosevelt's hunting trophies, not least the array of moose- and deerheads. The spacious but cozy wood-paneled rooms provided the setting for Roosevelt's peace-brokering between warring Russia and Japan in 1905, for which he was awarded the Nobel Peace Prize. Further exhibits, and a short film detailing Roosevelt's life, can be viewed in the adjoining Old Orchard Home Museum, which was added by Roosevelt's son in 1938.

Continuing east on Route 25A is the **Whaling Museum** at **Cold Spring Harbor►**, which remembers the nine-ship whaling fleet based here during the mid-1880s. The exhibits include one of the few existing complete whaling vessels, and numerous smaller pieces—examples of scrimshaw, harpoons, and the grisly tools used to separate blubber from bone.

When the Cold Spring Harbor whaling fleet was still sailing the high seas, Walt Whitman—born in 1819, 2 miles away in Huntington—was busy overturning the rules of traditional verse to create *Leaves of Grass*, the work that sealed his place among America's literary greats. The two-story shingled dwelling built in 1816 by Whitman's father is now the **Walt Whitman Birthplace State Historic Site►►**. One room has been reassembled as it was during Whitman's boyhood, and exhibits on the upper floor recount his adventure-filled life.

North of Centerport is the Spanish-style **Vanderbilt Mansion►**, which belonged to William K. Vanderbilt II, great-grandson of Cornelius Vanderbilt. He combined his taste for opulent living with an interest in natural history, acquiring the 17,000 specimens of stuffed and mounted creatures that make a strange addition to the antiques and original furnishings on display in this shrine to luxury living. The adjacent Vanderbilt Planetarium has views of the heavens, which fail to match those across Long Island Sound from the mansion's elegantly landscaped gardens.

Stony Brook and Setauket An almost too perfectly preserved village, Stony Brook▶▶ was saved from neglect by wealthy philanthropist Ward Melville during the 1930s. Melville also financed the **Museums at Stony Brook▶▶▶**, a complex that focuses on 19th-century Long Island life. Pride of place goes to the vintage carriages, and the paintings by William Sidney Mount, a Stony Brook resident who emerged as one of the country's most original and daring artists during the mid-1800s. First known as a portraitist, particularly noted for his painting of prominent statesmen such as Daniel Webster, Mount acquired more lasting fame by capturing rural scenes—such as farm life and village dances—on canvas, and was the first major painter to produce sympathetic images of African-Americans.

Close to Stony Brook is the similarly pretty village of Setauket▶, which was a hotbed of espionage during the revolutionary years of the late 1700s, and the birthplace of what is believed to have been the nation's first spy cell. One technique employed to outwit the occupying British troops was the conveying of messages using a local housewife's clothesline. The combination of clothing on the line corresponded to a prearranged code and did most damage—as far as the British were concerned—when used to alert George Washington to the approach of the French Expeditionary Force in 1780.

A trip to Connecticut?
Should the combination of Long Island's sea air and nautical museums give you the urge to take to the waves, you can seize the opportunity at Port Jefferson, 3 miles east of Setauket. From here, a ferry (taking both cars and pedestrians) makes the 20-mile crossing of Long Island Sound to Bridgeport in Connecticut, several times daily.

Framed by formal gardens, the 24-room Vanderbilt Mansion near Centerport sits at the heart of a 43-acre estate and provides a taste of high-class living, although most visitors come for the excellent planetarium and natural history exhibits

211

Accommodations

Hotels: the facts
The New York Convention
and Visitors' Bureau (2
Columbus Circle, New York,
NY 10019; tel: 800/NYC–VISIT
or 397–8222) publishes a
free guide to hotels listing
their addresses, phone
numbers, and prices, and
indicating their location on
a map. More opinionated
descriptions of New York
hotels can be found on
pages 262–268.

From side-street fleabags with naked lightbulbs to world-class lodgings with en suite Jacuzzi and antique furnishings, the one thing all New York hotels share is inflated prices: you will easily spend twice as much in this city as you would for similar hotel accommodations elsewhere in the U.S.

Budget hotels Any hotel room priced under about $75 is unlikely to offer anything more than the basic necessities: a roof over your head and a mattress under your back, with the bathroom likely to be a shared one at the end of a corridor and equipped with erratic plumbing.

Shabby though they may be, hotels at the rock-bottom end of the market are usually safe, though some near Times Square are an exception and should be approached with caution.

Basic comforts For $75–$150, you can expect a room to which you will be pleased to return, with color T.V. (television addicts should ensure their hotel has cable channels) and a bathroom and telephone to call your own.

As you dig deeper into your budget and spend $150–$200, rooms become larger and more elegantly furnished. The T.V. carries more channels, a good range of complimentary soaps and shampoos should be found in the bathroom, and sometimes a complimentary newspaper will be delivered to your door each morning.

Spoiling yourself To really start tasting the New York good life means kissing goodbye to at least $200 a night. Do this, and you will be able to stretch out on a cozy giant-sized bed in a matching-sized room, with a fully equipped bathroom. Further spending will be encouraged by 24-hour room service. You will, however, be spared from the irksome task of turning down your own sheets: a maid will do this, leaving a complimentary piece of chocolate on your pillow.

You will need to have a taste for opulent living, and ample funds, to enjoy a stay at the large and plush Helmsley Palace on Madison Avenue

ACCOMMODATIONS

The Warwick is just one of many comfortable hotels conveniently located in northern Midtown, where some of the city's top luxury establishments are also to be found

Hidden extras For all but the most affluent visitor, the basic rates quoted by hotels (and given above) are frightening enough. Believe it or not, there is also a string of taxes to be added: sales tax (8.25 percent), New York City hotel tax (5 percent), and a $2 occupancy tax, per room, per night.

Therefore, what might seem an $80 bargain will actually cost $92.60, and stretching your budget to its limits for a $250 treat will land you with a bill close to $285.

Not only do quoted rates not include tax, they do not usually include breakfast either. Some hotels have restaurants, but breakfasting at a nearby coffee shop is always cheaper and more fun—and is a quintessentially New York way to start the day.

Special deals Slightly better news on the financial front is that hotel prices are lower on weekends, when many establishments seek to attract suburb dwellers with cut-rate weekend deals. Such packages can bring savings of up to 40 percent on regular prices and are chiefly advertised in New York area newspapers. It is always worth inquiring whether a package is available during your stay.

A few hotels also give discounts for long stays—two weeks or more—which can bring considerable savings.

Seasonal factors New York never runs short of visitors, but the peak tourist seasons match the clemency of the weather. The prime months are April, May, and June. In the fall, many hotels are filled by some of the 1.8 million delegates who attend the city's numerous business conventions each year, and the months up to Christmas are spectacularly busy.

Even if you are arriving in the sweltering heat of summer or the freezing temperatures of January, do not turn up in New York without prearranging accommodations, at least for your first night, and do so well in advance.

Accommodations for women
Women traveling alone in New York are liable to experience problems that will not affect their male counterparts. The area west of Ninth Avenue near Times Square (where many hotels are situated) is especially unwelcoming for lone females. Another possible source of harassment is the staff of some upscale hotels who may suspect that an unaccompanied female is a prostitute. The good news is that several hotels provide safe accommodations exclusively for women (see pages 262–268 for some examples).

The Upper East Side is a fittingly exclusive setting for the art-deco Carlyle, a truly grand hotel

Credit cards
Most hotels accept credit cards as payment. All major cards are widely accepted.

The Raines Hotel Law
In an effort to cut down the level of alcohol consumption among the city's down-and-outs, the Raines Hotel Law of 1896 made it illegal to sell liquor in New York on a Sunday, except in hotels to accompany meals. To circumvent this law, every seedy bar with a few spare rooms declared itself a hotel and offered inedible sandwiches to its oblivion-seeking customers. The law was soon repealed.

Reservations and payment To secure a room in advance, you will be asked to place a deposit. The simplest way of doing this is by quoting your credit card number by phone (or by fax). If you reserve a room without a deposit during a busy period and arrive after 6 PM you may find the room has been allocated to another guest.

Payment for your full stay (or at least a large part of it) is expected on arrival by credit card, traveler's check or cash (though carrying large amounts of money is not advisable in New York—see pages 54–55).

Areas of the city Manhattan is quick and simple to travel around, so you can be selective about where you stay. By far the densest concentration of hotels is in the section of Midtown Manhattan bordered by 44th and 57th streets. Some of the grandest and priciest accommodations in the city can be found here, in a knot around Grand Central Terminal and at the southern end of Central Park. The cheaper Midtown hotels (mostly around Times Square) can be very unappealing, and you will get better value for money elsewhere.

In the southern reaches of Midtown Manhattan, where noise and traffic levels are more bearable, residential areas such as Chelsea and the Gramercy Park district hold several hotels full of character with attractive rates.

If you can afford them, a handful of classy hotels with sky-high rates sit in the moneyed environs of the Upper East Side. On the other side of Central Park, the limited number of hotels on the Upper West Side are better value, especially if you like a large room.

In Lower Manhattan, several high-rises in the Financial District are squarely aimed at the international expense-account business traveler. You'll find more affordable and interesting lodgings among the hotels dotted (albeit very thinly) through Chinatown, SoHo, and Greenwich Village.

Bed and breakfast Bed-and-breakfast accommodations are an increasingly popular alternative to staying in a hotel, but prices are not significantly lower: such is the demand for accommodations of every kind in the city that real bargains are hard to come by.

New York B.& B.s fall into two categories. "Hosted" means that guests occupy a spare room or two in the apartment of a New Yorker who will provide at least a modest breakfast. Hosted B.& B.s can be a source of useful insider information on the city, but there is always the risk that you might find yourself at odds with the host. With "unhosted" accommodations, guests get the run of a New York apartment whose owner is out of town.

B.& B. prices naturally vary according to the facilities and neighborhood. Many B.& B.s are in outlying locations, so bear this in mind when booking. A hosted bed and breakfast is generally cheaper ($60–$150) than its unhosted equivalent ($80–$200). Rooms should be booked well in advance for the widest choice, although you can book the day before if necessary. Among a growing number of bed-and-breakfast agencies are City Lights (P.O. Box 20355, Cherokee Station, New York, NY 10028; tel: 737–7049) and Urban Ventures (P.O. Box 426, New York, NY 10024; tel: 594–5650).

Student dorms
Further inexpensive accommodations are available (during short vacation times) in the student dorms of New York University. There is a minimum stay of three weeks, and the cost per week is around $70. These accommodations are extremely limited and are quickly snapped up. If you are interested, consult the New York telephone book and contact the housing office listed under the university entry.

215

Cheap and cheerful If hotels and B.& B.s are beyond your budget but you are still determined to see the Big Apple, the city has three Y.M.C.A.s that, for slightly less than the cost of the cheapest hotel room, offer single, double, and family rooms plus a range of facilities to men, women, and family groups. The West Side Y.M.C.A. occupies an elegant historic building at 5 West 63rd Street (tel: 787–4400).

You do not have to be a youth to stay at Hostelling International—New York's stylish and well-equipped New York hostel (891 Amsterdam Avenue; tel: 932–2300), although you do have to be a member of the International Youth Hostel Federation. Prices depend on whether you opt for a dormitory bed or a private room, but either way are substantially lower than hotels or B.& B.s. It is wise to make reservations in advance.

Home comforts, attractive bedrooms, and excellent value for money make the Wyndham popular with New York regulars, so book well in advance

Food and drink

City that never sleeps it may be, but New York is also a city that never seems to stop eating. This gastronomic obsession is easily explained: no city on earth has such an abundance or such a variety of food available—from burgers, blintzes, and catfish to dim sum and goulash—around the clock and at prices most people can afford.

Meals on the move The busier the street, the more vendors it will have! Most street vendors serve hot dogs—even the humble frankfurter in a bun has a place in New York culinary legend, and is regarded as a must-eat snack when visiting Coney Island (see page 75)—and also knishes (a doughy pastry filled with meat or potatoes), bags of roasted chestnuts, and huge soft pretzels, crusted with salt—each for around a dollar ($1.50 in the pricey heart of Midtown). In the morning, you'll often see stands stuffed with breakfast pastries, oversized bagels, and the like—breakfast-on-the-run.

You are never far from the next snack in Manhattan

In the Financial District, traders and other money men are to be seen not at chic restaurant tables, but eating their midday meal from rows of ethnic vendors lining the main thoroughfares. These pushcarts are the most convenient and quickest places to grab a bite. Here steaming piles of meat or seafood and noodles are sold for a few dollars.

The deli: a New York institution Street vendors apart, what New York has more of than any other American city is delis. The old-timers of the breed, known for their mile-high sandwiches stuffed with Eastern European meats such as pastrami, are nowadays few and far between. However, they have given their name to food sources all over the city where overstuffed sandwiches are served. More recently, Korean immigrants have given the word a whole new meaning, installing extensive salad bars holding dozens of trays of cooked meats, seafood dishes, stir-fries, hot and cold vegetables, casseroles, salads, fruit, even sushi.

Just fill a plastic container and pay by the weight. Depending on the price per pound and how much you eat, you can eat your fill for between $4 and $10. Many of these establishments have tables, but you may prefer to

Tipping
In any eating place that has waiter or waitress service, you are expected to leave a tip. Restaurant and coffee-shop staff depend on tips for a large part of their income, which is why the majority will eagerly attend to your needs. The precise amount that you leave should be judged according to the standard of service, but a tip of around 15 percent of the bill is considered average. One way to estimate a tip is to double the amount of sales tax (which is 8¼ percent) shown on your bill.

eat your salad outside on the nearest bench while people-watching.

Most New York delis also serve a mind boggling variety of sandwiches. Along with the traditional corned beef and pastrami on rye, you can also get heros (a.k.a. submarine sandwiches), as well as sandwiches based on food specialties of the individual deli owner's own native land. In delis owned by Greeks and Middle Easterners, for instance, you may find gyros—spit-roasted beef or pork stuffed inside a pita bread envelope. Even ordinary sandwiches, such as turkey or tuna fish, are often unbelievably thick, with at least an inch of meat between the slices of bread.

Bagels are served everywhere with many weird and wonderful toppings, but it is hard to beat the traditional New York way of eating them: smothered in (or with just "a schmear" of) cream cheese.

Every New Yorker has a favorite deli. Once you have found yours, start exploring the other traditional deli delights such as thick soups, chicken soup with the dumplings known as matzoh balls, sponge cakes and mile-high meringue pies, and blintzes—similar to crêpes wrapped around cream cheese or fruit fillings.

Coffee-shop breakfasts If, unlike the typical New Yorker, you are not in a rush in the morning, linger over breakfast in a coffee shop or diner. Such establishments are as prevalent as delis and street vendors and draw an equally devoted clientele.

Sit at a table or at the coffee shop's counter and make your selection from a menu which is likely to include sausages, bacon, lox (smoked salmon), pancakes, waffles, French toast, scrambled eggs, omelets with a host of mix-and-match fillings, and fried eggs. Coffee-shop breakfasts are usually served with hash browns (a.k.a. home fries), and toast. Often your cup of coffee will be refilled for free, for as long as you like to linger there.

Eating with children
The upper-crust restaurants of the Upper East Side might be an exception but otherwise many other New York restaurants welcome children. Young diners may even be handed toys or coloring books as soon as they sit down, and those who are old enough to read may find they have their own section of the menu, where child-sized portions and perennial children's favorites such as burgers, fries, onion rings, and ice cream feature strongly.

217

*A New York legend—
the original Jewish
deli*

A coffee-shop breakfast will cost around $5. For a dollar or two more, you will find something less dependent on the frying pan in a more health-conscious eatery, chosen simply by scanning the selections listed on the menu outside. Here the options might include oatmeal with raisins and hazelnuts or fruit slices with freshly squeezed orange juice.

Lunchtime fare Lunchtime in New York usually begins at 11 and ends around 2, though it isn't hard to find something to eat the rest of the afternoon. Sandwiches and salads are popular choices for lunch, and several establishments, such as the **Burke & Burke** and **Mangia** food shops, have turned sandwich and salad making into an art. Here you can find savory items such as fresh mozzarella and sun-dried tomatoes on a whole wheat baguette, and smoked turkey and avocado on Russian black bread; sometimes these sandwiches are so large you can barely fit them into your mouth.

Among New York's sandwich specialties are the "Reuben" (corned beef with Swiss cheese and sauerkraut on rye bread) and the "Monte Cristo" (French bread toast with turkey and ham topped by melted Swiss cheese). Coffee shops also serve salad plates that could feed an army and offer variations on the plain and simple hamburger such as bacon-and-cheese burgers, chili-cheese burgers, and pizzaburgers.

Lunch in a coffee shop is unlikely to cost more than $8 or so per head. An even cheaper lunch may be found at a neighborhood pizza joint, where you usually have a choice of toppings. Several pizza parlors also offer Italian hero sandwiches filled with meatballs, chicken cutlets, or eggplant.

Many New York restaurants, whatever their culinary leaning, offer specially priced lunch menus or lunch buffets for under $8, which not only means good eating at a great price but also makes lunchtime a golden opportunity to begin your investigation of the city's innumerable ethnic cuisines. Seldom will you have the chance to sample so wide a choice of restaurant fare at such affordable prices.

Italian restaurants Throughout the city, Italian restaurants can be relied upon for excellent food at very fair prices, but it is to Little Italy that most New Yorkers travel if they are seeking something special. What is special about Little Italy, however, is much less the food—though there are exceptions among the tiny area's predominantly Sicilian and Neapolitan eateries—than the immensely enjoyable atmosphere.

Little Italy's prices are also higher than they deserve to be. If money is no object and you are neatly dressed, head instead for the gourmet Italian restaurants recently opened on the Upper East Side.

Chinese food Within a toothpick's throw of Little Italy are the restaurants of Chinatown, which are unmatched for value. Because their trade is largely drawn from New York's Chinese community, Chinatown's eateries can stay in profit without compromising their quality to suit western tastes.

Although they may at first seem slightly intimidating places, packed with locals exchanging animated gossip and gesticulating at scurrying staff, nobody should leave New York without dropping into a Chinatown restaurant during its hours of dim sum service. Usually served until mid-afternoon, dim sum comprises steamed dumplings and baked buns filled with meat, seafood, and/or rice and noodles. Diners choose from trolleys pushed between the dining tables (don't bother grappling with the language difficulties; just point at what looks good—even though it might be chicken feet). When you cannot eat another thing, let the waiter or waitress know and the bill will be assessed by the number of empty plates on your table.

People who think they know their way around a Chinese menu will relish returning to Chinatown at night, when the dinner options span Cantonese, Hunan, and Szechuan specialties as well as a few more obscure regional cuisines.

Japanese food New Yorkers first got excited by Japanese sushi and sashimi during the late 1970s when a rash of new restaurants appeared. These were intended to serve the city's fast-growing Japanese population but found themselves besieged by locals entranced by the exotic combination of raw fish and tatami mats.

The city is still an excellent place for sushi and sashimi (ask any New Yorker for their suggestions), although the latest craze among devotees of Japanese food are the *okonomiyaki* restaurants, where large crêpes containing your choice of meat, seafood, vegetables, or noodles are prepared on a hot slab in full view.

Affordable food to suit most tastes

Mealtimes
To avoid crowds, or to avoid having a restaurant to yourself, be aware of the city's popular dining times. Most coffee shops open for breakfast around 6 AM and are at their busiest around 8 AM. By 10 AM, the pace has slowed as most New Yorkers are already planning their lunch. Some people eat their midday meal as early as 11:30 AM but around 1 PM is more common. By 2:30 or 3 PM coffee shops start preparing for the dinner rush, from around 5 PM to 7 PM. In restaurants, lunch hours tend to be similar to those of coffee shops but the peak restaurant dinner period is between 7 and 10:30 PM. Some noted after-theater dining spots do most of their business between 11 PM and midnight.

Head for 6th Street in the East Village for a dazzling array of Indian restaurants

Korean and Indian Korean is the other Asian cuisine firmly established in New York, even though few out-of-towners ever stumble on the Korean business district. Here, within a few blocks of the Empire State Building, off Fifth Avenue in the West 30s, a number of Korean restaurants maintain around-the-clock service.

With its emphasis on barbecued beef and pork, Korean eating might be less gastronomically adventurous than Chinese or Japanese, but anyone with a liking for spicy meat should enjoy Korean *jeyuk gui,* strips of barbecued pork smothered with a very hot sauce.

Indian food has been popular in New York for decades. The section of 6th Street between First and Second avenues in the East Village is packed with Indian restaurants, and another group is to be found in Midtown Manhattan, around Lexington Avenue between 27th and 30th streets.

Spanish and Greek New Yorkers often combine dining out with a trip to the theater, but not if they are planning to tackle one of the gargantuan helpings of paella (which might well take most of the evening to devour) served at the convivial Spanish restaurants dotted throughout the city, with several notable examples in Greenwich Village and Chelsea.

Outside the strongly Greek-populated Astoria area of Queens, Greek food is surprisingly hard to find or disappointing, although simple Greek dishes such as spinach pie and moussaka often appear in coffee shops, many of which are managed by Greeks. The dessert choice might well include Greek pastries.

Crossbred cuisines
New York's ethnic cuisines are quick to mix with one another. To become a gastronomic explorer at the frontiers of culinary adventure (which is sometimes a long way from culinary excellence), seek out the city's Chinese pizzerias, Kosher-Italian delis and Indian-Mexican fast-food outlets, among dozens of bizarre crossbreeds.

South American and Caribbean food You're assured of a lively evening in any of the city's increasingly well-regarded Brazilian restaurants, which between them represent most of the country's regional cuisines. Several Puerto Rican restaurants are along 116th Street in East Harlem, and they will be able to serve you barbecued pig (the island's national dish).

Less daunting Puerto Rican specialties are also served, but East Harlem can be intimidating after dark and it is sensible to restrict your food forays into the area to lunchtime.

Eastern Europe In the Yorkville district, in the 70s and 80s streets of the Upper East Side, several Hungarian, German, and Czech-Slovak restaurants are reminders of the Eastern European communities that settled here before departing for the suburbs. Look no farther for rich, heavy soups, stuffed cabbage, and very large portions of goulash.

Similarly solid but tasty fare turns up in the Ukrainian eateries of the East Village and in the Polish cafés that survive on the Lower East Side. In Brighton Beach's Russian restaurants, meanwhile, be ready for a Cyrillic menu—or choose from a buffet table and be prepared to dodge the vodka-sozzled dancers as you are doing so.

New York may be hard to beat for ethnic cooking, but the great all-American snack still has plenty of devoted fans

Recipes from the regions With the foods of the world providing such competition, the regional cuisines of the nation battle hard to be noticed. Nonetheless Cajun, Tex-Mex, and southwestern cooking all have their devotees. Fried catfish, grilled swordfish, jambalaya, gumbo soup, and even stuffed armadillo are among their offerings.

Being hungry in Harlem is a perfect excuse to discover soul food. Order a plateful of fried chicken or beef ribs coated in gravy, and don't skimp on the side dishes, such as black-eyed peas, corn bread, and grits.

Vegetarian food Street vendors, delis, and coffee shops are by no means no-go areas for vegetarians, who will (provided they eat fish) also find plenty of dishes to tempt them among the regular menus of most of New York's restaurants.

Those with stricter diets, such as lacto-vegetarians, are provided for by a number of usually excellent special restaurants, where very inventive and tasty dishes are concocted. Some specialize in meat-free ethnic cuisine—vegetarian Vietnamese food is one example.

Steak houses One kind of establishment into which veg-etarians *will* fear to tread is the New York steak house. Carnivores, however, will soon be salivating in these citadels of meat-eating, where large, thick, and juicy hunks of prime beef are served with a baked potato and a side salad.

The crème de la crème At the top end of the dining spectrum, New York's finest restaurants not only employ some of the world's best chefs, they also engage the top waiters (some of whom are famously surly) and leading interior designers and have a maître d' who is liable to put the fear of God into staff and diners alike.

To experience New York eating at this rarefied level requires much more than mere appetite and a strong bank balance. You will also need to make a reservation (preferably a few days in advance) and be ready to tip the maître d' handsomely. Unless you are an extremely famous face (and sometimes even then), you will be shown the door (or, at best, a table completely out of view of the other diners) if you are not dressed in your best for the occasion.

Expensive restaurants sometimes allow you to sample their premier offerings with fixed-price *menus dégustation,* or "tasting menus." These menus enable you to try a few dishes, usually up to 10, but the price may still

Smoking in restaurants
Any smoker who can survive without a puff for the duration of a restaurant visit would be well advised to do so. Most New Yorkers are very aware of health issues and their fear of passive smoking has helped make tobacco addicts the scourge of the city. In January 1995, smoking was made illegal in restaurants seating 35 or more people, except at separate bar areas or rooms with independant ventilation.

A revered New York institution: the steak house

be steep. Three-course, *prix fixe* menus often are more economical than choosing your meal à la carte, although they don't usually include drinks; you also have to watch out for extra charges. Perhaps a better way to save money is to sample these fine restaurants at lunch, when prices are usually considerably lower than at dinner (see page 218).

Coffee and tea Coffee is always freshly brewed and available in caffeinated and decaf (decaffeinated) forms. Cappuccino and espresso coffee, costing $2–$3 per cup, are also popular, especially on the sidewalk tables of Italian cafés. All types of coffee may be ordered to go from delis and street vendors, at prices graded according to the size of the cup or container. Ask for "regular" coffoo if you want milk but no sugar — to get sweetened brew, ask for "regular with sugar."

A recent phenomenon in Manhattan is coffee bars, which specialize in serving several different fine coffee blends (and usually a variety of teas). Customers order their drinks at a counter rather than being served. Although convenient, these places are more suitable for brief stops. rather than for lingering in.

Some New Yorkers have developed a taste for iced coffee, although far more have a liking for iced tea. Both are great drinks for cooling you down after a hot day on the city streets.

Most coffee shops and delis will serve hot tea if asked, but it is generally best avoided (unless you like it weak and made with lukewarm water) if it is not featured on a menu. Where it is a house specialty, tea will be offered in a variety of Chinese, Indian, and herbal blends. Serious tea drinkers should make themselves known at the city's handful of tearooms (see the panel).

Juice bars Sodas are fast declining in popularity among some of the more health-conscious New Yorkers, who, after a workout at the gym or a jog, refresh themselves instead with the nutritious fruit juices sold in the city's

Sample the wide variety of worldwide fare available in New York

223

Tearooms
There are few more welcoming sanctuaries from the mayhem of Manhattan's streets than the city's elegant tearooms (usually in deluxe hotels are recognized by their rather pretentious French names) between 2 and 5PM on a weekday afternoon. At this time, for a price ranging from $15 to $20, you can partake of tea— the list of blends usually spans Chinese, Indian, and Russian—and nibble selectively from a silver tray laden with chicken, ham, and smoked salmon sandwiches, chocolate cakes, delicate pastries, and scones topped with Devonshire thick cream.

FOOD AND DRINK

Relaxing outside the Victory Café on the Upper East Side

New York's new beers
Partly as a reaction against mass-produced beers and partly because New York loves a new trend, microbrewed beers (produced in small batches, often by the bar that serves them) have become increasingly common through the late 1990s. Hop enthusiasts can sample the likes of Brooklyn Brewery Black Chocolate Stout, Weinhard's Red, Rockefeller Red, Hudson River Porter, Gotham City Gold, Empire State Bitter, and Lady Liberty Light. At the Fraunces Tavern (see page 107) they can imbibe the creamy Swig Tavern Keeper, supposedly similar to that brewed when George Washington propped up the bar.

specialized juice bars. As well as fresh orange, grapefruit, and carrot juice, some juice bars offer power-packed juices blended from parsley, ginger, spinach, and root vegetables; expect to spend $1–$4 for a glassful.

Bars and beers New York can suddenly look very different when you have a glass of alcohol in your hand, not because of blurred vision brought on by overindulgence but because you are bound to be among socializing New Yorkers.

Bars, which stay open from around midday to the early hours (legally they must stop serving at 4 AM), range from the chummy neighborhood variety to those patronized almost exclusively by a particular social set be it stockbrokers, art dealers, or punk rockers. For more insights into the diversity of New York bars, see pages 114–115.

Most bars, especially larger ones and those with outdoor tables, have waiter or waitress service, though usually you can go to the bar and order drinks directly from the bartender—as you can if you sit at the bar.

Particularly in less crowded establishments, opting to sit at the bar means that you will probably not need to pay until you indicate to the bartender that you are ready to leave, at which point you will be presented with a bill. In all bars, the bartender will expect you to leave a tip when buying a round of drinks or when leaving.

Mass-market beers such as Budweiser, Miller, and Rolling Rock are on tap and in bottles in virtually every bar. Many establishments also carry a commendable selection of bottled European beers (occasionally found on tap) and Mexican beers.

Adventurous beer-drinkers should also investigate the output of the nation's many micro-breweries: Anchor

Steam Beer, brewed in California, is not the best of the bunch but is the most commonly found (for more beer, see panel opposite).

Sports bars Watching the playoffs at the neighborhood local bar is a way of life across America, but New Yorkers enjoy a variation on this theme: sports bars with multiple extra-large television screens. Some favorite ones in the city include **Entourage Sports** (1571 Second Avenue between 81st and 82nd Street), **Polo Grounds** (1472 Third Avenue between 83rd and 84th streets), **Sporting Club** (99 Hudson Street at Franklin Street), **Sports Page** (90 Second Avenue at 5th Street), baseball-mad **Mickey Mantle's** (42 Central Park South), Runyons (932 Second Avenue between 49th and 50th streets), and **Rusty's** (1271 3rd Avenue at 73rd Street), owned by former Met Rusty Staub.

Wines and liquor Alongside the beer, New York bars also stock a selection of wines from Europe and the United States—many available by the glass. The more elegant the bar, the more extensive (and expensive) its wine stocks will be. Some good restaurants produce wine lists on regularly updated computer print-outs. Behind every bar will be a very well-stocked rack of liquor, usually including a selection of malt whiskies, Russian vodka, and various types of bourbon.

Cocktails Any bar describing itself as a cocktail lounge —particularly in parts of Midtown Manhattan and in the Upper East Side—is likely to be a watering hole for the wealthy. For eavesdropping on high-society gossip and poodle grooming tips, cocktail lounges are unrivaled, but to spend an evening inside one you will need to be very well dressed and not afraid to spend $10 or more on a single drink—and on no account should you topple drunkenly from your stool.

Vintage classics
Hotel bars provide exhausted sightseers with some of the best places in Manhattan. The **Plaza Hotel's Oak Bar** (5th Avenue and 59th Street.) continues to age well with its plummy, dark-wood furnishings; it draws sophisticates, shoppers, and celebrities. The **Carlyle** (35 East 76th Street) contains the charming **Bemelman's Bar** with whimsical animal murals and live jazz piano music at night. At the art-deco style **Essex House** (160 Central Park S.), **Journeys** bar has pure English country-style decor with rich carved wood, sporting scenes on the walls, and large fireplace. One of the most elegant, venerable spots in New York to have a glass of wine (or a cup of tea) remains the **Algonquin Hotel Lounge** (59 W. 44th Street), with its many literary associations.

225

Views across to South Street Seaport and Lower Manhattan complement the food and wine at Brooklyn's River Café

Shopping

226

One way to keep warm in New York during January is to pay a visit to the Winter Antiques Fair, held at the Seventh Regiment Armory (see page 187). With all of New York's antiques dealers and antiques lovers gathered under one roof, you might not be able to afford anything, but eavesdropping on the chit-chat can be fascinating. There are plenty of fine antiques to admire, too.

Union Square now teems with shoppers choosing fresh produce at the popular Farmers' Market, which is held several times a week

From the ultra-exclusive antiques stores of the Upper East Side to the discount clothing stores that proliferate in Lower Manhattan, New York is not only the most exciting place in the world to buy things, but also the easiest and sometimes even the cheapest. Not surprisingly, New Yorkers often like to shop till they drop.

Antiques The New York millionaires who plundered the treasures of Europe and the Far East to furnish their mansions contributed to the city's emergence as the center of the international antiques trade. For serious buyers, there is no better place to locate that elusive Japanese watercolor or Swiss music box. There is plenty to drool over in the upscale antiques stores of the Upper East Side. The more affordable stuff, meanwhile, can be found elsewhere.

Among the city's top-range antiques stores, **A La Vieille Russie** (Fifth Avenue at 59th Street) highlights the achievements of czarist Russian craftsmen with Fabergé enamelware, jewel-encrusted icons, snuff boxes, clocks, and assorted silverware—none of which would disgrace the finest palace.

Prints, books and ornaments from 18th- and 19th-century Japan are among the Far Eastern treasures that can be found at **Things Japanese** (60th Street between Park and Lexington avenues). Well-heeled connoisseurs of art deco will find plenty to please amid the pricey rarities at **De Iorenzo** (Madison Avenue between 75th and 76th streets).

Several hours might be needed for a thorough exploration of **Asia House** (56th Street between Sixth and Seventh avenues), packed with porcelain, lamps, vases

and much more from points East. Meanwhile, **America Hurrah Antiques** (Madison Avenue at 66th Street) elevates the untutored skills of early U.S. settlers—displayed in everything from weather vanes to decoy ducks—to the status of fine art and prices it accordingly.

Antiquated melodies accompany browsing at **Rita Ford Music Boxes** (65th Street between Madison and Fifth avenues), a colossal collection of music boxes and miniature handmade carousels, which the staff are easily persuaded to demonstrate.

If you lack the nerve to pose as a genuine customer in the more exclusive antique stores, you might aim instead for the friendlier environs of the **Manhattan Art & Antiques Center** (Second Avenue between 55th and 56th streets). At the **Laura Fisher Gallery**, one of the center's 104 separate shops, you will learn more about American quilts than you thought you could know.

Another low-key spot high on potential is the **Chelsea Antiques Building** (110 W 25th Street), where 150 dealers are spread across twelve floors, and sell items ranging from 18th and 19th-century furnishings to toys, books, and comics.

The mood in SoHo antiques outlets, typically set in warehouse-like stores, is much less stuffy than that of the Upper East Side shops and the prices are far lower. Among the inventory of **Back Pages** (Green Street between Prince and W. Houston streets) you will find Wurlitzer jukeboxes, vintage pool tables, and vending machines.

Big Apple detritus forms the eclectic stock of **Urban Archeology** (285 Lafayette Street). This is just the place to pick up a bizarre bathroom fitting or a vintage barber shop chair. Similar ephemera fills **Secondhand Rose** (275 Lafayette Street), among it neon-lit Coke signs and dilapidated peep show machines. There are also some bizarre specialist stores: see panel.

Books Bookstores are abundant in New York. They include independently run stores with specialized fare; nationwide chains such as **B. Dalton Bookseller** (main branch on Fifth Avenue at 52nd Street), **Doubleday** (main branch on Fifth Avenue at 57th Street), each with formidable stocks of general fiction and nonfiction titles, and **Barnes and Noble** (whose main branch is at Fifth Avenue and 18th Street; tel: 807–0099). The store is said to contain over 3 million volumes, but giving it a run for its money as the world's biggest bookstore is the **Borders** bookstore (57th Street and Park Avenue; tel: 980–6785). With four floors, it is just slightly larger than the tri-level branch downtown in the World Trade Center.

Bookworms also gravitate to Manhattan's many independent operations, among them **Gotham Book Mart** (47th Street near Sixth Avenue), and **Coliseum Books** (Broadway between 57th and 58th streets). The city's most comfortable place to browse, however, is the oaken interior of **Rizzoli** (57th Street between Fifth and Sixth avenues). Check out also **Shakespeare & Co.** (2259 Broadway and 81st Street).

A change of identity? Anything is possible in the stores of Greenwich Village

Unusual stores
New York has an unusual store at every turn. Among the curiosities you might stumble across are: New York Firefighter's Friend (Lafayette Street between Prince and Spring streets), selling fire-fighting paraphernalia from model fire engines to helmets and hose nozzles; Maxilla and Mandible (82nd Street at Columbus Avenue), packed with skeletons and individual bones from humans, animals, and birds; Little Rickie (First Avenue at 3rd Street). where an extraordinary assortment of tasteless merchandise includes Elvis Presley clocks and lamps; and Tender Buttons (62nd Street between Third and Lexington avenues), with nothing but buttons—tens of thousands of them.

SHOPPING

Buying records and C.D.s
With 75,000 square feet of floor space, the Virgin Megastore (Broadway between 45th and 46th streets) claims to be the world's largest music and entertainment store. As you pore through rack after rack of records, C.D.s, laser disks, and cassettes, and pass through a classical section that includes space for a concert pianist, the claim is easy to believe. Other only slightly smaller shops are the several branches of Tower (692 Broadway; Trump Tower, 725 Fifth Avenue; and Broadway at 66th Street); and the four branches of HMV (in Midtown Manhattan at Fifth Avenue and 46th Street).

Museum shops
Many of New York's museums have excellent shops attached. The Museum of Modern Art (pages 158–160) and the Guggenheim Museum (pages 122–124), in particular, are excellent places to find art books, unusual badges, T-shirts, and other souvenirs marking their major exhibitions. A branch of the Guggenheim Museum in SoHo (575 Broadway) also has a good range of art-related merchandise, and the Cooper-Hewitt Museum (page 95) has tomes covering all aspects of the decorative arts.

Among the genre bookstores, crime-fiction fans are guaranteed to find their favorite authors represented in the **Mysterious Bookshop** (56th Street between Sixth and Seventh avenues) and **Murder Ink** (Broadway between 92nd and 93rd streets).

The Biography Bookshop (400 Bleecker Street), stocks plenty of what its title suggests, plus autobiographies, books of letters, journals, and travelogues from names spanning the very famous to the surprisingly obscure.

Art books are best sought in museum gift shops (see panel), although the SoHo branch of **Rizzoli** (West Broadway between Prince and Houston streets) carries a strong complement of fine art tomes. Nearby, **A Photographer's Place** (133 Mercer Street) stocks new and used books on photographic techniques and photographers. Art-related titles that are hard to find elsewhere sometimes turn up at **Hacker Art Books** (57th Street between Fifth and Sixth avenues).

It may not be the oldest bookstore in the city, but the **Oscar Wilde Memorial Bookstore** (15 Christopher Street) is claimed to be the world's first gay bookstore: it opened in 1969 and stocks books and magazines of interest to gay men. **Creative Visions** (548 Hudson Street) covers much the same subject matter but also has a lesbian section. Meanwhile, **Drougas Unoppressive Nonimperialist Bargain Books** (34 Carmine Street) is the perfect place for the politically correct to acquire new reading matter.

C.D.s and records C.D.s and tapes can be found to fit all tastes amid the eclectic and vast stocks of **Tower Records** (Broadway at 4th Street), **J.& R. Music World** (23 Park Row, in the Financial District) and those listed in the panel on this page.

Clothing The latest in leather, rubber, and plastic street fashions can be seen being worn around the East Village,

but New Yorkers on the whole are conservative dressers, despite the fact that every name in international high fashion has at least one outlet in the city. Dozens of discount stores sell tried and tested American casual clothing for a song.

Clothes-conscious folk who do not need to worry about their credit limits—or about being patronized by snooty

staff—do their shopping amid the designer-name stores of Midtown Manhattan and the Upper East Side, areas cluttered with the stores of world-famous names such as **Giorgio Armani** (Madison Avenue at 65th Street), **Gucci** (two stores on Fifth Avenue at 54th Street—numbers 685 and 689), **Hermès** (57th Street, between Madison and Fifth avenues) and **Yves St. Laurent** (Madison Avenue at 71st Street).

One pedigree designer you should visit for the setting alone, however, is **Polo/Ralph Lauren** (Madison Avenue at 72nd Street. The company occupies a French Renaissance-style Upper East Side mansion that is a show in itself.

Giorgio Armani also has a downtown store, **Armani A/X** (Broadway at Prince Street). This is pitched at the younger designer-dresser, though you will probably need much more than your weekly allowance to afford anything inside.

The person of average income in search of quality clothing should aim instead for the scores of discount outlets, where designer togs are unceremoniously discounted for as little as half their regular prices. Although their prices may be comparatively inexpensive, the stores themselves can be as classy as any. Among them are **Moe Ginsberg** (162 Fifth Avenue), offering mostly mens' clothing and footwear spread over four floors; **Michaels'—The Consignment Shop For Women** (1041 Madison Avenue), a favorite of well-heeled Upper East Side ladies; and **Pretty Plus Plus** (1309 Madison Avenue), with bargain designer wear for the larger woman.

There are some lower-priced (but not inexpensive) designer stores which specialize in chic clothes and accessories for the style-conscious traveler. One such place is **Betsey Johnson** (130 Thompson Street, one of three Manhattan branches), which adapts New York street fashion into loud and colorful garments.

Lower Manhattan is a good area for bargain clothing stores and stalls such as this one on West Broadway

A note for bargain-hunters
Photographic and electrical goods can bring real bargains in New York. It is vital, however, to know exactly what you want before entering a store and to resist the seductive patter of the salesperson. This is especially true of electrical goods, even if the sales pitch suggests otherwise.

The largest photographic discount store is 47th St. Photo (main branch on 47th St. between Fifth and Sixth avenues; others listed in the Yellow Pages). It also carries a large range of videos, computers, and all kinds of electrical gadgets.

Mainstream American-made clothing, particularly Levi jeans, represents exceptionally good value (especially for the European visitor); prices are lowest in the scores of discount stores on and around the SoHo section of Broadway: the biggest is **Canal Jean** (between Broome and Spring streets), with a massive stock of jeans, T-shirts, jackets, sunglasses, beachwear, loud ties, and all kinds of practical traveling accessories at extremely tempting prices.

Army/Navy (328 Bleecker Street, one of three Manhattan branches) is another dependable provider of items such as jeans, plaid shirts, T-shirts, and well-priced leather jackets.

Department stores Immortalized in film, fiction, and folklore, Manhattan's department stores are the stuff of legend. Generations of New Yorkers have grown up unable to imagine life without these totems to 20th-century consumerism, and while they are superficially similar, each one has a character and cachet very much its own and its own band of loyal supporters.

Among them is **Macy's** (34th Street and Sixth Avenue), famously described as the world's largest department store. The claim seems justified as you wind up its 10 floors and find half a million items for sale. There is even a section for buying pets and a branch of the Museum of Modern Art's gift shop. Large it may be but, despite revamping its image during the 1970s, Macy's is far from being the world's most exciting department store, having built its reputation by supplying middle-income family purchasers with the most middle-of-the-road tastes.

By contrast, **Bloomingdale's** (Third Avenue at 59th Street) is consummate high-style New York consumerism. A glamorous cross between a trendy disco and a Middle Eastern bazaar, visiting Bloomies (as it is widely called) is always something of an adventure, not least because of the special promotions that regularly transform the whole store.

Bloomingdale's was the first department store to feature now-established designers such as Yves St. Laurent, Calvin Klein and Ralph Lauren, and it supports many newer ones. Elsewhere, there are cosmetics, the latest in electrical gadgetry, a well-stocked bookstore, and a food level that devotes a whole section to caviar.

More opulent still is **Bergdorf Goodman** (Fifth Avenue between 57th and 58th streets). This is where the ladies of the Upper East Side shop beneath crystal chandeliers for clothes, jewelry, perfumes, and other luxury items. Their latest husbands, meanwhile, sift through the $100-a piece tie racks of **Bergdorf Goodman Men**, directly across Fifth Avenue.

Spread over nine artfully designed floors, **Barneys** (660 Madison Avenue) offers everything the stylish and

successful Manhattanite could wish for: designer names by the score and even a gym to help make customers look good in their new clothes.

The antidote to glitz and ostentatious wealth is **Saks Fifth Avenue** (Fifth Avenue between 49th and 50th streets), which simply offers tasteful, stylish and high-quality merchandise—clothing, linens, cosmetics—in an orderly setting with efficient service.

Jewelry Dozens of jewelers occupy Manhattan's "diamond district," which fills a block of 47th Street immediately west of Fifth Avenue. This wholesale jewelry trading district is where diamonds are cut and polished, jewelry is repaired, gems are set and deals are done above the ground level shops. More famous stores include **Tiffany & Co** (Fifth Avenue between 56th and 57th streets), with three floors of highly desirable pieces, not all of which cost the earth, and the more conservative **Cartier** (Fifth Avenue at 52nd Street), worth a call not least for the landmark building which it occupies. Another, less classy, stalwart is the **World's Largest Jewelry Exchange** (55 W 47th Street), more than a hundred retailers and repairers under a single roof providing ample opportunity for browsing and comparing prices.

Shoes Shoe stores abound in New York, and if you cannot find what you want (whether it's handmade Italian loafers or streetwise sneakers), you are simply not trying. Aside from numerous upscale outlets on the Upper East Side, and the extensive stocks of most department stores, many Lower Manhattan discount stores offer good deals in footwear. Manhattan also has two "shoe districts," where you will see rows of shoe stores—on West 8th Street and on 34th Street between Fifth and Sixth avenues.

At **Susan Bennis/Warren Edwards** (Park Avenue and 56th Street), the handmade, limited-edition footwear for men and women comes in all manner of styles.

Everything under one (huge) roof: Macy's

Personal shopping
If the prospect of many hours of roaming the city's department stores fills you with dread, each store has a team of personal shoppers who will make your purchases for you. All you have to do is pay for the goods—and for the personal shopper. Telephone for details: Bergdorf Goodman (tel: 753–5300); Bloomingdale's (tel: 800/777–0000); Macy's (tel: 560–4181); Saks Fifth Avenue (tel: 753–4000).

Nightlife

New York nightlife is never boring, and it's more plentiful and more diverse (and often of a higher standard) than you will find almost anywhere else in the world. To enjoy it, all you need is energy and, in most cases, plenty of money.

Most New York-based publications carry extensive nightlife listings. The most thorough are the *Village Voice* and the Friday and Sunday editions of *The New York Times*. For new movies and plays, the *New Yorker* is also an excellent source of opinionated, searching reviews and information.

Theater From the *Ziegfeld Follies* to *The Phantom of the Opera*, the theater has been an integral part of New York nightlife for years. The section of Broadway nearest sleazy Times Square has long been established as the flag-carrier of commercial American theater.

Big-time New York theater has hit a rough patch, however. Incredibly high production costs have resulted in high seat prices (as much as $75) and only financially low-risk plays seem to be contemplated. The result is an

endless stream of lavish musicals, comedies, and unadventurous drama, usually with a big name or two to spark interest. The hit shows continue to be packed every night, but overall, Broadway theaters have been hit by declining attendances and have had more flops than ever before.

Nonetheless, even if the show could be a little better, a good reason for splurging on a night inside one of the 34 official Broadway theaters is to enjoy the sumptuous auditorium and get a taste of a little of the history and folklore that every Broadway theater has in abundance.

Regularly hosting the city's major shows are the **Eugene O'Neill Theater** (230 W 49th Street), probably the biggest and best of the neighborhood playhouses; the **Broadway Theater** (1681 Broadway); the **Neil Simon Theater** (250 52nd Street); the **Palace Theater** (1564 Broadway); the **Richard Rogers Theater** (226 W 46th Street); and the **Roundabout Theater** (1530 Broadway). Another worth trying is the **Walter Kerr** (219 W 48th Street), as much for a renovation job that has brought back something of the 1920s' grandeur of the place as for the shows themselves.

Smaller than their Broadway counterparts, Off-Broadway theaters (seating 100–499) are a little more adventurous and among them they offer an excellent choice of musicals, comedies, revivals, classics, and new works that few cities can equal. Top playwrights and

Theater tickets

For most Broadway and Off-Broadway productions, New York theater goers usually order tickets by phone (Tele-Charge and Ticketmaster) or buy tickets through a ticket agent (listed in the Yellow Pages and local newspapers) rather than going to the theater box office.

Half-price day-of-performance tickets are sold from Manhattan's two branches of TKTS (on 47th Street between Broadway and Seventh Avenue, and in the south tower of the World Trade Center). All sales are cash only, in person.

Another way to cut costs is with a "two-fer"—a coupon entitling the holder to two tickets for the price of one. These are commonly used to boost audience numbers at otherwise poorly attended shows and are handed out at ticket lines and found in hotel lobbies.

leading professional actors are no strangers to Off-Broadway productions, and many of the more successful make the transition to Broadway.

Most of the leading Off-Broadway theaters are located in and around Greenwich Village, and they include the **Circle Repertory Theater** (159 Bleecker Street; tel: 254–6330); **Orpheum** (Second Avenue at 8th Street; tel: 477–2477) and **Actor's Playhouse** (100 Seventh Avenue South; tel: 239–6200).

The dozens of tiny Off-Off-Broadway theaters (seating under 100) are often housed in places like converted churches or vacant schoolrooms. It is here that daring and experimental plays are performed by unknown but often very talented actors. Seldom will you pay more than $15 for a seat.

Off-Off-Broadway venues also stage performance art and alternative cabaret. Among the longer-lasting are **The Kitchen** (19th Street between Tenth and Eleventh avenues; tel: 255–5793); Castillo Theatre (500 Greenwich Street; tel: 941–1234), and **P.S.122** (First Avenue at 9th Street; tel: 477–5829).

Another venerable New York dramatic institution is the **Public Theater** (425 Lafayette Street; tel: 260–2400—formerly the Joseph Papp Public Theater). Here you will discover provocative new plays and controversial adaptations of the classics in six separate theaters. Originally named for Joseph Papp, the director and producer whose credits included *A Chorus Line* and *Hair*, and who saved the building from demolition, the Public Theater hosts the New York Shakespeare Festival in Central Park for over six weeks each summer.

Big names and bright lights in the theater district

Theater information
Besides the listings in the *New Yorker, New York Times* and *Village Voice*, 24-hour recorded information on what is playing where, and on ticket availability, can be found by calling the NYC/ON STAGE hotline (tel: 768–1818).

Shakespeare in the Park
The Public Theater's former director, Joseph Papp, instigated the popular "Shakespeare in the Park" series, bringing two of the bard's plays to Central Park's open-air Delacorte Theater (near the 81st Street entrance on the Upper West Side) between June and August. Tickets are free but limited to two per person. A very long line begins forming around noon—the waiting is part of the fun; entertainers stroll and everyone chats and picnics—and the tickets are distributed at 6 PM.

233

The golden age of neon may be long since gone, but the gaudy excitement of Times Square remains legendary

The New York Film Festival
Each September, specially selected new American and foreign-made films are screened at the New York Film Festival, held at Alice Tully Hall at Lincoln Center. The festival is organized by the Film Society of Lincoln Center, and tickets tend to be in short supply (tel: 875–5610).

Films New York has always had a special relationship with the cinema, playing a part in countless films over a period of more than 60 years (see pages 14–15 and 188). The city is also a great place to watch movies. Not only do most high-budget Hollywood features get their first screenings here in state-of-the-art cinema complexes, but dozens of smaller film houses specialize in new independent films and rarely seen foreign movies. Nostalgia buffs are in for a treat, too, with oldies—from world cinema classics to kitsch 1940s musicals—regularly showing.

Multiscreen complexes show the latest releases all over the city; most art house and revival cinemas are downtown in the Village, Soho, and Tribeca. They include the six-screen **Angelika Film Center** (Houston Street at Mercer Street; tel: 995–2000); the **Anthology Film Archives** (Second Avenue at 2nd Street; tel: 505–5181); **Cinema Village** (12th Street between Fifth and Sixth avenues; tel: 924–3363); **Cineplex Odeon Art Greenwich** (971 Greenwich Avenue, tel: 505–CINE), **Film Forum** (Houston Street at Varick Street; tel: 727–8110); **The Screening Room** (Varick Street; tel: 334–2100); **Theatre 80** (80 St. Mark's Place between First and Second avenues; tel: 254–7400); and the **Walter Reade Theater** (70 Lincoln Center Plaza; tel: 875–5600).

Many of the city's museums have projection facilities and mount film series linked to a particular exhibition. The **Museum of Modern Art** and the **Metropolitan Museum of Art** also have extensive film archives of their own, and the **Museum of Television and Radio** (see page 161) is another potential source of delight for movie-lovers.

Classical music From free open-air recitals to concerts featuring the biggest in big names, the serious music lover will find plenty to cheer about.

Lincoln Center's Avery Fisher Hall is the home of the **New York Philharmonic,** whose season runs from mid-September to May (for information, tel: 875–5656). During July, the orchestra undertakes a free concert series in the parks of each of the city's five boroughs.

The Mostly Mozart Festival
For six weeks each July and August, New Yorkers shake off their summer slumbers with the enormously popular Mostly Mozart Festival, held at Lincoln Center's Avery Fisher Hall. Featuring many star performers and conductors, the festival is also the only chance many people get to afford front row seats: for the festival, all seats are charged at a single (low) price.

The **New York Chamber Symphony** (tel: 226–6927) is based at the 92nd Y (92nd Street at Lexington Avenue). The oak-walled **Kaufmann Theater** (also 92nd Street Y) is strong on both acoustics and atmosphere and is a popular venue with visiting soloists and other chamber groups.

At Lincoln Center, **Alice Tully Hall** (tel: 875–5050) is another important place for chamber music and all around the city numerous other venues regularly give all forms of classical music an airing. Historic **Carnegie Hall** (Seventh Avenue and 57th Street; tel: 247–7800) offers steady diet of chamber music and solo recitals; the compact **Merkin Concert Hall** (67th Street between Broadway and Amsterdam Avenue; tel: 362–8719) showcases more unusual fare, such as ethnic music; a broad-ranging program is offered at the **Town Hall** (43rd Street between Sixth Avenue and Broadway, tel: 840–2824).

Music fans of meager means should scan the newspapers' listing section for free concerts, held at the Financial District's **St. Paul's Chapel,** the Upper West Side's **Riverside Church**, and at the city's numerous schools of music—the major one being the **Juilliard School of Music** at Lincoln Center.

Ballet and dance Some of the world's most respected companies and most accomplished directors are in the city. New York's leading ballet company is the world-renowned **New York City Ballet**, based at Lincoln Center's **New York State Theater** (tel: 870–5570). Their performance seasons run from November to February and from April to June, with special performances of the *Nutcracker* during the Christmas season. Tickets vary widely in price and sell out in advance, although you can sometimes pick up tickets at the box office on the day of the performance, or snag a stray single (sold at face value or less) outside the theater just before curtain time.

Many of the world's finest dancers perform at the Met

NIGHTLIFE

The first Met
Generation after generation of New York's longstanding wealthy would demonstrate their social aloofness by occupying all of the few boxes available during the opera season at the Academy of Music (on Irving Place), leaving the *nouveau riche* of the mid- to late-19th century to face the social indignity of sitting below them. In retaliation, millionaires William Henry Vanderbilt and Jay Astor financed the first Metropolitan Opera House. The huge building that arose, opening in 1883, was criticized for its ugliness, but did provide the grand boxes from which the city's self-made millionaires could symbolically flaunt their affluence.

The Gate is just one of Greenwich Village's many popular nightspots

Based at Lincoln Center's **Metropolitan Opera House**, the **American Ballet Theater** (tel: 362–6000) garners rave reviews for its interpretations of classical and contemporary pieces. The season runs from April to June. In summer, top international guest companies, such as the Bolshoi or the Paris Opera, often come for a two-week run. Bear in mind that the cheaper seats are very high and very far from the stage, not really a great bargain in the theater.

Another important but much more intimate dance venue, **City Center** (55th Street between Sixth and Seventh avenues; tel: 581–1212), hosts a trio of innovative companies: the **Alvin Ailey American Dance Theater**; the **Dance Theater of Harlem**; and the **Merce Cunningham Dance Company**. A further small but interesting venue is the **Bessie Schonberg Theater** (19th Street between Seventh and Eighth avenues; tel: 924–0077), where the **Dance Theater Workshop** pioneers experimental dance. Bigger and more mainstream than the DTW, but smaller than the City Center, the **Joyce Theater** (175 8th Avenue) has the Feld Ballet in residence amongst others. The promising talent of many future dance stars can be seen in the student shows of the prestigious **American School of Ballet** (tel: 877–0600) at Lincoln Center's **Juilliard School of Music**.

Such is the quality of its productions that dance-loving Manhattanites regularly cross the East River to attend shows at the **Brooklyn Academy of Music** (tel: 718/636–4100). The U.S.'s first center for the performing arts, the Academy was founded in 1861 and moved to its current site in 1908. Artists from Enrico Caruso to Laurie Anderson have graced its boards. Established as a major center of modern dance, the academy hosts the spectacular Next Wave festival each fall.

Opera During its late September to mid-April season at Lincoln Center's vast **Metropolitan Opera House**, the **Metropolitan Opera** company's performances (tel: 362–6000) are as much social as musical occasions, especially Monday evenings. The company is criticized as unimaginative but seldom turns in anything other than exceptionally polished performances. Tickets are highly priced and can be hard to get without booking a long time in advance. Standing room tickets are available.

Also based at Lincoln Center is the increasingly innovative **New York City Opera** (tel: 870–5600), usually performing at the **New York State Theater**.

Among a sprinkling of smaller opera companies, with lower prices and cozier settings, is the **Amato Opera Company** (319 Bowery; tel: 228–8200). Also worth catching is the **Opera Orchestra of New York**, which performs at the atmospheric Carnegie Hall (57th Street at Seventh Avenue; tel: 747–7800). From June to August, **New York Grand Opera** (tel: 245–8837) mounts free shows at Central Park's Summer Stage.

Comedy clubs New York's comedy clubs have given a break to the careers of Eddie Murphy, David Letterman,

Robin Williams, and innumerable others over the years. Don't expect Las Vegas-style gags and routines—New York comedy clubs can be boisterous places and the crowds may be cruel if they take a dislike to a particular performer.

Most clubs have two shows nightly. It is wise to make a reservation for performances on Fridays and Saturdays. Expect to pay more (if you can get tickets) for an established name, but "open mike" nights (when amateurs take a turn, usually on Mondays) are almost always free. The most extensive comedy club listings are carried by the *Village Voice*.

With a range of well-chosen up-and-coming talent, and the occasional big name, the most reliable clubs are **Caroline's Comedy Club** (Broadway between 49th and 50th streets); the **Comic Strip Inc** (Second Avenue between 81st and 82nd streets; tel: 861 9386); **Dangerfield's** (First Avenue between 61st and 62nd streets; tel: 593 1650); and **Stand Up N.Y.** (78th Street and Broadway; tel: 595 0850).

The Poets' Slam
Listening to unknown poets reciting their latest verse can be an unexciting way to pass an evening, but at the Nuyorican Poets' Café (3rd Street between avenues B and C; tel: 505 8183), the Friday night "Poets' Slam" finds a bunch of rowdy poets locked in combat, each one hoping to impress the audience—and a panel of invited judges—with their work. A winner is chosen at the end of this lively and bizarre—but very New York event.

Music is a way of life for many New Yorkers. The city offers plenty of scope for talented performers

Nightclubbing at the Palladium

Nightclubs New York nightclubs are in a permanent state of flux. The last 15 years have seen the rise and fall of the jet-set chic Studio 54; the arty Mudd Club, which helped rejuvenate SoHo; and a batch of punky East Village clubs that reshaped many New Yorkers' notions of what a night out could be.

The city's nightclub scene in general is thriving. One recent development is that the action has tended to move downtown, but there are still scores of places of different kinds where you can dress up (or dress down), pose, preen, or just dance—well into the small hours.

For nonregulars, the biggest potential hazard at any club is the doorman, who will decide whether you are a suitable person (judged by your clothes and general manner) to be admitted. The arrogance of doormen is legendary, but if you are turned away, simply try somewhere else.

No nightclub worth its salt gets into gear before 1 or 2 AM in the morning (most are open until 4 AM). Arrive before midnight and you will probably have the place to yourself. One advantage of arriving early, however, may be a reduced admission charge. Drinks in nightclubs are more expensive than in bars, and sometimes extortionately so. Many clubs have different entertainment, and therefore an entirely different crowd, on particular nights of the week: always phone ahead to check.

New York nightclubs open, close, and change address with incredible rapidity; the following suggestions are intended as a representative cross-section.

One of the longer-established upscale clubs, the polo-stick-and-croquet-mallet-decorated **Au Bar** (58th Street between Madison Avenue and Park Avenue; tel: 308–9455) attracts a designer-dressed and rather staid crowd, dancing primly to fairly bland disco music.

Occasionally visited by rock-and-roll celebrities, the **China Club** (Broadway at 75th Street; tel: 877–1156) is an enjoyable mainstream rock-and-roll disco. Likewise, **Webster Hall** (11th Street between Third and Fourth avenues; tel: 353–1600) is unadventurous, but appreciated by its regular crowd of suburbanites.

Lively and youthful, and packed to the gills on busy nights, **Tunnel** (220 Twelfth Avenue; tel: 695–4682) is an entertainingly varied club with different rooms featuring different sounds, from hip-hop to acid jazz, the audience can be similarly eclectic. Also boasting diverse music is **Coney Island High** (15 St. Mark's Place), a spacious dance spot for specialist sounds ranging from 1950s rockabilly to 1970s funk and soul. There are more Latin American rhythms—and mambo lessons—at **S.O.B.s** (Varick Street at Houston Street; tel: 243–4940).

The Bank (Houston Street at Essex Street; tel: 505–5033), is a slick if sometimes run-of-the-mill disco, and makes for a reasonable night out—or try the **Palladium**

Radio City Music Hall is a popular rock venue

(14th Street between Third and Fourth avenues; tel: 473–7171), a cavernous room and dance-floor with video monitors designed by leading architect Arata Isozaki.

Opening in the mid-1980s, the subdued ambience of **Nell's** (14th Street between Seventh and Eighth avenues; tel: 675–1567) was intended as an antidote to flashing lights and pulsating music; this Victorian-style living room has faded from fashion but is still worth a visit. However, a new trend is rapidly evolving: the "lounge", a quiet place where the more sedate nocturnal New Yorker can just lounge and chat.

Rock music Rock music's big names always include New York on their international touring schedules. If they are not popular enough to fill the 55,000-capacity Shea Stadium in Queens, they are most likely to be found in venues such as the **Beacon Theater** (Broadway at 75th Street; for ticket info tel: 307–7171), **Madison Square Garden** (Seventh Avenue between 31st and 33rd streets; tel: 465–6741), or **Radio City Music Hall** (Sixth Avenue at 50th Street; tel: 247–4777) which stages musicals, dance and rock music shows.

Up-and-coming bands from the U.S. and Europe who have outgrown the small club scene but are not yet ready for the large concert halls turn up most nights of the week in mid-sized venues such as **Irving Plaza** (17 Irving Place; tel: 777–6800), the **Roxy** (515 W 18th Street; tel 714–8001), and **Roseland** (52nd Street between Eighth Avenue and Broadway; tel: 249–8870), the legendary ballroom of the Big Band era.

Other venues worth checking out are **The Bottom Line** (4th Street near Fifth Avenue; tel: 228–7800), showcasing new signings to major labels and also booking some aging 1960s cult names, and **Wetlands** (Hudson Street, three blocks south of Canal Street; tel: 966–4225), with 1960s psychedelic décor, organic food, and books and pamphlets on ecological issues—as well as a full roster of rock, reggae, and funk bands.

Another dependable spot for local talent and sometimes more, is **Brownies** (169 Avenue A, between Tenth and Eleventh Streets; tel: 420–8392).

New York's own rock music scene is highly incestuous—some bands might be huge in a particular neighborhood but unknown outside it. Plenty of exotically named hopefuls can be heard every night for free, or a few dollars, in dozens of tiny clubs secreted throughout the East Village and SoHo. For details, read the ads in the *Village Voice* or look for the handwritten notices pinned up in local cafés and bars.

Talking Heads and Blondie were just two of the big names that emerged from the New York punk scene of the mid-1970s, which centered on the still-surviving **C.B.G.B.** (Bowery at Bleecker Street; tel: 982–4052). Unknown bands play here every night of the week, while performance art and readings are also billed at the **C.B.'s 313 Gallery** next door (tel: 388–2529).

Experimentally minded musicians explore rock's avant-garde fringe at the **Knitting Factory** (Houston Street near Mulberry Street; tel: 219–3055).

Jazz and blues Since the 1940s, New York has been well endowed with smoky jazz clubs, usually occupying basements in Greenwich Village. Their floorboards will have been trodden by many of jazz's most illustrious figures.

Most jazz clubs have two or three nightly shows. Cover charges range from around $8 to $20 or more. Sometimes there will also be a two-drink minimum charge (around $6).

The long-established **Village Vanguard** (Seventh Avenue at 11th Street; tel: 255–4037) epitomizes the dark-and-smoky Greenwich Village basement jazz club. Many top names play here regularly. Major jazz stars are also frequent visitors to the atmospheric **Blue Note** (3rd Street

A popular jazz venue, Birdland is named after a club that was a 1940s legend

at MacDougal Street; tel: 475–8592), where cover charges can sometimes be very steep. Among the city's newer jazz venues is **Iridium Room** (48 W 63rd Street; tel: 582–2121), highly rated for its excellent roster of live acts and its quirky architecture, designed to resemble frozen music. An older venue in a fresh setting is **Birdland** (315 W 44th Street; tel: 581–3080) which aims to re-create the style of a 1940s supper club. It offers three nightly jazz sets as well as a Sunday jazz brunch.

A couple of lower-key Greenwich Village venues are **Sweet Basil** (Seventh Avenue at Bleecker Street; tel: 242–1785) and **55 Bar** (55 Christopher Street; tel: 929 9803), where quality piano and bass duos and more thrive in an intimate atmosphere.

Elsewhere around town, the pricey **Michael's Pub** (118 W 57th Street; tel: 758–2272) specializes in New Orleans-style jazz. On Monday nights, Woody Allen usually adds his clarinet to the exuberant musical melee. An appreciative audience helps make **Smalls** (183 W Tenth Street; tel: 929–7565) a likely place to catch emerging talents, and the **Knickerbocker Bar and Grill** (9th Street and University Place; tel: 228–8490) offers some line-ups that include established jazz stars.

Blues and R.& B., meanwhile, seldom come rawer or raunchier than the nightly acts at **Manny's Car Wash** (1558 Third Avenue at 87th Street; tel: 369–BLUES) or **Terra Blues** (149 Bleeker Street; tel: 777–7776).

Folk Greenwich Village was the epicenter of the early 1960s folk revival. Judy Collins, Bob Dylan, and other legends started here. The days of hootenannys are long gone, but legendary folk venues such as the **Bitter End** (147 Bleecker Street; tel: 673–7030) remain, alongside newer ones such as the small and welcoming **Centerfold Coffeehouse** (Church of Sts Paul and Andrew, 263 W 86th Street; tel: 866–4454).

Greenwich Village jazz: a costlier night out than 50 years ago, but the atmosphere remains the same

Country music
Listening to country music seems somewhat incongruous in ultra-urban New York, but the large and brassy Full Moon Saloon (Eighth Avenue at 46th Street) features a mixture of new wave and traditional country sounds. Smaller country venues are O'Lunney's (44th Street near Fifth Avenue; tel: 840–6688) and the Rodeo Bar (Third Avenue at 27th Street; tel: 683–6500).

New York for children

For children in the Outer Boroughs

Brooklyn's Children's Museum (145 Brooklyn Avenue) is an architecturally innovative affair, with exhibits to encourage understanding of the basics of science and nature. Older children might prefer a romp through the vintage subway cars displayed at the New York Transit Museum (see page 76).

A ride on the Staten Island Ferry is enjoyable in its own right and, once ashore, the Richmondtown Historic Restoration (see page 179) has traditionally attired guides bringing local history to life in a colorful and informative way.

Elsewhere, the Bronx Zoo (see pages 70–71) has a children's section; in Queen's, the New York Hall of Science (page 171) has a mass of entertaining hands-on exhibits.

Alice and friends in Central Park

A number of Manhattan museums have sections intended for children but only the **Children's Museum of Manhattan** (in the Tisch Building, 83rd Street between Broadway and Amsterdam Avenue) is purpose-designed: a wonderful play-as-you-learn facility using computerized interactive exhibits and displays. The Children's Museum's four floors of informative fun include the Brainatarium, exploring the functions of the human brain, and the Time Warner Center for Media, where children can film, edit, and star in their own videos. Outside, the Urban Tree House explores the environmental conflicts between city life and the natural world.

Still with an educational role, the **American Museum of Natural History** (see pages 63–64), with its dinosaur skeletons, giant model whale, and scores of stuffed creatures, is usually popular. At the **Sony Wonder Technology Lab** (550 Madison Avenue), the multinational media corporation has regular programs for children, which explore the mysteries of animation and other media-related subjects with the aid of interactive computers and special weekend workshops.

For city views, the **World Trade Center**, with its speedy elevator ride, wins out over the **Empire State Building**, although the latter's **New York Skyride** provides thrills. A boat trip (page 67) can be combined with a clamber around the historic ships of the **South Street Seaport** (page 178).

In Central Park, the main **Central Park Wildlife Center** is behind the Arsenal at 64th Street and Fifth Avenue (tel: 408–0271). Sea lion feeding times are at 11:30 AM, 2 PM, and 4 PM. Storytelling takes place Saturdays at the Hans Christian Andersen statue by Conservatory Water (tel: 794–6564 for details). On the northern edge of Central Park are the exhibits of the **Charles A. Dana Discovery**

Center (110th Street and Fifth Avenue), which explore environmental themes. Special events include beginners' birdwatching and walks.

When it is time for treats, go to the **Enchanted Forest** (85 Mercer Street), where expensive stuffed animals inhabit a make-believe medieval forest, or **F.A.O. Schwarz** (Fifth Avenue between 58th and 59th streets), packed from floor to ceiling with the kind of toys children dream about—including top-of-the-line items not regularly found at your local Toys "R" Us.

Above: Getting to grips with the game in Central Park

Above left: The Bronx Zoo, described on pages 70–71

Left: Rollerblading in Central Park

New York for free

Free in the Outer Boroughs
The Brooklyn Historical Museum is free every day. Throughout the summer, the Brooklyn Arts Council (for details, tel: 718/625–0080) hosts free musical events at several locations, including Brighton Beach. The Bronx's Hall of Fame for Great Americans (page 72) is always free, as is the Bronx Zoo (pages 70–71) from Tuesday to Thursday, although a voluntary donation is expected. In Queens, the New York Hall of Science (page 171) does not have an admission charge but suggests a donation. Staten Island's Garibaldi Meucci Museum (page 180) has free admission, and there is no charge for the July concert series at Snug Harbor (tel: 718/448–2500).

244

Even paupers can have fun in the Big Apple. Many of New York's finest things—architecture, pulsating streetlife, distinctive neighborhoods, fantastic department stores—can be seen without spending a cent. Study the suggestions below for even more ways to enjoy New York for free.

Free in Manhattan Several of the city's major museums described in the A to Z section of this book offer free admission on selected weekday evenings: the **Cooper-Hewitt Museum** (*Open* Tue 5–9 PM); the **Guggenheim Museum** (*Open* Fri 5–8 PM. *Admission charge* donation); the **Museum of Modern Art** (*Open* Thu 5–8:30 PM. *Admission charge* donation); and the **Whitney Museum of American Art** (*Open* Thu 6–8 PM). Among the smaller institutions with temporary shows, the **National Academy of Design** allows free entry to its exhibitions on Tuesday evenings (5–8 PM), as does the **International Center of Photography** (*Admission charge* donation).

Museums and galleries to which admission is always free are the **American Numismatic Society** (page 65); the **American Bible Society** (page 61); the **Forbes Magazine Galleries** (pages 107); the **Hispanic Society of America** (page 126); the **Museum of American Folk Art** (page 155; there is a suggested donation of $2); the **Museum of American Illustration** (see page 62); the **Nicolas Roerich Museum** (page 189); and the **Police Academy Museum** (page 152).

Visiting **Federal Hall** (page 102) and the **General Grant Memorial** (page 110) costs nothing, and both **Lincoln Center** (page 134) and the **Stock Exchange** (page 182) offer free guided tours. When tickets are available, you can listen for free to delegates' speeches at the **U.N. General Assembly** (page 184).

Free musical and theatrical entertainment can be found in the summer in **Central Park** (tel: 794–6564), at **Rockefeller Center** (tel: 632–4000), on the plazas of **Lincoln Center** (tel: 875–5350) and the **World Trade Center** (tel: 435–4170), and at **South Street Seaport** (tel: SEA PORT).

Window-shopping, Manhattan-style: a live window display at Macy's department store

TRAVEL FACTS

Arriving
By air Flights into New York land at John F. Kennedy Airport (in Queens, about 15 miles east of Manhattan), at La Guardia (also in Queens, 8 miles east of Manhattan), and at Newark (in New Jersey, about 15 miles west of Manhattan). La Guardia Airport is almost exclusively for domestic flights.

Wherever you land, travel into Manhattan should be fairly straightforward if somewhat time-consuming: Allow at least an hour and a half to travel from the airport to the city. Each airport has a Ground Transportation Desk where you can check routes, times and fares into the city.

Besides the public transportation services detailed below, taxis operate from each of the three airports and should be taken from the clearly signposted official taxi dispatch lines, which will be pointed out by uniformed airport staff. Any taxi driver who approaches you in person is likely to be unlicensed. Never ride in independent cabs; stick with yellow cabs, and look for the medallion—the official flat bronze-colored disk affixed to the vehicle's hood.

Taxi fares from the airports into Manhattan are high: expect to spend around $40–$50 (road and bridge tolls are extra) from Newark, $20–$30 from La Guardia. From JFK there is a flat fare of $30 plus tips and tolls. Bear in mind, too, that traffic can be dense around each airport and can add further to taxi charges.

Use only licensed yellow cabs

From J.F.K. Free shuttle buses run to the nearest subway station, at Howard Beach, which leaves a 60-minute ride into Manhattan. Other buses link the airport to other subway lines, intended for New Yorkers who want to get home without changing lines. (See **Public transportation** on pages 252–253.)

Nervous tourists arriving in New York for the first time and carrying luggage should use the Carey Airport Express bus service (tel: 800/284–0909). Buses depart for six stops in Midtown Manhattan every 30 minutes between 6 AM and midnight. You buy a one-way ticket, for less than half the cost of a taxi, from the uniformed attendant at the "Ground Transportation" desks inside the terminals.

Another option slightly more expensive but potentially quicker is to use a shared minibus. Gray Line Air Shuttle (tel: 800/451–0455) operates minibuses from J.F.K. to any address in Manhattan, available between 7 AM and 11 PM.

If money is no object, you can zip between the airport and Manhattan by helicopter. The helicopter service takes 10 minutes to reach the 34th Street Heliport (tel: 800/645–3494).

From Newark The New Jersey Transit Bus (tel: 201/762–5100) runs to Manhattan's Port Authority Bus Terminal (42nd Street and Eighth Avenue) around the clock. The journey takes about 30 minutes. Alternatively, you could take the Olympia Trails Airport Express (tel: 964–6233), which travels from Newark to three locations in Midtown and Lower Manhattan between 6:15 AM and midnight, departing roughly every 20 minutes.

As from J.F.K., Gray Line Air Shuttle (tel: 800/451–0455) operates shared minibuses from Newark airport to any address in Manhattan.

From La Guardia Local buses run to the rest of Queens, but to reach Manhattan the choice is between the Carey Express Airport Coach (tel: 800/451–0909), which departs for six Midtown Manhattan stops every 30 minutes between 6:30 AM and midnight, and a shared Gray Line Air Shuttle minibus (tel: 800/451–0455)

Helicopters provide a speedy but costly way to sightsee or reach the airport. Most travelers prefer to use the bus

to any address in Manhattan, available between 7 AM and 11 PM.

By boat New York's great days as a seaport may be long gone, but the *Q.E.2* keeps the tradition and the sheer luxury of transatlantic ocean-liner travel very much alive. After the ocean crossing, you will glide into New York beneath the Statue of Liberty and put ashore at Midtown Manhattan's gleaming Passenger Ship Terminal, which is situated on Twelfth Avenue between 50th and 52nd streets.

By bus Long-distance buses into New York complete their journeys at the country's largest and busiest bus station: Port Authority Bus Terminal (tel: 564–8484), which is found at the junction of 42nd Street and Eighth Avenue.

By train Most local commuter trains pull into Grand Central Terminal, at 42nd Street and Park Avenue, while Amtrak's long-distance trains pull into New York's other station, Penn Station, at 31st Street and Eighth

Avenue. For information on train travel, tel: 800/872–7245.

Car breakdown
In the unlikely event of your rental car breaking down, simply phone the car rental firm you rented from. With luck, the rental company representative will shortly arrive with another car in which you can continue your journey.

Should you be break down far from a phone, stay with your vehicle and wait for a police officer to come by. If a passing motorist stops to offer help, there is every chance that the approach will be genuine—but treat the offer with caution. Usually, the best help such a person can provide is driving on to a public telephone and making a call on your behalf.

Car rental

With traffic lights on almost every block and a lack of affordable parking, as well as the constant threat of gridlock, Manhattan—and New York City generally—is a difficult place in which to drive. For excursions outside the city, however, a rental car is almost essential. A few taxi rides cost less than a space in an overnight parking lot, so no Manhattanite drives his own car in the city unless he has to. If you're planning an excursion, consider renting a car just before departure.

You will save time and money if you travel out of the city by public transportation and then rent a car in a smaller town. But, all the major international car-rental companies have desks at New York's airports (and offices in the city), where you can collect a prebooked car or rent one on the spot.

The address of the nearest major car-rental outlet can be found by calling the following toll-free numbers: Avis (tel: 800/331–1212); Budget (tel: 800/601–5383); Hertz (tel: 800/654 –3131); National (tel: 800/227–7368); Thrifty (tel: 800/367–2277). Many more rental firms are listed in the Yellow Pages, though the big international companies are often safest.

Wherever you rent a car, check the small print very carefully, particularly with regard to Collision Damage Waiver (C.D.W.), a compulsory form of insurance that can add considerably to costs. Check also whether or not the vehicle has to be returned with a full tank of gas.

Without booking ahead, anyone under the age of 25 and/or without a credit card may have problems renting a car in New York.

Climate

Although there's an occasional bone-chilling winter day, with winds blasting in off the Hudson, snow is hardly ever a problem in the city (the skyscrapers trap enough heat to melt most snowfalls). Summer is the only unpleasant time of year, especially the humid, hot days of July and August, when many Manhattanites vacate the island for summer homes. Most hotels are air-conditioned, but if you're traveling in summer and choosing budget accommodations, it's a good idea to ask whether your room has an air conditioner. Air-

The view that confirms you have really arrived in the Big Apple

conditioned stores, restaurants, the-aters, and museums provide respite from the heat; so do the many green expanses of parks. Subways and buses are usually air-conditioned, but subway stations in summer can be as hot as saunas (and considerably dirtier).

For advice on when to travel outside New York City, where summers are much more pleasant, see the panel on page 194.

Crime
New York is among the world's most notorious cities for crime against the person. Stay alert and read the Survival Guide on pages 54–55 of this book, and you will reduce what is already a statistically very slender chance of your being robbed or attacked.

Don't leave money and valuables in your hotel room: simply hand them over to the staff for safe keeping. Street robbery can be reduced by not carrying easily snatched handbags and not having your wallet sticking out of your back pocket.

Lost or stolen traveler's checks are relatively easy to replace (read the instructions when you buy the checks and make a note of the relevant details).

Driving tips
It is never a good idea to bring a car into Manhattan—not least because New Yorkers drive like maniacs, and parking can be very expensive. Where less-expensive parking lots do exist, they are rarely the most central. Free parking on the street is almost impos-sible to find in Midtown, except on Sunday mornings. If you *do* bring a car into Manhattan, note that parking infringements attract stiff fines or worse (your car could be towed), so read the signs carefully. Never park within 10 feet of a fire hydrant. If pos-sible, avoid leaving valuables in the car: if you can't take them with you, make sure that they are out of sight.

Venture beyond the city to the Catskill Mountains, the remoter parts of the Hudson Valley, Long Island, or New Jersey—or farther afield—and wheels of your own become essential (see pages 194–211).

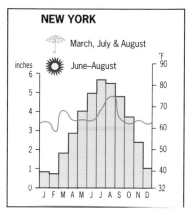

NEW YORK

March, July & August

June–August

There is a speed limit of 55 m.p.h. or 65 m.p.h. in force on interstates (in some places there may also be a minimum limit). In built-up areas, lower speed limits are indicated. An extremely dim view is taken of drinking and driving—it is not unusu-al for hefty fines and prison sentences to be frequently imposed.

Be warned that tolls are charged for some Manhattan bridges and for some stretches of road in the Outer Boroughs.

If you are a member of an auto-mobile club, such as A.A.A., be sure to have its emergency road service phone number handy in case of a breakdown.

Emergency telephone numbers
For **ambulance**, **police** or **fire**, dial 911 (no money required) and ask for the relevant service.

Other emergency numbers include **Crime Victim's Hotline** (tel: 577–7777), **New York Gay and Lesbian Anti-violence Unit** (tel: 807–0197), **Rape Helpline** (tel: 267–7273).

Lost property
Lost at J.F.K. Airport, tel: 718/656–4120.
Lost at La Guardia Airport, contact relevant airline.
Lost at Newark Airport, tel: 201/961–2230.
Lost in a taxi, tel: 840–4734.
Lost on a bus or the subway, tel: 718/330–3000.

Media

New York has hundreds of T.V. and radio channels and newspapers and magazines. Free publications aimed at visitors litter every hotel lobby, the best source of what's-on information being the new *Critic's Choice*. Also excellent are the weekly *Village Voice* and *New York* magazine. For a full run-down on the city's media, see pages 132–133.

Money matters

Automated-teller machines (A.T.M.s) are proliferating; many are tied to international networks such as **Cirrus** and **Plus**. You can use your bank card at A.T.M.s away from home to withdraw money from your checking account and get cash advances on a credit-card account (providing your card has been programmed with a personal identification number, or P.I.N.). Check in advance on limits on withdrawals and cash advances within specified periods. Remember that finance charges apply on credit-card cash advances from A.T.M.s as well as on those from tellers. And note that transaction fees for A.T.M. withdrawals outside your home turf will probably be higher than for withdrawals at home. For specific Cirrus locations in the United States and Canada, call 800/424–7787 (for U.S. Plus locations, 800/843–587), and press the area code and first three digits of the number you're calling from (or the

Elevated subway in Williamsburg

calling area where you want an A.T.M.). American Express Company's **Express Cash** system lets you withdraw cash and/or traveler's checks from a worldwide network of 57,000 American Express dispensers and participating bank A.T.M.s. You must enroll first (call 800–CASH–NOW for a form and allow two weeks for processing). Withdrawals are charged not to your card but to a designated bank account. You can withdraw up to $1,000 per seven-day period on the basic card, more if your card is gold or platinum. There is a 2% fee (minimum $2.50, maximum $10) for each cash transaction made, and 1% fee for traveler's checks (except for the platinum card), which are available from American Express dispensers.

At AmEx offices, cardholders can also cash personal checks for up to $1,000 in any seven-day period; of this $200 can be in cash, more if available, with the balance paid in traveler's checks, for which all but platinum cardholders pay a 1% fee. Higher limits apply to the gold and platinum cards.

Older travelers

The **American Association of Retired Persons** (A.A.R.P., 601 E. St, N.W., Washington, DC 20049, tel: 202/434–2277) provides independent travelers the Purchase Privilege Program, which offers discounts on hotels, car rentals, and sightseeing, and the A.A.R.P. Motoring Plan, provided by Amoco, which furnishes domestic trip-routing information and emergency road-service aid for an annual fee of $39.95 per person or couple ($59.95 for a premium version). A.A.R.P. membership is open to those aged 50 and over; annual dues are currently $8 per person or couple.

Two other membership organizations offer discounts on lodgings, car rentals, and other travel products, along with such nontravel perks as magazines and newsletters. The National Council of Senior Citizens (1331 F. St. N.W., Washington, DC 20004, tel: 202/347–8800) is a nonprofit advocacy group with some 5,000 local clubs across the United

States; membership costs $12 per person or couple annually. Mature Outlook (6001 N. Clark St., Chicago, IL 60660, tel: 800/336–6330), a Sears Roebuck & Co. subsidiary with 800,000 members, charges $9.95 for an annual membership.

Note: When using any senior-citizen identification card for reduced hotel rates, mention it when you are booking, not when checking out. At restaurants, show your card before you're seated; you may find that discounts are limited to certain menus, days or hours. If you are renting a car, ask about promotional rates that might improve on your senior-citizen discount.

Saga International Holidays (222 Berkeley St., Boston, MA 02116, tel: 800/343–0273), which specializes in group travel for people over 60, offers a selection of variously priced tours and cruises.

Opening hours

New York store opening hours vary greatly. Many big stores will open on weekdays and Saturdays from 9 AM to 5 or 6 PM, but smaller or more specialty stores may open as late as 11 AM or noon and close at 9 PM or 10 PM.

Museum opening times also vary. Many are open from 10 or 11 AM to 6 PM on weekdays and Saturdays (though several are closed on Monday). Some also open on Sundays, and several keep late hours on Tuesdays.

Bank opening hours are Monday to Friday from 9 AM to 3 or 3:30 PM (6 PM on Thursday at some branches).

Places of worship

New York's places of worship are many and varied. Some of the principal ones are described in the A to Z section of this book and on pages 120–121. Your hotel reception desk will be able to advise of those in your immediate neighborhood, and the telephone book carries a comprehensive list.

Police

Popularly known as "New York's Finest," the city's police are helpful and efficient in almost every situation. Besides patroling in cars, officers are regularly seen on the street, and the police are well represented in crowd situations.

CONVERSION CHARTS

FROM	TO	MULTIPLY BY
Inches	Centimeters	2.54
Centimeters	Inches	0.3937
Feet	Meters	0.3048
Meters	Feet	3.2810
Yards	Meters	0.9144
Meters	Yards	1.0940
Miles	Kilometers	1.6090
Kilometers	Miles	0.6214
Acres	Hectares	0.4047
Hectares	Acres	2.4710
U.S. Gallons	Liters	3.7854
Liters	U.S. Gallons	0.2642
Ounces	Grams	28.35
Grams	Ounces	0.0353
Pounds	Grams	453.6
Grams	Pounds	0.0022
Pounds	Kilograms	0.4536
Kilograms	Pounds	2.205
U.S. Tons	Tonnes	0.9072
Tonnes	U.S. Tons	1.1023

MEN'S SUITS							
U.K.	36	38	40	42	44	46	48
Rest of Europe	46	48	50	52	54	56	58
U.S.	36	38	40	42	44	46	48

DRESS SIZES						
U.K.	8	10	12	14	16	18
France	36	38	40	42	44	46
Italy	38	40	42	44	46	48
Rest of Europe	34	36	38	40	42	44
U.S.	6	8	10	12	14	16

MEN'S SHIRTS						
U.K.	14	14.5	15	15.5	16	16.5 17
Rest of Europe	36	37	38	39/40	41	42 43
U.S.	14	14.5	15	15.5	16	16.5 17

MEN'S SHOES						
U.K.	7	7.5	8.5	9.5	10.5	11
Rest of Europe	41	42	43	44	45	46
U.S.	8	8.5	9.5	10.5	11.5	12

WOMEN'S SHOES						
U.K.	4.5	5	5.5	6	6.5	7
Rest of Europe	38	38	39	39	40	41
U.S.	6	6.5	7	7.5	8	8.5

251

If you are unfortunate enough to be the victim of theft, you will need to visit a police station to have your insurance claim authorized. Every New York neighborhood has a police station. To find the one nearest you, dial 374–5000. If you need the police in an emergency, dial 911.

Post offices

New York's main post office, at Eighth Avenue and 34th Street, stays open around the clock, every day of the week. Elsewhere in the city, larger post offices are open Monday to Friday from 8 AM to 6 PM and Saturdays from 8 AM to 1 PM. Smaller post offices keep shorter hours.

Stamps can also be bought, sometimes at inflated prices, through vending machines found in some stores and in many hotel lobbies.

Public transportation

Spending most of your time in Manhattan will leave you much less reliant on public transportation than you might expect. Not only are distances small, but much of Manhattan is best seen on foot. If you are exhausted, in a rush, planning to visit the Outer Boroughs or simply commuting between nightclubs, however, you will need to make use of the city's buses, subway, or taxis.

City buses Substantially slower than subway trains, New York buses at least allow passengers to view the city as they travel through it. Many people find them less intimidating than the subway system. The bus network is comprehensive (free maps are available from the tourist information office listed on page 255), and the majority of routes run north–south, with free transfers provided to change on to east–west "crosstown" buses.

Bus stops are close to street corners—marked by a blue sign and a yellow painted section of curb—and most have a route map and frequency schedule for the buses that use that stop. The route is displayed on the front of each bus. Most buses stop every two or three blocks; those marked "limited" (which only run at rush hour) make fewer stops, usually only at major junctions.

It is illegal to pass a stationary school bus

As with the subway, there is a flat fare (currently $1.50) for all journeys. This can be paid in coins (exact change only; no dollar bills) or with a subway token (see below), either of which should be dropped into the box beside the driver.

If you need a transfer, ask the driver as you pay and he or she will hand you a transfer slip. Transfers can be used only for continuing travel, not as round-trip tickets. They are valid for a few hours from the time punched on them and can be used only on the bus routes printed on the back of the transfer slip.

Especially during rush hours, New York buses can become solidly packed. If you are wedged in a crowded bus and think your stop may be coming up soon, start making your way towards the exit doors (which are in the middle of the bus—though you can also get off at the front door where you entered) in plenty of time; otherwise there is every chance you will not reach the doors before they shut and the bus moves on.

The subway The much-maligned New York subway system is a swift, inexpensive, and largely efficient way to get about the city.

A tangle of lines denoted by numbers and letters, the subway system map (available free from subway station token booths and from the tourist information office listed on page 255) initially seems hopelessly confusing. In fact, the system is relatively easy to use provided you remember that "Uptown" trains go north (toward the Upper West and East sides and Harlem) and "Downtown" trains travel south (toward Lower Manhattan). Any train labeled "Brooklyn Bound" is indeed bound for Brooklyn but will make stops in Lower Manhattan on the way.

What can be more confusing is the choice between "Express" and "Local" trains. While local trains stop at all stations on a particular line, express trains stop only at selected stations. Board an express train by mistake and you can sometimes could find yourself some distance from where you want to be, and possibly in a dangerous neighborhood. If this happens, cross over to the other platform and take the next train back.

Provided you know which line and which direction you want before entering the station, follow the relevant signs to the platform. If you do not know, inquire at the ticket booth or ask a uniformed transit police officer. Each train has the relevant letter or number and its destination shown along its side, in a color that corresponds to the colors on the subway map.

During the day, trains arrive every 10–15 minutes (more often in rush hours). Between midnight and 5 AM (the service operates around the clock), the usual wait is 20–30 minutes.

To enter the subway system, you will need to drop a subway token (which currently costs $1.50) into a slot, or swipe your Metrocard through an electronic reader, and pass through a turnstile. Subway tokens can be bought from the token booths found at every station (their opening hours are shown above the station entrance) and also from a few major museums. Tokens are gradually being replaced by electronic metro cards. The subway, like other locations in New York and other large cities, does have its share of crime—but providing you stay with the crowds and stay alert, you should have no problems (see pages 54–55). On fares, check the latest details with the New York Convention and Visitors Bureau (see page 255).

City streetlife takes many forms in the Big Apple

253

Taxis New York taxis are expensive and liable to be stuck in traffic for long periods of time. Sometimes cabs are the best and least expensive way to get where you are going, however. When you want one, simply raise your hand to hail the next empty one to pass by. You know a cab is empty if the sign on its roof is lighted.

Once under way, it is a good idea to ask the driver what route he intends to take, and, if you are going any distance, to follow your route on a map. This helps if the driver gets lost and also prevents any unwanted "scenic detours" intended to increase the fare.

Always wear the seat-belts provided—the security barriers can be lethal to teeth in sudden stops—and get a receipt from the driver before leaving. If you leave something in the cab, you may then have a marginally less slim chance of getting it back.

Use only the official "medallion" cabs. These are yellow with "N.Y.C. Taxi" stenciled on the side, a light on the roof, and a medallion on the hood. Any other vehicle looking for passengers will be unlicensed (known colloquially as a "gypsy cab") and should be ignored. Official taxi charges currently begin at $1.50 and gain 25¢ for each 1/5 mile traveled and 25¢ for

Street advertising is an art form New York could call its own

each minute stopped in traffic; a 15–20 percent tip is the norm.

Rest rooms
Public rest rooms in New York run the gamut when it comes to cleanliness. Facilities in Penn Station, Grand Central Terminal, and the Port Authority bus terminal are often inhabited by homeless people. Do not use rest rooms in subway stations. Instead, try Midtown department stores such as Macy's, Lord & Taylor, and Bloomingdale's, museums, and large hotels. Public atriums, such as the Citicorp Center and Trump Tower, also provide reasonable public facilities. Restaurant rest rooms are usually for patrons. If you're dressed well and look as if you belong, you can just sail right on in. Be aware that cinemas, Broadway theaters, and concert halls have limited amenities, and there are often long lines before performances, as well as during intermissions.

Student and youth travel
Students in full-time education and anyone under 26 may qualify for discounted flights offered by travel agents that specialize in youth and

student travel. Students carrying International Student Identity Cards (I.S.I.C.s) will also find themselves entitled to reduced admission to many New York museums and other attractions.

While not exclusively for young and student travelers, the city's Y.M.C.A.s and youth hostels (see page 215) offer budget-priced accommodations and a chance to socialize with other young New York visitors from around the world.

Telephones
You'll find payphones in the street, in hotel lobbies, in train and bus stations, in bars and restaurants, and in most public buildings.

Almost without exception, hotel room telephones have charges much higher than those of public telephones. Sometimes hotels even charge for dialing toll-free numbers!

Emergency calls (dial 911) and calls to the operator (dial 0) or the international operator (dial 1-800/874-4000) are free.

Throughout this book, toll-free numbers are given where available. The area code for Manhattan, (212), is omitted on the assumption that you are calling from another Manhattan number.

Time
New York uses Eastern Standard Time, three hours ahead of the West Coast.

Tipping
How much you tip is entirely up to you, but the general rule in a restaurant or coffee shop is to leave the person who served you 15-20 percent of the total bill. (An easy way to calculate the approximate amount is to double the sales tax figure—which is 8.25 percent—shown at the bottom of the bill.) Do not leave a tip at any food outlet where you serve yourself or where the food is sold to be taken out.

After a taxi ride, it is customary to tip the driver around 15-20 percent of the fare. The amount need not be

St. Paul's Chapel on Fulton Street was built in 1766

exact, however, and most people (if the amount works out within reason) allow the driver to keep the change.

Tipping hotel porters is also expected. Again, the amount you tip is entirely discretionary, but plan on $1 per bag. If a porter simply helps move your luggage from the lobby into a taxi outside the hotel, a total of $1-$2 should usually be sufficient. Leave the chambermaid $1 per day if you wish.

Tourist information
The multilingual staff of the New York Convention and Visitors' Bureau, 2 Columbus Circle, at the junction of 59th Street and Broadway, are able to answer visitor queries and provide free bus and subway maps. The office (*Open* on weekdays from 9 AM to 6 PM and on weekends from 10 AM to 6 PM; tel: 800/NYC-VISIT or 397-8222) also has racks of free leaflets and brochures detailing New York hotels, restaurants and tourist attractions.

255

Tours on foot

There are many guided tours on offer in New York. **Sidewalks of New York** (tel: 212/517–0201; 212/662–6300) take various thematic tours on weekends year-round and on weekdays by appointment. Other guided tour companies include **Adventures on a Shoestring** (tel: 212/265–2663), **Citywalks** (tel: 212/989–2456), **Urban Explorations** (tel: 718/721–5254), and the **Big Apple Greeters** (tel: 669–2362), who specialize in showing New York to out-of-town visitors. See also page 56.

Travelers with disabilities

In New York, facilities for travelers with disabilities are not only impressive, but are also improving all the time. By law, public buildings have to be at least partially wheelchair-accessible, and all must provide accessible toilet facilities. Almost all New York buses have rear-door "elevators" for wheelchair-users, and most are also able to "kneel" to make it easier to get onto the bus from the curb.

Trains and airlines are obliged to provide services for travelers with disabilities if requested, and Amtrak has earned a reputation for doing this well. Though less comfortable than the trains, Greyhound buses are more frequent and will allow a companion to travel free provided that you have a doctor's certificate stating that this is necessary.

Some major car-rental companies can arrange vehicles with hand controls provided they receive advance notice.

For brochures and further information, contact the **Mayor's Office for People with Disabilities** (52 Chambers St., Office 206, New York, NY 10007, tel: 212/788–2830). Blind or visually impaired visitors may appreciate a visit to the **Andrew Heiskell Library for the Blind and Physically Handicapped** (40 W. 20th St., tel: 212/206–5400), a public library branch with a large collection of Braille, large-print, and recorded books, housed in a layout specially designed for easy access by the visually impaired.

The Information Center for Individuals with Disabilities (Fort Point Pl., 27-43 Wormwood St., Boston, MA 02210, tel: 617/727–5540; in MA, 800/462–5015 between 11 AM and 4 PM, or leave message; T.D.D./ T.T.Y., 617/345–9743) is a private, nonprofit organization providing information, referral and problem-solving assistance on all issues of disability. The company publishes a monthly newsletter, *Disability Issues*, and *Tips For Traveling With Disabilities*, which includes state-by-state listings of tour and travel operators providing services for people with disabilities, useful voice and T.D.D. telephone numbers, general advice for travel planning, and recent travel articles from *Disability News*. *Tips For Traveling With Disabilities* is available for $10 per copy (inclusive of shipping and handling).

Mobility International U.S.A. (Box 3551, Eugene, OR 97403, voice and T.D.D. tel: 503/343–1284) is the U.S. branch of an international organization based in

Stamps can be bought from vending machines

Britain and present in 30 countries. It coordinates exchange programs for people with disabilities, especially programs with an educational, work, or community-service component; provides travel information; and publishes and sells *A World of Options for the '90s*, a guide to travel for people with disabilities ($16). Annual membership costs $20 and includes a quarterly newsletter and access to a referral service.

The **Society for the Advancement of Travel for the Handicapped** (S.A.T.H., 347 5th Ave., Suite 610, New York, NY 10016, tel: 212/447–7284, fax: 212/725–8253) provides lists of tour operators specializing in travel for people with disabilities, an information sheet on traveling with specific disabilities and to specific countries, and a quarterly newsletter. Annual membership is $45, $25 for students and senior citizens. Nonmembers may send $5 and an S.A.S.E. for information on specific destinations. S.A.T.H. members receive a color magazine, *Access to Travel*, which provides a wide range of travel information for travelers with all kinds of disabilities.

Travelin' Talk (Box 3534, Clarksville, TN 37043, tel: 615/552–6670) is a network of people with disabilities worldwide ready to provide the up-to-date lowdown on accessibility in their area. To join, there is a one-time registration fee (on a sliding scale of $1–$10 for individuals, $15–$50 for organizations) that also entitles you to a quarterly newsletter.

The **Big Apple Greeters**, who show visitors around (see **Tours on foot** page 256), extend their service to those with disabilities.

Traveling with cameras, camcorders, and laptops

About film and cameras

If your camera is new or if you haven't used it for a while, shoot and develop a few rolls of film before leaving home. Pack some lens tissue and an extra battery for your built-in light meter, and invest in an inexpensive skylight filter, to both protect your lens and provide some definition in hazy shots. Store film in a cool, dry place—never in the car's glove compartment or on the shelf under the rear window.

Films above I.S.O. 400 are more sensitive to damage from airport security X-rays than other films; very high speed films, I.S.O. 1,000 and above, are exceedingly vulnerable. To protect your film, don't put it in checked luggage; carry it on your person in a plastic bag and ask for a hand inspection. Such requests should be honored at American airports.

Don't depend on a lead-lined bag to protect film in checked luggage— the airline's security may very well turn up the dosage of radiation to see what you've got in there. Airport metal detectors do not harm film, although you'll set off the alarm if you walk through one with a roll in your pocket. Call the Kodak information Center (tel: 800/242–2424) for details.

Take care on the subway

257

About camcorders

Before your trip, put new or long-unused camcorders through their paces, and practice panning and zooming. Invest in a skylight filter to protect the lens, and check the lithium battery that lights up the L.C.D. (liquid crystal display) modes. As for the rechargeable nickel-cadmium batteries that are the camera's power source, take along an extra pair, so while you're using your camcorder you'll have one battery ready and another recharging.

About videotape

Unlike still-camera film, videotape is not damaged by X-rays. However, it may well be harmed by the magnetic field of a walk-through metal detector. Airport security personnel may want you to turn the camcorder on to prove that that's what it is, so make sure the battery is charged when you get to the airport.

About laptops

Security X-rays do not harm hard-disk or floppy-disk storage. Most airlines allow you to use your laptop aloft but request that you turn it off during takeoff and landing so as not to interfere with navigation equipment.

Make sure the battery is charged when you arrive at the airport, because you may be asked to turn on the computer at security checkpoints to prove that it is what it appears to be. If you're a heavy computer user, consider traveling with a backup battery.

Further reading

Many a famous writer has set down his or her impressions of this fascinating city. Some of the best full-length accounts are Christopher Morley's *New York*, a mid-1920s essay; *Walker in the City*, by Alfred Kazin; and *Apple of My Eye*, a 1978 account of writing a New York guidebook, by Helene Hanff. *New York Style*, by Suzanne Slesin, Stafford Cliff, and Daniel Rozensztroch, has several sections devoted to the city. Dan Wakefield recalls his early literary days in *New York in the 50s*. Perhaps the best of all is E.B. White's 1949 essay "Here is New York."

The early history of New York is wittily told in the classic *Knickerbocker's History of New York*, by Washington Irving. For a fine historical introduction to the city, find the heavily illustrated *Columbia Historical Portrait of New York*, by John Kouwenhoven. *New York, New York*, by Oliver E. Allen, is a well-rounded, up-to-date history of the city. *You Must Remember This*, by Jeff Kisseloff, is an oral history of ordinary New Yorkers early in this century. *The Park and its People*, by Roy Rosenzweig and Elizabeth Blackmar, tells how Central Park evolved.

Fiorello H. La Guardia and the Making of Modern New York, by Thomas Kessner, is a biography of the charismatic Depression-era mayor. *The Power Broker* by Robert Caro is a fascinating biography of Robert Moses, one of the city's most influential parks commissioners. Robert Daley's *Prince of the City* is a true-life drama of New York police corruption.

Highly critical accounts of the city's recent politics can be found in *The Streets Were Paved with Gold*, by Ken Auletta; *The Rise and Fall of New York City*, by Roger Starr; *Imperial City*, by Geoffrey Moorhouse; and *City for Sale*, by Jack Newfield and Wayne Barrett. *A License to Steal*, by Benjamin J. Stein, concerns Wall Street's notorious Michael Milken, as does *Den of Thieves*, by James B Stewart.

Theater lovers may want to read *Act One*, the autobiography of playwright Moss Hart; for more up-to-date essays on the city's theater scene, try David Mamet's *The Cabin*. *The Kingdom and the Power*, by Gay Talese, offers a behind-the-scenes look at the *New York Times*; life at one of the city's most venerable magazines is recounted in *Here at the New Yorker*, by Brendan Gill. Speaking of that august publication, *Up in the Old Hotel* brings together Joseph Mitchell's *New Yorker* stories, which deal with colorful New York characters.

From Manet to Manhattan, by Peter Watson, explores the city's art world. *Literary New York*, by Susan Edmiston and Linda D. Cirino, traces the haunts of famous writers, neighborhood by neighborhood. *The Heart of the World*, by Nik Cohn, is a block-by-block history of Manhattan's most famous street, Broadway.

A.I.A. Guide to New York City, by Elliot Willensky and Norval White, is the definitive guide to the city's many building styles; Paul Goldberger's *The City Observed* describes Manhattan building by building. John Kieran's

From a restaurant meal to a shoe-shine ... don't forget that tipping is expected

A Natural History of New York explores the wildlife of the city's parks, while Eugene Kinkead concentrates on the most famous park in Central Park: *The Birth, Decline, and Renewal of a National Treasure*.

Perhaps because so many writers have lived in New York City, there is a wealth of fiction set here. Jack Finney's *Time and Again* is a delightful time-travel story illustrated with 19th-century photos; *Winter's Tale*, by Mark Helprin, uses surreal fantasy to create a portrait of New York's past. Novels set in 19th-century New York include Henry James's *Washington Square*, Edith Wharton's *The Age of Innocence*, and Stephen Crane's *Maggie, A Girl of the Streets*.

O. Henry's short stories depict the early years of this century, while Damon Runyon's are set in the

259

raffish underworld of the 1930s and 1940s. F. Scott Fitzgerald (*The Beautiful and Damned, 1922*), John Dos Passos (*Manhattan Transfer*, 1925), John O'Hara (*Butterfield 8*, 1935), and Mary McCarthy (*The Group*, 1938) also wrote about this city. J. D. Salinger's *Catcher in the Rye* (1951) partly takes place here, as does Thomas Pynchon's *V* (1965). Truman Capote's 1958 novella *Breakfast at Tiffany's* is a special favorite of many New Yorkers.

Many current New York models include *Bonfire of the Vanities*, by Tom Wolfe; *The Mambo Kings Play Songs of Love*, by Oscar Hijuelos; *The New York Trilogy*, by Paul Auster; and *People Like Us*, by Dominick Dunne. For portraits of gay life, try Larry Kramer's *Faggots*, David Leavitt's *The Lost Language of Cranes*, and Sarah Schulman's *After Delores* and *People in Trouble*.

The experience of black people in Harlem has been chronicled in Ralph Ellison's *Invisible Man*, James Baldwin's *Go Tell It on the Mountain*, and Claude Brown's *Manchild in the Promised Land*. For a portrait of Harlem during the 1920s, there's *When Harlem Was in Vogue*, by David Levering Lewis.

The history of New York's Jewish population can be traced through such books as *World of Our Fathers*, by Irving Howe; *Call It Sleep*, by Henry Roth; *The Promise*, by Chaim Potok; *Enemies, A Love Story*, by Isaac Bashevis Singer; and *Our Crowd*, by Stephen Birmingham.

Greenwich Village and How It Got That Way is a fascinating study of that neighborhood by Terry Miller. Francine Prose's *Household Saints* is a fictional portrait of life in Little Italy. *The New Chinatown*, by Peter Kwong, is a recent study of the community across Canal Street. Kate Simon's *Bronx Primitive*, Laura Cunningham's autobiographical *Sleeping Arrangements*, and E.L. Doctorow's novel *World's Fair* are set in the Bronx.

Brooklyn's history is beautifully illustrated in *Brooklyn: People and Places, Past and Present*, by Grace Glueck and Paul Gardner. Anna Quindlen's *Object Lessons* is set in the Westchester suburbs; while Susan Isaac's *Compromising Positions* takes place on Long Island.

Mysteries set in New York City range from Dashiell Hammett's urbane 1933 novel *The Thin Man*, to Rex Stout's series of Nero Wolfe mysteries (continued by Robert Goldsborough) to more recent picks: *While My Pretty One Sleeps*, by Mary Higgins Clark; *Greenwich Killing Time*, by Kinky Friedman; *Dead Air*, by Mike Lupica; and *Unorthodox Practices*, by Marissa Piesman.

Beneath Brooklyn Bridge

HOTELS AND RESTAURANTS

HOTELS AND RESTAURANTS

The following recommended hotels and restaurants have been divided into three price categories:

- **budget ($)**
- **moderate ($$)**
- **expensive ($$$)**

Prices do not include taxes (see page 213). Note also that telephone numbers prefixed 800 are free outside the 212 code area when dialed within the United States (dial "1" first); local toll numbers follow the toll-free number, the code for Manhattan being 212 (see also page 255).

ACCOMMODATIONS

CHINATOWN
Holiday Inn Downtown ($$) 138 Lafayette Street, at corner of Howard Street (tel: 800/HOLIDAY; 966 8898). The only hotel in Chinatown, with very small rooms offering two telephones, in-room movies and individual climate control. Eat in the excellent Pacifica restaurant, or head for the many cheaper alternatives in the busy streets around.

FINANCIAL DISTRICT
Cosmopolitan Hotel ($) 95 West Broadway (tel: 888/895 9400; 566 1900). Comfortable and well-equipped rooms at a very tempting price inside an historic building almost in the shadow of the World Trade Center and on the edge of TriBeCa.
Millenium ($$$) 55 Church Street (tel: 800/752 0014; 693 2001). A black-glass tower rising 55 stories opposite the World Trade Center, the Millenium was designed for the downtown business exec, with room rates to match. In return, you get an impressive array of services including a sky-lit swimming pool and choice of two restaurants—the Taliesin and the less formal Grille, both offering 24-hour full-menu room service. Ask for an upper-floor room—the view is unforgettable.
New York Marriott Financial Center ($$$) 85 West Street (tel: 800/242 8685; 266 6145). A traditional hotel catering mainly to business people, the Marriott Financial Center exudes the confidence of knowing exactly what it is trying to do and doing it well. Service is speedy and professional, and public rooms have plenty of soul. The Liberty Lounge serves snacks and cocktails, or you can dine in J.W.'s restaurant. Rooms are small, with the compensation of generously sized bathrooms and spectacular views. Weekend rates are very low and make this a good base for exploring southern Manhattan.
Marriott World Trade Center ($$$) 3 World Trade Center (tel: 800/228 9290; 938 9100). Another state-of-the-art shrine to the needs of the high-flying corporate business traveler, the hotel provides a fitness center and

indoor swimming pool to hone the muscles before clinching those crucial Wall Street deals.

GREENWICH VILLAGE
Washington Square Hotel ($) 103 Waverly Place (tel: 800/222 0418; 777 9515). There is no better placed or better priced Greenwich Village base, this hotel being situated just opposite a corner of Washington Square Park. The rooms tend to be small but are clean and pleasantly furnished, and the staff is helpful. In a previous life as the Hotel Earle, this was the first New York home of Bob Dylan and was where a homesick John Phillips of the Mamas and the Papas penned the hit song "California Dreamin.'"

LITTLE ITALY AND SOHO
Off-SoHo Suites ($$) 11 Rivington Street (tel: 800/ OFF SOHO; 979 9808). These mini-apartment-style suites are good value if you want to be within walking distance of SoHo, Little Italy, and the Lower East Side. Rates are inexpensive, but the suites are tiny, and the area, just the wrong side of the Bowery, can be chancy. For budget accommodations, though, this is well worth considering. Each suite has cable T.V. and V.C.R., and there is a laundry and fitness room on the premises. Make use of the hotel's 24-hour discount cab service.

MIDTOWN MANHATTAN
Algonquin ($$) 44th Street between Fifth and Sixth avenues (tel: 800/548 0345; 840 6800). It took a Japanese company to restore this literary landmark (home of the Round Table, presided over by Dorothy Parker and friends from 1919) to its former glories. Above the sumptuous lobby and bar areas, however, the Algonquin's rooms are only adequate, and there are plenty of better-value alternatives in the area.
Allerton House ($) 57th Street at Lexington Avenue (tel: 753 8841). A women-only and largely residential hotel with tiny but clean, tidy, and very low-priced rooms. Private bath-rooms are a few dollars extra.
Ameritania ($) Broadway at 54th Street (tel: 800/922 0330; 247 5000). A glitzy, inexpensive hotel on the Great White Way, next to the Ed Sullivan Theater and six blocks from Central Park. Everything is brand new, from the black marble bathrooms to the neon-lit lobby with waterfall. There is also an Italian restaurant and a busy pizza parlor and coffee shop on the premises. The low prices are a major attraction—book early.
Beekman Tower ($$$) 3 Mitchell Place at First Avenue and 49th Street (tel: 800/ME SUITE; 689 5200). The 1928 Gothic-style Beekman Tower rises above the East River and holds an all-suite hotel providing sensibly priced accommodations especially attractive for long-term stays—which explains its popularity with officials from

262

the nearby United Nations. All the suites have kitchenettes with microwave ovens and coffee-makers, and there is a fully equipped fitness center.

Best Western Manhattan ($) 32nd Street between Fifth Avenue and Broadway (tel: 800/567 7720; 736 1600). Now part of the Apple Core chain of reasonably priced hotels, the Aberdeen offers unelaborate but functional rooms in the heart of the compact Korean business district, almost in the shadow of the Empire State Building.

Beverly ($$) 50th Street between Lexington and Second avenues (tel: 800/ 223 0945; 753 2700). Some much-needed renovations are helping The Beverly, whose spacious, one-bedroom suites, equipped with kitchenettes, are very good value. Also on the premises is a 24-hour pharmacy.

Box Tree ($$$) 49th Street at Second Avenue (tel: 758 8320). The perfect place for an indulgent weekend, The Box Tree fills two (soon to be three) adjoining brownstones in the Turtle Bay area of Midtown. Trompe-l'oeil decorate the walls, and a Gaudiesque main staircase leads from the restaurant to a series of tiny private dining rooms, most on Versailles-like themes, upstairs. The 13 bedrooms are decorated in different styles—take your pick from Chinese, Egyptian, or Japanese—and although bathrooms are tiny, you are again paying for style rather than space.

Carlton Arms ($) 25th Street at Third Avenue (tel: 679 0680). Each wacky, threadbare room is designed and decorated by a different (unknown) artist, and what the Carlton Arms lacks in cleanliness and creature comforts (which is quite a lot) it just about makes up for through its sheer eccentricity. If this sounds like it's for you, book well in advance for a room with a bathroom. Many struggling artists make this their New York home, so expect bizarre fellow guests and exceptionally low prices. If you pay for six nights, you get a seventh for free.

Chelsea Hotel ($$) 23rd Street between Seventh and Eighth avenues (tel: 243 3700). Arthur Miller reputedly relocated here from the Plaza Hotel because he was fed up with having to put on a tie to go down to the front desk to collect his mail. The Chelsea still attracts refugees from more formal establishments, with its laid-back but solicitous service and the atmosphere of a run-down but arty apartment building. For the full story of the writers and artists who have stayed in this landmark New York hotel, see the feature on page 85.

Chelsea Inn ($) 46th West 17th Street (tel: 645 8989). Good value rooms with kitchenettes in a 19th-century townhouse; the least expensive have bathrooms shared with one other room.

Comfort Inn Murray Hill ($$) 35th Street between Fifth and Sixth avenues (tel: 800/228 5150; 947 0200). This branch of the nationwide chain predictably has higher rates than its far-flung counterparts but nonetheless represents good value for New York City, with tidy, comfortable rooms.

Doral Inn ($$$) Lexington Avenue at 49th Street (tel: 800/22 DORAL). A deservedly popular hotel in an excellent location. Public rooms are decorated in a stylish 1990s version of Grecian architecture, and the staff is helpful and friendly. If tramping the New York streets has left you with any energy, you can use the inn's private squash courts—or simply relax in the fitness center's sauna.

Drake Swissotel ($$$) Park Avenue at 56th Street (tel: 800/DRAKENY; 421 0900). The lobby's wood and brass fittings (and the bowls of complimentary Swiss chocolates) set a comfortable, low-key mood that continues into the comfortable, airy rooms.

Edison ($$) 47th Street at Eighth Avenue (tel: 800/637 7070; 840 5000). A partial refurbishment has made some of the Edison's rooms bright, airy and welcoming affairs, while others remain rather shabby and depressing. The good rooms come at a fair price although the hotel's sheer size (1,000 rooms) and its theater-district site means it is very much a tourist hotel, with little atmosphere.

Elysée ($$) 54th Street between Madison and Park avenues (tel: 753 1066). Recent refurbishment has sadly obliterated the highly individual "Lucy goes to Hollywood" older rooms, but some of the original furnishings have been kept and have been incorporated into the brand-new, Regency-inspired rooms. Most of the doubles are small—opt for a suite if you want to spread out. V.C.R.s are standard features, as are marble bath-tubs and in-room safes.

Essex House Hotel Nikko ($$$) Central Park South between Sixth and Seventh avenues (tel: 800/654 5687; 247 0300). From the etched brass and black marble features of the art-deco lobby to the amply proportioned and tastefully furnished rooms, the Essex House is stylish and enjoys an enviable position facing Central Park. To get the best views, however, splurge on one of the luxurious suites.

Four Seasons ($$$) 57th Street between Park and Madison avenues (tel: 800/ 332 3442; 758 5700). The Four Seasons is not only the tallest hotel in New York—designed by the celebrated I.M. Pei, it rises 52 stories high—but also the most opulent. On average, each room cost a million dollars to deck out in stylish contemporary art-deco form and acquire amenities such as bathtubs that fill within 60 seconds and are large enough to wash an elephant.

Gorham New York ($$) 55th Street between Sixth and Seventh avenues (tel: 245 1800). An excellent location to enjoy the best features of Midtown Manhattan. The staff is noted for courtesy and friendliness, and the more costly of the very comfortable rooms feature whirlpools, kitchenettes with microwave ovens, and the latest in temperature-controlled baths.

Gramercy Park ($$) 21st Street and Lexington Avenue (tel: 800/221 4083; 475 4320). Facing Gramercy Park (keys to this private park are available to hotel guests from the porter), this gracefully aging hotel may have slow elevators and few recent furnishings, but it does have character in large amounts, offers discounts at weekends and for long stays, and is usefully placed on the borders of Midtown and Lower Manhattan.

Helmsley Middletowne ($$) 48th Street between Lexington and Third avenues (tel: 800/221 4982; 755 3000). Owned by the controversial hotelier Leona Helmsley (but not to be confused with the Helmsley Palace), the Middletowne occupies a 17-story former residential apartment house not far from the United Nations. The property has a mellow, homey ambience, and the pleasant rooms have kitchenettes and fridges. Some rooms open on to terraces.

Herald Square ($) 31st Street near Fifth Avenue (tel: 800/727 1888; 279 4017). Occupying the 1893 *Life* magazine building, with mementoes of the publication easy to spot, the rooms here are small and spartan but with clean, tiled bathrooms. Most have color T.V. and phones, but you probably wouldn't want to spend too much time in the room. The main attractions are the cheap prices, offset by the noisy and relatively uninteresting location.

Holiday Inn on 57th Street ($$) 440 West 57th Street (tel: 800/231 0405; 581 8100). Unexciting but dependable branch of a nationwide chain, this is near the Midtown Manhattan sights but occupies a lackluster location.

Howard Johnson's 34th Street ($) 34th Street between Seventh and Eighth avenues (tel: 800/ 633 1911; 947 5050). Small, functional rooms are adequate for a night's rest if you don't mind the slightly sleazy location, opposite Penn Station. Each room has cable T.V. and a private bathroom, with the low prices being the main attraction.

Iroquois ($) 44th Street between Fifth and Sixth avenues (tel: 800/332 7220; 840 3080). A much-needed refurbishment greatly improved this always dependable but once very shabby hotel. The pricier rooms are equipped with kitchenettes; almost all are nowadays tastefully decorated in relaxing pastel shades. People who have stayed here recently say that the service sometimes leaves a lot to be desired.

Lexington ($$) Lexington Avenue at 48th Street (tel: 800/448 4471; 755 4400). Beyond the marble-floored lobby with its rosewood pillars and beautiful flower arrangements are two types of accommodations—the dated older rooms and the newly decorated (and more expensive) Tower rooms.

Although both types are small, there is plenty of space in which to spread out elsewhere. A coffee shop, a northern Italian restaurant, a highly acclaimed Chinese restaurant, and the western-style nightclub, Denim and Diamonds, are on the premises.The Winter Citysaver rates are by far the best value.

Macklowe Broadway ($$$) 44th Street between Sixth Avenue and Broadway (tel: 800/MACK LOWE; 768 4400). Though situated in the heart of the Times Square theater district, the Macklowe is geared more toward business travelers than tourists. But if the price is affordable, there are few better-appointed or more up-to-date options in the vicinity.

Mansfield ($) 44th Street between Fifth and Sixth avenues (tel: 800/255 5767; 944 6050). A place with few pretensions, it offers very affordable rooms in a prime Midtown Manhattan location (the more famous Algonquin Hotel is just across the street). The turn-of-the-century building was designed by noted New York architect Stanford White.

Marriott East Side ($$$) Lexington Avenue at 49th Street (tel: 800/242 8684; 755 4000). Erected as an apartment house slightly more recently than the medieval-style gargoyles on the facade might suggest, the 34-story Marriott East Side has successfully molded spacious 1920s New York residential rooms into comfortable hotel accommodations. Each room contains useful extras such as an iron and a filter-coffee machine, though if you prefer not to do all this for yourself, the service is helpful and there is a club-like bar downstairs.

Martha Washington ($) 30th Street between Park and Madison avenues (tel: 689 1900). Women-only accommodations in a semi-residential area. The rooms are gloomy and range from small to comparatively spacious; pay extra for a private bathroom and T.V. Bookable by the night or at very tempting weekly rates; additional discounts for longer stays (one month maximum).

Michelangelo ($$$) 51st Street at Seventh Avenue (tel: 800/237 0990; 765 1900). Genuine 18th- and 19th-century European art and a wealth of marble and crystal help the Michelangelo to rank among New York's most luxurious hotels. The large rooms come in art deco, Empire or country French styles with seemingly every possible amenity, including T.V. in the bath room. There is even a free unpacking service if you have too much luggage to tackle alone. The atmosphere is a bit hushed, but this deluxe, self-styled palazzo is one of the fanciest places to stay around Broadway.

Milford Plaza ($$) 45th Street at Eighth Avenue (tel: 800/221 2690; 869 3600). Not the most characterful or luxurious of hotels (in fact reminiscent of an airport lounge), the Milford Plaza has its share of cramped rooms, but a prime location on Times Square makes it a hit with money-conscious tourists and business travelers alike. The immediate area can be dangerous at night, but hotel security is good.

Morgans ($$$) Madison Avenue between 37th and 38th streets (tel: 686 0300). The brainchild of the former owners of the extremely chic Studio 54 nightclub, Morgans has a minimalist design and a color scheme based on black, gray and white. The bathrooms feature unique stainless steel basins and fittings, and every room has a video player. The clientele is predominantly young and fashionable—and not short of a dollar or two.

Parker Meridien ($$$) 56th Street between Sixth and Seventh avenues (tel: 800/ 543 4300; 245 5000). From the glitzy interior architecture to the pricey French nouvelle cuisine served in its restaurant, everything about Le Parker Meridien symbolizes conspicuous wealth. The ideal guest must be rich, beautiful, and inclined to pose for hours at the rooftop swimming pool.

Pickwick Arms ($) 51st Street between Second and Third avenues (tel: 800/ PIC KWIK; 355 0300). A sumptuous lobby, a cocktail lounge and a roof garden go some way towards compensating for the small rooms. This is a well priced option for the area, just a few minutes' walk from the heart of Midtown Manhattan.

Plaza ($$$) Fifth Avenue at Central Park South (tel: 800/759 3000; 759 3000). New York's leading hotel since it opened in 1907, the Plaza's past guests have included Teddy Roosevelt, F. Scott and Zelda Fitzgerald, the Beatles, and Solomon Guggenheim, who lived in one of the Plaza's suites and decorated its walls with the art that later became the core of the Guggenheim Museum's collection. Property tycoon Donald Trump snapped up the Plaza for $400 million in 1988 and put his then wife Ivana in control of a $100-million face-lift. Still the epitome of class, the Plaza has every facility you can think of. Some of the infamously tiny viewless rooms have been converted into suites; the pricier accommodations have unbelievable panoramas of Fifth Avenue or Central Park.

Portland Square Hotel ($) 47th Street between Sixth and Seventh avenues (tel: 800/382 0600). An unknown James Cagney was just one among many struggling actors who used this long-established budget-priced hotel in the heart of the Broadway theater district. The rooms have a few more frills than the Portland's sister hotel, Herald Square: there are places to sit in the lobby, lockers, and a drinks- and ice-machine. Parts of the immediate area can be intimidating after dark.

Quality Hotel ($$) 40th Street between Fifth and Madison avenues (tel: 800/ 228 5151; 447 1500). Unfancy but crisply decorated

rooms here offer all the usual amenities in a good location at a very fair price.

Remington ($) 46th Street between Broadway and Sixth Avenue (tel: 221 2600). Clean, no-frills accommodations in the theater district. The cheapest rooms lack private bathrooms, but all are fair value for their low price. Very close to Times Square, which is not a place for aimless nighttime strolling.

Roger Smith ($$) Lexington Avenue at 47th Street (tel: 800/445 0277; 755 1400). Tucked just north of Grand Central Terminal, the Roger Smith offers attractively furnished rooms and the intimate, personal atmosphere most Midtown Manhattan hotels can only strive for.

Roger Williams ($) 31st Street between Madison and Park avenues (tel: 800/ 637 9773; 684 7500). Located in a quiet semi-residential area of Midtown, the Roger Williams is one of the friendlier budget hotels. Every room has a kitchenette and cable T.V., and there is a good choice of suite accommodations for families. The furnishings may have seen better days, but the hotel is good value.

Roosevelt ($$) Madison Avenue at 45th Street (tel: 800/223 1870; 661 9600). Once a preeminent New York hotel catering to the thousands of train travelers who poured into the city at nearby Grand Central Terminal, the Roosevelt has matured into a slightly down-at-the-heels but dependable hotel. Renovations are now in progress—one of the first areas to be spruced up was the beautiful, vast, neo-classical lobby. Many of the rooms have been upgraded too; with the very reasonable room rate, this is one of Midtown's better deals.

Royalton ($$$) 44th Street between Fifth and Sixth avenues (tel: 800/635 9013; 869 4400). Another ultra-trendy hotel from the team that created Morgans (see page 265), the Royalton is designed with a cool artistry throughout and finds favor with the young and good-looking.

St. Moritz on the Park ($$) Central Park South at Sixth Avenue (tel: 800/221 4774; 755 5800). You will pay the usual high rates for a park view, but in general this is one of the less exclusive and more affordable hotels facing Central Park. The St. Moritz draws a mixture of guests, ranging from airline crews to people on intensive Fifth Avenue shopping sprees, and there is usually a busy crowd milling around the lobby, the bar, and Rumpelmayer's ice-cream parlor. Rooms are small, but fine for a stay of a couple of days.

Salisbury ($$) 57th Street between Sixth and Seventh avenues (tel: 800/223 0680; 246 1300). A welcoming, professionally run, small hotel across the road from the Russian Tea Room, it is convenient for shopping. Decor is frumpy, but rooms are spotless and comfortable, the most recently renovated ones offering brand-new microwaves and fridges. If you want even more space, opt for one of the apartment sized suites.

San Carlos Hotel ($$) 50th Street between Lexington and Third avenues (tel: 800/ 722 2012; 755 1800). Little sets it apart from other Midtown Manhattan hotels, but the San Carlos offers good quality rooms with ample cupboard space and adequately equipped kitchenettes.

Sherry Netherland ($$$) Fifth Avenue at 59th Street (tel: 355 2800). One of the grand French chateau-style buildings put up along Fifth Avenue across from Central Park during the 1920s, the Sherry Netherland offers soaring park views and impeccable service. Rooms are spacious and individually decorated, with V.C.R.s and microwaves, and plenty of personal touches. The sky-high rates are worth it if you have a huge range of hard-to-satisfy demands. Room service is by the acclaimed restaurant, Harry Cipriani, located at ground level.

Tudor ($$$) 42nd Street between First and Second avenues (tel: 800/879 8836; 986 8800). This stylish hotel is in a planned Tudor-style residential section of Midtown Manhattan, a few minutes' walk from the Chrysler Building, Grand Central Terminal and the U.N. Rooms are spacious and furnished in deep, rich colors, and offer trouser press, minibar, cable T.V. and safe. The corporate discounts and dual-line phones with data ports favor the business traveler, but there is plenty for others, from the balustraded Regency Lounge and Carvery to the sauna and fitness center.

U.N. Park ($$$) First Avenue at 44th Street (tel: 800/233 1234; 758 1234). The rooms in this modern, architectural-award-winning structure do not begin until the 28th floor, the lower levels being U.N. office space. Chrome, marble, and mirrors are prevalent throughout, and every room has a stunning view. The sports facilities are excellent. You will find many a U.N. delegate using the indoor tennis courts, swimming pool, and sauna.

Vanderbilt-Y.M.C.A. ($) 47th Street between Second and Third avenues (tel: 755 9600). Make an early booking to stay at the most popular and best-located of New York's Y.M.C.A.s. Open to men and women, it has newly renovated small single and double rooms at very low prices plus extra facilities such as a brand-new restaurant, luggage lockers, a swimming pool, a gym, and a laundromat.

Waldorf-Astoria ($$$) Park Avenue between 49th and 50th streets (tel: 800/WALDORF; 355 3000). After the Plaza, the Waldorf-Astoria is New York's most famous hotel. It was the birthplace of the charity ball and the prime rendezvous for New York high society from the 1930s—although it has taken a $150-million restoration to bring back the grandeur of times gone by. A sense of opulence strikes as soon as you enter the art-deco lobby, and all the rooms

are stylishly appointed with marble bathrooms. Only in the top-price suites, however, will you encounter a level of luxury to match the hotel's rich history.

Warwick ($$$) 65 West 54th Street (tel: 800/223 4099; 247 2700). Built by William Randolph Hearst in 1927, the recently renovated Warwick is popular with business travelers. It has over 400 rooms (all with T.V. and telephone), plus a restaurant and fitness facilities, and it is convenient for all the main Midtown sights.

Wellington ($$) Seventh Avenue at 55th Street (tel: 800/652 1212; 247 3900). Except perhaps for the lobby, there is nothing fancy about the sizeable Wellington, where the rooms are clean and simple and reasonably priced for their prized central location.

Wolcott ($) 31st Street at Fifth Avenue (tel: 268 2900). For a remarkably low rate, the Wolcott offers smallish but well furnished, comfortable rooms complete with private bathrooms and cable T.V., and some interesting photos of New York on the walls. The mirror-lined, baroque-style lobby is an unexpected bonus in this impressive budget hotel.

Wyndham ($$) 58th Street between Fifth and Sixth avenues (tel: 753 3500). The Wyndham feels more like an apartment building than a hotel and is especially popular with Broadway performers who could easily afford to stay elsewhere. Such good-sized rooms in this area and price bracket are very unusual; all are individually and taste-fully decorated. The low prices mean early booking is essential.

UPPER EAST SIDE

Barbizon ($$) 63rd Street at Lexington Avenue (tel: 800/ 753 0360; 838 5700). By the standards of the high-priced Upper East Side, the Barbizon is remarkably good value for its smallish but cozy rooms and the dozen terraced suites (some with good views) that occupy the red-brick building's Gothic tower. Until 1981, the Barbizon was a women's residential hotel, and its roll-call of famous former guests includes Grace Kelly, Candice Bergen, and Liza Minnelli.

Carlyle ($$$) 76th Street at Madison Avenue (tel: 800/227 5737; 744 1600). For years, the understated elegance of the Carlyle has provided a home away from home for high-ranking international dignitaries and those so accustomed to being fabulously wealthy that they have no need to flaunt their affluence. Crystal chandeliers hang above the public spaces, and the guest rooms are decorated with antiques, tapestries, and fresh flowers. Most also have fax machines. Sink into the marble bathtub and you will find that you have a phone at your elbow.

Lowell ($$$) 63rd Street between Park and Madison avenues (tel: 838 1400). A small, luxurious hotel, the Lowell occupies an art-deco building in the landmark district of the

Upper East Side. Chinese porcelain, 18th- and 19th-century prints, and wood-burning fireplaces decorate the rooms; service is personal (staff greet you by name within minutes of checking in). There is a fitness room for the use of all guests, but if you like your workouts to be private then go for the Gym Suite, said to be inspired by one-time guest Madonna.

Mark ($$$) 77th Street at Madison Avenue (tel: 800/ 843 6275; 744 4300). In-room whirlpools, video players (select the film you want to watch from a well-stocked library) and reliable and courteous staff help the Mark attract a fashionable, jet-setting clientele.

Mayfair Hotel Baglioni ($$$) Park Avenue at 65th Street (tel: 800/223 0542; 288 0800). With its turn-of-the-century-style public rooms, white-gloved elevator attendants, and plenty of thoughtful extras, the Mayfair Hotel Baglioni is one of the city's consistently top places to stay. The spacious rooms are decked out in chintz and fresh flowers; many of the world's great and good arrive for repeat stays.

Pierre ($$$) Fifth Avenue at 61st Street (tel: 800/332 3442; 940 8101). There is absolutely nothing surreal about the mural-lined corridors or the enormous, well-furnished rooms of the Pierre, even though this was Salvador Dali's favorite New York hotel. Packed with antiques and lined by lush carpets, the hotel's aristocratic ambience is heightened by the after-noon tea served daily beneath the rotunda.

Plaza Athénée ($$$) 64th Street between Park and Madison avenues (tel: 734 9100). With Louis XIV-style furniture filling every corner and marble and crystal fittings wherever you look, the Plaza Athénée is intended to evoke the grandeur of a European royal palace. Even though some find it pretentious, plenty of wealthy guests bask happily in the pre-revolutionary Versailles atmosphere, and standards of service are high.

Regency ($$$) Park Avenue between 60th and 61st streets (tel: 800/23 LOEWS; 759 4100). The lobby may be stuffed with French antiques, but the Regency, while extremely stylish, is a lot less snooty than many of its Upper East Side rivals. Be they financial wheeler dealers or rock stars on the rise, the clientele appreciate the tastefully furnished, airy rooms and the efficient, attentive staff.

Stanhope ($$$) Fifth Avenue at 81st Street (tel: 800/828 1123; 288 5800). With high-quality reproduction Louis XIV furniture filling the lobby and antique porcelain sitting beside state-of-the-art electronic gadgets in every guest room, the Stanhope is an interesting blend of old and new but has a rather hushed and hallowed atmosphere.

Surrey ($$$) 76th Street at Madison Avenue (tel: 800/ ME-SUITE; 288 3700). A small, quiet, and welcoming hotel, where all the rooms include kitchenettes—though it is hard to imagine the tidily bank-rolled guests opting for self-made snacks when room service operates around the clock and an acclaimed French restaurant is located on the premises.

Wales ($$) Madison Avenue at 92nd Street (tel: 800/428 5252; 876 6000). One of New York's longest-serving hotels, the Wales has been in business since 1900, and the attractive rates reflect its location on the northern edge of the neighborhood—though public transportation links to Midtown and Lower Manhattan are swift. The price of the nicely but not opulently furnished rooms includes afternoon tea and a light breakfast.

Westbury ($$$) Madison Avenue at 69th Street (tel: 800/321 1569; 535 2000). Elegance takes on an English appearance at the Westbury, where genuine Chippendale furniture decorates the lobby and a generous number of top-class reproductions fill the guest rooms. Splurge on a deluxe room and you can stretch out on a four-poster bed. Extras include a well-equipped gymnasium for guests' use.

267

UPPER WEST SIDE

Beacon ($$) Broadway at 75th Street (tel: 800/572 4969; 787 1100). A bustling, professionally run, small hotel, 10 blocks north of Lincoln Center and within easy reach of most Upper West Side attractions. The large rooms all come with cable T.V. and kitchenette, and Zabar's, the city's best gourmet deli, is just up the street. A very good deal, especially the newly renovated rooms.

Broadway ($) Broadway at 77th Street (tel: 362 1100). Mid-sized hotel with competitive rates. All rooms come with color T.V. and fridges. A few dollars can be saved by opting for a shared rather than a private bathroom.

Esplanade ($) West End Avenue at 74th Street (tel: 874 5000). Filling a large, red-brick building in a residential part of the Upper West Side, the Esplanade is an attractively priced, mainly suite-oriented hotel. All rooms are well proportioned; those facing west get views of the sunset across the Hudson River. Be aware, however, that the area, while safe during daylight, can be empty and rather spooky at night.

Excelsior ($) 81st Street between Central Park West and Columbus Avenue (tel: 800/368 4575; 362 9200). Standard but entirely acceptable rooms with spotless, old-fashioned bath-rooms make this a good standby, in a residential section of the Upper West Side. Central Park, the American Museum of Natural History, and the Columbus Avenue bars and restaurants are all within easy walking distance.

Hostelling International New York ($) Amsterdam Avenue at 103rd Street (tel: 932 2300). The largest youth hostel in the U.S.

occupies an architectural landmark—dating from 1883, the building was designed by the man responsible for the base of the Statue of Liberty. Very clean and welcoming, with small dormitory rooms and a host of additional services for the budget traveler.

Malibu Studio ($) Broadway between 102nd and 103rd streets (tel: 800/647 2227; 222 2954). Bordering a district that can be intimidating at night, though close to Columbia University and the Cathedral Church of St. John the Divine, the Malibu offers student-residence-style accommodation at very low rates. Rooms are unelaborate but homey, and a few extra dollars bring a color T.V., kitchen facilities and private bathroom.

Mayflower on the Park ($$) Central Park West at 61st Street (tel: 800/223 4164; 265 0060). On the border with Midtown Manhattan, and with some rooms overlooking Central Park, the Mayflower offers tidily appointed rooms a stone's throw from Lincoln Center. Stars of stage and screen sometimes number among the guests.

Milburn ($) 76th Street near Broadway (tel: 800/833 9622; 362 1010). One of the Upper West Side's best budget choices, the Milburn offers not only a quiet, graceful lobby and rooms with brand-new kitchenettes (with microwaves), but also prompt, friendly service. The spacious suites make ideal family accommodations (children under 12 stay with their parents free); there is a self-service laundry on the premises.

Olcott ($) 72nd Street between Central Park West and Columbus Avenue (tel: 877 4200). Worn furnishings and offhand service may put some off, but others—including theatrical and musical performers—stay here for the inexpensive weekly rates. Shorter stays are subject to availability; early booking is essential (no credit cards).

Radisson Empire ($$) Broadway at 63rd Street (tel: 800/221 6509; 265 7400). A luxury chain hotel, recently refurbished to the tune of $30 million, it offers small, well-furnished rooms all with C.D. and tape deck as well as color T.V. and V.C.R. . The grand, high-ceilinged lobby displays a beautiful collection of model stage sets—appropriate for a hotel a few steps from Lincoln Center.

Riverside Tower ($) Riverside Drive at 80th Street (tel: 800/724 3136; 877 5200). Located in an unexciting residential section of the Upper West Side, the Riverside Tower's spartan and somewhat dreary rooms have phones, color T.V.s and superb views over the Hudson River. There are no other facilities—use this as a low-cost place to sleep.

West Side Y.M.C.A. ($) 63rd Street near Central Park West (tel: 787 4400). Book well ahead for these simple but usefully situated and reasonably priced rooms, which are available as singles or doubles in a large, echoey building close to Lincoln Center.

The price includes use of a well-equipped gym and a large swimming pool, safe-deposit boxes, coin-op laundromat and 24-hour security.

RESTAURANTS

THE BRONX
Dominick's ($$) 2335 Arthur Avenue (tel: 718/733 2807). The southern Italian cuisine is far from exceptional, but dining at Dominick's is strong on atmosphere, not least because the place is usually crowded with noisy diners and the menu is not written, but recited by the harassed waiters.

Mario's ($$) 2342 Arthur Avenue (tel: 718/584 1188). Often as busy as Dominick's (above), but with a slightly better standard of food, much of it Neapolitan.

BROOKLYN
Cucina ($) 256 5th Avenue, between Carroll Street and Garfield Place (tel: 718/230 0711). Even Manhattanites travel to this Park Slope trattoria for the friendly atmosphere, flavorful pastas, and large entrées.

Junior's ($) 386 Flatbush Avenue Extension, at DeKalb Avenue (tel: 718/852 5257). A Brooklyn institution known for its large breakfasts, corned beef and pastrami sandwiches, and award-winning cheesecakes. Near the Brooklyn Academy of Music.

Lemongrass Grill ($) 61A Seventh Avenue, between Berkeley and Lincoln places (tel: 718/399 7100). Inexpensive Thai food that's flavorful, fresh and fast. Nice garden.

Mrs Stahl's Delicious Knishes ($) 1001 Brighton Beach Avenue (tel: 718/648 0210). Delivers exactly what its name suggests: expertly made knishes available with a host of fillings. Buy several.

New Prospect Café ($) 393 Flatbush Avenue (tel: 718/ 638 2148). Lively locals' eating spot, near the Brooklyn Museum.

Odessa ($$) 1113 Brighton Beach Avenue (tel: 718/253 1470). Come with several friends. One price buys a bottle of vodka and all you can eat from the Russian–Georgian buffet table. Be ready to dance.

Patsy Grimaldi's ($) 19 Old Fulton Street, between Front and Water streets (tel: 718/858 4300). Pizza aficionados consider Patsy's among the city's best. Red-checkered tablecloths and plenty of Sinatra provide the perfect atmosphere to enjoy large, thin-crust pies with myriad toppings.

Peter Luger Steak House ($$$) 178 Broadway, at Driggs Avenue (tel: 718/387 7400). Considered by many to be the best steak house in the country, what it lacks in its turn-of-the-century German beer hall ambiance it makes up for in dry-aged porterhouse, warm onion rolls, buttery home fries, and creamed spinach. Cash only.

Santa Fe Grill ($$) 60 Seventh Avenue, corner of Lincoln Place (tel: 718/636 0279).

Large portions of spicy Cajun and Tex-Mex food are served at lunchtime, but the place really gets into gear during the evenings, when it is also used for drinking.
Slades 107 ($–$$) 107 Montague Street, Brooklyn Heights (tel: 718/858 1200). Pleasantly informal yet stylish bistro serving pastas, salads, and sandwiches for lunch, and more inventive dishes at dinner.
Teresa's ($) 80 Montague Street, Brooklyn Heights (tel: 718/797 3996). Very filling, very well-priced Polish food.

CHINATOWN

Bo Ky ($) 80 Bayard Street (tel: 406 2292). Nothing fancy about the decor but nourishing bowls of noodle soup with seafood or duck served at rock-bottom prices.
First Taste ($$) 53 Bayard Street (tel: 962 1818). Serves an eclectic mix of Hong Kong favorites and, as the name suggests, makes a good spot to begin exploring the intricacies of this regional cuisine.
Golden Unicorn ($$) 18 East Broadway (tel: 941 0911). A favorite for large family banquets or big parties. Large selection of dishes, from savory appetizers through dim sum to duck, fresh fish, and tofu.
Hong Fat ($) 63 Mott Street (tel: 962 9588). Locals come here for steaming noodles and meat dishes, served in a boisterous but friendly eat-and-run setting.
HSF ($$) 46 Bowery (tel: 374 1319). This is a fair bet for lunchtime dim sum, especially for first-time western visitors who will not feel as left out here as they might in some Chinatown eateries, thanks to a picture chart showing some of the options.
Hunan House ($$) 45 Mott Street (tel: 962 0010). One of the first places to make spicy Hunan fare available in predominantly Cantonese Chinatown, it still carries a good range of tasty, fiery dishes.
Joe's Shanghai ($) 9 Pell Street, between Bowery and Mott streets (tel: 233 8888). One of the best Chinese restaurants in the city, known for its rich and satisfying Shanghaiese cooking—soup, dumplings, braised pork shoulder, lion's head, handmade Shanghai noodles, and more. Worth the long wait. Cash only.
King Fung ($$) 20 Elizabeth Street (tel: 964 5256). Good choice of well-prepared Cantonese food in a setting that is a cut above most neighborhood eateries; also lunchtime dim sum.
Mandarin Court ($) 61 Mott Street, near Canal Street (tel: 608 3838). Wonderfully chaotic dim sum parlor, busiest on Sundays when the communal tables are packed. Once you are seated, be ready for a lot of shouting and pointing to get what you want from the passing trolleys.
Mueng Thai ($$) 23 Pell Street (tel: 406 4259). A variety of tantalizing Thai dishes. Anyone who wants to keep the roof on their mouth should take care when venturing among the spicier items.

New Indonesia and Malaysia ($) 18 Doyers Street (tel: 267 0088). Hundreds of Indonesian and Malaysian dishes to choose from in this tiny but cozy diner, where everything from gado gado to fish head curry is spiced to the customer's wishes.
New York Noodle Town ($) 28 Bowery (tel: 349 0923). Providing plenty of what its name suggests in many more varieties than you ever imagined possible.
Nha Trang ($) 87 Baxter Street, between Bayard and Canal streets (tel: 233 5948). Excellent, inexpensive Vietnamese. BBQ pork chops, crispy squid, and other regional specialties never disappoint.
Nom Wah Tea Parlor ($) 13 Doyers Street (tel: 962 6047). Long-established and immensely popular, it serves a wonderful selection of dim sum throughout the day. Plenty of gastronomically thrilling and exotically filled dumplings and pastries fill the passing trays, although regulars claim standards have dropped.
Saigon House ($–$$) 89–91 Bayard Street (tel: 732 8988). Small and unpretentious venue for enjoying highly regarded Vietnamese specialties at a bargain price.
Sun Say Gay ($) 220 Canal Street (tel: 964 7256). This hole-in-the-wall rice shop dispenses simple dishes—bits of meat, vegetables and pickles on generous piles of rice—at absurdly cheap prices.
Sweet 'n' Tart Café ($) 76 Mott Street, at Canal Street (tel: 334 8088). The menu is arranged according to rules of traditional Chinese medicine. Expertly prepared, fast, and super-inexpensive.
Thailand Restaurant ($) 106 Bayard Street (tel: 349 3132). Inexpensive Thai favorites, and some lesser-known dishes, fill a lengthy, mouthwatering menu.
Triple 8 Palace ($$–$$$) 59 Division Street (tel: 941 8886). On the top floor of a building beneath the Manhattan Bridge, this is wildly popular with locals who show up mostly for the lunchtime dim sum, although the menu carries a large and appetizing range of Hong Kong cuisine.
20 Mott Street ($$) 20 Mott Street (tel: 964 0380). Spread over three floors and offering a massive and (to Westerners) largely indecipherable menu, this is one of Chinatown's most celebrated restaurants. Its reputation is definitely for the food rather than the service—often you will need to be very determined to get your order taken. Come for the lunchtime dim sum or for a memorable dinner, even though you may not be certain what you are eating.
Vegetarian's Paradise ($) 68 Mott Street (tel: 406 6988). A vegetarian cubby hole does wondrous things re-creating regular Chinese dishes but using nothing that ever walked, crawled, or swam.
Viet-Nam ($) 11 Doyers Street (tel: 693 0725). An unpretentious setting for the best and probably most authentic Vietnamese cuisine in New York.

HOTELS AND RESTAURANTS

Wong Kee ($) 113 Mott Street (tel: 966 1160). Fine selection of Cantonese dishes at irresistible prices; deservedly crowded.

EAST VILLAGE AND LOWER EAST SIDE

Acme Bar and Grill ($$) 9 Great Jones Street (tel: 420 1934). Cajun cooking and lots of it—gumbo, jambalaya, and deep fried oyster are among the choices—plus a range of hot sauces.

Angelica Kitchen ($) 12th Street between First and Second avenues (tel: 228 2909). Tasty and very inexpensive natural foods.

Benny's Burritos ($) Avenue A at 6th Street (tel: 254 2054). Burritos with a host of inventive fillings are dispensed here to a lively East Village crowd before or after they spend the night clubbing.

Caffè della Pace ($) Seventh Street between First and Second avenues (tel: 529 8024). This low-key spot is worth seeking out for its stylishly presented Italian food at very reasonable prices.

Christine's ($$) Lexington Avenue at 40th Street (tel: 953 1920). Serves omelets, salads, and sandwiches, but knowing regulars choose the Polish dishes—tripe, homemade pirogi or blintzes—and leave room for the babka as dessert.

Dojo ($) 24 St. Mark's (tel: 674 9821). An intriguingly combined Japanese and health-food restaurant, with a predominantly youthful and trendy clientele.

Emerald Planet ($) 2 Great Jones Street (tel: 353 9727). Exotic variations on the humble Mexican burrito with a mouth-watering range of creative fillings and garnishing such as jasmine rice and mango salsa.

First ($) 87 First Avenue, between 5th and 6th streets (tel: 674 3823). This clubby East Village bistro serves an intriguing menu of whimsically updated American favorites until 4AM. Everything is made on the premises and brought to your table by waiters wearing black vinyl aprons.

Great Jones Café ($$) 54 Great Jones Street (tel: 674 9304). This is where you will find the cutting-edge East Village faces selecting their late-afternoon breakfasts from the daily specials—hearty and homely American fare—chalked on a blackboard.

Il Bagatto ($) 192 East 2nd Street, between Avenues A and B (tel: 228 0977). Surprisingly authentic homemade pastas and entrées at bargain prices in a lively setting. Always busy; always good.

Indochine ($$) Lafayette Street between Astor Place and 4th Street (tel: 505 5111). Dine amid palm fronds on a tremendous mix of Vietnamese, Thai, and Cambodian fare; open for dinner only.

Katz's Delicatessen ($) East Houston Street near Orchard Street (tel: 254 2246). Legendary for providing pastrami and corned beef sandwiches for over a century, Katz's found additional fame in the 1989 film *When Harry Met Sally*.

Kiev ($) Second Avenue at 7th Street (tel: 674 4040). Eastern European specialties such as pirogi and generously filled blintzes are served around the clock, also a selection of more familiar omelets and burgers.

Miracle Grill ($) 112 First Avenue, between 6th and 7th streets (tel: 254 2353). Among the first in the wave of ambitious, inexpensive restaurants in the area, the Southwestern food at this trendy restaurant still satisfies. Lovely garden.

Mitali ($$) 6th Street between First and Second avenues (tel: 533 2508). The quality Indian cuisine brings adventurous diners from all over New York; reserve a table on Friday and Saturday evenings.

Opaline ($$) 85 Avenue A, between 5th and 6th streets (tel: 475 5050). A recent upscale entry in the East Village scene, the cutting-edge ambiance is more satisfying than the food, but overall, this restaurant works.

Pommes Frites ($) 123 2nd Avenue, between 7th and 8th streets (tel: 674 1234). The smell of Belgian-style French fries crisping in peanut oil and the wide selection of homemade mayonnaises attracts lines to this new East Village take-out shop.

Ratner's Dairy Restaurant ($) Delancey Street between Norfolk and Suffolk streets (tel: 677 5588). Established in 1905, Ratner's is well past its prime for kosher Jewish dairy specialties, but the hush-hush Lansky Lounge in the back room attracts a beautiful East-Village crowd for specialty cocktails and definitively New York scene.

Second Avenue Kosher Deli ($$) Second Avenue at 10th Street (tel: 677 0606). This landmark family-run Jewish deli is one of the last remaining places where you can sample kasha, kugel, knishes, and knaidels in authentic forms. The back room features memorabilia from the Lower East Side's Yiddish Theater.

Two Boots ($) Avenue A at 2nd Street (tel: 505 2276). Enterprising and successful mixing of Italian and Cajun cookery: shrimp pizza is just one example.

Veselka ($) Second Avenue at 9th Street (tel: 228 9682). Earthy, filling Ukrainian and Polish fare is served around the clock and in large quantities to a surprisingly diverse East Village crowd. For something comparatively light, stick to the blintzes.

Yaffa Café ($) 97 St. Marks Place (tel: 674 9302). This is a hangout for East Village characters, happily grazing on croissants or burgers inside or out in the garden.

FINANCIAL DISTRICT, SOHO, AND TRIBECA

Aquagrill ($$$) 210 Spring Street, at 6th Avenue (tel: 274 0505). Fresh fish and seafood in a trendy SoHo setting. Creative entrées balance simple preparations. Try the signature snail snaps and roasted cod. Great desserts.

Au Mandarin ($) World Financial Center (tel: 385 0313). A well-priced selection of

Chinese meals is offered on the first floor of this bustling, architecturally innovative structure, notable for its indoor palm trees.

Bridge Café ($$) Water Street at Dover Street (tel: 227 3344). If you have just crossed the Brooklyn Bridge on foot, reward yourself with a lunch in this cozy red-brick dining room sited just beneath the bridge itself. Along with the usual lunch and dinner favorites, there is an appetizing selection of well-prepared seafood.

Ceci Cela ($) 55 Spring Street, at Lafayette Street (tel: 274 9179). This tiny French bakery with six tables at the back has the best croissants and classic French pastries this side of the Atlantic.

Balthazar ($$$) 80 Spring Street, at Crosby Street (tel: 965 1414). The closest you'll come to a Parisian brasserie. The hottest restaurant at the moment, where power-brokers and celebutantes enjoy chilled seafood platters, roasted chicken, braised short ribs, and other brasserie fare. Reservations necessary.

Bar 89 ($$) 89 Mercer Street, between Broome and Spring streets (tel: 274 0989). Though competently prepared, the food isn't the draw here, the bathrooms are. Clear glass stall doors flood with opaque light before you expose yourself to the world. Don't leave without sipping a beautiful martini or cosmopolitan.

Blue Ribbon ($$) 97 Sullivan Street, between Prince and Spring streets (tel: 274 0404). Open from 4PM to 4AM, this small SoHo bistro offers everything from chicken soup with matzo balls to fondue to Asian noodles, all skillfully prepared. A favorite hangout for New York City chefs.

Bouley Bakery ($$$) 120 West Broadway, at Duane Street (tel: 964 2525). Under the direction of one of the city's best chefs, this tiny, elegant bakery/restaurant offers exquisite, deceivingly simple French food with an unmatched selection of breads.

Cellar in the Sky ($$$) 1 World Trade Center (tel: 524 7033). Although it is on the 107th floor, nobody comes to Cellar in the Sky for the views. The attraction is a specially chosen, fixed-price, multi-course dinner served with selected wines; the details change every two weeks. The price is astronomical, classy attire is necessary, and you will need to make a reservation.

Duane Park Café ($$) Duane Street between West Broadway and Hudson Street (tel: 732 5555). This fashionable dining spot has an impressive menu bearing culinary influences from Italy, Japan, and California.

Franklin Station ($$) 222 West Broadway (tel: 274 8525). A creative mixture of French and Southeast Asian cooking finds many discerning locals making this their favorite neighborhood dinner spot.

Fraunces Tavern ($$) 54 Pearl Street (tel: 269 0144). A reconstruction of a landmark 18th-century tavern (see page 107), the Fraunces Tavern is an atmospheric dining

place, but the food, regular American fare, is seldom above average.

Harry's at Hanover Square ($) 1 Hanover Square (tel: 425 3412). Essential stop for seekers of the ultimate burger: Harry's hamburgers are lovingly grilled over charcoal and apple wood and come with a range of toppings from caviar to avocado.

Honmura An ($$$) 170 Mercer Street, between Houston and Prince streets (tel: 334 5253). Handmade soba is the highlight of this serene outpost of a Tokyo favorite.

Lombardi's ($) 32 Spring Street, between Mott and Mulberry streets (tel: 941 7994). The 1905 coal-fired oven gives the pizza at this parlor an unusually flavorful crust. Many consider it the best on the island.

Montrachet ($$$) 239 West Broadway, between Walker and White streets (tel: 219 2777). One of the first TriBeCa destination restaurants, this cozy bistro features terrific French-inspired food, great service, and a reasonably priced wine list of unusual, hard-to-find selections.

Nobu ($$$) 105 Hudson Street, at Franklin Street (tel: 219 0500). Sister to London's latest hotspot and L.A.'s movie-star hang out, this Japanese-inspired restaurant has won awards both for design and for food.

Odeon ($$$) West Broadway at Thomas Street (tel: 233 0507). A longtime favorite for its contemporary American cuisine and its art-deco and neon-decorated setting.

Omen ($$) Thompson Street between Spring and Prince streets (tel: 925 8923). A stylish place to soothe stressed nerves, this relaxed Japanese restaurant's house specialty is indeed Omen—a spicy soup dish with vegetables and noodles.

Quilty's ($$$) 177 Prince Street, between Thompson and Sullivan streets (tel: 254 1260). Named for a character in Nabokov's *Lolita*, this elegant bistro serves wonderfully creative contemporary fare.

Raoul's ($$) Prince Street between Sullivan and Thompson streets (tel: 966 3518). A winning New York version of a French restaurant, it has a tempting selection of main courses, devilish desserts, an impressive wine list, plus comfortable seating and a convivial atmosphere.

Rialto ($$) 265 Elizabeth Street, between Houston and Prince streets (tel: 334 7900). The beautiful crowd at this east SoHo newcomer enjoys the reasonably priced, upscale American menu, charming garden, and hip atmosphere.

Soho Steak ($$) 90 Thompson Street, between Prince and Spring streets (tel: 226 0602). Don't be put off by the wait or the sardine-like seating in this tiny bistro. The menu—which features more than just steak—is expertly prepared and exceptionally well priced.

TriBeCa Grill ($$) Greenwich Street at Franklin Street (tel: 941 3900). Co-owned by actor Robert de Niro and set in what is now a film company building, the TriBeCa Grill draws a star-spotting crowd but its real attraction is the gourmet-pleasing food, especially the carefully crafted fish dishes.

GREENWICH VILLAGE

Anglers and Writers ($) Hudson Street at St. Luke's Place (tel: 675 0810). Plays up the neighborhood literary links and serves snacks, tea, and coffee amid antiques and rows of frequently thumbed books.

Artepasta ($) 81 Greenwich Avenue, at Bank Street (tel: 229 0234). Inexpensive pastas with the traditional accompaniments in a cozy setting. Great lunch bargains.

Bar Six ($) 502 Sixth Avenue, between 12th and 13th streets (tel: 691 1363). Serious bar scene with American fare. Airy and light during the day, smoky and dark at night.

Benny's Burritos ($) 113 Greenwich Avenue (tel: 727 0584). Like the branch in the East Village (see above), its burritos are stuffed with as much cheese, beans, meat, or vegetables as they will hold.

Café Loup ($$) 13th Street between University Place and Fifth Avenue (tel: 255 4746). A delightful French bistro provides classy food with a minimum of fuss and welcoming prices.

Caffè Lure ($$) 169 Sullivan Street, between Bleecker and West Houston streets (tel: 473 2642). This small, French bistro has real French flare. Hip crowd and high-value.

Caffè Rafaella ($) 134 Seventh Avenue, between Charles and 10th streets (tel: 929 7247). Sandwiches, salads, and desserts tempt in this living-room setting, where people-watching is as good as it gets.

Caffè Reggio ($) 119 MacDougal Street (tel: 475 9557). Claimed to be the country's oldest coffee shop, it has a dark, atmospheric interior and a selection of pleasing coffees and cakes.

Chumley's ($$) 86 Bedford Street (tel: 675 4449). A one-time speakeasy, Chumley's is a compact and atmospheric location for either a drink or a meal chosen from a menu of dependable American fare.

Clementine ($$$) 1 Fifth Avenue, at 8th Street (tel: 253 0003). The chef of Midtown's acclaimed Monkey Bar has just taken over this cursed space. If his creative contemporary menu and attention to service details can't make it work, nothing can.

Corner Bistro ($) 331 West 4th Street (tel: 242 9502). Busy, no-frills stop for chicken wings, burgers (served on paper plates), and beer.

Cowgirl Hall of Fame ($) 519 Hudson Street (tel: 633 1133). Photos of famous cowgirls grin down from the walls and country music plays on the jukebox as plaid–shirted staff dispense substantial helpings of Tex-Mex fare—and potent margaritas.

Cucina Stagionale ($) 264 Bleecker Street (tel: 924 2707). Simple, inexpensive and very pleasing Italian food; be prepared to wait in line and make sure you bring your own alcohol.

Drover's ($$) 9 Jones Street, between Bleecker and West 4th streets (tel: 627 1233). Home-style American menu features meatloaf, fried chicken, mashed potatoes, crispy fries, and satisfying desserts.

Elephant and Castle ($$) 68 Greenwich Avenue (tel: 243 1400). Great selection of breakfast omelets; plus other healthy fare at lunch or dinner times. The mellow setting encourages relaxed eating.

Est! Est! Est! ($$–$$$) 64 Carmine Street (tel: 255 6294). From dependable fresh pasta dishes to seasonal game and specialties, the food and service rarely disappoint.

Florent ($$) 69 Gansevoort Street (tel: 989 5779). Bistro specializing in, but not limited to, delectable meat dishes. Being open around the clock with a breakfast menu available from midnight finds an intriguing assortment of club-going New Yorkers arriving through the small hours.

Gotham Bar and Grill ($$$) 12th Street at Fifth Avenue (tel: 620 4020). From the perfect architecture to the perfectly presented food, the Gotham Bar and Grill is impeccably stylish and a real place to be seen.

Home ($$) 20 Cornelia Street, between Bleecker and West 4th streets (tel: 243 9579). The reasonably priced food is surprisingly elegant and delicious. Accompaniments like homemade relishes and sausages are a bonus.

Il Cantinori ($$$) 32 East 10th Street, between Broadway and University Place (tel: 673 6044). Upscale Italian with fine pasta and Tuscan specialties. Although the service can throw attitude, the overall experience is lovely, if slightly overpriced.

Indigo ($$) 142 West 10th Street, between Greenwich Avenue and Waverly Place (tel: 691 7757). Inexpensive, contemporary American bistro offering creative food at very reasonable prices.

Japonica ($$) 100 University Place (tel: 243 7752). Spartan setting for substantial helpings of sushi and other Japanese fare.

John's Pizzeria ($) 278 Bleecker Street (tel: 243 1680). Long popular—not least with Woody Allen—it serves perfect oven-baked pizzas in more than 50 varieties. Also a great place to eavesdrop on Greenwich Village gossip.

Le Gigot ($$) 18 Cornelia Street, between Bleecker and West 4th streets (tel: 627 3737). Tiny French bistro with excellent food and very reasonable prices. Inexpensive wine list and warm, friendly service.

Mama Buddha ($) 57 Hudson Street (tel: 924 2762). Meat, seafood, and numerous vegetarian options make up a tempting menu of efficiently served Chinese dishes.

Marquet Patisserie ($) 15 East 12th Street, between 5th Avenue and University Place (tel: 229 9313). Charming French bakery and cafe with fresh salads, soups, pastries, and cafe au lait served in bowls. Breakfast and lunch only.

Minetta Tavern ($$) Minetta Lane and MacDougal Street (tel: 475 3850). A historic Greenwich Village saloon decorated with artworks and memorabilia of local life in the 1930s, the Minetta Tavern provides an informal place for very satisfying Italian lunches and dinners.

Mirezi ($$) 59 5th Avenue, between 12th and 13th streets (tel: 242 9708). Korean-inspired contemporary cooking in a beautiful room. Flavors and presentations are top notch. Lounge downstairs.

Moustache ($) 90 Bedford Street, between Barrow and Grove streets (tel: 229 2220). There's always a wait for one of the 10 tables at this Middle Eastern restaurant, where freshly baked pittas come to the table hot out of the oven and puffed like pillows.

Pink Teacup ($$) 42 Grove Street (tel: 807 6755). Should a craving for black-eyed peas or collard greens suddenly strike, this long-running soul-food restaurant has both—and much more. The prices, however, reflect the fashionable location.

Ray's Original Pizza ($) Sixth Avenue at 11th Street (tel: 243 2253). Ray's Pizza outlets are all over New York, but this is the first and best of the lot. It serves pizza by the slice to go or to eat at one of the few tables.

Sammy's Noodle Shop ($) 453 6th Avenue, at 11th Street (tel: 924 6688). Bustling Chinese restaurant where everything is made from scratch, including the noodles, baked buns, and barbecued duck.

Sông ($–$$) 107 Macdougal Street (tel: 529 3808). From sugarcane shrimp to crispy fish, the Vietnamese fare comes tasty and good at this likable spot which also offers numerous daily specials.

Taka ($$) 61 Grove Street, between Bleecker Street and 7th Avenue (tel: 242 3699). Unusual because the sushi chef is a woman, this beloved Japanese restaurant has a strong following.

Tanti Baci Caffè ($) 163 West 10th Street, between 7th Avenue and Waverly Place (tel: 647 9651). Inexpensive Italian trattoria with the feel of a grotto. Combine your favorite pasta and sauce or choose from one of the daily specials.

Tea and Sympathy ($) 108 Greenwich Avenue (tel: 807 8329). Comfort food—especially for homesick Brits—as well as the traditional high tea, they also serve shepherd's pie, fish cakes, and stodgy "school dinner" desserts.

Thali Indian Vegetarian ($) 28 Greenwich Avenue, between 10th and Charles streets (tel: 367 7411). There are no options at this closet-sized vegetarian restaurant. $10 gets you the delicious *thali* platter of the day.

Tortilla Flats ($) Washington Street at 12th Street (tel: 243 1053). There is rarely a dull moment at this shaking Tex-Mex eatery, where the emphasis is on rowdy good times as much as on consuming fiery food and alcohol in very large amounts.

White Horse Tavern ($) Hudson Street at 11th Street (tel: 243 9260). Famous as the bar where Dylan Thomas drank one too many whiskeys, the Tavern also has a fair range of food. Regulars swear by the burgers.

HARLEM

Copeland's ($$) 145th Street between Broadway and Amsterdam Avenue (tel: 234 2356). Where the high-flyers of Harlem don their finery and dine on a creative mix of soul food and nouvelle cuisine.

Sylvia's ($$) Lenox Avenue between 126th and 127th streets (tel: 996 0660). A landmark soul-food restaurant, seemingly as popular with busloads of tourists as with locals, Sylvia's serves massive helpings of southern favorites, such as spicy barbecued ribs and chicken, and follows the main courses with devilishly stodgy desserts.

LITTLE ITALY

Assaggio ($$) 178 Hester Street (tel: 226 2686). Not as rowdy as some Little Italy establishments, it has much that is good among its southern Italian staples.

Bellato's ($$) 55 E Houston Street (tel: 274 8881). While there might be better Neapolitan food at other restaurants, few can match this one for Little Italy atmosphere.

Benito's ($) 163 and 174 Mulberry Street (tel. 226 9012 and 226 9171). Two branches of the same trattoria, each with dependable, fairly priced dishes.

Caffè Biondo ($) 141 Mulberry Street (tel: 226 9285). At this popular spot, arty, dressed-in-black SoHo types choose from a wide selection of coffees and pose by the oversized front window.

Caffè Roma ($) 385 Broome Street (tel: 226 8413). In business since the 1890s, Caffè Roma offers excellent coffee and freshly baked pastries.

Ferrara ($) 195 Grand Street (tel: 226 6150). Lacks the atmosphere of Caffè Roma (see above), but a nice place to sip a cappuccino and nibble your selection from a tempting array of baked goods while watching the world go by from a sidewalk table.

Taormina ($) 147 Mulberry Street (tel: 219 1007). A touch pricier and classier than its neighbors, Taormina serves Neapolitan dishes in a sedate setting conducive to pleasant eating.

MIDTOWN MANHATTAN
East and West Midtown
Aquavit ($$$) 13 West 54th Street, between 5th and 6th avenues (tel: 307 7311). It's not easy to make Swedish food alluring but this elegant restaurant raises herring and smoked fish to new gastronomic heights.

Carnegie Delicatessen ($$) 854 7th Avenue, at 55th Street (tel: 757 2245). Mile-high sandwiches and oversized portions are priced to match, but the food's still good at this perpetually busy deli.

273

Cosi Sandwich Bar ($) 165 East 52nd Street, between Lexington and 3rd avenues (tel: 758 7800). Hot-out-of-the-oven flatbread filled with your choice of creative stuffings is the draw at this favorite lunch spot.

Delegates' Dining Room ($$) United Nations, First Avenue at 46th Street (tel: 963 7626). Armed with a reservation and proper attire, the general public can rub shoulders with United Nations officials and delegates (those who eat here are unlikely to be famous faces, however) on any weekday lunchtime. Top value is the buffet.

Four Seasons ($$$) 52nd Street between Park and Lexington avenues (tel: 754 9494). At the helm of contemporary American cuisine, the Four Seasons rarely offers anything from its changing daily menu that will fail to delight the true gourmet. What is more, the restaurant has an entrance decorated by a large Picasso and sits inside the architecturally significant Seagram Building, designed by Mies van der Rohe and Philip Johnson.

Hangawi ($$) 12 East 32nd Street, between 5th and Madison avenues (tel: 213 0077). If you don't know what "vegetarian mountain Korean food" is, order the Emperor's Menu. Some 12 courses later you will understand the allure of this unusual and enticing restaurant.

Harley Davidson Café ($–$$) 56th Street at 6th Avenue (tel: 245 6000). Very few genuine bikers are found at this theme restaurant devoted to the legendary motorcycle; serves American staples such as burgers, chicken wings, and sandwiches.

Jean George ($$–$$$) 1 Central Park West (tel: 299 3900). It isn't often that a new restaurant immediately skyrockets to the top of the critics' lists. But the neoclassic *haute* French menu at this hotspot has gourmets clamoring for reservations. Even given the astronomical prices, nothing disappoints. A less expensive, less formal cafe is no less intriguing.

Judson Grill ($$$) 152 West 52nd Street, between 6th and 7th avenues (tel: 582 5252). Somewhere between a casual American bar and a fancy French restaurant, the creative, contemporary fare makes this atmospheric restaurant popular at lunch and dinner.

Kang Suh ($) 1250 Broadway, at 32nd Street (tel: 564 6845). Skip the sushi bar and head straight upstairs for the Korean menu. Oyster and scallion pancakes, tableside barbecue, and a stunning array of *kim chee* are served into the wee hours.

Kaplan's Deli ($$) 59th Street between Park and Madison avenues (tel: 755 5959). An unexciting but reliable standby, it has sandwiches, soups, and the usual deli fare in an otherwise pricey area.

Keens Chophouse ($$) 36th Street between Fifth and Sixth avenues (tel: 947 3636). Keens has been providing no-fuss meat-and-potatoes fare since 1885; mutton chop

with mint is what they do best, although there is a wide choice of other meat dishes and some hearty seafood options.

Le Bernadin ($$$) 155 West 51st Street, between 6th and 7th avenues (tel: 489 1515). Recently tapped by a national magazine as the best restaurant in America, this midtown mecca elevates fish and seafood to the *haut*est level of cuisine. Doting service and an exceptional wine list round out the package.

Le Cirque 2000 ($$$) 455 Madison Avenue (tel: 794 9292). New outer-space setting for one of the city's best and most expensive restaurants, regularly packed with celebrities and well-heeled gourmets.

Lespinasse ($$$) St. Regis Hotel, 2 East 55th Street, between 5th and Madison avenues (tel: 339 6719). The Asian-inspired food and extremely formal dining room make this one of New York's most exciting French restaurants.

Lou G. Siegel ($$) 38th Street between Seventh and Eighth avenues (tel: 921 4433). Kosher deli established since 1917 and still serving chopped liver, gefilte fish, chicken soup—and much more, to local workers and long-distance regulars.

Lutèce ($$$) 50th Street between Second and Third avenues (tel: 752 2225). The kitchen torch has been passed and the classic French menu has been streamlined and updated. Service has an attitude but some of the modern French innovations make the suffering worth it.

Maloney & Porcelli ($$$) 37 East 50th Street, between Madison and Park avenues (tel: 750 2233). Bring a large appetite to this whimsical American eatery, a new favorite of the power-lunch crowd.

Marichu ($$) 342 East 46th Street, between 1st and 2nd avenues (tel: 370 1866). Around the corner from the U.N., this charming restaurant offers authentic Basque cooking.

Motown Café ($–$$) 104 West 57th Street (tel: 581 8030). Another theme restaurant, this one styled around the 1960s Motown sound, with decor of the decade and a largely soulfood menu.

Oceana ($$$) 55 East 54th Street, between Madison and Park avenues (tel: 759 5941). Although the dining room makes you feel as though you are on a cruise ship, the inspired cooking breaks the metaphor. Elegant seafood preparations. Warm service.

Osteria del Circo ($$$) 120 West 55th Street, between 6th and 7th avenues (tel: 265 3636). An offspring of Le Cirque, this upscale Italian trattoria mixes contemporary cooking with traditional Tuscan fare. A favorite of celebrities and power brokers.

Planet Hollywood ($–$$) 140 West 57th Street (tel: 333 STAR). Celebrity-owned worldwide chain that is always busy and is probably the most enjoyable of Manhattan's theme restaurants.

Rainbow Room ($$$) 65th floor, 30 Rockefeller Plaza (tel: 632 5000). The food may be no more than reasonable value for the money, but the restored art deco setting is a delight and comes complete with roaming cigarette girls and a 12-piece band providing 1940s favorites. You will need a reservation, chic attire, and 20-20 vision to enjoy to the full the stunning views of New York stretching out below.

Secret Harbor Bistro ($$) Lexington Avenue at 37th Street (tel: 447 7400). Chic place to start the day, with pastries, yogurt and fresh juices, or to end it with a choice of well-prepared dishes ranging from vegetable lasagna to blackened tuna in lemon-leek sauce.

Sushi Bar ($$) 256 East 49th Street, at 2nd Avenue (tel: 644 8750). Traditional and innovative Japanese food in an intriguing space. Sashimi is the highlight of the long menu.

"21" Club ($$$) 21 West 52nd Street, between 4th and 5th avenues (tel: 582 7200). A new chef has updated the menu at this historic restaurant, where the lounge and bar room are favorite haunts of New York power brokers.

Vong ($$$) 200 East 54th Street (tel: 486 9592). Well-known to choosy New Yorkers and the brainchild of one of the city's most talented chefs, Jean-Georges Vongerichten. You must call in advance if you want to make a reservation to sample the French/Thai food.

Zarela ($$) Second Avenue between 50th and 51st streets (tel: 644 6740). Zarela's raises Mexican cuisine to lofty heights with exotic creations stressing subtlety in taste and texture.

Theater District

Becco ($$) 355 West 46th Street, between 8th and 9th avenues (tel: 397 7597). All-you-can-eat antipasti and homemade pasta arrive as soon as you sit down. If you have room for an entrée, you won't be disappointed.

Cabana Carioca ($$) 45th Street between Sixth and Seventh avenues (tel: 581 8088). Hefty servings of Brazilian food, well-cooked meat, and black beans by the bowlful. The bar serves lethal cocktails, and the diners come in party mood.

Churrascaria Plataforma ($$) 316 West 49th Street, between 8th and 9th avenues (tel: 245 0505). An amazingly authentic Brazilian barbecue restaurant, where one price gets you a lavish salad bar and an endless parade of marinated and grilled meats.

Firebird ($$$) 365 West 46th Street, between 8th and 9th avenues (tel: 586 0244). Prerevolutionary, aristocratic Russian cooking in an ornate setting. Blini, caviar, kasha, and other delicacies haven't been so good since the rise and fall of Communism.

India Pavilion ($–$$) 56th Street between Broadway and Eighth Avenue (tel: 489 0035). Very fairly priced and extremely good quality Indian and Pakistani food, served in an intimate setting.

Jezebel ($$) Ninth Avenue at 45th Street (tel: 582 1045). Soul-food favorites, such as fried chicken, catfish, and grits, feature in a setting themed as a Deep South bordello.

Joe Allen ($$) 46th Street between Eighth and Ninth avenues (tel: 581 6464). Burgers, bowls of chili, and other simple American food are served in large portions amid Broadway show posters.

Landmark Tavern ($$) Eleventh Avenue at 46th Street (tel: 757 8595). Hearty lunches and dinners—fish-and-chips, and shepherds' pie alongside the ubiquitous burgers and sandwiches—are served to appreciative diners in wood-paneled rooms dating from 1856.

Little Saigon ($) 374 West 46th Street (tel: 956 0639). A useful pre- or post-theater stop for very well-priced Vietnamese dishes.

Russian Tea Room ($$$) 57th Street between Sixth and Seventh avenues (tel: 265 0947). Founded by homesick Russian ballet dancers in the 1920s, the Russian Tea Room is a fixture for New York showbiz high society, serving top-notch caviar, borscht, and smoked salmon— plus champagne, vodka, and tea from the samovar. (At the time of writing, it is undergoing a total renovation and expansion.)

Sardi's ($$) 44th Street between Broadway and Eighth Avenue (tel: 221 8444). A noted theatrical hangout and gossip-columnists' lair, Sardi's is well past its prime, but the caricatures of Broadway stars still line its walls and the service is still as off-hand as ever. Choose from an Italian menu.

Stage Deli ($$) Seventh Avenue at 54th Street (tel: 245 7850). Long time rival of the Carnegie Deli (see above), the Stage Deli provides much the same staple deli fare in equally generous portions, though the staff can often be less than gracious.

Virgil's Real BBQ ($) 152 West 44th Street, between Broadway and 6th Avenue (tel: 921 9494). Casual American barbecue joint with tender, tasty ribs, chicken, shrimp, corn bread, and other favorites.

Murray Hill, Gramercy, Chelsea and Flatiron District

Alva ($$) 36 East 22nd Street, between Broadway and Park Avenue (tel: 228 4399). American bistro at its best; roast chicken, lamb, fish, mashed potatoes, and a neighborhood atmosphere.

An American Place ($$) Park Avenue and 32nd Street (tel: 684 2122). Some innovative and exciting American nouvelle cuisine is inspired by U.S. regional cooking.

Bendix Diner ($) 219 8th Avenue, at 21st Street (tel: 366 0560). The menu has a little of everything—American, Thai, Italian, you name it—and it's all good and inexpensive Hot brunch spot.

Bolo ($$$) 23 East 22nd Street, between Broadway and Park Avenue South (tel: 228

2200). Creative Spanish food, deftly flavored and skillfully prepared.

Bright Food Shop ($) 216 8th Avenue, between 21st and 22nd streets (tel: 243 4433). Unusual Asian/Southwestern food in a 1930s coffee-shop. Odd-sounding menu selections turn out to be delicious.

Chat 'n' Chew ($) 10 East 16th Street, between 5th Avenue and Union Square West (tel: 243 1616). Huge helpings of American classics in a comfortable setting. Sandwiches, entrées, and desserts are tops. Late-night dining.

Chelsea Bistro & Bar ($$$) 358 West 23rd Street, between 8th and 9th avenues (tel: 727 2026). A neighborhood French bistro that attracts gourmets from around the city. Foie gras ravioli and other innovative dishes are not to be missed.

The City Bakery ($) 22 East 17th Street, between 5th Avenue and Union Square West (tel: 366 1414). The architecturally urban setting of stainless steel and cement showcases beautiful sandwiches, salads, soups, cookies, tarts, and other luncheon items.

Coffee Shop ($$) 16th Street and Union Square West (tel: 243 7969). Eat-and-run coffee shops abound around Union Square, but this, despite its name, is actually a lively and fashionable spot for consuming American-Brazilian food and generally being seen by the right faces.

Ess-a-Bagel ($) 359 1st Avenue, at 21st Street (tel: 260 2252). Contender for the city's best bagels. Smoked salmon, cream cheese, and other accompaniments are worth lining up for.

Follonico ($$) 6 West 24th Street, between 5th and 6th avenues (tel: 691 6359). Among the most authentic-feeling trattorias in town. A wood-fired oven gives the Tuscan fare a welcome rustic flavor.

Food Bar ($) 149 8th Avenue, between 17th and 18th streets (tel: 243 2020). In the heart of Chelsea's gay scene, this jam-packed eatery offers standard American fare and entertaining people-watching.

Frank's ($$) 14th Street between Ninth and Tenth avenues (tel: 243 1349). Operating in the so-called "meat-packing district" since 1912, this honest-to-goodness steak and seafood spot offers food of far higher quality than the sawdust-on-the-floor decor might suggest. Local butchers feature prominently among the lunchtime diners.

Gramercy Tavern ($$$) 42 East 20th Street, between Broadway and Park Avenue South (tel: 477 0777). They set out to redefine 4-star dining and succeeded with prix-fixe, multicourse menus of inspired modern French cooking. Lighter and less expensive tavern menu available in the bar.

Le Madri ($$$) 168 West 18th Street, at 7th Avenue (tel: 727 8022). *Alta* Italian in a beautiful "villa" setting. Homemade pastas, tasty entrées, and an elegant ambiance make this one of the city's best Italian bets.

Le Singe Vert ($$) 160 7th Avenue, between 19th and 20th streets (tel: 366 4100). Brand new French bistro with classic menu. Great ambiance.

Live Bait ($$) 23rd Street between Madison and Fifth avenues (tel: 353 2400). Styled as a rustic southern fishing shack, Live Bait is a busy bar and also dispenses filling southern-style sandwiches, burgers, and salads.

Lola ($$) 22nd Street between Fifth and Sixth avenues (tel: 675 6700). American food bearing a West Indian influence, and some genuine Caribbean and South American dishes, is prepared to an exceptional standard. A "gospel brunch" is also served on Sundays.

Merchants, NY ($) 112 7th Avenue, at 17th Street (tel: 366 7267). Pub-like atmosphere with good bar food and outdoor seating.

Mesa Grill ($$) 102 5th Avenue, between 15th and 16th streets (tel: 807 7400). Considered the city's best Southwestern. Hefty portions and friendly service make this a favorite among well-dressed Yuppies. Funky, award-winning design.

Negril ($$) 362 West 23rd Street, between 8th and 9th avenues (tel: 212/807 6411). Traditional and innovative Jamaican food served in a bustling, noisy setting. Always a wait on the weekends.

Newsbar Inc ($) 19th Street between Fifth and Sixth avenues (tel: 255 3996). Serves breakfast, lunch, and early dinner, but the real reason to visit this minimalist-designed café is to sip coffee, people-watch, and scan the racks of international newspapers.

Park Bistro ($$) Park Avenue between 28th and 29th streets (tel: 689 1360). Among the better of New York's many French bistro-style restaurants, this is deservedly popular for providing lovely food in a lovely setting.

The Parlour Café at ABC ($) 38 East 19th Street, between Broadway and Park Avenue South (tel: 677 2233). Charming spot for breakfast or lunch on the ground floor of the elegant ABC department store. If you like the table you're at, you can buy it.

Patria ($$$) 250 Park Avenue South, at 20th Street (tel: 777 6211). Inspired, boldly flavored and stunningly presented "Nuevo Latino" cooking keeps this trendy restaurant packed. Lunch is a bargain.

Periyali ($$$) 35 West 20th Street, between 5th and 6th avenues (tel: 463 7890). As upscale as Greek gets. Simple food with a few creative touches served in a friendly Mediterranean setting.

Pete's Tavern ($$) 18th Street at Irving Place (tel: 473 7676). A bar popular with the after-work crowd, it's an ideal place for sidewalk dining. The food includes the usual American fare and a wide choice of pasta dishes.

Union Square Café ($$) 16th Street and Union Square West (tel: 243 4020). Contemporary American cookery has made this restaurant a favorite among well-heeled New Yorkers.

Zen Palate ($) 34 Union Square East (tel: 614 9291). Delicious vegetarian food with an Asian accent presented in delicately arranged portions.

QUEENS

Elias Corner ($) 24-02 31st Street, at 24th Avenue, Satoria (tel: 718/932 1510). Simple grilled fish and other traditional Greek fare make this a favorite destination for adventurous Manhattanites.

Happy Dumpling ($) 135–29 40th Road, Flushing (tel: 718/445 2163). Chinese fare, and rarely bettered for stuffed dumplings or noodle dishes.

Jackson Diner ($) 74th Street between Roosevelt and 37th avenues (tel: 718/672 1232). Probably the best priced of a glut of Indian restaurants in this section of the borough. The food is far better than the decor might suggest.

Ko Hyang ($) 42–96 Main Street, Flushing (tel: 718/ 463 3837). Informal Korean restaurant with a wide selection of meals and snacks.

Lefkos Pyrgos ($) 22–85 31st Street, Astoria (tel: 718/932 4423). The pick of Astoria's many Greek cafés, it offers an array of sweet things certain to alarm your dentist.

Penang Malaysian Cuisine ($) 38 04 Prince Street, at Roosevelt Avenue, Flushing (tel: 718/321 2078). Related to, but much better than, the two Manhattan outposts, the original Flushing locale features an exotic menu of Malaysian specialties that range from Indian curry and roti to coconut shrimp.

Yao Han ($) 135–21 40th Road, Flushing (tel: 718/359 2828). Chinese and Vietnamese food makes this another great find for noodle-lovers.

UPPER EAST SIDE

Arcadia ($$$) 62nd Street between Madison and Fifth avenues (tel: 223 2900). Few New Yorkers would dispute that Arcadia is among the finest restaurants in the city. Its selective menu is adjusted according to ingredients in season and may include anything from smoked lobster to roast quail on dandelions.

Arizona 206 ($$$) 60th Street between Second and Third avenues (tel: 838 0440). The American Southwest is re-created on Manhattan's Upper East Side, with desert-style decor and southwestern cuisine of exceptional quality.

Aureole ($$$) 34 East 61st Street, between Madison and Park avenues (tel: 319 1660). The exquisite upscale American food and startling presentations make this one of the city's best restaurants. Elegant dining room and courteous service. Don't miss the multifaceted dessert extravaganzas.

Brother Jimmy's ($) 1644 Third Avenue (tel:426 2020). Sometimes rowdy spot for substantial sandwiches, soups, barbecued ribs, and other accompaniments to beer drinking and watching sports TV.

Club Macanudo ($$) 26 East 63rd Street, between Madison and Park avenues (tel: 752 8200). A cigar bar where the food is incidental, but the atmosphere is comfortable and the crowd is, well, made up of cigar smokers.

Coco Pazzo ($$–$$$) 23 East 74th Street, between 5th and Madison avenues (tel: 794 0205). The first in an upscale, city-wide chain of Italian eateries, this one is still the best. Pastas and entrées don't disappoint, but the check can be a shock.

Daniel ($$$) 76th Street between Fifth and Madison avenues (tel: 288 0033). The French chef from Le Cirque (see below) already had such an exalted reputation among New York foodies that this, his own restaurant, was an instant success when it opened in 1993. Dinner reservations entail an eight-week wait; alternatively, hope for a lunch cancellation.

E.A.T. ($) Madison Avenue between 80th and 81st streets (tel: 772 0022). Yuppies come here after racquetball, shoppers come on the weekend, and locals come all the time for the Continental Jewish snacks and sinful desserts.

277

Fred's at Barneys ($$–$$$) 10 East 61st Street, at Madison Avenue (tel: 833 2200). In the basement of Manhattans trendiest upscale department store, this is a favorite of the "ladies who lunch" (and shop) and Upper East Side socialites.

India Grill ($$) 240 East 81st Street (tel: 988 4646). Well-priced menu of Indian fare, and often offering daily specials.

J.G. Melon ($) Third Avenue at 74th Street (tel: 744 0584). Its American diner fare is a cut above the average, served at low cost in the homey environment of a wood-paneled bar.

Jo Jo ($$) 160 East 64th Street, near Lexington Avenue (tel. 223 5656). Superb "international" dining; prices are remarkably low for the quality so reservations are a must. Choose between the main dining area—usually loud and packed—and the more serene rear room.

Lenox Room ($$$) 1278 3rd Avenue, between 73rd and 74th streets (tel: 772 0404). The smooth service and sophisticated contemporary cooking at this new favorite make it a perfect place to rest after a day of shopping.

Mesa City ($$) 1059 3rd Avenue, between 62nd and 63rd streets (tel: 207 1919). They finally accept reservations at this bustling, downscale, uptown cousin of Mesa Grill. Southwestern specialties and margaritas are the order of the day.

Ottomanelli's Café ($) York Avenue between 81st and 82nd streets (tel: 737 1888). One of several Upper East Side branches of this well-known New York eatery. This particular one has a tempting selection of freshly baked goods among the usual range of salads, pastas, burgers, and sandwiches.

HOTELS AND RESTAURANTS

Park Avenue Café ($$$) 100 East 63rd Street, at Park Avenue (tel: 644 1900). You can't help but laugh at the witty and whimsical interpretations of modern American cooking. Everything tastes even better than it looks. A favorite for weekend brunch.
Petaluma ($$) First Avenue at 73rd Street (tel: 772 8800). Mesquite-grilled swordfish, boneless chicken in garlic, and fried calamari are among the options in this inventive California-style Italian restaurant.
Pig Heaven ($$) Second Avenue between 80th and 81st streets (tel: 744 4333). Pig-themed decor as well as intriguing pig dishes alongside a host of stylish Chinese dishes make this place a local favorite.
Post House ($$$) 63rd Street between Park and Madison avenues (tel: 935 2888). If you have an ample budget but detest French food, this might be the answer: a classy place, but best for no-nonsense portions of seafood and steak.
Rosa Mexicano ($$–$$$) 1063 1st Avenue, at 58th Street (tel: 753 7407). The Mexican food at this venerable restaurant is painstakingly authentic. Tableside guacamole with fresh corn tortillas and braised lamb shank with 3-pepper sauce are not to be missed. Downscale bar area in front with more formal restaurant in back.
Senza Nome ($$) 1675 3rd Avenue, between 93rd and 94th streets (tel: 410 4900). Simple, sophisticated Italian fare in a stark, award-winning setting.
7th Regiment Mess ($) 643 Park Avenue between 66th and 67th streets (tel: 744 4107). American home-cooking in an old wood-paneled restaurant inside the Seventh Regiment Armory. This place is great for children; booking is advisable.
Sign of the Dove ($$$) 1110 3rd Avenue, at 65th Street (tel: 861 8080). Romantic restaurant featuring top-notch creative American cooking. Courteous service and an excellent wine list round out the experience.
Syrah ($$) 1400 Second Avenue (tel: 327 1780). Stylish spot with a large menu of classy American dishes, mostly served to a local clientele.
Trois Jean ($$) 154 East 79th Street, between Lexington and 3rd avenues (tel: 988 4858). Classic French cooking in a classic French bistro setting. Lunch prix fixe is a bargain.
Vinegar Factory Restaurant ($$) 431 East 91st Street, between 1st and York avenues (tel: 987 0885). While the bustling market carries on below, enjoy a terrific brunch in this weekend-only restaurant. The bread basket alone is worth the schlep.
Wilkinson's Seafood Café ($$$) York Avenue between 83rd and 84th streets (tel: 535 5454). Mouthwatering variety of always-fresh seafood. Usually the choice includes lobster, red snapper, crab cakes, swordfish, and salmon—all stylishly presented to well-dressed, appreciative and mostly local diners.

UPPER WEST SIDE
Baci ($$) 412 Amsterdam Avenue (tel: 496 1550). Cramped and often crowded, but has some of the best Italian food in the area.
Barney Greengrass (The Sturgeon King) ($$) Amsterdam Avenue between 86th and 87th streets (tel: 724 4707). The epitome of a New York Jewish deli-diner and in the ownership of the Greengrass family since 1908. The proud claims for the sturgeon are justified, and salmon is another house specialty; breakfast and lunch only.
Blue Nile ($$) 77th Street at Columbus Avenue (tel: 580 3232). One of New York's few Ethiopian restaurants, it's an essential call for adventurous eaters. The food is scooped up and devoured with spongy chunks of injera bread.
Café des Artistes ($$$) 67th Street at Central Park West (tel: 877 3500). The 1930s Howard Chandler Christy murals of ethereal nudes add to the joy of consuming what might well be the best food in New York. Reservations are essential for dinner and also for the divine Sunday brunch.
Café La Fortuna ($) 71st Street between Central Park West and Columbus Avenue (tel: 724 5846). Sip from one of the coffees and sample an excellent pastry to feel at home in this neighborhood favorite.
Café Lalo ($) 83rd Street at Amsterdam Avenue (tel: 496 6031). This trendy spot attracts would-be neighborhood writers, artists, and media folk who drink cappuccino and gorge themselves on a selection of irresistible cakes.
Café Luxembourg ($$$) 70th Street between Amsterdam and Columbus avenues (tel: 873 7411). This is an art-deco bistro aiming for a 1930s Parisian ambiance. The top-rated food—a mix of French, Italian, and regional U.S. cuisines—draws fashionable faces from all New York.
E.J.'s Luncheonette ($) Amsterdam Avenue between 80th and 81st streets (tel: 873 3444). Retro diner complete with chrome fittings and historic Coke advertisements. The sandwiches (try the grilled Cajun chicken breast) could feed an army.
Empire Szechuan ($) Broadway at 97th Street (tel: 663 6005). Immense choice of Szechuan and Hunan fare. Dim sum is available weekend lunchtimes.
Fishin Eddie ($$) 71st Street between Central Park West and Columbus Avenue (tel: 874 3474). A dinner-only seafood restaurant with a strong reputation for unusual Italian dishes such as cioppina—a type of fish stew—served in large portions.
Gabriela's ($) 685 Amsterdam Avenue, at 93rd Street (tel: 961 0574). Inexpensive Mexican eatery that's always packed. The posole is particularly good, but for the price, you can't go wrong with anything.
Gennaro ($–$$) 665 Amsterdam Avenue, at 92nd Street (tel: 665 5348). What is such delicious, homemade Italian food doing up here? Don't ask, just enjoy.

Good Enough To Eat ($$) Amsterdam Avenue between 83rd and 84th streets (tel: 496 0163). Grand selection of ever-popular American staples, from ham and eggs to strawberry waffles, for breakfast, lunch, or dinner in cozy surroundings.

India Garden ($$) Amsterdam Avenue between 90th and 91st streets (tel: 787 4530). Distinguished from the neighborhood Indian restaurants by its goat dishes, available in biryani, vindaloo, saag, and badami forms.

Indian Café ($$) Broadway at 108th Street (tel: 749 9200). Competitively priced Indian food includes especially inventive vegetarian selections, such as chickpeas with spinach and tomato, and sauteed lentils with garlic and ginger. Alternatively, feast on a selection of appetizers.

It's a Wrap ($) 2012 Broadway, between 68th and 69th streets (tel: 362 7922). The twist on the increasingly popular wrap sandwich here is that the bread (like an Indian naan) is homemade. Fillings include B.L.T., turkey club, and roasted lamb.

Joe's Fish Shack ($–$$) 520 Columbus Avenue (tel: 873 0341). Sophisticated decor is not a feature of this intentionally ramshackle dining room that specializes in clams, crab cakes, and fish.

John's Pizzeria ($) 48 West 65th Street, between Columbus Avenue and Central Park West (tel: 721 7001). A cousin of the original Greenwich Village John's, it has pizzas that are every bit as good and the atmosphere is a little more pleasant.

Josie's ($–$$) 300 Amsterdam Avenue, at 74th Street (tel: 769 1212). The health-food-inspired menu has a number of vegetarian options. Salads are fresh and vegetables and whole grains abound.

La Caridad ($) Broadway at 78th Street (tel: 874 2780). Intriguing and inventive Chinese-Cuban dishes are served without fuss in informal surroundings.

La Traviata ($) 101 West 68th Street (tel: 721 1101). This hole-in-the-wall outlet is popular with locals and dispenses tasty pizza by the slice.

Lucy's ($$) Columbus Avenue between 84th and 85th streets (tel: 787 3009). Tex-Mex food is boisterously consumed in the back room as the fashionable faces of the Upper West Side fill the bar.

Mad Fish ($$) 2182 Broadway, between 77th and 78th streets (tel: 787 0202). Among the first of the new wave of restaurants in the neighborhood, this trendy seafood spot is packed late into the night.

Museum Café ($$) Columbus Avenue at 77th Street (tel: 799 0150). Facing the American Museum of Natural History, it offers a delicious assortment of generous salads and melt-in-the-mouth pasta dishes.

Ollie's Noodle Shop ($) Broadway at 84th Street (tel: 362 3712). No-nonsense Chinese fare prepared in full view of diners. The noodle soups are flavorful and very cheap.

Picholine ($$$) 35 West 64th Street, between Broadway and Central Park West (tel: 724 8585). Expertly prepared modern French food in a country French setting. The restaurant boasts its own cheese cave for aging and storing.

Popover Café ($) Amsterdam Avenue between 87th and 88th streets (tel: 595 8555). Salads, soups and sandwiches, and popovers (served with generous helpings of jam and butter) are the specialties of this quaintly decorated place.

Presto's Pasta Pizza ($$) Amsterdam Avenue at 82nd Street (tel: 721 9141). The Italian standards are cooked with flair and accompanied by great fresh-baked bread.

Rain ($) 100 West 82nd Street, between Amsterdam and Columbus avenues (tel: 501 0776). The Thai-inspired menu fills this bustling eatery with a young crowd. The wait on weekends can be tiresome.

Rancho Mexican Café ($$) Amsterdam Avenue between 82nd and 83rd streets (tel: 362 1514). Potent margaritas accompany the Mexican fare—for a free one, order during happy hour. Sunday brunch is riotous.

Sarabeth's Kitchen ($$) Amsterdam Avenue between 80th and 81st streets (tel: 496 6280). A refined place for smoked salmon sandwiches and fluffy omelets. Has a scintillating selection of homemade cakes.

Savann ($$) 414 Amsterdam Avenue, between 79th and 80th streets (tel: 580 0202). American bistro with a French accent. Upper West Siders flock to this imaginative, but crowded, restaurant.

Sesso ($$) 285 Columbus Avenue, between 73rd and 74th streets (tel: 501 0607). Italian trattoria with the typical neighborhood crowd. Reasonably priced for the area.

Shark Bar ($) 74th Street between Columbus Avenue and Broadway (tel: 874 8500). Tallahassee grilled shrimp, Louisiana fried crab cakes, or pan-blackened catfish—the Shark Bar has the tastiest fare from all over the south.

Shun Lee ($$$) 43 West 65th Street, between Columbus Avenue and Central Park West (tel: 595 8895). Upscale Chinese served by tuxedoed waiters. The chef is talented, but the bill can be a shock.

Symposium ($) 113th Street at Amsterdam Avenue (tel: 865 1011). Authentic, inexpensive Greek fare popular with students from nearby Columbia University. In summer, you can dine in the garden.

Tavern on the Green ($$$) 67th Street at Central Park West (tel: 873 3200). More famous as a New York landmark than as a home of fine dining, the tavern serves erratic—but usually excellent—meals beneath the Venetian chandeliers of the Crystal Room or outside in the garden.

Vince and Eddie's ($$$) 70 West 68th Street, between Columbus Avenue and Central Park West (tel: 721 0068). A cozy, American bistro that's a favorite of quiet celebrities and Lincoln Center regulars.

279

Index

a

Abby Aldrich Rockefeller Sculpture Garden 159
Abigail Adams Smith Museum 60
abstract expressionist art 128–129
Abyssinian Baptist Church 121
accommodation
  bed and breakfast 215
  Chinatown 262
  Financial District 262
  Greenwich Village 262
  hostels 215
  hotel guide 212
  hotels 212–214, 262–268
  Little Italy and SoHo 262
  Midtown Manhattan 262–266
  rates and taxes 212, 213
  reservations and payment 214
  seasonal factors 213
  special deals 213
  student halls of residence 215
  Upper East Side 266–267
  Upper West Side 267–268
  women travelers 213
Adams, Franklin P. 153
African-Americans 73
Agee, James 116
airports and air services 54, 246
  John F. Kennedy 170, 246
  La Guardia 170, 246
  Newark 246
Akeley, Carl 63
Albany 200, 204, 205
  Albany Institute of History and Art 205
  Corning Tower 205
  Empire State Institute for the Performing Arts 204
  Empire State Plaza 205
  New York State Capitol 205
  New York State Museum 205
  Schuyler Mansion 205
Algonquin Hotel 153
Alice Austin House 180
Alice Tully Hall 134, 235
Allen Street 138
Allen, Woody 14, 77, 188
Alphabet City 54, 60–61
American Academy and Institute of Arts & Letters 61
American Ballet Theater 236
American Bible Society 61, 244
American Craft Museum 62
American Crafts Festival 27
American Federation of the Arts 62
American Immigrant Wall of Honor 100
American Museum of the Moving Image 172
American Museum of Natural History 52, 63–64, 189, 242

Akeley Gallery 63
  Hall of Human Biology and Evolution 64
  Hall of Minerals and Gems 64
  Hall of Ocean Life and Biology of Fishes 64
  Hayden Planetarium 64
  Highlights Tour 63
  Nature Max Cinema 64
American Numismatic Society 61, 65, 244
American Radiator Building 163
Amityville 207
Annex Antiques Fair and Flea Market 140
apartment buildings 10, 24, 52, 123, 189
  Dakota Apartments 24, 83, 96, 189
  Kenilworth Apartments 189
Apollo Theater 126
architecture
  apartment buildings 24
  art-deco 162–163
  beaux-arts style 25
  brownstones 24, 39, 76, 77
  Federal style 24
  Greek revival style 24
  International style 25
  plazas 25
  skyscrapers 24–25
  zoning laws 24, 162
Arkville 198
Armory Show 128, 149
art galleries
  art gallery listings 176
  57th Street 176
  guided tours 177
  nonprofit galleries 177
  SoHo 176–177
  Upper East Side 176
art museums
  free admission 244
  Frick Collection 20, 36, 52, 110, 187
  Guggenheim Museum 21, 52, 122–124, 129
  Metropolitan Museum of Art 20, 52, 92, 142–148, 162
  Museum of Modern Art (M.o.M.A.) 21, 25, 129, 158–160
  National Academy of Design 164, 244
  New-York Historical Society 20, 21
  Whitney Museum of American Art 20, 52, 129, 187, 191
Asia Society 65, 187
Asimov, Isaac 100
Astor, John Jacob 36, 98, 168
Astor Place 98, 99
Astoria 172
A.T. & T. Building 25
Auden, W.H. 23
Audubon, John James 61
Audubon Terrace 61
Austin, Alice 180
Avery Fisher Hall 134, 234

B

Bacall, Lauren 15, 96
Bainbridge 154
Balanchine, George 105

Balducci's 113, 118
Baldwin, James 23, 116
ballet and dance 235–236
Barclay-Vesey Building 163
Barnum, P.T. 66, 80
Barrymore, John 118
bars 114–115, 224–225
  All State Café 115
  Bar Six 115
  d.b.a. 114
  Cedar Tavern 114, 119, 128
  Coffee Shop 114
  Conservatory Bar, Mayflower Hotel 115
  Costello's 115
  Fifty Seven Fifty Seven 115
  Greatest Bar on Earth 114
  happy hours 224
  hotel bars 115
  King Cole Bar 115
  Live Bait 115
  Marie's Crisis Café 115
  McSorley's Old Ale House 99, 114
  Peculier Pub 114
  SoHo Brewery 114
  sports bars 91
  Top of the Sixes 114
  Top of the Tower 114
  White Horse Tavern 114
Bartholdi, Frédéric Auguste 181
baseball 70, 90, 152
basketball 90–91
Battery Park 66
Battery Park City 18–19
  Esplanade 19
  World Financial Center 19, 25
Beame, Abe 46–47
Beat Generation 119
Bedford Avenue 78
Bedford Street 118
Beecher, Henry Ward 76, 78
Behan, Brendan 85
Belmont Park 91
Berlin, Irving 100
Bernard, George Gray 92
Bernstein, Leonard 96
Big Apple nickname 11
bike hire 195
Black History Month 26
Bleecker Street 118, 136
boat trips 67
Bohemian National Hall 131
bookstores 99, 140, 227–228
Booth, Edwin 152
Bow, Clara 77
Bowery Savings Bank 150
Bowling Green 33
Bowne House 170
Bowne, John 170
bridges
  Brooklyn Bridge 39, 59, 80
  Kosciuszko Bridge 105
  Pulaski Bridge 105
  Verrazano-Narrows Bridge 59
Brighton Beach 53, 75, 139
Broadway 38, 68–69
Bronx 52, 53, 70–72
Bronx Community College 71–72

Bronx Museum of the Arts 70
Bronx Zoo (Bronx Wildlife Conservation Park) 53, 70–71, 242
Brooklyn 53, 74–79
Brooklyn Academy of Music 236
Brooklyn Botanic Garden 79
Brooklyn Bridge 39, 59, 80
Brooklyn Heights 53, 59, 74, 76, 79
Brooklyn Heights Promenade 59, 76
Brooklyn's Historical Museum 76, 244
Brooklyn Museum 53, 79
Brooklyn-Battery Tunnel 66
Brown, James 126
brownstones 24, 39, 76, 77
Bruno Hauptman House 71
Bryant, William Cullen 82
Burgee, John 161
Burnham, Daniel H. 106
Burroughs, John 196, 199
Burroughs, William 23, 85, 114, 118, 119
buses
  airport services 246
  city 252
  long-distance 247

C

Café des Artistes 108
Caffè Reggio 113
Calvary Church 121
Canal Street 86, 87
Canal Street Flea Market 140
Capote, Truman 22, 79
Carnegie, Andrew 36, 95, 202
Carnegie Hall 80, 235
Carnegie Hall Museum 80
Carrère and Hastings 168
Carter, Betty 76
Castle Clinton 35, 66
Castro, Fidel 119
Cathedral of St. John the Divine 52, 81, 94
Cather, Willa 23, 116
Catskill Mountains 195, 196–199
cemeteries
  Green-Wood Cemetery 74
  St. Raymond's Cemetery 71
  Woodlawn Cemetery 72
Central Park 52, 54, 82–84
  Belvedere Castle 84
  Bethesda Terrace 83
  carriage tours 84
  Central Park Wildlife Center 242–243
  Concert Ground 83
  Conservatory Garden 84
  Dairy 82
  Great Lawn 84
  Hans Christian Andersen statue 242
  Lake 83
  Literary Walk 83
  Mall 82–83
  Naumberg Bandshell 83
  personal safety 84
  The Ramble 84

280

281

INDEX

INDEX

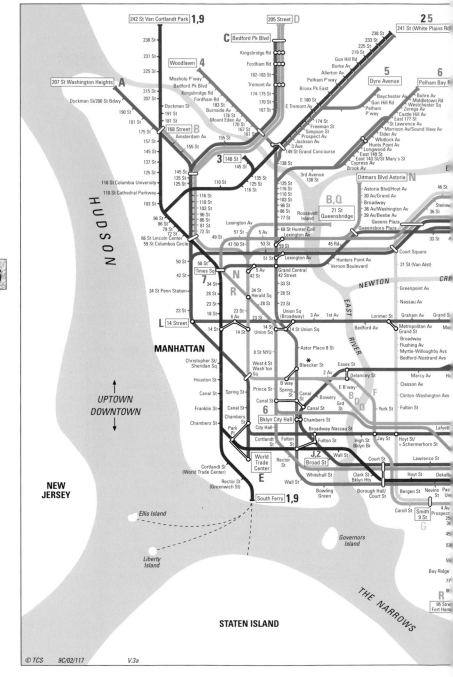

© TCS 9C/02/117 V.3a

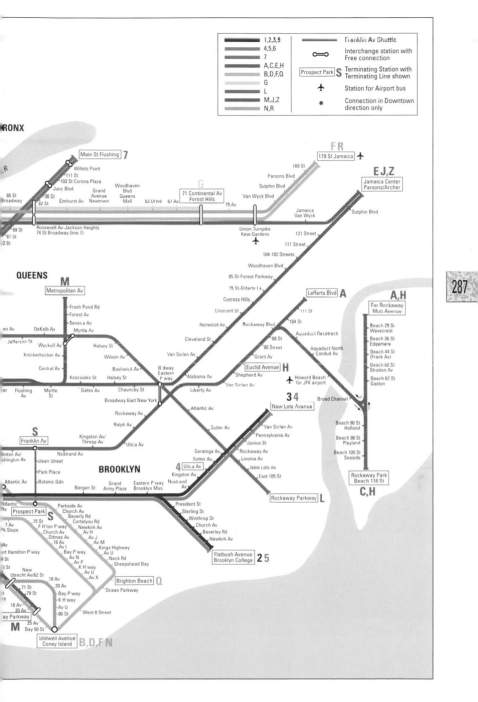

Picture credits

The Automobile Association would like to thank the following photographers, libraries and associations for their assistance in the preparation of this book:
J ALLAN CASH 127a Market. ALLSPORT UK LTD 90a American Football (S Dunn). AMERICAN CRAFT MUSEUM 62 Museum interior (Dan Cornish). BETTMANN ARCHIVE 22b Damon Runyon (UPI/BETTMAN NEWSPAPERS), 42b *The Brains* (THE BETTMAN ARCHIVE), 43a William O'Dwyer (THE BETTMAN ARCHIVE), 44b East River (THE BETTMAN ARCHIVE), 46 Ed Koch (UPI/BETTMAN), 119a P Orbvsky & A Ginsberg, 119b A Poole in our time (THE BETTMAN ARCHIVES). BRIDGEMAN ART LIBRARY LTD 29a Irish immigrants disembark at the Battery in New York, 1855 (Museum of the City of New York, 1855/Bridgeman Art Library, London), 32a New York after Independence, seen from East River by George Torino (18th C) (Private Collection/Bridgeman Art Library, London), 36a Cartoon depicting Andrew Carnegie, 1903 (Private Collection/Bridgeman Art Library, London), 97b *Campbell's Soup* by Warhol, Andy (1930–87) (Wolverhampton Art Gallery, Staffs/Bridgeman Art Library, London). D CORRANCE 92 The Cloisters, 110 Frick Museum, 123 Guggenheim Museum, 177 Soho Martin Lawrence Gallery, 179 Staten Island Ferry, 241 Greenwich Village Jazz. J HENDERSON 127b Puerto Rican. HULTON DEUTSCH COLLECTION LTD 16b,17a Riots in Harlem, 46a,b Labour Strikes, 47a New York Strike, 73b Malcolm X. KOBAL 15a King Kong. MAGNUM PHOTOS LTD 16c Dinkins, 97a Eyes Warhol (Philipe Halsam), 188a Woody Allen (Ernst Haas). MARY EVANS PICTURE LIBRARY 22a Manhattan Transfer, 23 Henry James,(Mary Evans/J Morgan) 30a Dutch Land on Staten Island, 33 Declaration of Independence, 34–5 Immigration, 41a,b Wall St Crash, 105a Immigrants at Ellis Island. METROPOLITAN MUSEUM OF ART 143a Egyptian Funerary Customs – Coffins (Rogers Fund 1915 (15.2.2), 145a Islamic Eastern Mediterranean Glass (Rogers Bequest of Edward C Moore 1891 (91.1.1530), 147a Henri Matisse painting (Robert Lehman Coll. 1975 (1975.1.194), 147b Jacopo Bellini painting (Gift of Irma N Straus 1959 (59.187). MUSEUM OF MODERN ART NEW YORK 129 Jackson Pollock painting, 158b *The Starry Night* Van Gogh. MUSEUM OF TV & RADIO 161 Int Lonsdale Room. PICTURES COLOUR LIBRARY 24–5 East 47th Street. RONALD GRANT ARCHIVES 15b *Saturday Night Fever*, 188b *Manhattan* Woody Allen. P SLATTERY 8b Mick Sinclair. SPECTRUM COLOUR LIBRARY Spine Statue of Liberty, 26b Chinese New Year, 27 Flute Player, 154a St Patrick's Day, 154b Pipe Band, 240 Birdland Jazz Club. THE MANSELL COLLECTION 30/1 New Amsterdam, 31 Landing of Hendrick Hudson, 32 P Stuyvesant, 34b Entering a New World, 36 Andrew Carnegie, 37 Pierpont Morgan, 38b Brooklyn Bridge, 38–9 New York 1851, 45 SS *Queen Mary*. UNITED NATIONS 184 Int, UN Building. ZEFA PICTURE LIBRARY (UK) LTD Cover Park Avenue at night, 11 Tompkins Sq Park, 14 Times Sq, 18 Times Sq, 39 Harlem, 40 Wall St, 69 Broadway, 73a Boy & Water, 138 Delancey St, 155 Folk Art Mus, 173 Rockefeller Plaza, 176 Soho Gallery, 185a U N Building,189 Central Park, 203 West Point Parade, 205 Albany, 237 Musician & bike, 255 St Paul's Chapel.

All remaining pictures are from the Association's own picture library (AA PHOTO LIBRARY) with contributions from:
P BAKER 127c. D CORRANCE 4, 6–7, 13, 20, 25, 55, 58–9, 67a, 72, 76, 78, 79, 87, 89, 96, 101, 106, 118a, 126, 128–9, 135, 137, 146, 148, 159, 160a, 162a, 171c, 175, 181b, 182, 185b, 192, 214, 215, 217, 222, 225, 229, 232, 233, 234–5, 236, 242, 246, 257, 259b, 263, 266, 280. R ELLIOTT 3, 5a, 7, 10a, b, 12–3, 16a, 17b, 19, 20a, 21, 24, 28, 43, 44, 45, 50, 51, 52, 53, 54b, 56, 60, 61a, 63, 64, 66a, 68, 70, 74, 80, 81a, b, 83, 86, 88a, b, 90b, 94, 99, 100, 104, 112, 113, 114a, 115, 116, 117a, b, 124a, b, 125, 131, 132, 139a, b, 140, 141a, b, 142, 143b, 144, 149, 150, 151, 153, 156, 157, 158a, 160b, 163, 164, 165a, b, 167, 168, 169, 171a, b, 172, 174b, 178, 180, 183a, b, 187, 190, 191, 193a, b, 194, 195, 196, 197, 198, 199a, b, 200, 201, 202, 206–7, 208, 209, 210, 211, 212, 216, 220, 223a, 226, 227, 228, 238a, b, 239, 244, 247a, 250, 253, 254, 256a, 258. P KENWARD 2, 5b, 5c, 6c, 9, 12, 18a, 23, 26, 54a, 57, 66b, 67b, 71a, b, 75a, b, 84a, b, 91, 93, 102, 103, 118b, 120a, 132a, 134, 136a, b, 152, 162b, 166a, 170, 174a, 181a, 186, 213, 218, 219, 221, 224, 231a, b, 235, 243a, b, c, 245a,b, 247b, 248, 252, 259a, 260, 261b, 279. D.POLLACK 65, 85a, b, 108, 111, 120b, 121a, b, 261, 275. E ROONEY 9b, 29b, 49b. C SAWYER 8a, 105b.

Contributors

Revision copy editor: Sean Connolly
Original copy editor: Donna Dailey
Revision verifier: Mick Sinclair